HANDBOOK OF DISCOURSE ANALYSIS

VOLUME 1
Disciplines of Discourse

HANDBOOK of DISCOURSE ANALYSIS

HANDBOOK
of DISCOURSE ANALYSIS

VOLUME 1
Disciplines of Discourse

Edited by

TEUN A. VAN DIJK

Department of General Literary Studies
Section of Discourse Studies
University of Amsterdam
Amsterdam, The Netherlands

1985

ACADEMIC PRESS, INC.
Harcourt Brace Jovanovich, Publishers

London   San Diego   New York
Austin   Boston   Orlando   Sydney
Tokyo   Toronto

ACADEMIC PRESS INC. (LONDON) LTD.
24–28 Oval Road
LONDON NW1 7DX

United States Edition published by
ACADEMIC PRESS, INC.
Orlando, Florida 32887

Library of Congress Cataloging in Publication Data

Main entry under title:

Handbook of discourse analysis.

    Includes indexes.
    Contents: v. 1. Disciplines of discourse -- v. 2.
Dimensions of discourse -- v. 3. Discourse and dialogue --
[etc.]
    1. Discourse analysis. I. Dijk, Teun Adrianus van,
Date   . II. Title.
P302.H343 1985   001.51   84-6482
ISBN 0-12-712001-7 (v. 1 : alk. paper)

PRINTED IN THE UNITED STATES OF AMERICA

    86 87 88   9 8 7 6 5 4 3 2

Contents

1

Introduction: Discourse Analysis as a New Cross-Discipline
Teun A. van Dijk

2

Linguistics as a Tool for Discourse Analysis
Charles J. Fillmore

3
Text Linguistics in Discourse Studies
Robert de Beaugrande

4
Cognitive Psychology and Text Processing
Gordon H. Bower and Randolph K. Cirilo

5
Social Psychology and Discourse
W. P. Robinson

6
Artificial Intelligence: Modeling Memory for Language Understanding
Roger Schank and Mark Burstein

7
Sociological Approaches to Discourse Analysis
William A. Corsaro

8
Sociocultural Dimensions of Discourse
Alessandro Duranti

9
Philosophy and Discourse Analysis
Asa Kasher

10
Historical Discourse
Nancy S. Struever

11
Legal Discourse
Brenda Danet

Contributors

Numbers in parentheses indicate the pages on which the authors' contributions begin.

ROBERT DE BEAUGRANDE (41), Department of English, University of Florida, Gainesville, Florida 32611

GORDON H. BOWER (71), Department of Psychology, Stanford University, Stanford, California 94305

MARK BURSTEIN[1] (145), Department of Computer Science, Yale University, New Haven, Connecticut 06520

RANDOLPH K. CIRILO[2] (71), Department of Psychology, Stanford University, Stanford, California 94305

WILLIAM A. CORSARO (167), Department of Sociology, Indiana University, Bloomington, Indiana 47401

BRENDA DANET (273), Communications and Sociology, Hebrew University of Jerusalem, Jerusalem, 91905, Israel

ALESSANDRO DURANTI (193), Instituto di Glottologia, Universita degli Studi di Roma, Rome, Italy

CHARLES J. FILLMORE (11), Department of Linguistics, University of California at Berkeley, Berkeley, California 94720

ASA KASHER (231), Faculty of Humanities, Department of Philosophy, Ramat Aviv, Tel Aviv 69978, Israel

W. P. ROBINSON (107), School of Education, University of Bristol, Bristol, England

ROGER SCHANK (145), Department of Computer Science, Yale University, New Haven, Connecticut 06520

NANCY S. STRUEVER (249), Humanities Center, The Johns Hopkins University, Baltimore, Maryland 21218

TEUN A. VAN DIJK (1), Department of General Literary Studies, Section of Discourse Studies, University of Amsterdam, Amsterdam, The Netherlands

---

[1] Present address: Bolt, Beranek, and Newman, Inc., Cambridge, Massachusetts 02238.
[2] Present address: Century University, Beverly Hills, California 90212.

Preface to the Four Volumes

One of the most conspicuous and interesting developments in the humanities and the social sciences in the past decade has undoubtedly been the widespread, multidisciplinary attention paid to the study of discourse. This development began to take shape in the early 1970s, after some scattered attempts in the late 1960s, in such disciplines as anthropology, linguistics, semiotics, poetics, psychology, sociology, and mass communication research. This shared interest for various phenomena of language use, texts, conversational interaction, or communicative events soon became more integrated, under the common label of discourse analysis (or, e.g., *Textwissenschaft* in German).

The variety of theoretical and descriptive approaches in this new interdisciplinary field is impressive: for example, the study of narrative in nearly all disciplines mentioned above, the attention paid to natural forms of language use in the social context in sociolinguistics, the experimental or computer-simulated study of text processing in psychology and artificial intelligence, the construction of text grammars in linguistics, the ethnography of speaking in anthropology, as well as the continued attention to the analysis of style, rhetoric, argumentation, and persuasive communication in several branches of the humanities and the social sciences.

To document the development and the current state of this new field of discourse analysis, it became imperative to unite these various directions of research in one multidisciplinary publication. The present *Handbook of Discourse Analysis*, in four volumes, is the result of this enterprise. This *Handbook* provides surveys of and introductions to the respective approaches in discourse analysis. In concrete sample analyses, its chapters show how discourse analysis actually works at several levels of description. It summarizes our insights into the structures and functions of various discourse types or genres. And it demonstrates for a number of important social domains and problems how discourse analysis can be usefully and critically applied. The four volumes deal, respectively, with these major aims: presentation of the various disciplines of discourse analysis, introduction to descriptive methods, study of important genres of (dialogical) discourse, and application in critical social analysis.

For each topic we have invited leading scholars to contribute essays in their area of specialization. Most of these scholars are widely known, in and beyond their own fields. Young researchers have also been invited to write about the topic in which they have become specialists. To make the *Handbook* not only interdisciplinary but also international, care has been taken to include scholars from several countries.

The *Handbook* has been set up according to a few basic leading principles. First, as an introductory state of the art, its chapters satisfy a number of didactic criteria so that it is accessible at least to advanced and interested students in all disciplines of the humanities and the social sciences, and not only to specialists in some area of research. Second, the *Handbook* has a descriptive and analytic bias, to allow more direct application in concrete discourse research. Detailed attention to theoretical issues, as well as excessive formalization, have been avoided. Third, in line with the important interest in spontaneous uses of language, illustrations are given predominantly of natural discourse forms. Fourth, within the constraints of the thematic setup of the *Handbook*, authors are free to present their own perspectives and to summarize their own research findings. The variety of approaches, however, guarantees that the major directions, theories, or methods of research are represented.

Despite its multidisciplinary and wide-ranging scope, even a four-volume handbook must have self-imposed limitations. There are, of course, more disciplines involved in discourse analysis than could be represented here. Thus, space limitations forced us to exclude, for example, the study of mass communication and literary scholarship. Similarly, of the hundreds of discourse genres, only some of the most important could be treated here. The same holds for various details of discourse structures. And, finally, not all directions of research or schools of thought could be covered (such as discourse analysis in France). Yet the selection we made should result in a coherent, representative, and up-to-date state of the (new) art of discourse analysis.

The preparation and editing of this *Handbook* have been a considerable task that would have been impossible to perform without the help, the advice, and the assistance of many people—too many to mention here. I hereby thank them all for their cooperation.

University of Amsterdam   TEUN A. VAN DIJK
Autumn, 1984

Preface to Volume 1: Disciplines of Discourse

In this first volume of the *Handbook of Discourse Analysis*, the major disciplines involved in the development of discourse analysis are presented. The chapters provide backgrounds, surveys, and introductions to the methods and results of discourse analysis of each of these disciplines in the humanities and the social sciences. Besides the central discourse disciplines of linguistics, psychology, social psychology, sociology, and anthropology, more recent interest in discourse analysis in history, law, artificial intelligence, and philosophy is represented. It may be expected, however, that future developments in the field will also involve disciplines such as mass communication, political science, and other social sciences. The methods of discourse analysis developed in poetics (literary scholarship), stylistics, rhetoric, or content analysis (e.g., in mass communication research) receive attention in the subsequent volumes of the *Handbook*, although the findings of these approaches are so voluminous that they require treatment in separate studies. Indeed, specialization in discourse analysis have increased enormously in the past decade, as the chapters in this volume show in more detail. Yet, at the same time, the boundaries between the many disciplines involved have become blurred through the attention to a common object of research—discourse (or texts, conversations, messages, etc.)—despite a large variety of theories, descriptive approaches, and empirical methods. This increasing multidisciplinary integration has led to the emergence of the new interdiscipline of discourse analysis as an independent field in the humanities and social sciences. The chapters in this first volume of the *Handbook of Discourse Analysis* bear witness to this important development in the study of language use and communicative interaction.

Contents of Volumes 2, 3, and 4

Volume 3: Discourse and Dialogue

Volume 4: Discourse Analysis in Society

CHAPTER 1

Introduction: Discourse Analysis as a New Cross-Discipline

Teun A. van Dijk

HISTORICAL BACKGROUND

Discourse analysis is both an old and a new discipline. Its origins can be traced back to the study of language, public speech, and literature more than 2000 years ago. One major historical source is undoubtedly classical rhetoric, the art of good speaking. Whereas the *grammatica,* the historical antecedent of linguistics, was concerned with the normative rules of correct language use, its sister discipline of *rhetorica* dealt with the precepts for the planning, organization, specific operations, and performance of public speech in political and legal settings. Its crucial concern, therefore, was persuasive effectiveness. In this sense, classical rhetoric both anticipates contemporary stylistics and structural analyses of discourse and contains intuitive cognitive and social psychological notions about memory organization and attitude change in communicative contexts.

After some important revivals in the Middle Ages and the seventeenth and eighteenth centuries, however, rhetoric lost much of its importance in the curricula of schools and in academic research. The emergence of historical and comparative linguistics at the beginning of the nineteenth century and the birth of structural analysis of language at the beginning of the twentieth century replaced rhetoric as the primary discipline of the humanities. Fragments of rhetoric survived only in school textbooks of speech and communication, on one hand, and in stylistics or the study of literary language, on the other.

Yet, parallel to this decline of rhetoric as an independent academic discipline, new developments in several fields of the humanities and the social sciences took place that would eventually lead to the emergence

1

of discourse analysis. First, the young revolution in Russia witnessed concomitant new ideas in anthropology, poetics, and linguistics, an interdisciplinary development known under the label of "Russian formalism." Apart from research by literary scholars and linguists (and related new experiments in the theory and practice of art and film), one of the (later) most influential books of that time appeared to be *Morphology of the Folktale* by Vladimir Propp (1928, first English translation 1958). Major structural principles of early linguistics (phonology, morphology) were here paralleled with a first structural analysis of discourse, namely, the Russian folktale, in terms of a set of fixed thematic functions in which variable contents of different tales could be inserted. Although it may be arbitrary to specifically select this work in this brief historical survey, its wide-ranging though often indirect influence in the study of narrative in several disciplines (semiotics, poetics, anthropology, and psychology) 40 years later bears witness to its importance.

Indeed, part of the inspiration of (initially French) structuralism in the 1960s came through the translation of this and other work of the Russian formalists (and Czech structuralists) of the 1920s and 1930s. Lévi-Strauss' structural analysis of culture, and especially his analysis of myths, in part inspired by Propp and by the further development of structural linguistics in Europe, was at the same time one of the sources for renewal in anthropology, poetics, and other branches of the humanities and the social sciences. These early interdisciplinary developments of the middle 1960s were often captured under the new (or rather, renewed) label of "semiotics," to which is associated the names of Barthes, Greimas, Todorov, and many others engaged in the structural analysis of narrative and other discourse forms or cultural practices.

STRUCTURALISM AND THE ANALYSIS OF TEXTS (1964–1972)

Although of course historical developments are more continuous than is suggested here, it seems warranted to locate the origins of modern discourse analysis in the middle 1960s. The first publication of structural analyses of discourse in France, by some of the authors mentioned above, appeared in 1964 (*Communications* 4): a new critical analysis of Propp by Bremond, an application of modern linguistics and semantics to literature by Todorov, the well-known extension to the analysis of film by Metz, the famous rhetorical analysis of publicity pictures by Barthes, and finally, the first introduction to the new discipline of semiotics *sémiologie*, also by Barthes. This issue of *Communications* was followed 2 years later by another special issue (*Communications* 8), which was completely dedicated to the structural analysis of narrative (with contributions by the same authors, but also by Greimas, Eco, and Genette, among others). Although the background, orientations, objects of research, and methods of all these authors were still far from homogeneous, the common interest in discourse analysis within the wider framework of a linguistically inspired semiotics influenced and provided coherence in these first attempts.

At the same time, on the other side of the ocean, 1964 also saw the publication of another influential book of readings: Hymes' *Language in Culture and Society.* Although notions such as 'discourse' or 'text' do not yet dominate the contributions to that voluminous book, there is attention to forms of 'speech', 'communication', and to specific topics such as 'forms of address', which would later develop into the discourse analytical orientation of the so-called ethnography of speaking in anthropology. Of course, there are obvious differences between this and the French brands of structuralism in the 1960s. Yet on both sides the interaction between structural linguistics and anthropology appeared to be very fruitful for the initial interest in the study of language use, discourse, and communication forms. At the same time, Hymes' collection not only contained the great names of linguistic anthropology (or anthropological linguistics), such as Boas, Greenberg, Goodenough, Lévi-Strauss, Malinowski, Firth, Sapir, and many others, but also the first collection of work from what soon would be called sociolinguistics (Brown, Bernstein, Gumperz, Bright, and others). That is, not only discourse, style, forms of address and verbal art, but also the social, cultural, and historical contexts, and the variations of language use came to be studied systematically.

From a methodological point of view, it is interesting to note that the new linguistic paradigm that also came to be established in the mid-1960s, Chomsky's generative–transformational grammar, hardly appears in this book of classics. His name is mentioned only once in the index, merely referring to a 1955 article by him, although his *Syntactic Structures* figures in the general bibliography.

One other name that appears in Hymes' collection is that of Pike, whose tagmemic approach to language and human behavior would soon also provide background for new developments in discourse analysis (Pike, 1967). The study of narratives in indigenous languages by him and his followers had always been closely related to the analysis of discourse (Grimes, 1975; Longacre, 1977).

Back in Europe again, 1964 also was the year in which the first linguistic appeals were made in favor of a so-called text linguistics or text grammar, first by Hartmann in a small paper, and soon by his students, such as

Schmidt and others in the Germanies and the surrounding countries. In Europe, more than in the United States, the original plea by Harris (1952) for a linguistic discourse analysis was taken seriously and eventually led to a new, generative–transformational approach to the grammar of discourse.

Similarly, the functional orientation of linguistics in Czechoslovakia, such as the interest in notions such as "topic" and "comment" in the study of functional sentence perspective, also provided a natural stimulus to take discourse structures into account (see for instance, the work by Palek [1968] on hyper-syntax). Ten years later, this work would be one of the sources for American work on the functional analysis of topic and the discourse dependence of grammar (Givón, 1979).

Another functional approach, finally, is characterized by the "systemic grammar" developed by Halliday (1961), in which not only the thematic organization of sentences, but also the relations between sentences and discourse, were analyzed. This work gave rise to several studies at the boundaries of linguistics, stylistics, and poetics, both by Halliday himself and by Leech and Crystal. Besides poetry, conversation, advertising, and news received systematic attention in these English studies.

From this brief historical review of the origins of modern discourse analysis, we may draw several conclusions. First, the early interest in systematic discourse analysis was essentially a descriptive and structuralist enterprise, mainly at the boundaries of linguistics and anthropology. Second, this interest primarily involved indigenous or popular discourse genres, such as folktales, myths, and stories, as well as some ritual interaction forms. Third, the functional analysis of sentence and discourse structure as well as the first attempts toward text linguistics often took place independently of or against the increasingly prevailing paradigm of generative–transformational grammars. Both the formal sophistication and the inherent limitations of this approach to language would decisively influence the development of discourse analysis and other studies of language during the 1970s.

THE EMERGENCE OF DISCOURSE ANALYSIS AS A NEW DISCIPLINE (1972–1974)

Whereas the 1960s had brought various scattered attempts to apply semiotic or linguistic methods to the study of texts and communicative events, the early 1970s saw the publication of the first monographs and collections wholly and explicitly dealing with systematic discourse analysis as an independent orientation of research within and across several disciplines.

This development, however, did not come alone. Part of its theoretical and methodological inspiration was shared by other paradigm shifts in the study of language, for example, a critical extension or refutation of formal, context-free transformational grammars. Thus, sociolinguistics, which had also begun to take shape in the late 1960s (Fishman, 1968), emphasized that the theoretical distinction between competence and per-formance, as it had been reintroduced by Chomsky (after Saussure's distinction between *langue* and *parole*), was not without problems. Against notions such as 'ideal speakers' and 'homogeneous speech community', sociolinguistic work stressed the importance of language variation in the sociocultural context. Apart from variations in phonology, morphology, and syntax, and the dependence of stylistic variation on social factors, this reorientation also soon began to pay specific attention to discourse, for example, the work of Labov (1972a, 1972b). His studies of Black English also involved analyses of forms of verbal dueling among ado-lescents, and his other sociolinguistic work featured analyses of natural storytelling about personal experience. This latter research was in marked contrast to the structuralist analysis of written stories mentioned above because of its interest in spoken language and the functions of discourse in the social context.

A second important development in the early 1970s was the discovery in linguistics of the philosophical work by Austin, Grice, and Searle about speech acts. Whereas sociolinguistics stressed the role of language variation and the social context, this approach considered verbal utterances not only as sentences, but also as specific forms of social action. That is, sentences when used in some specific context also should be assigned some additional meaning or function, an illocutionary one, to be defined in terms of speaker intentions, beliefs, or evaluations, or relations between speaker and hearer. In this way, not only could systematic properties of the context be accounted for, but also the relation between utterances as abstract linguistic objects and utterances taken as a form of social interaction could be explained. This new dimension added a pragmatic orientation to the usual theoretical components of language. This de-velopment of linguistics toward a study of language use also appeared in published form between 1972 and 1974 (e.g., Maas & Wunderlich, 1972; Sadock, 1974), although the integration of speech act theory and discourse analysis was to be paid attention to only some years later.

Third, within the framework of grammatical theory itself, it was re-peatedly maintained that grammars should not merely provide structural characterizations of isolated sentences. This and other arguments led to the development of text grammars, mainly in the Germanies and other European countries. The study of pronouns and other cohesion markers, of semantic coherence, presupposition, topic and comment, overall semantic macrostructures, and other typical features of texts, understood as sequences of sentences, began to be studied in linguistics within a new, integrated perspective. Though demonstrating a more formal point of view, this new orientation shared with sociolinguistics and pragmatics its interest for an account of the structures of actual language use. The first books in the field, after a few articles in the 1960s, also began to appear in the early 1970s (Dressler, 1972; Petöfi, 1971; Schmidt, 1973; van Dijk, 1972), soon leading to a more widespread, interdisciplinary and broader study of textlinguistics and discourse, often independently in various countries (e.g., Halliday & Hasan, 1976).

At the same time psychology and the new field of artificial intelligence rediscovered discourse, after the early, and later influential, work on memory for stories by Bartlett (1932). More than other neighboring disciplines, psychology and psycholinguistics developed in the shadow of transformational grammar, so that much work was concerned with the experimental testing of the psychological reality of, for example, syntactic rules. The early 1970s brought not only a decisive breakthrough—conditioned by Chomsky, Miller, and others—of the cognitive and information processing paradigm against the prevailing behaviorism of the previous decades, but also a greater interest in semantic memory and the representation of knowledge (Carroll & Freedle, 1972; Lindsay & Norman, 1972). The extension of this cognitive research to models of memory for texts and of processes for text understanding and production was a natural step, and the collection edited by Carroll and Freedle, just mentioned, represents the first attempts in that direction. Work done by Kintsch, Bower, Rumelhart and others marked the beginnings of the psychological study of discourse (e.g., Kintsch, 1974) and at the same time demonstrated renewed interest for the earlier work by Bartlett (1932).

Artificial intelligence, the computer simulation of language understanding, at the same time started its important work about knowledge representations in memory. Thus, Charniak (1972) in his dissertation on children's stories showed the relevance of the vast amounts of world knowledge and the great numbers of knowledge-activation strategies needed for the understanding of even very simple children's stories. Bartlett's early notion of 'schema' now had the more sophisticated company of similar notions in artificial intelligence, such as 'script', 'scenario', 'frame', in the work by Schank, Abelson, Rumelhart, and others in this new sister discipline of cognitive psychology (e.g., Schank & Abelson, 1977).

Apparently, paradigmatic shifts seldom come alone in a single discipline. The early 1970s also witnessed important developments in sociology, such as the increasing attention to the analysis of everyday conversations and other forms of natural dialogue in social interaction. Here too, the late 1960s saw a critical refutation of the prevailing macrosociological approaches to social structure: Attention was turned to everyday social interaction and to commonsense interpretation categories at the microlevel of social reality. This interpretative, phenomenological sociology was advocated by Goffman, Garfinkel, and others. Work by the late Harvey Sacks (through his unpublished lecture notes and an occasional paper) primarily initiated and stimulated the soon quickly spreading analysis of everyday conversation. The early 1970s also saw the first published and widely read versions of this work (Cicourel, 1973; Sacks, Schegloff, & Jefferson, 1974; Sudnow, 1972). With this approach, the predominant interest in monological discourse genres (texts, stories, myths, etc.) had found its necessary complement. Natural, mundane, and spontaneous language use was primarily identified with conversation and other forms of dialogue in the social situation. People not only have implicit knowledge of the rules of grammar, but also of the rules of, for example, turn taking in conversation. In this respect, this conversational analysis recalls the early structural and formal approaches to the structures of sentences and provides the first elements of a grammar of verbal interaction. Thus, not only was a new dialogical dimension added to the earlier monological studies of discourse structures, but also a plea was made for the study of language and language use as a form of social interaction, as pragmatics or speech act theory had done in more formal and philosphical terms. Soon this work in sociology found its way into linguistics and other neighboring disciplines. Not only conversations but also dialogues in the classroom or in other institutional settings received extensive interest, such as in the discourse analysis approach to classroom talk by Sinclair and Coulthard (1975) in England.

And finally, the circle of these independent beginnings of contemporary discourse analysis can be closed by returning again to the discipline where much of it had started in the first place: anthropology. The work by Hymes, Gumperz, and others had yielded an increasingly autonomous orientation of ethnographic research on communicative events, labeled the "ethnography of speaking" (or the "ethnography of communication"). Under the inspiration of the influential and programmatic work of Hymes in the 1960s, new theories and fieldwork were collected in two readers (Bauman & Scherzer, 1974; Gumperz & Hymes, 1972). The boundaries between the sociolinguistics of discourse and this new branch of anthropology were fuzzy: the study of "real" language use in the sociocultural context no longer stopped at form of address, rituals, or myth, but also began to pay attention to the mundane forms of talk in different cultures, such as greetings, spontaneous storytelling, formal meetings, verbal dueling, and other forms of communication and verbal interaction.

CONCLUSION

This brief survey of the emergence of new directions in the study of language use and discourse at the beginning of the 1970s shows that there was both continuity and change with respect to the previous decade. Formal sentence grammars had been challenged from several sides and were at least complemented with new ideas about language use, linguistic variation, speech acts, conversation, other dialogues, text structures, communicative events, and their cognitive and social contexts. Most of the paradigmatic shifts in the various language disciplines also brought a natural extension toward discourse phenomena. And soon, this common interest in the respective disciplines led to a more integrated, autonomous, and interdisciplinary study of discourse in the following decade (1974–1984). Work during this decade is exemplified and reviewed in the respective chapters of this first volume of the *Handbook of Discourse Analysis,* which itself may be interpreted as a signal of the independence and autonomy of the new cross-discipline.

Whereas the respective chapters of this volume pay detailed attention to the major notions, theories, results, and some of the historical background of current discourse analysis, this introduction has shown the sources, contacts, and early interdisciplinary work of the 1960s that led to the current approaches that emerged in several countries at the beginning of the 1970s. Much of the still burgeoning variety of orientations, methods, characteristic objects of research (e.g., genres of discourse or dimensions of context), and styles of theory formation and description finds its origin in the different historical backgrounds of each of the disciplines engaged. Thus, conversational analysis and interaction theories in many respects had to develop as an anti-(macro-)sociology, text grammar as a antisentence grammar, speech act theory as an antigrammar *tout court,* and much of current psychology and sociology of language as antilinguistics. Much formal rigor and theoretical sophistication had to be temporarily bracketed out in order to formulate completely new approaches, to set out new areas of research, and to introduce new and sometimes strange notions. But from the initial paradigm shifts briefly described above, we now seem to have entered the stage of normal science for the field of discourse analysis. The chapters of this volume provide ample evidence for this view of the field, as well as introductions and a description of the current state of insights into the structures and functions of discourse and its contexts. Yet 10 or maybe 20 years after the first modern studies of discourse is not much, and it will therefore also be apparent that the discipline is still in the first stage of its normal development.

In the meantime, the four or five central disciplines of discourse have received company elsewhere. In the field of law studies it has been realized that much of its object domain, such as laws, legal (inter-)action, and legal documents, has a textual or dialogical nature. The same holds for history and historiography, of which both the sources and the products are mostly texts and, more recently, also oral discourse forms. The study of mass communication, dealing with mass-mediated messages and their conditions of production and reception, also is developing from early content analysis to more sophisticated discourse analysis of media texts and talk. Here, as well as in semiotics, the relation between discourse and pictures, photographs, or film also are systematically analyzed. Poetics, interested in literary texts but also in dramatic dialogue, has been closely associated with the structuralist beginnings of discourse analysis and continues to be influenced by it. Clinical psychology has paid attention to therapeutic discourse, and social psychology to the interaction of cognitive and social aspects of persuasive communication and attitude change, to the situational analysis of verbal interaction, and to the discourse-mediated formation of social representations and attributions.

It is not difficult to continue this list of social sciences that have, since the 1970s, paid attention to text and talk. Some of these disciplines are also presented in this volume; others—such as the political analysis of discourse—receive more specific attention in later volumes. It may be expected, thus, that in the 1980s discourse analysis will on the one hand lead to further integration and expansion, while on the other hand it will differentiate into inevitable specialization.

SELECTED BIBLIOGRAPHY

This list of references is merely a selective bibliography of the major works and names of the people mentioned in this historical survey of the emergence of discourse analysis. Further references and bibliographic details of the historical backgrounds in the respective disciplines can be found in the following chapters.

Bartlett, F. C. (1932). *Remembering*. London: Cambridge University Press.
Bauman, R., & Sherzer, J. (Eds.). (1974). *Explorations in the ethnography of speaking*. London: Cambridge University Press.
Carroll, J. S., & Freedle, R. O. (Eds.). (1972). *Language comprehension and the acquisition of knowledge*. Washington, D.C.: Winston.
Charniak, E. (1972). *Towards a model of children's story comprehension*. Unpublished doctoral dissertation, Massachusetts Institute of Technology, Cambridge.
Cicourel, A. V. (1973). *Cognitive sociology*. Harmondsworth: Penguin Books.
Communications 4 (1964). *Recherches sémiologiques*. Paris: Seuil.
Communications 8 (1966). *Recherches sémiologiques. L'analyse structurale du récit*. Paris: Seuil.
Dressler, W. U. (1972). *Einführung in die Textlinguistik*. Tübingen: Niemeyer. (new version, with R. de Beaugrande, published as *Introduction to text linguistics*. London: Longman, 1981).

Fishman, J. (Ed.). (1968). *Readings in the sociology of language*. The Hague: Mouton.

Givón, T. (Ed.). (1979). *Discourse and syntax. Syntax and semantics* (Vol. 12). New York: Academic Press.

Grimes, J. E. (1975). *The Thread of discourse*. The Hague: Mouton.

Gumperz, J. D., & Hymes, D. (Eds.). (1972). *Directions in sociolinguistics. The ethnography of communication*. New York: Holt, Rinehart & Winston.

Halliday, M. A. K. (1961). Categories of the theory of grammar, *Word, 17*, 241–292.

Halliday, M. A. K., & Hasan, R. (1976). *Cohesion in English*. London: Longman.

Harris, Z. S. (1952). Discourse analysis. *Language, 28*, 1–30.

Hartmann, P. (1964). Text, Texte, Klassen von Texten. *Bogawus, 2*, 15–25.

Hymes, D. (Ed.). (1964). *Language in culture and society*. New York: Harper & Row.

Kintsch, W. (1974). *The representation of meaning in memory*. Hillsdale, NJ: Erlbaum.

Labov, W. (1972a). *Language in the inner city*. Philadelphia: University of Pennsylvania Press.

Labov, W. (1972b). *Sociolinguistic patterns*. Philadelphia: University of Pennsylvania Press.

Lindsay, P. H., & Norman, D. A. (1972). *Human information processing*. New York: Academic Press.

Longacre, R. E. (Ed.). (1977). *Discourse grammar* (Vols. 1–3). Dallas: Summer Institute of Linguistics.

Maas, U., & Wunderlich, D. (1972). *Pragmatik und sprachliches Handeln*. Frankfurt: Athenaeum.

Palek, B. (1968). *Cross-reference*. Prague: Charles University.

Petöfi, J. S. (1971). *Transformationsgrammatiken und eine ko-textuelle Texttheorie*. Frankfurt: Athenaeum.

Pike, K. L. (1967). *Language in relation to a unified theory of human behavior*. The Hague: Mouton.

Propp, V. (1958) *Morphology of the folktale*. Bloomington, IN: Indiana University Press. (Original work published 1928)

Sacks, H., Schegloff, E., & Jefferson, G. (1974). A simplest systematic of turntaking for conversation. *Language, 50* 696–735.

Sadock, J. M. (1974). *Towards a linguistic theory of speech acts*. New York: Academic Press.

Schank, R. C., & Abelson, R. P. (1977). *Scripts, plans, goals and understanding*. Hillsdale, NJ: Erlbaum.

Schmidt, S. J. (1973). *Texttheorie*. Munich: Fink (UTB).

Sinclair, J. McH., Coulthard, R. M. (1975). *Towards an analysis of discourse. The English used by teachers and pupils*. London: Oxford University Press.

Sudnow, D. (Ed.). (1972). *Studies in social interaction*. New York: Free Press.

van Dijk, T. A. (1972). *Some aspects of text grammars*. The Hague: Mouton.

CHAPTER 2

Linguistics as a Tool for Discourse Analysis

Charles J. Fillmore

LINGUISTIC RELATIONS

The science of linguistics concerns itself with discovering, describing, and (where relevant) explaining (1) the units of linguistic form or content, (2) the structures or patterns in which these units are defined and situated, (3) the roles or functions that these units serve in these structures, and (4) the dependencies or interpretive links that obtain between different units in the same text. Since some of the units I speak of provide the substance, or make up the constituents, of higher-level units, we find that we can speak of units, roles, structures, and intratextual connections at many levels in the description of a language and in the description of texts.

For maximum generality I allow myself to use the word 'text' to designate any whole product of human linguistic capacity, including, thus, words and tone groups at the narrow end of its scope, novels and bodies of law at the wide end. The organization of users' knowledge of their language can be seen as having intertextual, intratextual, and extratextual dimensions. Intertextually, we recognize relations between what we actually find in a given segment of text and what might have been there in its place. That is, we deal intertextually with relations between the piece of text at hand and other potential texts or text segments that are partly like it and partly unlike it. Intratextually, we have to do with relations between given pieces of a single text. And extratextually, we are concerned with the connection between a text and its "worlds."

We can discern at least seven major types of relations involving units of linguistic form. Among the intertextual relations are those which hold

HANDBOOK OF DISCOURSE ANALYSIS, Vol. 1
Disciplines of Discourse

between

1. a given unit and other units that are structurally mutually substitutable with it,

and those which hold between

2. a given unit and other units that can be thought of as coming from the same repertory or linguistic domain as the observed unit.

Relations of types 1 and 2 may be spoken of as relations of 'alternativity' and 'association', respectively, the vagueness and boundarylessness of the latter not unintended.

Intratextual relations are those that hold between

3. a given unit in a text and a larger unit of which it can be seen as a part,
4. a given unit in a text and its companions or co-constituents, that is, the other units found in its containing structure,

or between

5. a given unit in a text and other units in the same text with which it holds the relation of obligatory or potential co-interpretation.[1]

With respect to extratextuality we can distinguish

6. the world within which the text is produced, or what I have elsewhere called the text-external world (Fillmore, 1976),

and

7. the world whose properties the text represents, the text-internal world.

In general, relations of the first four types are found at every linguistic level; relations of the fifth through seventh types are found only at the level of structures capable of receiving semantic interpretation.

Analogous to but distinct from the contrast made here between the intertextual and intratextual is a more traditional distinction between the paradigmatic and the syntagmatic dimensions (Saussure, 1976). Briefly, the paradigmatic dimension is that within which one speaks of contrast and alternation (to which our category 1 is the closest approximation),

---

[1] The term *co-interpretation* is from Halliday and Hasan, 1976. I include in this category (1) the lexicogrammatical markers of grammatical constructions, (2) the separate pieces of discontinuous constituents, and (3) 'phoric' elements that have relations of coreference or cosignificance with other elements of the same text.

while the syntagmatic dimension is that within which one speaks of structure, co-occurrence, dependencies, and the like—in short, the "combinatorics" of language—represented here by categories 3–5, but also much of 2. The distinction made here between intertextual and intratextual can be phrased as the difference between (1) knowledge that a text interpreter brings to the text in order to achieve an interpretation of it and (2) an awareness of the text itself and the data which it provides.

With respect to intratextual relations, there are two possible directions of dependencies: 'anaphoric', leading from a presented unit to something earlier in the text, and 'cataphoric', leading from a presented unit to entities appearing later in the text. In familiar discussions within linguistics, these terms are generally restricted to discourse about pronominalization phenomena and various other reduction or deletion processes. But I am generalizing the two terms, for our purposes, to the two situations of (1) recognizing what something is, or seeing how it is to be interpreted, through an awareness of its connection to something earlier in the text and (2) recognizing what something is and, by virtue of that recognition, sensing its connectedness to something found later in the text.

The categories of linguistic skills and knowledge suggested by the above classification of linguistic relations can be illustrated as follows:

1. Knowledge of phonemic contrast (knowing precisely how and where *live* and *love* differ at the phonological level), awareness of the contrasting categories of an inflectional system (having distinct strategies for interpreting present-tense and past-tense fictional narratives, for example), sensitivity to morphologically related or phonosymbolically related words, knowledge of minimal semantic contrasts in lexical fields (knowing, for example, that *girl* is simultaneously 'not boy' and 'not woman'), knowledge of both within-frame contrasts (such as one finds between *stingy* and *generous* or between *thrifty* and *wasteful*) as well as cross-frame contrasts (as one finds when there is a question of whether the same behavior should be evaluated by the *stingy–generous* scale or by the *thrifty–wasteful* scale.

2. Abstract knowledge of the grammatical requirements of individual lexical items, knowledge of the occurrence of items in phraseological units, knowledge of the joint fitting into common semantic schemata of given sets of lexical and phraseological units (as with *buy, sell, pay, cost, spend,* fitting each in a unique way onto a commercial-event schema), awareness of the 'happiness conditions' for speech acts of given types.

3. Knowledge of the function of phonemes of given types in the text's well-formed syllables, recognition of word-forming patterns exhibited in the text and the functions of the constituents of these patterns, knowledge of the grammatical roles of words and headed phrases within larger

phrases or sentences, knowledge of the grammatical structure of the text's constituent sentences, recognition of genres and text types through recognition of their constituent elements, awareness of the situatedness of given speech acts in larger communicating events.

4. Knowledge of the connection between a syllable nucleus and its onsets or codas, awareness of the fit between given prefixes or suffixes and given lexical stems in word composition, relations of government and agreement between words and phrases in presented syntactic structures, sensitivity in semantic structure to relations of predication, modification, quantification, negation.

5. Knowledge of distant dependencies in syntax, awareness of discontinuous constituents, relations of anaphora and cataphora between elements of the text requiring co-interpretation, recognition of such narrative-structural matters as the moment of the introduction of a problem in a narrative and the moment of its resolution.

6. The ability to establish exophoric relations (in the sense of Halliday & Hasan, 1976): *deixis* (the relation between linguistic choices and systematic aspects of the communicative act, such as the identity of the participants, the time of the communicative act, the location of the participants at the time of the communicative act, the social relations between the participants, etc.), register (the fit between linguistic choices and the acts, discourse topics, and personnel in the associated activities), pragmatics (the relation between the formation of an utterance and the acts that a performer of the utterance is capable of accomplishing within given contexts).

7. The ability to construe a text by constructing the characteristics of the world or situation that is most compatible with it (i.e., the world that contains the objects, behaviors, or institutions that the text implies or refers to, that has the history presupposed by the text).

LINGUISTICS AND LANGUAGE PROCESSING

It has not been a part of established linguistic tradition to see as a proper object of study the time-bound processes of producing or interpreting linguistic texts, or even to see the workings of such processes as included in the scope of what a science of linguistics is about. Asymmetries in anaphoric and cataphoric processes have long been noted, and functionalist explanations have occasionally been proposed to account for left–right asymmetries in syntactic 'movement' and 'depth of embedding'. Such notions as 'anticipation' and 'perseveration' of articulatory gestures have long figured in explanatory accounts of phonological processes. But in general, the temporal development of text, in production or comprehension, has not been seen as providing a fruitful organizing principle for the description of linguistic units and their structures. Linguists have traditionally been interested in patterns found in the products of linguistic abilities (and in the abstract competence of speakers that underlies the knowledge of such patterns), much more than they have had any interest in the behaviors and strategies language users avail themselves of in producing and understanding language. (Linguistic and other work committed to the procedural approach is briefly surveyed in Beaugrande & Dressler, 1981, Chap. 3.)

For anyone who is explicitly interested in the description and analysis of texts or discourse, of course, attention to processes and to the time line that the operation of such processes presupposes is indispensable. If we wish to see whether the concepts, notations, and analytic tools of linguistics can figure in such inquiry, we will find it useful to examine some of these in new ways. In particular, by making the effort to see any linguistic product as growing or developing through time (the product itself at the sending end, the experience of constructing its interpretation at the receiving end), we need to reformulate many of the standard linguistic concepts to make them into tools that can aid in the understanding of such processes. If a static description of a language allows us to describe a particular element as cataphoric, a dynamic description will allow us to speak of its role in inducing an interpreter to expect the ongoing text to proceed in a particular way. An anaphoric element induces the interpreter to review earlier portions of the text to complete its interpretation. Paradigmatically contrasting elements are often perceived or interpreted by bringing the relevant framework of contrast into awareness, and the activation of that framework may itself establish further expectations and conclusions about the ongoing text.

Taking as an ideal interpreter of a linguistic text someone who has supreme command of the knowledge and interpreting abilities represented by the seven categories of linguistic knowledge identified above, we can show something of the ways in which linguistic structures figure in the linear time development of the processes of speaking, writing, or understanding by constructing a series of questions that could be asked, during the processing of a text, on the part of such a supremely competent interpreter, and by considering how and whether the text provided answers to those questions.[2]

---

[2] The general approach to the study of the dynamics of text interpretation followed here is discussed, with somewhat different emphasis, in Fillmore (1981). The approach was developed in collaborative work with Paul Kay and a number of students in Berkeley.

At each step, our interpreter's questions can be imagined as having some such form as the following:

1. What is the unit that I have just encountered?
2. Am I helped in knowing what this unit is by remembering interpretations I gave to something earlier in this text? That is, did some cataphoric element cause me to be ready for this? Alternatively, am I able to draw anaphoric links from this to something I've already encountered earlier in the text?
3. Is the current unit a part of a larger unit in this text? If so, in what role is it situated, or what function is it serving, in that larger unit?
4. What things might have occupied this position in place of the unit I have just encountered? What conclusions can I justifiably draw from the fact that the creator of this piece of text chose to use this unit rather than any of its possible substitutions?
5. What things have already appeared that are also part of the thing this is a part of? What things can I assume might appear later in the text that are also part of the structure that this is part of?
6. What might the thing this is a part of be a part of? What role does it play (or might it turn out to play) in that larger thing?
7. Does the presence of this unit in this place signal the copresence of some corresponding unit at another level of linguistic structure?

It can be seen that an answer to question 6 leads to a cycle through the same set of questions with respect to a more inclusive unit in the structural hierarchy of a text (where decisions about a phoneme have led to conclusions about a syllable or morpheme, or where decisions about the role and function of a sentence have led to conclusions about the nature of an episode, etc.), while an answer to question 7 leads to a cycle through the same questions for a unit in a different domain (i.e., crossing the domains of form, meaning, usage, etc., as where the correct recognition of a lexical unit has led to the positing of an active semantic unit, or where the correct semantic interpretation of a sentence has led to decisions about the kind of illocutionary act the sentence is being used to perform, etc.).

It is helpful to think of the process of working one's way through a text as a kind of game with moves and states. A move consists in accepting an increment in the text and making the changes, additions, and so on, that the text and the rules dictate. A state is the full set of expectations, questions, and registered conclusions that a player has formed after a particular move has been completed. At each point in this imagined step-by-step development of an ongoing text we can attribute to the interpreter of a text one or more of those cognitive states expressed by the following statements:

I have a current set of hypotheses about the text as a whole: its point, its content, its source, its setting, and so on.

I am now expecting a specific element. (e.g., The latest increment was the word *blithering;* I am now expecting to see the word *idiot*).

I have brought into play a framing context, the one introduced by a unit just encountered. (e.g., Sensing that the topic in the current text is a musical one, and having just encountered the phrase *acoustic guitar,* I am prepared to see the setting of the text at this point as one in which a contrast between ordinary musical instruments and electrically amplified versions of these is relevant.)[3]

I am expecting to find soon a syntactic structure of a particular kind because of a dependency associated with some previously encountered syntactic element. (e.g., Having encountered the verb *put* and a direct object for that verb, as in *The child refused to put his toys . . . ,* I know that a locative or directional adverb is now due.)

I have just resolved a previous uncertainty or answered a question that had been posed or left unanswered with a previous move. (e.g., I had needed to know in what sense and about which object *put* was being used. The nounphrase *his toys* has just answered those questions for me.)

I have now reopened a question about a previously processed element. (e.g., I had believed that an earlier quoted section of text was to be taken as spoken by the princess in the story, but now I am not so sure.)

I have just had to revise a previous decision that I have just learned was in error. (e.g., The author tricked me into believing that the surgeon was a man; the last increment of the text revealed to me that it was a woman.)

In short, we attribute to the interpreter of an ongoing text an awareness of at least certain properties of what is currently "in the buffer," a memory of what complex state the interpreter was in just previously, the knowledge of repertories of items and structures (at many levels, and simultaneously), the knowledge of a set of principles characterizing the language in question, and the ability to generate expectations from this complex of awarenesses and knowledge.

DIVISIONS OF LINGUISTICS

Without being overly concerned about the psychological reality of the implied online processing claims that accompany the manner of speaking

---

[3] I am indebted to Mark Hansell for making me aware of the acoustic–electric contrast.

I have adopted, I nevertheless find it useful to think of standard linguistic analysis as making explicit the layers of questions, expectations, and conclusions that an interpreter of linguistic texts experiences, these layers corresponding more or less to the familiar levels of linguistic structure. The notion of 'levels of structure', in fact, is understandable in terms of the ways in which the act of closing one line of questioning (by identifying a new unit of a particular kind) opens up new questions and new expectations. (A resolution of questions about a given complex structure at one level often results in the recognition of an elementary unit at another level—a unit about which questions of functions, companions, and the rest can now begin.)

The technical divisions one finds in the science of synchronic linguistics can be thought of as separate assemblies of the kinds of knowledge that work together in the processes we have been considering.

Phonology

Knowledge of allowed phonetic sequences is used when one closes or creates expectation chains in speech perception. Recognition of phonetic segments (phonetics), identification of their potential role in the syllable or other phonotactic structures (phonemics), knowledge of the combinatorial possibilites of phoneme units (phonotactics), and so on make up the segmental phonology of a language. Paradigmatic alternation among phonological units in corresponding parts of morpheme variants as these figure in the recognition of morphemes and their roles in larger morphological structure is part or all of morphophonemics.

Grammar and Lexicogrammatical Categories

Knowledge of category contrasts among inflected forms of words participates in the recognition of operating grammatical categories and thus in the recognition of grammatical structures. The formal difference between the following two German texts is only that between the indicative *war* and the subjective *sei*.

> *Im Büro sass nur die Sekretärin. Der Chef war auf einer Konferenz.*
> *Im Büro sass nur die Sekretärin. Der Chef sei auf einer Konferenz.*

In each of the two texts, however, the role played by the second sentence is dramatically different. In the former text the statement about the boss' absence is offered as an explanation of why the secretary is alone. In the latter text, however, the second sentence represents something that the secretary said. The transition from word-form recognition, to grammatical-category recognition, to knowledge of use, to contexted application is generally instantaneous in the comprehension experience.[4]

Knowledge of word-forming and phrase-forming principles in the language leads to the ability to create appropriate expectations and arrive at appropriate conclusions in the processing of complex words, phrases, and sentences. Knowledge of the valence of verbs, nouns, and adjectives, and knowledge of the co-occurrence requirements associated with lexical items that serve as markers of specific grammatical constructions create structures of expectation and resolution at many levels of sentence complexity. Moved or displaced constituents (as with interrogative word questions, relative clauses, or topicalized sentences) alert the interpreter to seek the gap in the constituents that follow.

Semantics and the Lexicon

Knowledge of contrast sets and the various other kinds of semantic relations studied in lexical semantics makes it possible to bring into the interpretation of a text the entire framework within which the related lexical items have their motivated existence. The semantic valencies of individual lexical items invite interpreters to look for (in earlier text) or expect (in later text) the relevant dependent information.

Pragmatics and Text Linguistics

Knowledge of the principles of conversational cooperation lead to questions, expectations, and conclusions about illocutionary force. (Asking a question puts the person asked under an obligation to answer the question in good faith. Thus, if in the state of having been asked "Can you take me to Hawaii?" one is heard saying, "Am I a millionaire?," we are empowered to interpret that as a negative answer to the question.) Portions of a text expressing presuppositions lead the interpreter either to verify the presupposed proposition in the previous text segments or, where that is impossible, (1) to assume that what the text presupposes is true in the text's inner world and (2) to draw appropriate conclusions about the text's outer world from the fact that the information was revealed only through presupposition.

SAMPLE TEXT ANALYSIS: *LA BOHÈME*

As material on which to demonstrate some of the linguistic notions mentioned above, I have chosen what might be considered an unnatural

---

[4] For the German examples I am indebted to Knud Lambrecht.

text, that of an opera resume. My text is the synopsis of the Puccini opera *La Bohème* distributed by the San Francisco Opera company in its 1978 fall season. My interest in such texts comes from the fact that they tend to be uncommonly difficult to understand and from my suspicion that this difficulty is to be explained by their special purpose.

Texts of the type from which our synopsis was chosen are monological, written, semicontextualized, narratives with a fixed point of view. In virtue of their being monological, they lack expressions anchored in the difference between sender and receiver; as written texts, they are at least partly decontextualized, meaning that they do not interact fully with the ongoing activities that engage sender or receiver; in describing them, nevertheless, as semicontextualized, I mean that they require an amount of awareness of something going on (in particular, what is happening on the stage during the opera's performance) relatively greater than for ordinary written texts; that they represent narratives goes without saying; and the fixed point of view is determined necessarily by the spatial relation between the audience and the stage. There are clear pragmatic constraints on their production and interpretation, and an awareness of those constraints is essential to giving them their correct interpretation. Essential to an understanding of the genre is the knowledge that these texts are not structured to make the story maximally easy to grasp; rather, their purpose is to represent the sequence in which things happen, on the stage, during the opera's performance, and to let the readers know at least something about what the performers are saying or singing to each other. The consequences of constructing texts required to satisfy this condition will come out in much that is said below.

Here is the full text of the *La Bohème* synopsis.

Act I—(A garret). In their cold Paris attic, two of the Bohemians are trying to keep a fire burning in their stove; the painter Marcello is prevented from burning a chair by the poet Rodolfo, who instead sacrifices one of his own manuscripts. Their friend Schaunard arrives with food and drink, having just been paid for a music lesson; they are also joined by Colline, the philosopher. After a visit by the landlord Benoit, who demands payment of the long overdue rent, all except Rodolfo leave for the Cafe Momus. There is a knock at the door and a neighbor, Mimi, comes in, hoping to light a candle which went out in the draft. A little later, she returns for the key to her room, which she lost. As she and Rodolfo look for it, their hands touch. He tells her about himself and his dreams, followed by Mimi's charming narration about her own life and longings. They are attracted to each other and go out together to join Rodolfo's friends.

Act II—(A square in the Latin quarter). Christmas Eve. At the Cafe Momus, situated in a square filled with a happy crowd, Marcello is embarrassed by the arrival of his old flame Musetta with her wealthy "protector" Alcindoro. In spite of their attempts to appear indifferent, it is obvious that Musetta and Marcello still care for each other. She sings a provocative song deliberately directed at

Marcello, after which they embrace and she joins the friends at the table. After the arrival of the guards, the Bohemians depart, leaving Alcindoro with the unpaid bill.

Act III—(A tollgate on the outskirts of Paris). The pale and distraught Mimi looks for Marcello. She tells him how difficult life has become with the jealous Rodolfo. Then, hiding, she overhears Rodolfo complaining about her. A sudden coughing fit reveals her presence. While they talk of parting Marcello and Musetta quarrel. Mimi and Rodolfo, however, decide to stay together until spring.

Act IV—(A garret). Back in their attic, Rodolfo and Marcello long for their girl-friends, Musetta and Mimi, who have left them. Schaunard and Colline bring food and drink and for a while, the four friends together forget their sorrow and poverty. Musetta helps Mimi in; she is very ill and had asked to be brought to the attic, where she has been so happy with Rodolfo. Colline decides to sell his only coat in order to provide for some medicine. Left alone, Rodolfo and Mimi recall their happy days together. After the friends return with medicine and a muff for Mimi's cold hands, Rodolfo is the last one to realize that Mimi has died.

(A breakdown of the text into numbered and annotated segments is to be found in the Appendix to this chapter. The segment numbers in the following paragraphs refer to the segmentation given in the Appendix.)

Background Information

What we know about the text–external world of our synopsis is that it is to be read by people who are about to see an opera, and that most of the people who read it are doing so in order to make sure that they will know what is happening on the stage and what the people on the stage are singing about. In many cases, readers will know the story but will nevertheless appreciate being reminded of which episode appears in which act. Many background facts and situations in the story of an opera are not presented in the performance itself. When such background information makes it into the printed resume, it is usually by way of presupposition or subordination of various kinds, especially if its full elaboration would interfere with the main purpose of such pieces of writing, which is to represent the action of the opera scene by scene.

First Mention

Since the table identifying the cast in any particular performance generally gives only the names of the characters, it is usually up to the text of the synopsis to identify the characters' roles or professions. True to that tradition, our text identifies each character, on first introduction, with a name-and-role two-part formula. We are introduced, by turn, to *the painter Marcello* (6), *the poet Rodolfo* (8), *their friend Schaunard* (11), *Colline, the philosopher* (16), *the landlord Benoit* (17), *a neighbor, Mimi* (23), *(Marcello's) old flame Musetta* (41), and *(Musetta's) wealthy "protector" Alcindoro* (42). An ordinary narrative might allow the prior setting up of a network of relationships as knowledge that could be built on later (*There lived in Paris, around 1830, a group of artists and intellectuals who . . .*). It is typical of texts of the kind we are examining, however, that participants are described and situated only as they individually first appear on the scene. This is often accomplished through the special use of nominal apposition constructions of the kind we have just seen.

It is significant that the central character in the opera (Mimi) is the only one introduced with an indefinite noun phrase—*a neighbor, Mimi* (23). This fact is compatible with the view that the other characters are to be seen as making up the setting within which Mimi's story unfolds.

Informing via Presupposition

Throughout the text we find instances of information that is introduced by way of presuppositions—through the back door, so to speak. I use the term "presupposition" informally, referring merely to uses of language that suggest that some of the information it communicates is seen as taken for granted rather than being conveyed as fresh information. I have in mind, of course, the use of definite noun phrases, factive verbs, and the like, but also the depiction of situations that presuppose contexts or backgrounds that the text itself has not introduced. The frequency of this practice is presumably due to the particular communicative goals of texts in this genre. The phenomenon is by no means unusual in other sorts of narrative text, but it appears to be particularly useful for authors of opera resumes.

The practice and its effect can be seen in perspective by noting the pragmatic differences between different ways of preparing directions for someone finding his way for the first time in a new city. If I say something like

> *Go north on Fourth Street. You will eventually come to a huge First National Bank building. Turn left on that corner.*

I am introducing new objects into the text world in the usual way. If, however, I say something like

> *Go north on Fourth Street and turn left at the First National Bank building.*

I am asking you to construe my text in a slightly unusual way. The language of this second text is constructed as if by the time you need to know when to turn, you will have become aware of the existence of the relevant landmark. Similarly, in opera resumes, texts are often constructed in such a way as to suggest that the readers will be aware of the individuals, events, and landmarks referred to in them at the time they play an anchoring role in the text. The language of these texts gives the impression that they are designed to be read at the time the opera is being performed; from examining these texts and knowing their purposes, one might predict flashlights going on and off at each seat in the auditorium as the audience consults the synopsis during the performance.

From (4–5) (*two of the Bohemians are trying to keep a fire burning in their stove*) we learn that the flat has a stove, that there is a fire burning in it, that the characters are having difficulty in keeping it going— all by way of presupposition. From (6–8) (*the painter Marcello is prevented from burning a chair by the poet Rodolfo*) we learn, again by presupposition, that Marcello had intended and prepared to add a chair to the fire. From (9–10) (*who instead sacrifices one of his own manuscripts*) we learn that Rodolfo has more than one manuscript about, and that the one he assigns to the fire is one he would have preferred to keep; these facts we learn from *one of* and *sacrifices*. In (13–14) (*having just been paid for a music lesson*) the text lets us conclude, again indirectly, that Schaunard is a musician. In segment (17) (*After a visit by the landlord Benoit*) we learn, by a presuppositional device presumably used for brevity rather than for any reason dictated by the needs of the genre (we see this because of a tense conflict in (18), that the landlord paid a visit. Segments (18–19) *who demands payment of the long overdue rent*) tells us that the Bohemians were behind in their rent. Where Mimi enters, *hoping to light a candle which went out in the draft* (24–25), we learn, by presupposition, that her once-lighted candle had been extinguished and, by implicature, that her flat is drafty.

The sentence in (31–32) presupposes prior knowledge of what is here described as *Mimi's charming narration;* only by assuming that and by recalling the purpose of our text can we even make sense of the grammar of this sentence (*He tells her about himself and his dreams, followed by Mimi's charming narration about her own life and longings.*). We must realize that the purpose of the first clause is to let the readers know what Rodolfo is singing about in this scene, and that *Mimi's charming narration* is in fact the well-known aria "Mi chiamano Mimi." Someone who did not know the function of the text would find the grammatical form of this sentence quite unmotivated.

In segment (43) (*In spite of their attempts to appear indifferent*) we learn, indirectly, that Marcello and Musetta had been pretending to ignore each other. From segment (48) (*and she joins the friends at the table*) we learn for the first time that the friends are on stage. The fact that the audience will already know that (given the pretense that the text is to be read while the performance is going on), even if the innocent reader does not, allows the text to fit its external world satisfactorily. In the next segment, (49) (*After the arrival of the guards*), we learn that there has been a military parade. Except for the need to conserve space, this should have appeared as a separate sentence, at least, because the parade does make up an important scene in this act. Since it is not deemed necessary for the audience to understand what is being sung in this scene, subordinating the parade in this way does not go against the goals of the genre; the same seems to be true of the information, revealed presuppositionally in (51) (*leaving Alcindoro with the unpaid bill*), that the revelers had not paid their bill.

We learn that Rodolfo and Mimi have been living together, and that Rodolfo is a jealous mate, from (55–56) (*She tells him how difficult life has become with the jealous Rodolfo.*).

When in the last act we see that *Musetta helps Mimi in* (72), we feel ourselves invited to assume that Mimi is too ill to walk easily by herself. When in (78–79) we read that *Rodolfo and Mimi recall their happy days together* we learn, presuppositionally through *recall,* that the couple had happy times when they were together. And when, at the very end, we find out that Mimi is dead, we learn it by being told that Rodolfo finally realizes that she is dead. The audience, of course, knows before Rodolfo does that Mimi has died.

Reading between the Lines

In a great many places throughout the text, understanding by implicature, or "reading between the lines," is necessary. The text invites us to believe that the characters are poor by the reports of their need to make great personal sacrifices just to keep warm in the winter. Mimi comes to the garret *hoping to light a candle* (24). The text does not tell us whether she got her needed flame, and it does not tell us whether she then left the flat. But in segment 26 we learn that *A little later, she returns.* To make the text cohere (i.e., to motivate *return*), we have to believe that she went away after getting her candle lit, and that she is now returning to the garret for some other purpose. In an ordinary narrative such an omission would seem uncooperative.[5]

In Act II we learn that Musetta, after her song, *joins the friends at the table* (48), although we have not been told in advance that the friends

---

[5] I do not remember whether in the 1978 SFO version Mimi actually left the flat. The libretto does not require it.

were there. The reader can assume (as the audience will simply know) that this scene in the cafe is to be understood as immediately following Act I, and that, in fact, the Bohemians who left the garret at the end of Act I are together in the cafe in Act II.

Between (53–54) (*The pale and distraught Mimi looks for Marcello*) and (55) (*She tells him how difficult life has become*) we have to assume that Mimi found Marcello. From the description of Mimi *hiding* (57) we infer that Rodolfo has appeared (an inference immediately verified in the text, but of course known prior to Mimi's hiding by the audience). In a scene in which we know of the presence of Marcello, Mimi, and Rodolfo, we read (62) that *Marcello and Musetta quarrel*. But the text gave us no reason, before (62), to believe that Musetta was nearby. In a scene in Act IV in which all six friends are present and from which we have just learned of Colline's intention to sell his coat to get money for Mimi's medicine, we read (78) that Rodolfo and Mimi were *left alone*. The text does not tell us directly that all four of the others left, but we have to believe that anyway.

Some of the inferences we make in understanding the text are made in conformity with the results of the anaphoric processes. In (9–10), for example, the word *instead* has to be taken as linking back to Marcello's plan to use one of the friends' chairs for fuel, so we conclude easily that the sacrifice of Rodolfo's manuscript is as fuel to keep the fire going. In (15–16) we read *they are also joined by Colline, the philosopher*. Just before this point Marcello and Rodolfo were called on by Schaunard. Without *also* the *they* of (15–16) could easily refer to all three friends; but *also* requires the reader to schematize the visits of both Schaunard and Colline as events of people joining Marcello and Rodolfo, as opposed to the alternative of accepting Schaunard into the group and then seeing Colline as joining that group of three.

The phrase *a little later, she returns* (26) (already discussed in connection with the presuppositions associated with *returns*) makes sense only if we allow ourselves to believe something that the text itself did not tell us, namely, that she had left the flat. That this judgment belongs in the topic 'anaphora' comes from the interpretation of *a little later*: The question "later than what?" forces itself upon us.

Point of View

The fact that the text reports what happens on the stage, before the audience's eyes, determines the selection of point of view for the writer and reader. In ordinary third-person narrative, the point of view is created by the author through the use of deictic elements, expressive language, and so on; but in our case the point of view is fixed for us. When Schaunard *arrives* (11), we do not need to be told where he arrives. When we learn of the landlord's *visit* (17), we have no doubts about where he paid his visit. Everything we read about is to be understood as revealing what happens before our eyes literally. The source of motions, whenever they are not mentioned in the text, is always the place where the actors are moving about. The Bohemians *leave for the Cafe Momus* (21); a neighbor *comes in* (23); later she *returns* (26). We read of the *arrival* of Musetta (40), of the *arrival* of the guards (49), and of the Bohemians' departure (50). The friends *bring food and drink* (69), Mimi asks to be *brought to the attic* (74), and the shoppers *return* with the medicine (80). The scenes that the stage allows us to see determine the focal point of all of the coming and goings, the appearances and the experiences, that we learn of through the text.

Conclusion

I am not sure whether, strictly speaking, we should say that linguistic concepts directly provide the tools and framework for describing in processual terms the structure of the *La Bohème* text, or whether the notions of contrast, intratextual links, and the rest, as taken from standard linguistics, merely provide models and metaphors for the deeper and richer kind of interpretation that goes on in analyzing a text. For the purposes of text analysis, I suspect that it does not matter. What I think does matter is that the practice of linguistics tends to force analysts of textual material to see their object of study through particular filters, to ask questions in certain habitual ways, and to look for explanations along particular lines. I feel certain that at least some of this is likely to be fruitful.

APPENDIX: THE TEXT SEGMENTED, WITH COMMENTS

(1)   La Bohème

We may assume readers' familiarity with the title and knowledge that it refers to a community of unconventional artists and intellectuals living in nineteenth-century Paris.

(2)   *ACT I—(A garret)*

(3)   *In their cold Paris attic*

Their is a coreferential pronoun with no antecedent, and deictic reference is out of the question. For the text to be coherent, we need to find out very soon who 'they' (of *their*) are. We note also that the pronoun is possessive, modifying *attic*. We may have an interest in knowing which of the various kinds of relations, codable by the possessive construction is intended here. Are we to believe that they own the attic, or that they merely live in it, paying rent to someone else? The adjective *cold* is a paradigmatic alternate of its opposite 'warm', and *attic* is a paradigmatic alternate of its superordinate 'flat' (or the like). Why is the flat described as cold and as an attic? Both must be relevant. From knowing the meaning of *attic* and the purpose of attics, we make use of the facts that attics are not desirable places to live if one can afford to live elsewhere and that one does not live in a cold flat if one can afford to heat it. The joint categorizing of the flat as cold and as an attic immediately suggests poverty. And poverty is known to be characteristic of the Bohemian life.

(4)   *two of the Bohemians*

The phrase answers the question about the antecedent of *their* above. The definite article suggests that the reader must have been likely to have in mind the class of people nameable by *Bohemians,* presumably from the title. From the phrase *two of the Bohemians* we know that the episode involves two Bohemians and we are made aware that there are still more. We do not yet know whether other Bohemians will figure in our story, though we are inclined to think that they will by knowing the author could have written simply *two Bohemians* in this place instead of *two of the Bohemians.*

(5)   *are trying to keep a fire burning in their stove*

Trying presupposes obstacles, inviting the reader to imagine various sources of difficulty in keeping the fire going: faulty stove, inconvenient drafts, shortage of fuel, and so on. A problem with the supply of fuel would support the suspicion of poverty, already well supported by the title of the drama and the phrase *cold Paris attic*. The reader is made aware in this segment that the narrative is given in the present tense. The reader knows that the present tense is appropriate for descriptions of ongoing events and is willing to accept this text as something usable in those terms. The *their* of *their stove* must be anaphoric either to *the Bohemians* or *two of the Bohemians*. Should it be the case that the phrase *the Bohemians* in the very first sentence of our text refers specifically to the four male friends of the narrative, then it is possible that the *their* in this phrase refers to this group and that all four of them live together in the attic.

(6)   *the painter Marcello*

Presumably Marcello is one of the *two* mentioned in segment (4). The
apposition here should not be taken restrictively, since we have no reason
to believe there are two people named Marcello. (That is, we have no
need to distinguish *the painter Marcello* from, say, *the egg chandler
Marcello.)*

(7)   *is prevented from burning a chair*

Burning a chair relates to keeping the fire burning. Since we know, from
knowing the meaning of *chair,* that chairs are not for burning, and since
we know that burning destroys things and it is not generally desirable
to destroy chairs, the earlier interpretation of fuel shortage as the source
of difficulty in keeping the fire burning is supported. All of this—supported
by a cultural stereotype linking poverty with the burning of furniture—
emphasizes the desperateness, poverty, and discomfort in the scene before
us. The word *prevented* presupposes that Marcello wanted, intended, or
prepared to burn a chair. The passive form invites us to wonder who
stopped him from doing what he wanted to do.

(8)   *by the poet Rodolfo,*

This must be the second of the two Bohemians living in this attic. He
is then the one who prevented Marcello from burning the chair. The
manner of his introduction into the narrative matches that of Marcello's
and thus serves to establish a naming pattern for new characters.

(9)   *who instead sacrifices*

Instead is anaphoric, here pointing back to Marcello's attempt to use
the chair for the fire. The use of the verb *sacrifices* indicates that what
Rodolfo is going to offer is precious and is something that he really
wanted to keep. Since *sacrifice* is a transitive verb, we now expect the
direct object.

(10)   *one of his own manuscripts.*

From the phrase *one of his* we know that Rodolfo has more than one.
Since we have been told that Rodolfo is a poet, we assume that the
manuscript contains one of his writings; given the times and the conditions,
we can take it that it is his only copy—a presumption supported by the
fact that this phrase is the direct object of *sacrifices.*

(11)   *Their friend Schaunard arrives*

Their is obviously Marcello and Rodolfo, the only people on stage at
the moment. Zero anaphora with *arrives* refers to the attic apartment

seen on the stage. The language used to introduce Schaunard departs from the identification pattern used for the earlier two; will we find out what Schaunard does?

(12)   *with food and drink,*

The phrase *food and drink* is formulaic. The relevance of bringing things to eat and drink is high in view of the suggested poverty of the Bohemians.

(13)   *having just been paid*

This *having just* construction is used as an explanation for something previously mentioned. It must be an explanation for why Schaunard was able to bring food and drink. We conclude that Schaunard, also poor, could only buy food with money just earned. From this we learn both that he had no savings to speak of and that he was willing to spend money that he had just earned on food for himself and his friends.

(14)   *for a music lesson;*

The question of Schaunard's profession is now answered. He is a musician. The history we create is of someone who gives a music lesson, gets paid, takes the money he was just paid and buys food, and takes the food to his friends.

(15)   *they are also joined*

Which *they?* There are two possible groupings of people capable of bearing the antecedent relation to *they* at this point: (1) Marcello and Rodolfo, the two who were on stage from the start, and (2) Marcello, Rodolfo, and Schaunard, the three men currently on stage. It must be the original two, or the word *also* would not be usable here. The arrival of Schaunard is to be seen as an instance of somebody joining the other two, and we are now witnessing the arrival of a fourth character in the narrative but a second visitor to the garret.

(16)   *by Colline, the philosopher.*

This fourth member of the group represents a fourth calling. The four friends jointly fit the stereotype of Bohemians. Does this give us reason to believe that Colline is one of them, and that he, too, is a pauper?

(17)   *After a visit by the landlord Benoit,*

In a present-tense narrative it is slightly strange to skip an episode in the regular flow of the narrative and to introduce it by a backgrounding nominalization (*a visit by the landlord*). We recognize that the question of the possessive relation in *their attic* was not one of ownership. Given the assumed poverty, we believe we know the purpose of the landlord's visit.

(18)   *who demands payment*

With the last phrase we moved the time pointer to a point after the landlord's departure, but here, with a present-tense form, we have something more appropriate to the author's purposes: to tell us what people are singing about on the stage. We notice that the narrative appears to have skipped a step, moving the time pointer to a period after the landlord's visit; from this it must follow that in the next segment we are to understand that the landlord has left. The text here tells us that the landlord has made a demand. We are not told to whom the demand is addressed. (We actually do not know, from the text, whether this attic houses two or four.)

(19)   *of the long overdue rent,*

The presence of the article *the* shows that it is taken for granted that the rent is overdue. Here we are told that it is long overdue, long enough, apparently, to merit a personal visit by the landlord.

(20)   *all except Rodolfo*

Since Benoit has presumably left (in spite of the contradictions noted above), those included by this phrase must be all of those (minus Rodolfo) who are in the attic at the time of this move: Marcello, Schaunard, and Colline.

(21)   *leave for the Cafe Momus.*

The choice of the expression *leave for* rather than *go to* reinforced our viewpoint association with Rodolfo. We expect the next sentence not to tell us about what the three experience on their way to the cafe, but what Rodolfo experiences in the attic. The definite article in *the Cafe Momus* gives the impression that this place is already an object in the interpreters' version of the text's world. (Compare *leave for a night on the town.*)

(22)   *There is a knock at the door*

We were not told whether the previous two visitors knocked. Presumably they did not, hence the newcomer must be a stranger. Who is it?

(23)   *and a neighbor, Mimi, comes in,*

The text does not tell us whether she came in with or without permission. We assume, of course, that she was the one who knocked. The naming pattern continues to inform us of the role of each individual who appears on stage. Mimi is the only one of the five characters introduced so far to be identified with an indefinite noun phrase (*a neighbor, Mimi*).

(24)   *hoping to light a candle*

If we are told in an opera synopsis that one of the characters "hopes to light a candle," we have the right to suppose that words to that effect are being sung or spoken on stage. Her situation must be particularly bad if she lacks even the means to light a candle.

(25)   *which went out in the draft.*

From the fact that *go out* (said of a candle) is in paradigmatic opposition to *get lit* and *be lit,* we learn that her candle had once been lit. We also learn in this segment that Mimi's flat is drafty, all of this contributing to the picture of bad living conditions. We notice here that the simple past is used for what would be represented by the pluperfect in a past-tense narrative.

(26)   *A little later, she returns*

A little later is anaphoric; its interpretation depends on something earlier in the text. In this case it is not interpretable on the basis of something contained in the text's form, since the last event on record is that of Mimi's coming in. Since what she is doing here a little later is returning, we have to read between the lines to assume that after her visit to light her candle, she left. The text does not tell us whether she got the light for her candle, but we assume, from "principles of conversational cooperation" (Grice, 1975), that she did: If Rodolfo lacked a match, if the fire had no single remaining spark, or if Rodolfo had refused to give his neighbor what she requested, such a fact would have had too great a dramatic import to have been left out of the narrative.

(27)   *for the key to her room*

For, here, must be in the sense of 'in order to get'. If she came to the attic for her key, why is it likely to be here?

(28)   *which she lost.*

Once again, we see the simple past used for what would be pluperfect in a past-tense narrative. Mimi presumably lost her key (or believes that she lost it, or expects Rodolfo to believe that she lost it) here, in the attic.

(29)   *As she and Rodolfo look for it,*

She is Mimi and *it,* of course, is the lost key. Will they find it? (The fact, knowable from the libretto, that Rodolfo pocketed the key as soon as he found it in order to prolong Mimi's visit, is not revealed in this version of the tale.)

(30)   *their hands touch.*

The reader must know the significance of allowing the hands to touch. Is this a flirtation? On whose part? Was her losing the key here an accident?

(31)   *He tells her about himself and his dreams,*

For this to follow the report of the hands touching, we have to believe that that highly salient experience is what allowed the conversation to reach the level of intimacy described here.

(32)   *followed by Mimi's charming narration about her own life and
          longings.*

The sentence (31–32) is a strange one, capable of being made intelligible only to someone who knows that all of this is intended to present, in the order of their delivery, the content of a number of sung pieces. The definite expression *Mimi's charming narration* presupposes the advance knowledge of the ''charmingness'' of her discourse, a presupposition that can be satisfied by someone who knows that a particular aria (''Mi chiamano Mimi'') is being alluded to here.

(33)   *They are attracted to each other*

(34)   *and go out together*

(35)   *to join Rodolfo's friends.*

The phrase *Rodolfo's friends* must refer to the ones who earlier left to go to the cafe; we assume our lovers are joining their friends at that cafe.

(36)   *ACT II—(A square in the Latin quarter)*

(37)   *Christmas Eve.*

There appears to be a flaw in the text here. By having Act II shown as taking place on Christmas Eve and having Act I unmarked, the reader is inclined to see a time gap between the two acts. Actually, however, Act II merely represents what happens to our characters after they leave their garret at the end of Act I. Act I, too, takes place on Christmas Eve.

(38)   *At the Cafe Momus,*

(39)   *situated in a square filled with a happy crowd,*

It is odd to locate a square by such temporary phenomena as the size and happiness of the people in it. It must be that *filled with a happy crowd* is to be understood nonrestrictively, odd in the present circumstances because of the indefinite article and the lack of a comma. The phrase warns the operagoer of much dancing and milling about on the stage.

(40)   *Marcello is embarrassed by the arrival of*

Marcello has to be *at the Cafe Momus,* and since he is the subject of the sentence, he must be visible to the audience to whom the square is also visible. Familiarity with the conventions of opera staging may be necessary for the reader to get an appropriate image of the scene.

(41)   *his old flame Musetta*

Another character is introduced via the familiar naming pattern. Why is Marcello embarrassed? What are the two people going to do? How is this going to develop? We know of embarrassment as an emotion that generally makes its experiencer want to do something, and we are there-fore—from knowing that the author bothered to tell us about Marcello's embarrassment—expecting something to happen.

(42)   *with her wealthy "protector" Alcindoro.*

Still another character is introduced using the familiar naming pattern. *"Protector"* is in quotes, suggesting that the category into which we are to put this man Alcindoro is perhaps not best named by this word. What is he to her, really? (We think we know.) If Musetta needs such a man, she must not be moneyed herself. Is she one of the Bohemians? We notice that Alcindoro's wealth is being played off against the poverty of the Bohemians.

(43)   *In spite of their attempts to appear indifferent,*

At this point *their* could be Musetta and Alcindoro, since they were presented as entering together, or Musetta and Marcello, since they were described as former lovers. The rest of the sentence will have to tell us.

(44)   *it is obvious that Musetta and Marcello still care for each other.*

It is, of course, Musetta and Marcello who try to pretend not to know each other and who still obviously care for each other.

(45)   *She sings a provocative song*

They have stopped pretending—or at least she has. Why is the song described as *provocative?* Is she seeking to rearouse his passion for her?

(46)   *deliberately directed at Marcello,*

What is the effect of *deliberately* here?

(47)   *after which they embrace*

In seeking that antecedent of *which,* we find the event of segment (45). This version of the narrative does not tell us where Alcindoro is during this scene.

(48)   *and she joins the friends at the table.*

We learn for the first time that *the friends* are at *the table,* and that all of this has taken place in the presence of the whole group. *The friends* must include the five friends introduced in Act I.

(49)   *After the arrival of the guards,*

Who are the guards? Why is the arrival of the guards backgrounded? Does their arrival give the Bohemians a reason to leave? The text leaves all of these natural questions unanswered.

(50)   *the Bohemians depart,*

Here it is important to have an opinion on whether Musetta is a Bohemian. If she is, then we can believe that she went off with the others—that, in other words, the six friends went off together. Where did they go? Why did they leave?

(51)   *leaving Alcindoro with the unpaid bill.*

How exactly was this done? Had Alcindoro been sitting at the same table with the others? This is the first time we are told that the revelers had been drinking or eating in the cafe, and that they hadn't paid their bill yet.

(52)   *ACT III—(A tollgate on the outskirts of Paris)*

The text fails to motivate the place description. How much time passed between Act II and Act III?

(53)   *The pale and distraught Mimi*

We know from this description that something has gone wrong. We know that at least enough time has passed between Act II and now for some upsetting events in Mimi's life to have developed.

(54)   *looks for Marcello.*

Why is she looking for Marcello? What is her connection with him? Why does she expect to find him at the tollgate? (We are not told in this version that the two men were renting a hotel room at this location.)

(55)   *She tells him how difficult life has become*

We interpret a reported *how* + adjective clause as either descriptive or expressive. Descriptive use would be implied if our sentence were something like *She tells him how old her turtle is*, or *She tells him how long her telephone cord is*. But there are no appropriate measures of life's difficulty. We assume, therefore, that the clause is to be interpreted as a represented-speech version of *How difficult life has become!*

(56)   *with the jealous Rodolfo.*

We learn, through presupposition, that Rodolfo is the jealous type. We also learn for the first time, indirectly, that Mimi and Rodolfo have been living together.

(57)   *Then, hiding,*

Then must be 'after talking to Marcello'. Why does she hide? The valence of the verb *hide* has a slot for somebody the hider wishes to avoid. Who is that in this case? It must be that if she hides suddenly (as is suggested here by *Then, hiding*), the person she wishes not to be seen by has suddenly appeared, or that it has suddenly become apparent that he is about to appear. These events will be apparent to the opera viewer (at the time that they happen), but not to the reader.

(58)   *she overhears Rodolfo complaining about her.*

When did Rodolfo come? Is it from Rodolfo that she is hiding? The verb *complain* has in its valence a slot for an interlocutor; we ask, therefore, to whom Rodolfo's complaints are addressed. How does what Mimi overhears make her feel?

(59)   *A sudden coughing fit*

We know about a coughing fit that it is incompatible with successful hiding and that it is a symptom of illness. We predict that Mimi will be discovered. What will happen when she is discovered? Does this coughing signal serious sickness?

(60)   *reveals her presence.*

The verb *reveal* has in its valence a slot for a discoverer or witness. To whom is her presence revealed? Since Rodolfo is the only other person besides Marcello and Mimi we have been told about in this act so far, we must assume that she was hiding from Rodolfo and that it is he who now knows of her presence.

(61)   *While they talk of parting*

At this point *they* could refer to the group of three, or to Rodolfo and Mimi. But it is clear that we will need to wait until the end of the sentence to find out.

(62)   *Marcello and Musetta quarrel.*

Here we learn that the *they* of (61) refers to Musetta and Marcello. Until this moment we knew nothing about Musetta's presence on the scene. What are they quarreling about?

(63)   *Mimi and Rodolfo, however, decide to stay together*

The word *however* requires us to see the two couples' situations as parallel. The affair of Marcello and Musetta has taken one turn (61–62); here we are told that Rodolfo and Mimi have decided to stay together. The contrast revealed by *however* requires us to conclude that Marcello's and Musetta's quarrel led to a decision to break up.

(64)   *until spring.*

Until spring? Why such a limit? (To pool fuel?) When is it now? We assume that the events of Acts I–III take place in a single winter season.

(65)   *ACT IV—(A garret)*

The place descriptions follow slightly different conventions than those that govern the rest of the text. One might ordinarily expect that since *A garret* was the description given for the setting of Act I, and since Act IV takes place in the same room, we should find *The garret* here. But we do not.

(66)   *Back in their attic,*

This description supports the belief, in spite of the *a* in the place description, that we are now in the same attic as before. How soon after the events of the last act? Should the word *back* cause us to believe that it is very soon after that?

(67)   *Rodolfo and Marcello long for their girl-friends, Musetta and Mimi,*

If Mimi is also gone, is the current time after spring?

(68)   *who have left them.*

What happened between the time of the quarrels and now?

(69)   *Schaunard and Colline bring food and drink*

Now all four of the men are together again. Are they still poor?

(70)   *and for a while, the four friends*

The *for a while* must mean while they were enjoying the food and drink.

(71)   *forget their sorrow and poverty.*

Sorrow in particular because of the absent women? Do Schaunard and Colline share in this sorrow?

(72)   *Musetta helps Mimi in;*

It is strange to have the new appearance of somebody be expressed with just proper name references. Because of presuppositions connected with *help* we know that Mimi is not able to carry herself easily, and hence we believe that Mimi must be ill. This may answer the question we had earlier about Mimi's coughing.

(73)   *she is very ill*

At this point, grammatically speaking, either of the two women could be *she;* but since we already had reasons to suspect that Mimi was ill, the *she* here must refer to Mimi and Musetta. Why is she coming here if she is so ill?

(74)   *and had asked to be brought to the attic,*

This time we have a pluperfect, whereas earlier the simple past bore that function, that is, in the sentences that told us that the candle *went out* (25) and that Mimi *lost the key* (28). A difference is that in each of these earlier cases, the needed backgrounding was accomplished by occurrence in a relative clause. Why did she want to come to the garret?

(75)   *where she has been so happy with Rodolfo.*

And now we have a present perfect in the pluperfect function! Notice that we have not been told until now that Mimi had spent time with Rodolfo, except through the report of Mimi's complaints (55–56) about life with Rodolfo. The fact that the text says *where she has been so happy* indicates that her period here was longer than the one visit with the key and the candle.

(76)   *Colline decides to sell his only coat*

Another evidence of poverty. The text tells us that he *decides* to sell his coat. Will he do it? Who will he sell it to? What will he do with the money?

(77)   *in order to provide for some medicine.*

The purpose of his act is now known. Will he do it?

(78)   *Left alone, Rodolfo and Mimi*

When we learned, in the last segment, that Colline had decided to sell his coat to fetch some medicine, there were six people on stage. Now we find that Rodolfo and Mimi are alone. We have to believe that Colline did indeed go out to try to sell his coat, but also that the other friends went out too. Subtraction, not the text, leads us to that conclusion. Again, the text does not tell us that any of this happened.

(79)   *recall their happy days together.*

The verb *recall* in other contexts could merely refer to the experience of remembering. But since this is an opera resume, we have to believe that *recall their happy days together* represents the content of a certain amount of vocalizing. The purpose of this line is to let the audience know what the singing is about.

(80)   *After the friends return*

with the medicine?

(81)   *with the medicine and a muff for Mimi's cold hands,*

With the medicine and more. Something obviously happened between the lovers' vow to stay together until spring and now: the need for a muff suggests that spring is not yet here.

(82)   *Rodolfo is the last one to realize*

If Rodolfo is *the last one to realize,* then we must assume that the others on stage—and the audience—already know what the next clause will tell us.

(83)   *that Mimi has died.*

REFERENCES AND ADDITIONAL READING

Allén, S. (Ed.) (1982). *Text processing.* Stockholm: Almqvist & Wiksell.

Beaugrande, R. A. de, & Dressler, W. (1981). *Introduction to text linguistics.* London: Longman.

Fillmore, C. J. (1976). Pragmatics and the description of discourse. In S. Schmidt (Ed.), *Pragmatik II* (pp. 83–106). Munich: Fink Verlag. Reprinted in Peter Cole (Ed.). (1977). *Radical pragmatics* (pp.143–166). New York: Academic Press.

Fillmore, C. J. (1981). Ideal readers and real readers. In D. Tannen (Ed.), *Analyzing text and talk: Georgetown University Round Table in Languages and Linguistics,* (1981) (pp. 248–270). Washington, DC: Georgetown University Press.

Givón, T. (1979). From discourse to syntax: Grammar as a processing strategy. In T. Givón (Ed.), *Syntax and Semantics* (Vol. 12) (pp. 81–112). New York: Academic Press.

Grice, H. P. (1975). Logic and conversation. In P. Cole & J. L. Morgan (Eds.), *Syntax and semantics* (Vol. 3) *Speech acts* (pp. 41–58). New York: Academic Press.

Grimes, J. (1975). *The thread of discourse*. The Hague: Mouton.

Halliday, M. A. K., & Hasan, R. (1976). *Cohesion in English*. London: Longman.

Saussure, F. de. (1916). *Cours de linguistique générale*. Paris: Payot.

van Dijk, T. A. (1977). *Text and context: Explorations in the semantics and pragmatics of discourse*. London: Longman.

van Dijk, T. A. & Petöfi, J. S. (Eds.) (1977). *Grammars and descriptions*. Berlin: de Gruyter.

CHAPTER 3

Text Linguistics in Discourse Studies

Robert de Beaugrande

In memory of Peter Hartmann

HISTORICAL OVERVIEW

The evolution of the two fields, text linguistics and discourse analysis, forms a diverse, occasionally contrapuntal pattern. They were sometimes considered identical,[1] sometimes opposed, and sometimes unrelated. Since the 1970s they have expressly merged in concerted interaction. Both fields originally emerged from attempts to expand and extend the conventional linguistics of the sentence. But the two attempts appeared in different scientific contexts, each with its own peculiar pressures and results. Only when a considerable body of individual research had accrued did a consensus arise about the need for a general, self-sufficient research program on both text and discourse.

Historically, the concerns of language research were heavily determined by the context in which linguistics established its credentials as a science. Especially in America, the notion of 'science' is preempted by mathematics and the natural sciences, whose preoccupations are observation and measurement. Emulating that outlook, the human sciences, for example, linguistics, preferred to investigate artifacts, rather than the human processes that operate upon artifacts. Saussure (1916/1962, p. 317) concluded his famous *Course in General Linguistics* with the assertion: "Language,

---

[1] Some sources (e.g., Koch, 1972) treat discourse analysis as merely an English equivalent for the German Term Textlinguistik (Kalverkämper, 1981, p. 16), since American linguistics had no established designation for text research per se. I suggest a distinction by contrasting the main trends in the two areas—text linguistics was more predominantly concerned with grammatical structures—but rescind it later by defining a discourse as a set of mutually relevant texts (see p. 49). At present, the two designations are chiefly academic labels for the same domain.

HANDBOOK OF DISCOURSE ANALYSIS, Vol. 1
Disciplines of Discourse

viewed in and of itself, is the only object of linguistic science."[2] Early research centered on the aspects of language that seemed easiest to observe and measure. The success of phonology and morphology in cataloguing the sounds and forms of language with compact, orderly taxonomies decisively influenced the methods and projects linguistics was disposed to pursue later on. The analysis of samples into minimal units identified by their positions and distinctive features became the unchallenged focus of the linguistic enterprise. The motives for real utterances in communication and the processes that produce or receive them were not considered rewarding scientific issues. Yet in actual practice, this abstraction could not be upheld. Instead, linguists were supplying this context as an a priori (and invisible) step in their analysis (Beaugrande, 1984a). Data were derived partly from observation and partly from the mental constructs of the investigators. Human artifacts would be meaningless if they were genuinely isolated from human processes.

The sentence, which Saussure (1916, p. 172) had once excluded as belonging to language use, not to the language itself, soon became the central entity of linguistic theory. It was relatively easy to treat the sentence as an object (Morgan, 1975) because there was already a traditional consensus about its structural definition. Beyond the sentence, however, comparable structures proved much harder to find. The study of text and discourse started from attempts to extend the established descriptive–structural methods beyond the analysis of the single sentence. But due to the difference in structural frameworks, the methods used in this extension varied considerably.

This variation can be clearly shown with two illustrations. At one extreme, the tagmemic approach developed by Kenneth Pike and his associates was extremely broad. Tagmemists wanted to adopt a "multiple perspective, the recognition of parallel, simultaneous reactions to criss-crossing, intersecting vectors of experience, mental tools, values, and psychological pre-sets" (Pike, 1967, p. 10).[3] They recognized that the analysis of discourse was indispensable to effective anthropological field-work on little-known languages. The fieldworker faced the difficult task of analyzing a language without the aid of grammars or dictionaries, and many times without even a bilingual interpreter. Therefore, the only access to the language was to infer the nature and meaning of words or sentences from the ways they were uttered in a social context, where "language behavior and non-language behavior are fused" (Pike, 1967,

---

[2] I provide my own translation for all non-English citations.
[3] The foundations of Pike's (1967) theory were essentially stated in volumes produced at the Summer Institute of Linguistics in 1954 and 1955.

p. 26). The slot-and-filler approach of descriptive structural linguistics was adapted as a theoretical base for a unified theory for the totality of human behavior.

At the other extreme, the distributionalist approach developed by Zellig Harris and his associates was extremely narrow. Harris (1951) proposed to found linguistic inquiry wholly on "the distribution or arrangement within the flow of speech of some parts or features relative to each other" (p. 3). Along the same lines, Harris (1952) proposed to describe the regularity of discourse by uncovering equivalent formal units and structures from sentence to sentence. To increase the equivalences in discourse samples, Harris introduced the notion of 'transformations'. Harris resembled Pike in the concern for slots and fillers, but unlike Pike he excluded from study the larger context and purpose of discourse in human interaction.

Many lines of linguistic inquiry into discourse might have been adopted between the two extremes of Pike and Harris. In American linguistics, Pike's tagmemics remained isolated for some years while the majority followed the heritage of Harris. However, discourse itself disappeared from view when Chomsky (1957) put Harris' (1952) notion of 'transformation' to a new use. Chomsky's grammar of transformations was intended to describe sentence structures not in a single discourse, but rather in an entire language. This retreat away from language in use toward language in the abstract removed all motivation for Harris' project. If all sentences of the language can be described by means of rules of formation and rules of transformation, then the same is necessarily and trivially true of all sentences occurring together in a discourse; what applies to the complete set of sentences must apply to any subset. Moreover, if all grammatical sentences of the language are equally valid evidence for linguistic theory, it no longer seemed necessary to take samples from natural discourse as the descriptive structuralists had done. The new grammarians routinely invented their own sample sentences about John and Mary, the ideal, abstract pair whose star-crossed exploits provided the content of linguistic samples for years to come.[4]

While American linguistics was preoccupied with isolated, invented sentences, researchers in other countries saw no obstacle to the investigation of real discourse. Such studies had been advocated by the major founders of European language research, such as Bronislaw Malinowski (1923), Vladimir Propp (1928), Vilém Mathesius (1928), Frederick Bartlett (1932), Karl Bühler (1934), John Rupert Firth (1935/1957), and Louis

---

[4] This practice was already commonplace among philosophers and logicians.

Hjelmslev (1943). Peter Hartmann's (1963a, 1963b) advocacy of a science of language use encouraged new approaches and diverse, lively discussions of trends and projects among his students at the University of Münster, Germany.[5] A similar impulse came from the work of Harald Weinrich and his students at Münster, Cologne, and Bielefeld. Though it was not until the 1970s that text linguistics gained wide recognition,[6] individual scholars had long since used textual discourse as material for pursuing issues like these:

1. classification of language elements;[7]
2. grammatical relationships that can extend beyond sentence boundaries, as in complex syntactic units,[8] tenses,[9] ellipsis,[10] and proforms or other substitutions among different expressions for the same thing;[11]
3. recurrent language units, either inside a text[12] or in an exchange of texts;[13]
4. utterances as speech events, with regard to speech rhythm and intonation,[14] or emphasis and emotion;[15]
5. the constitution of meaning in context;[16]
6. the informativity of discourse;[17]
7. communicative settings and situations,[18] including special types such

---

[5] Harweg, 1968a; Koch, 1971; Schmidt, 1969; Wienold, 1971. All of these books issued from dissertation projects under Hartmann. My own thinking has been profoundly influenced by Hartmann's works, though I never had him as a teacher.

[6] The term 'text linguistics' first appeared, as far as I know, in Coseriu (1955-56, p. 33), as *lingüistica del texto*. The German term *Textlinguistik* was made current by Weinrich (1967, p. 109), and the English designation was a literal translation of the German.

[7] Glinz, 1952, 1965; Hartmann, 1963b; 1964; Hausenblas, 1964; Koch, 1965; Sumpf, 1969.

[8] Pospelov, 1948.

[9] Brinkmann, 1966; Weinrich, 1964; Žinkin, 1956.

[10] Isačenko, 1965; Karlsen, 1959.

[11] Borst, 1968; Brinkmann, 1965; Harweg, 1968a; Hasan, 1968; Palek, 1968; Roggero, 1968; Sevbo, 1966; Steinitz, 1974; Vater, 1968.

[12] Harweg, 1968a; Vardul', 1955. The work of Halliday and Hasan on lexical cohesion dates back to this period, but its planned publication was deferred until Hasan's (1968) dissertation was combined with further work in Halliday and Hasan (1976). The notion of 'cohesion' appears for the first time, as far as I know, in Halliday (1964), in a narrower sense than that used here (all factors holding the surface text together).

[13] Švedova, 1960.

[14] Beneš, 1958; Daneš, 1949, 1957, 1960; Halliday, 1967a; Pauliny, 1950; Pilipenko, 1965.

[15] Bečka, 1948; Filipec, 1955; Horálek, 1953; Šmilauer, 1940.

[16] Coseriu, 1955-56; Schmidt, 1969; Slama-Cazacu, 1961.

[17] Boost, 1955; Buttke, 1969; Firbas, 1957a, 1964, 1966; Halliday, 1967b, 1968.

[18] Brinkmann, 1967; Firbas, 1962; Leont'ev, 1969; Skalička, 1961; Slama-Cazacu, 1961; Zawadowski, 1956.

as bargaining,[19] myths,[20] novels,[21] anecdotes,[22] satire,[23] or news reports on the radio[24] and in newpapers;[25]

8. memory[26] and aphasia;[27]
9. language history;[28]
10. information-theoretical semiotics;[29] and
11. computer analysis of discourse,[30] including automatic abstracting.[31]

Within a few years, German-speaking scholars had expanded the enterprise of text linguistics and consolidated it in readers and surveys.[32] Scholars from other European cultures also presented surveys of broad scope (Conte, 1977; Coseriu, 1981; Enkvist, 1975; Mortara, 1974; van Dijk, 1978; van Dijk & Petöfi, 1977; Viehweger, 1976, 1981). This rich palette of inquiry showed how much linguistics could profit by recognizing texts and discourses as objects of inquiry in their own right. Proposals for a linguistics beyond the sentence had been raised from time to time (Hendricks, 1967; Hill, 1958; Pike, 1965). The usual sentence syntax was to be supplemented with what was variously called 'hyper-syntax' (Palek, 1968), 'macrosyntax' (Gülich, 1970), or 'text syntax' (Dressler, 1970). The most obvious tactics were to classify texts as structural units above the sentence (Ballmer, 1975; Heger, 1976; Pike, 1965) or as sentence sequences, usually sentence pairs (Isenberg, 1971; Lang, 1977; Wunderlich, 1974). An extension of transformational sentence grammar was explored as a possible foundation for a 'text grammar' (Heidolph, 1965; Isenberg, 1971; Jackson, 1971; Karttunen, 1968; Kuno, 1978; Mel'čuk & Žolkovskij, 1970; Petöfi, 1971; Sanders, 1970; van Dijk, 1972). Comparable foundations

---

[19] Mitchell, 1957
[20] Barthes, 1966; Bremond, 1964; Lévi-Strauss, 1960; Todorov, 1966.
[21] Wienold, 1969.
[22] Morin, 1966.
[23] Koch, 1967
[24] Harweg, 1968b.
[25] Harweg, 1968c; Weinrich, 1966.
[26] Kay, 1955; Smirnov, 1948.
[27] Cvetkova, 1968; Luria, 1961.
[28] Coseriu, 1958; Dressler, 1969; Firbas, 1957b; Šimko, 1957; Stempel, 1964.
[29] Bense, 1962.
[30] Pecheux, 1969.
[31] Sevbo, 1969.
[32] Beaugrande and Dressler, 1981a; Breuer, 1974; Dressler, 1972, 1978a, 1978b; Dressler and Schmidt, 1973; Fries, 1972; Gülich and Raible, 1972, 1977; Hartmann, 1975; Harweg, 1974; Heger, 1976; Jelitte, 1973-74, 1976; Kallmeyer, Klein, Meyer-Herman, Netzer, and Siebert, 1974; Kalverkämper, 1981; Koch, 1972, 1973; Kummer, 1975; Petöfi, 1975, 1979; Petöfi and Rieser, 1974a, 1974b; Plett, 1975; Rieser, 1977; Ruttenauer, 1974; Schmidt, 1970, 1973; Sitta and Brinker, 1973; Stempel, 1971; Weinrich, 1976; Wirrer, 1977.

were sought in logical theories of coherence (Bellert, 1970; Biasci & Fritsche, 1978; Dorofeev & Martem'janov, 1969; Petöfi, 1980). Logic-based grammars were less dependent on the linearity of sentences than were transformational grammars (Petöfi, 1972).

However, the transition from sentence grammar to text grammar encountered what Kuhn (1970) might call a scientific anomaly built into linguistic theory but seldom openly acknowledged before then. By postulating a separation between language and language use, conventional linguistics had obscured its access to the facts of language, namely, the real utterances or inscriptions occurring spontaneously in communicative interaction. In Chomsky's (1965) standard theory, for example, such utterances had to pass through a dense theoretical filter: (1) they were performance, whereas the grammar only addressed competence; (2) they were surface structure, whereas interpretation was based on deep structure; and (3) they might be judged ungrammatical or semi-grammatical. Thus, contrary evidence could not directly falsify the theory, though it could cause grammarians to add new rules or patch up old ones.

In sentence linguistics, this crucial problem of theory versus evidence was circumnavigated because linguists considered the nature and structure of the sentence to be obvious, even universal. But no such consensus obtained for the text. The task of accounting for text structures therefore brought the whole question of linguistic evidence into new focus. Hartmann demonstrated that the facts that any grammar represents are language events:

> The factual substrate, or the objective correlate of statements about grammar is
> . . . the linguistic facts 'contained' in formulations. . . . If we define the grammar
> of a language as 'living formative procedures for language expressions' created
> by combination, then our basic material consists in the fact or facts of combination.
> . . . We are concerned with a theoretical account of what a factual grammar can
> only *realize* by being an effect or consequence of these facts. (1963a, p. 391)

When linguists make statements about abstract grammar (*langue* or competence), they are in fact synthesizing, interpreting, and generalizing on the basis of their own experience with language events. To judge whether a sentence is grammatical, linguists try to imagine possible uses for it (Bolinger, 1968). This step is inescapable because grammar only defines itself reliably when it is used (Lenneberg, 1975).

It was inevitable that these considerations would become acute when texts replaced sentences as objects of inquiry. While a sentence can be minimally defined as 'noun phrase plus agreeing verb phrase', the constituents of a text are selected to meet the demands of a communicative context. Hence, the customary formal rules for sentence forms had no apparent equivalent for text forms. A frequent question for discussion was whether any exact linguistic or formal definition could be given for the text, that is, was there a set of abstract, formalized conditions every possible text must satisfy (Agricola, 1970; Bierwisch, 1965). Some linguistic forms or features were proposed as necessary parts of such a definition, such as sentence-linking conjunctions (Berry-Rogghe, 1970; Gleitman, 1965; Lang, 1977), relations between expressions that can be substituted in specified sequences (Harweg, 1968; Hasan, 1968; Roggero, 1968; Sevbo, 1966), logical-semantic deep structures (Bellert, 1970; van Dijk, 1971, 1972), and configurations of topics (Agricola, 1970; Buttke, 1969; Firbas, 1966; Halliday, 1967b, 1968; Karttunen, 1968; Koch, 1965). It was understood, however, that a general definition of the text must not conceal the need to classify different text types (Bense, 1962; Gülich & Raible, 1972; Koch, 1965; Sumpf, 1969).

Other researchers argued that no formal definition could be given in purely linguistic or logical terms, precisely because the text is partly formed and determined by its overall context and by the roles of communicative participants (Brinkman, 1966; Pecheux, 1969; Schmidt, 1973; Slama-Cazacu, 1961; Wienold, 1969). If context is necessary to define texts, it should presumably be necessary to define sentences as well.[33] The constitution of the smaller unit ought to follow the same principles as that of the larger. The consensus arose that the text should be defined as 'a natural language occurrence in a communicative setting', and the discourse as 'a set of mutually relevant texts' (Coseriu, 1955–56; Dubois, 1969; Hartmann, 1963a, 1963b, 1964; Schmidt, 1973; Slama-Cazacu, 1961; Weinrich, 1967); as such, a text is an event, the result of a human action in a dynamic situation (see also Rona, 1968; Schmidt, 1968; Svoboda, 1968; Weinrich, 1976). Empirically at least, the the sentence would have the status of a subevent: a format for placing words and expressions inside a sequence belonging to a larger linear action. Carried to its logical conclusion, the same line of argument that established the status of texts and discourses thus implied a fundamental reconsideration of linguistic perspectives (Coseriu, 1981; Schmidt, 1973).

The same trend was well under way in discourse analysis. Fieldwork on unwritten languages had to deal directly with contextualized events in discourse (Grimes, 1975, 1978; Longacre, 1976). Sociology explored the nature of conversational interaction (Garfinkle, 1967; Sacks, Schegloff, & Jefferson, 1974). Language education was reexamined as a special

---

[33] Compare Bolinger, 1968; Jackson, 1971; Petöfi, 1971; Sanders, 1970; van Dijk, 1972; Weinrich, 1971. Conversely, the formalized reconstruction of texts with methods used for sentences (e.g., Ballmer, 1975, Koch, 1971) has brought neither theoretical nor empirical progress, being after the fact, not of the fact.

mode of discourse centered on learning and performance (Cicourel, 1974; Coulthard, 1977; Jones, 1977; Leont'ev, 1969; Sinclair and Coulthard, 1975; Widdowson, 1978). Psychologists used discourse to study cognitive processing (Freedle, 1977, 1979; Kintsch & van Dijk, 1978; Meyer, 1975; Norman & Rumelhart, 1975; Schank & Abelson, 1977; also surveys in Beaugrande, 1980–81, 1982). These studies gradually converged into a domain known as 'discourse processing' (see outlines in Beaugrande, 1980a, 1980–81). The emerging role of text linguistics in that domain is sketched in the following section.

NEWER TRENDS AND PROBLEMS

Van Dijk (1979b) remarks that text linguistics is an overall designation for any linguistic exploration of the text. For some time, a unified definition of the text was not easy to agree upon. Such definitions as 'unit above the sentence' or 'sequence of sentences' are at best incomplete and at worst inadequate, because they bypass the status of the text as a communicative event. In addition, sentence research so far has by no means covered the issues text research must address. The syntactic dependencies are looser and more variable in texts than in sentences; semantic dependencies are constituted on a larger scale in a more elaborate hierarchy; contingencies and controls adapt steadily as the text evolves; factors such as attention, memory capacity, and situational goals are more crucial; and so on. Text research could bring new insights into the nature of the sentence, rather than vice versa. The sentence could be operationally defined as 'a preferential format for chunking word sequences during a discourse action', depending on setting, social roles, processing load, informativity, and so on (Beaugrande, 1980a, 1984a).

To be sure, the text is normally composed of cohesive phrases and clauses, and the concepts it represents and activates are normally coherent. However, what counts as cohesive and coherent depends also on the attitudes of communicative participants who intend and accept the text as such. The participants may tolerate lapses in cohesion or coherence as long as the communicative situation remains under control. A doubtful text in isolation may be a perfectly good contribution to an ongoing discourse, given appropriate motives, such as to be creative or humorous. The distinction between a text and a non-text therefore cannot be determined by formal definition; it can only be explored as a gradation of human attitudes, actions, and reactions. Normally, a non-text occurs only when someone deliberately blocks communication. The text is distinguished by its 'textuality', based not only on cohesion and coherence but also on intentionality, acceptability, situationality, intertextuality, and informativity (Beaugrande, 1980a; Beaugrande & Dressler, 1981a, 1981b).

Language events necessarily reflect the general conditions for human action and cognition. Theories for any one domain should be specifications of general theories of communication and cognition (Beaugrande, 1984a; Schmidt, 1982). Linguistic syntax is a special case of linear processing. Semantics is a special case of conceptual processing: creating, storing, recovering, and utilizing meaningful knowledge. Pragmatics is a special case of goal planning: setting up an intended state of the world and implementing steps to attain it. These definitions help to treat language as one mode of action and processing among human events at large.

In essence, theory and method are shifting from a logical to an operational outlook. The traditional philosophical or logical perspective placed the burden of discovery upon the investigator's efforts to invent classifications. This approach works best for narrow, uniform domains such as phonology and syntax and not very well for broad, variegated domains such as semantics and pragmatics. Research that relies so heavily on individual schemes and abstractions is not likely to be cumulative. In the experimental or operational perspective, on the other hand, the burden of discovery falls on modeling real events in communication and cognition. The fact that classifications and abstract categories are necessarily provisional and oversimplified is accepted as a natural consequence of the adaptability and variety of the human domain (Garfinkel, 1960, 1967). Research can be cumulative as long as investigators agree on data-gathering procedures for the events that merit consideration.

What a language entity is—a noun, phrase, sentence, statement, speech act, paragraph, text, or whatever—is empirically defined by what language users intend it to be. For the native speaker, the syntax and semantics of a language are sets of procedures for doing things with the language, and for giving other people instructions on what to do. Linguistics in the traditions of Saussure, Harris, and Chomsky assumes the invariance of the language element (phoneme, morpheme, word, meaning, etc.) within its respective subsystem. This invariance postulate, though crucial for a linguistics divorced from language use, is essentially a fiction resting on the common agreement among linguists about the proper categories and elements for classificational schemes. In real communication, an element is classified not by what it is in the linguist's scheme, but by what it does, that is, by its function in the processing of the participant. A single element may have several functions, and a single function may be assigned to several elements. Thus what we need is not grander, more elaborate lists of elements, but an account of how elements are selected and defined during ongoing processes.

The language element so defined need not have a stable, uniform, or exclusive identity. Instead of a unique place in a system of oppositions, as foreseen by Saussure, the nature of the element would be the intersection of functions and values situated on a set of gradations (parameters) selected and influenced by context. The word *last* by itself, for example, is neither noun, verb, adverb, adjective, nor ordinal; in context, it becomes one of these and assumes the appropriate meaning. One classification may dominate others (i.e., supervise processing) without by any means excluding them. For instance, in a statement such as

(1)   *The moon shone bright.*

the language user may construe *bright* as an attribute of *moon* (hence an adjective), as an attribute of *shone* (hence an adverb), or keep both possibilities side by side with one of them dominating, but not canceling, the other.

The enterprise of stating all potential word classes and meanings—the ultimate step in abstract linguistics—is doomed precisely because the results of contextual determination cannot be foreseen (predicted) merely on the basis of grammatical and lexical features a priori. A more auspicious enterprise would be to explore the processes of contextual determination, the nature of which must be reasonably controlled and uniform in order for communication to succeed among different people. Thus, the taxonomy of phrase structures would be replaced by the study of human intentions and actions that put words in order, meeting the constraints of phrase formating as well as those related to goals, ideas, concepts, and sounds or letters. A concept is a configuration of knowledge routinely stored and activated at once, and an idea is a concept or concept cluster that guides the assembling of content. What counts as an idea or concept is therefore whatever fulfills this function in processing. The use of the concept or idea may modify its status as a stored entity associated with particular expectations (Beaugrande, 1985).

In systems theory, we can distinguish between virtual systems and actualized systems (Beaugrande, 1980a, 1984a, and references there; Gülich & Raible, 1977; Hartmann, 1963a, 1963b). Since Saussure, linguists have addressed the virtual repertories of a language by generalizing from their own experience (see above). Text linguistics forced researchers to deal directly and openly with the realizations of language. Saussure's *langue* and Chomsky's 'competence' disregarded time, place, motivation, and resources—all the human factors that determine how language is empirically manifested. The price for these severe abstractions has been an enduring theoretical and methodological crisis whose resolution demands not a revision or extension of standard theories but a fundamentally new departure. Most of the significant progress in linguistics within the last decade has come from the return to real discourse and from the new methods that were developed for this purpose.

Unlike an abstraction, an operation has the potential for success, failure, or any degree in between. Language in use is subject to errors (Frith, 1980; Fromkin, 1981). The student who wrote:

(2)   *Education gives the student a sampling of each of the areas before making the decision is made on which area to pursue.*

was caught between two phrasal options, active versus passive, neither of which successfully dominated the other. Both options evidently arrived in the buffer of working memory from which the text was being read out during production, and either one by itself would have made a successful sentence format. But due to ongoing conditions that required resources elsewhere (e.g., for assembling content), the operation was a partial failure. Intriguingly, the writer overlooked the slip again during proof-reading, presumably because someone who already knows what the text is intended to convey is prone to rely on the mental representation at the expense of the surface text. Other readers might notice the slip and react negatively, even though there is no doubt about the content of the statement.

Since all language theories are ultimately abstracted from events, the factors that influence the success or failure of communicative actions must be investigated and included in the theories. The orderly nature of processing creates the order of language, not vice versa. We may not be able to find out what specifically caused the production of sample (2), but we can identify general principles that are responsible for typical sets of results. Each action consumes processing resources and thus limits what can be done elsewhere. Each process must have thresholds that trigger and terminate it according to the current state of the whole system, for example, the extent to which an action is judged to have adequately fulfilled an intention. Most operations involve a tradeoff: If some element or action is given an extreme value on its relevant parameters, the result is likely to revert to the opposite extreme. If you strive to make a text very simple and easy, for instance, the outcome may be so trite and boring that people find it very hard to read. If you repeat a statement, you may increase the audience's disposition to accept it; but after too many repetitions, the audience will reject it instead. Thus, it should be generally true that processing is normally constrained by the need to maintain a balance between extremes on such parameters as fast–slow, precise–fuzzy, certain–uncertain, general–specific, explicit–implicit, elaborate–plain, changing–repetitive, new–given or expected, innovative–commonplace, and so on. How the balance turns out in any one operation depends on what else is going on and how many resources are available.

The text linguist needs at least a working knowledge of psychological and social factors bearing on language use, but special concern will be devoted to the particularly linguistic (language-based) aspects of texts. This domain includes a system for identifying and exploring the sounds, forms, and patterns of language, as well as for relating the selected options to the communicative purpose of the discourse interaction. Any system of elements or features devised should serve both of these ends. Among the totality of linguistic features a given text can yield, we need to explore the borderline (or gradation) between the features trivially entailed in the use of the system per se and the features whose selection and arrangement are adapted to the current occasion. During text production, words must be retrieved from memory, placed in a buffer, and executed as configurations of sounds and letters. At each step, the words must be suitably processed according to the demands of the tasks involved. To express a concept, the processor must determine the specifications—meaning, connotations, style, and so on—that candidate words ought to meet. Slips of the tongue, where similar words are confused or interchanged (Fromkin, 1971), and the tip-of-the-tongue phenomenon, where some features but not the whole word are recovered (Rubin, 1975), suggest that memory searches need not work with whole words as units. Apparently, words appear as configurations of features or instructions that adapt to the needs of language processing. The actions of articulating or inscribing the surface text draw upon motor programs directed to obtaining a result that matches a spatial and temporal target (MacNeilage, 1970; Morton, 1980). Thus, the same phoneme or grapheme will have different implications depending on its environment of occurrence. As MacNeilage (1970) has shown, the invariance of phonemes cannot be based on a large catalogue of allophones for every possible environment (the total would exceed 100,000), but only on the targets which are skillfully adapted to fit whatever environments are required. Thus the traditional catalog of phonemes from descriptive linguistics is at best a point of orientation for the study of speaking or writing.

Similarly, the classification of words into categories (noun vs. verb, content vs. function word, concrete vs. abstract word, etc.) should take into account the processes that use the words for given purposes. These classes can probably be defined according to the procedures that recover and process them. Content words would have dense search grids and act as control centers; function words would have sparse grids and act as control adjuncts. Concrete words would have more consistent sensory associations than abstract words. In this way, what the processor does has the side effect of defining the status of the elements being processed.

Syntax is the operational consequence of any linear modality, that is, a modality in which only a single element can be executed at a time. This linearity needs general principles which, like the targets of sound–letter execution, can be specified to fit multifarious needs and settings. These principles could be subsumed under such headings as (1) distinguishing central elements from their adjuncts, (2) pausing or retarding the sequence, (3) assigning processing resources, (4) looking back, (5) looking ahead, (6) disambiguating, and (7) listing (Beaugrande, 1984a). Linguistic rules in use always entail one of these principles and often several. For instance, elements that heavily load the system tend to appear either toward the start or toward the end of clauses and sentences; hence the subject tends to convey the content immediately furnished by experience (Ertel, 1977; Osgood & Bock, 1977), or established in the prior text (Firbas, 1962, 1964, 1966; Halliday, 1967b, 1968). Whatever rules govern grammatical phrasing per se interact with these motives, which include perception, motivation, focus, plans, text types, and so on.

A complete model of language should have its levels stipulated in terms of processing phases: actions with characteristic consequences for cognition (see survey in Kintsch, 1977, pp. 229ff.). Goal planning should be the deepest stage because of its strong role in memory and action control. The other levels are less and less deep: ideation, conceptual development, expression, phrase linearization, and sound–letter linearization. This scheme can be justified by showing the individual contributions of the levels to human processing (Beaugrande, 1982a, 1982c). Though the levels interact extensively in everyday discourse, experimental methods can dissociate them. For example, the distinction between conceptual development (that creates coherence) and phrase linearization (that creates cohesion) is clear from findings on perception through noise (Marks & Miller, 1964), noticing changes (Bransford, Barclay, & Franks, 1972), and rate of memory decay (Begg & Wickelgren, 1974). In all these experiments, conceptual content had a more powerful effect than phrasing and must therefore belong to a deeper phase. These phases need not be discrete nor in fixed order; each phase may be unified in its procedural outcome, though dispersed in real time. For best efficiency, a processor might strive to work on the deepest feasible level (Drewnowski & Healy, 1977; Kintsch, 1979; Marcel, 1980). Having understood the conceptual content, for instance, might enable a bypassing of thorough analysis of phrasing. When obstacles (e.g., ambiguities, surprises) occur or when the processor is strongly motivated, the details of the shallower levels could receive more resources.

The brief sampling of issues in this section should suggest what some pressing concerns of text linguistics might be in future research on discourse. Such an enterprise is the linguistic (language-based) sector of a broad interdisciplinary study of cognition and communication. Real, spontaneously occurring texts are to be studied within theories of cognitive processing and human interaction, including factors such as mental resources, memory storage and search, scheduling, motor actions, feedback, attention, motivation, and many more. At present, we have little more than an outline of how the enterprise might eventually look. In the meantime, theory, research, and practice should be considered provisional. Work is necessarily exploratory, not assertive; approximative, not formal; qualitative, not quantitative; and probabilistic, not lawlike. The merit of the enterprise lies above all in the wide scope of its concerns.

A DEMONSTRATION

Though they would be an aid to research, mechanical discovery procedures requiring no intuition or interpretation from the investigator are not feasible for linguistics (Pike, 1967, pp. 224ff.). The linguist usually knows the language itself as well as the typical uses of languages in communicative interaction. Even the simple enumeration of morphemes and their distribution (see p. 43) incorporates the investigator's tacit assumptions about which morphemes are relevant, probable, and so on. Thus, the investigator should openly declare the purpose of the research in relation to the selection of relevant features as opposed to an exhaustive listing of all features in the discourse under study (the detailed line of argument in Beaugrande, 1983). Moreover, by working toward a firm empirical basis in real discourse, text linguistics can achieve a counterbalance against the dangers of circular proof and artifactual findings. The linguist's processes can serve as ongoing hypotheses about more general processes for further inquiry among nonspecialized language users. As a matter of principle, we should study real, naturally occurring texts rather than ones invented by the investigator to make a point. Though we cannot ignore or eliminate our own knowledge and experience regarding language, we can at least avoid interposing them at the production end as well as at the reception end. The occurrence of the text is both an empirical fact and an essential part of its definition. We ought not to cloud these factors by making up the examples we want to explore.

I offer a brief (not exhaustive or definitive) demonstration of the kind of questions text linguistics could pursue. The first step is for the investigator to listen to or read the text several times, first in the same fashion as the expected audience, then with steadily greater selectivity and attention. Anything special, marked, or predominant in comparison to everyday communication should be noted: patterns of sounds and letters, unusual vocabulary and phrasing, repetitions, redundancies, rhetorical devices, contradictions, evasions, allusions to speaker–writer and hearer–reader, type size, illustrations (photographs, drawings), place where the text is presented, relevant circumstances and motivations, and so on. Next, the investigator forms tentative hypotheses about the nature and intention of whatever was noted, that is, why these particular language options were selected and arranged to meet this particular occasion as contrasted with the options trivially entailed in using the language (see p. 52). Then the text should be presented to a larger audience in order to test how general the investigator's reactions and associations might be. Tasks such as free recall, cued recall, question answering, and evaluation provide several paths to access the audience's processes. However, some points may be relatable only to indirect evidence, because the naive language user's introspection is not likely to detect the more detailed, complex actions. At any stage of investigation, the evidence can be recycled back into the inquiry in order to narrow down, revise, or restate specific hypotheses for further exploration.

Here is the text from an advertisement for a hotel chain that appeared in *Time* (February 15, 1982):

We're changing
right before your eyes.

We're adding the finishing touches to exciting new Ramada rooms, lobbies and restaurants remodeled in our nationwide refurbishment program.

We're complementing new carpeting and furnishings in our lobbies with greenery and contemporary wall hangings.

We're finishing newly remodeled guest rooms with new bedspreads and draperies —in relaxing colors to make you feel welcome.

And in Ramada restaurants across the land, you'll enjoy cheerful atmospheres, with tasteful accents to spice your dining pleasure.

So, if you're tired of the hohums, come stay at Ramada for some very refreshing "Ah-haas!"

RAMADA INN

We're changing right before your eyes.

Above the text is a photo from which a covering is being peeled away; the still-covered portion is black and white and shows movers delivering chairs. The uncovered and larger portion to the right is in color and shows three men (one partly hidden by the edge of the wrapping) sitting in gold-colored armchairs; in the center of the picture is an empty chair facing the reader, probably to suggest that the reader would sit there and be in the middle of everything. In the background a young couple is arriving, followed closely by a uniformed bellhop with three suitcases. The woman is walking with her hand on the man's wrist, and both are staring outward and upward in evident wonderment at the refurbished premises. No one in the picture looks much older than 30. The scene is composed mainly of browns, tans, and yellows, imbued with gold-colored light.

I provide my own analysis first. On the deep level of plans and goals, the intention of the text producer(s) is to convince audiences that the hotel chain is radically changing. The goal would be attained when audiences believe the statement and obey the command to *come stay at Ramada*. Apparently, these inns consider their current image unfavorable enough to demand extensive recasting. (Perhaps the evaluation cards left in rooms for guests to fill out have been critical.) The management now assures us that any past deficiencies are disappearing in the wake of a *nationwide refurbishment program*. Perhaps customers are being asked to overlook inconveniences from reconstruction work going on while the hotels remain open.

The change may have a more pressing motive. The *Letter from the Publisher* opening the same issue of *Time* (p. 3) recounts the many signs that "the American economy had slid deeper into recession"—also the topic of the lead article (pp. 8–11). Tourism seems hard pressed. Sheraton and Marriott also ran costly full-page ads in this issue of *Time*. Four airlines did the same, including Laker's Airways, whose liquidation was, ironically, reported just three pages after his ad; the impending collapse of other airlines is rumored in the press. Being able to raise prices almost daily (whereas houses and apartments have long-term leases), the hotel industry is the most inflation-sensitive branch of real estate. Plainly, a large hotel chain in a depressed, competitive market cannot afford an unfavorable image, especially if forced to raise its rates.[34]

On the conceptual level, the message seems compact and yet evasive. The large print at the top and bottom announces the topic only vaguely. The first three paragraphs specify the most obvious meaning of the announcement: changing the decor all at once. The lobbies are getting *new*

---

[34] A single room at Ramada for one night costs, as of March 1982, $55–58 in Washington, D. C., and $60–70 in New York City. In comparison, the rates for Sheraton are $90–95 (Washington, D. C.) and $95–105 (New York City); and for Marriott, $85–124 (Washington, D. C.) and $105–160 (New York City). Prices vary according to the view.

carpeting and furnishings while the rooms rejoice in *new bedspreads and draperies*. The new items are being *complemented*—a word strongly reminiscent of *complimented*—by *greenery*, bringing to mind that the Ramada calls its dining area *The Greenery*. The photograph shows, off in the corner, a sign with that name and four plants. No *contemporary wall hangings* are shown, though, probably to allow each customer free choice of images.

As the text proceeds, the enumeration of new items becomes steadily less specific. The lobbies got more new equipment than the rooms, and there is no signal that the restaurants altered their material decor at all. The concrete items *carpeting, furnishings, bedspreads,* and *draperies* contrast starkly with the abstractions *atmospheres,*[35] *accents,* and *pleasures.* However, by leading off with the most complete and concrete renovations, the ad could leave the impression that everything has been replaced in all parts of the hotel.

After describing what *we're* doing in three short paragraphs, the text shifts to what *you'll* do, as if *your* arrival is imminent. As noted above, the attractions of the restaurant are vague in comparison to *new furnishings*. If read carefully, the fourth paragraph need not be about food at all; it could, for example, be about cheerful waiters with foreign accents distributing spice bottles.

Dining pleasure need not come from bread alone. Thus, it would be much harder to test the claims in this paragraph than those made before.

The final paragraph suggests that people who are *tired of the ho-hums* can expect *some very refreshing "Ah-haas!"* if they *stay at Ramada*. The use of sound words for states and events makes this assertion the oddest in the whole text. A literal translation for *ho-hums* might be 'boredom' or 'apathy', and one for *Ah-haas!* might be 'pleasant surprises'. However, the sound words, being less determinate than the translations, could be taken to suggest any change from dullness to excitement. The harried businessman, a chief patron of such hotels,[36] could find release from his humdrum routines at home. However, it is not obvious how new carpets and draperies could provide such thrills.

On the level of cohesion, the most striking feature is the insistent use of the present progressive for five of the eight finite verbs: *changing* (twice), *adding, complementing,* and *finishing.* According to Quirk, Greenbaum, Leech, and Svartvik (1972, p. 92), the progressive aspect

---

[35] The plural is strange in English. It may be intended to suggest variety or continual change.

[36] It is striking that the photo shows ten men (four patrons, four furniture movers, and two hotel staff), one woman, and no children.

indicates "process and continuation," as well as "simultaneity, vividness of description, emotional colouring, and emphasis." This text stresses new events *right before your eyes.* Thus verb forms are employed to give the impression that the changes are in progress this very minute. Reinforcement comes from the participials that, except for *dining,* refer only indirectly to actions: *finishing, exciting, relaxing,* and *refreshing.* Even nouns with no relation to action are selected with the *-ing* ending: *carpeting, furnishings, and wall hangings,* versus *carpets, furniture,* and *wall decorations.* A total of 12 *-ing* suffixes in a text of 100 words is noticeably higher than is normally entailed in the language system.

The prefix *re-* stands out as well: *remodeled* (twice), *refurbishment, relaxing, refreshing,* and (etymologically at least) *restaurants.* Just as the accumulation of *-ing* suffixes evokes dynamic events, the accumulation of *re-* prefixes arouses the impression of innovation. In most dialects of American English, the first syllable of *Ramada* sounds the same as the *re-* in those cited words where it is unstressed. In fact, the sound of *Ramada* and *remodel* are close enough to suggest, on an unconscious level, that the hotel is an institution of constant change—hence the recurrent prefix in this ad.[37] A message registered not by means of a statement but through subtle sound repetitions should be easier to present without fear of rejection. The recurring use of *new* four times adds support.

Another striking aspect is the use of parallelism. Five sentences appear as independent paragraphs beginning with *We're _____ing.* Two of them, the heading and conclusion, are identical. In the other three, the word *new* appears in each sentence predicate, in one case echoing *newly.* Since space is very expensive in national magazines and every word is costly, text producers do not repeat words and phrases without strong motives. Like the other features of the surface text, recurrence and parallelism must have been selected here to make the text memorable and persuasive. The intricate patterning lends the message itself a sense of necessity, or even of inevitability (Beaugrande & Dressler, 1981b, p. 160).

My own analysis outlined above indicates some hypotheses to be tested with groups of readers. One group of 5 graduate students and one of 23 undergraduate students at the University of Florida read the text carefully.[38] Then, the text was removed and they wrote, in their own words, everything they could remember. These free recall protocols were collected and then a series of specific questions was answered (see Appendix). Though

---

[37] *Ramada* itself was associated by most students with Italian food (*pizza, cheese, pasta*); *remodel* was named only once.

[38] The photograph should rightfully have been a part of the tests, but is excluded here as not being illustrative of the linguist's contribution to such a study.

most students had stayed at a Ramada, the groups were not fully representative of the general population of hotel customers; still, some directions emerged for further inquiry. These students had the advantage of knowing me well enough to be frank and forthright about their answers, at least most of the time.

All the graduates and 6 undergraduates reproduced the statement *We're changing right before your eyes.* By appearing both first and last, the statement enjoys both primacy and recency effects in recall. In contrast, readers were confused about what specific claims had been made about new furnishings. Seven readers thought new wallpaper was put up (maybe confused by *wall hangings?*), and two mentioned repainting the walls. Three incorrectly recalled that the guest rooms, not just the lobbies, had new carpeting and artwork. Fifteen asserted that the restaurants had changed the food, not just the atmosphere. The color suggested by *greenery* led readers to report green wallpaper and carpeting. Such findings illustrate that changes in comprehension and memory are important factors in communication. In this case, readers believed the hotel to have made more improvements than are asserted in the text itself.

Language typically elicits associations and images. I presented key phrases and asked readers to report what came to their minds. The opening and conclusion about *changing right before your eyes* was envisioned by twelve readers with construction workers, while nine reported visions of someone undressing. Three mentioned that the remodeling had to be done without closing the hotels, so that guests might run into some inconvenience. *Exciting rooms* were never imaged in terms of *bedspreads* and *draperies*: the readers reported a *stereo* (10 times); a *sexual encounter* (6); *full-length wall* or *ceiling mirrors* (for couples who want to watch their own activities in bed) (8);[39] a *waterbed* (7), preferably *heartshaped* (1); a *bar* (4); a *bathtub,* either *huge* (2) or *sunken* (3), or better still, a *whirlpool* (3); *plush carpets* (3); and *whips* (1). Four readers refused to respond—the only question so treated. I can only surmise that their excitements were not considered reportable.

The phrase *cheerful atmospheres, with tasteful accents to spice your dining pleasure* elicited mixed reactions. Some were quite positive: a *classy, nice, pleasant, peaceful,* and *quiet* restaurant offering *champaign and candlelight,* plus a *piano player.* Others were negative: *cardboard food,* that is, *mediocre motel food with no gourmet dishes* served by *a*

---

[39] One young lady wanted video as well for instant replay—a device Hugh Hefner of *Playboy* is reputed to have in his bedroom. Notice that sexual encounters were reported less often than obvious props like mirrors; this kind of inquiry is plagued with a margin of concealment by test persons, for example, those who refused to answer this question.

waiter or a waitress with a pasted-on smile. Still others focused on *spices,* for example, *salt, pepper, garlic, oregano, basil,* and *Accent* (a brand name for monosodium glutamate), or *Mexican food* and *tropical food.* Conceptual indeterminacy, though logically a disturbance, may be an operational strategy with advantageous results (cf. traditional view, p. 49).

Indeterminacy also proved useful in regard to readers' notions of *contemporary wall hangings.* There were basically two camps. One favored realism (*landscapes, houses*) and decried abstract art (*Geometric modern*) as a *blob of orange on blue green, splashed or dripped colors on a white canvas;* or *a bunch of rusty nails glued together.* The other camp welcomed abstraction and disdained *gold and tan flowers, bunches of trees,* and *romantic airbrushed nature scenes, seashores, sailing ships, forest paths.* Ramada was wise not to show an illustration in the photo; one camp or the other could easily have been alienated.

The photograph is dominated by beige, yellow, and brown, plus the green of the plants. Many readers listed these colors as *relaxing.* The color most often mentioned was *blue* (18 times), followed by *brown* (11), *green* (8), *yellow* (6), *beige* (5), *earth* (3), *white* (3), *pink* (3), and *orange* (2). Readers typically suggested that relaxing colors should be *pale, light, muted, mellow,* and *pastel*—again concurring with the photograph that they had not seen. These findings show once more that personal constitution of meaning is variable but not uncontrolled or random, thanks to cultural consensus.

The expression *ho-hum(s)* was recalled by 21 readers, giving proof that odd language is memorable even if unclear. Several students were reminded of the advertisements of rival hotel chains that picture a yawning guest (or a bear) about to sink into blissful slumber. *Exciting rooms, spiced pleasures,* and *Ah-haas!* have appeal for the harried business manager or representative bored with everyday routines. Intriguingly, one reader believed she had read *home,* and another *humdrum*—very apt sound confusions in this context. A hotel offers escape from the static home scene of the middle class, but only under certain conditions. Fancy furnishings may allow a brief feeling of grandeur by contrast to the wornout chairs and carpets at home. However, the students' response to *exciting rooms* signal that the advertisement could be taken as suggesting something quite different, something it would be rather awkward to spell out explicitly. Several students associated *Ah-haa,* which they spelled *Aaaah,* with physical pleasures, not with new drapes. The surface message nicely compromises between two middle-class attitudes. On the one hand, the belief that paradise on earth can be found in material goods (decor and furniture) is affirmed; on the other hand, a means of release from that same milieu is subtly suggested. The reverse strategy would have been sheer folly: to tell people their homes are dull and that a hotel offers the freedom and anonymity denied by conventional codes of respectability.

The above demonstration is intended merely as illustrative, not conclusive. The findings suggest the kinds of questions a more ambitious research program might want to explore: strategic use of linguistic forms, constitution of meaning, pursuits of communicative goals and reactions, and so on. Text linguistics can provide input into the larger enterprise of discourse studies in which social and psychological conditions are undeniably relevant, as I have tried to demonstrate. The fact that people put forms and meanings to special uses (and expand, alter, conflate, or disguise them) is as vital a part of communication as the structures that constitute the surface text itself. For instance, the accumulation of verb forms, affixes, and parallel phrase structures in this sample is an important part of the overall plan (see pp. 57ff). A narrow analysis of linguistic or logical structures would overlook the dynamics of textual communication and impoverish the results of research. An operational approach, on the other hand, tries to find out what happens to texts in real situations. We stand to learn the most about language by adopting a broad scope on the interactive event and its human implications.

APPENDIX: PROBE QUESTIONS

1. What did they do to the lobbies?
2. What did they do to the guest rooms?
3. What did they do to the restaurants?
4. What do you see as *contemporary wall hangings*?
5. What are *relaxing colors*?
6. What impression do you get from *cheerful atmospheres, with tasteful accents to spice your dining pleasure*?
7. What are you *tired of* if you should stay at Ramada?
8. What image do you associate with the statement, *we're changing right before your eyes*?
9. What do you consider an *exciting room*?
10. What do you think a room at Ramada looks like?
11. Why do you think they are remodeling?
12. What do you associate with the word *Ramada*?
13. Have you ever stayed there yourself?

REFERENCES

I provide translations for titles that do not obviously resemble their English renderings.

Agricola, E. (1970). Textstruktur aus linguistischer Sicht [Text structure in a linguistic perspective]. *Wissenschaftliche Zeitschrift der Pädagogischen Hochschule Potsdam, 7*, 85–88.

Ballmer, T. T. (1975). *Sprachrekonstruktionssysteme* [Language reconstruction systems]. Kronberg/Taunus: Skriptor.

Barthes, R. (1966). Introduction à l'analyse structurale des récits [Introduction to the structural analysis of discourse]. *Communications, 8*, 1–27.

Bartlett, F. (1932). *Remembering*. Cambridge: Cambridge University Press.

Beaugrande, R. de. (1980a). *Text, discourse, and process*. Norwood, NJ: Ablex.

Beaugrande, R. de. (1980b). Text and discourse in European research. *Discourse Processes, 4*, 287–300.

Beaugrande, R. de. (1980–81). Design criteria for process models of reading. *Reading Research Quarterly, 16*, 261–315.

Beaugrande, R. de. (1981). Linguistic theory and meta-theory for a science of texts. *Text, 1*, 113–161.

Beaugrande, R. de. (1982). The story of grammars and the grammar of stories. *Journal of Pragmatics, 6*, 383–422.

Beaugrande, R. de. (1984a). *Text production*. Norwood, NJ: Ablex.

Beaugrande, R. de. (1984b). Learning to read and reading to learn in the cognitive science approach. In H. Mandl, N. Stein, & T. Trabasso (Eds.), *Learning and comprehending text* (pp. 159–191). Hillsdale, NJ: Erlbaum.

Beaugrande, R. de. (1985). Written meaning in real time. In A. Matsuhashi (Ed.), *Writing in real time*. New York: Longman

Beaugrande, R. de, & Dressler, W. (1981a). *Einführung in die Textlinguistik*. Tübingen: Niemeyer.

Beaugrande, R. de, & Dressler, W. (1981b). *Introduction to text linguistics*. London: Longman.

Bečka, J. (1948). *Úvod do česke stylistiky* [An introduction to Czech stylistics]. Prague: Mikuta.

Begg, I., & Wickelgren, W. (1974). Retention functions for syntactic and lexical versus semantic information in recognition memory. *Memory & Cognition, 2*, 353–359.

Bellert, I. (1970). On a condition of the coherence of texts. *Semiotica, 2*, 335–363.

Beneš, E. (1958). Větná rámcová construkce a její uvolňování v odborném stylu současné spisovné němčiny [The frame sentence construction and its relaxation in the specialist style of contemporary standard German]. *Cizí jazyky ve škole, 2*, 244–252.

Bense, M. (1962). *Theorie der Texte*. Cologne: Kiepenheuer.

Berry-Rogghe, G. (1970). The conjunction as a grammatical category. *Linguistics, 63*, 5–18.

Biasci, C., & Fritsche, J. (Eds.). (1978). *Texttheorie–Textrepräsentation*. Hamburg: Buske.

Bierwisch, M. (1965). Rezension zu Z. S. Harris, 'Discourse Analysis'. *Linguistics, 13*, 61–73.

Bolinger, D. (1964). Intonation as a universal. In H. Lunt (Ed.), *Proceedings of the Ninth International Congress of Linguistics*, (pp. 833–847). The Hague: Mouton.

Bolinger, D. (1968). Judgements of grammaticality. *Lingua, 21*, 34–40.

Boost, K. (1955). *Neue Untersuchungen zum Wesen und zur Struktur des deutschen Satzes: Der Satz als Spannungsfeld* [New investigations on the nature and structure of the German sentence: The sentence as a field of tension]. Berlin: Akademie.

Borst, E. (1968). Pro-Infinitive. *Englische Studien, 39,* 413–418.

Bransford, J., Barclay, J. R., & Franks, J. (1972). Sentence memory: A constructive versus interpretive approach. *Cognitive Psychology, 3,* 193–209.

Bremond, C. (1964). Le message narratif. *Communications, 4,* 4–32. Also in W. Koch (Ed.). (1972). *Strukturelle Textanalyse* (pp. 75–103). Hildesheim: Olms.

Breuer, D. (1974). *Einführung in die pragmatische Texttheorie* [Introduction to pragmatic text theory]. Munich: Fink.

Brinkmann, H. (1965). Die Konstituierung der Rede [The constitution of discourse]. *Wirkendes Wort, 15,* 157–172.

Brinkmann, H. (1966). Der Satz und die Rede [Sentence and discourse]. *Wirkendes Wort, 16,* 376–390.

Brinkmann, H. (1967). Die Syntax der Rede [The syntax of discourse]. In Brinkmann, *Satz und Wort im Heutigen Deutsch* (pp. 74–94). Düsseldorf: Schwann.

Bühler, K. (1934). *Sprachtheorie: Die Darstellungsfunktion der Sprache* [Language theory: The representational function of language]. Jena: G. Fischer.

Buttke, K. (1969). *Gesetzmässigkeiten der Wortfolge im Russischen* [Regularities in the word order of Russian]. Halle: Niemeyer.

Chomsky, N. (1957). *Syntactic structures.* The Hague: Mouton.

Chomsky, N. (1965). *Aspects of the theory of syntax.* Cambridge: MIT.

Cicourel, A. (Ed.) (1974). *Language use and school performance.* New York: Academic Press.

Clark, H., & Haviland, S. (1977). Comprehension and the given-new contract. In R. Freedle (Ed.). *Discourse production and comprehension* (pp. 1–40). Norwood, NJ: Ablex.

Conte, M. E. (1977). *La linguistica textuale* [Text linguistics]. Milan: Feltrinelli.

Coseriu, E. (1955–56). Determinación y entorno [Determination and setting]. *Romanistisches Jahrbuch, 7,* 29–54.

Coseriu, E. (1958). *Sincronía, diacronía, y historia.* Montevideo: Universidad de la Republica Facultad de Humanidades y Ciencias.

Coseriu, E. (1981). *Textlinguistik: Eine Einführung* [Text linguistics: An introduction]. Tübingen: Narr.

Coulthard, M. (1977). *Introduction to Discourse Analysis.* London: Longman.

Cvetkova, L. K. (1968). Teorii vosstanovitel'noe obučenija [On the theory of rehabilitative instruction]. *Prace Psychologisne-Pedagogiczne, 204,* 81–90.

Daneš, F. (1949). Intonace otázky [The intonation of interrogative sentences]. *Naše reč, 33,* 62–68.

Daneš, F. (1957). *Intonace a věta ve spisovné čestině* [Intonation and sentence in standard Czech]. Prague: Czechoslovakian Academy of Sciences.

Daneš, F. (1960). Sentence intonation from a functional point of view. *Word, 16,* 34–54.

Daneš, F. (Ed.). (1974). *Papers on functional sentence perspective.* Prague: Academia.

Daneš, F., & Viehweger, D. (Eds.). (1976). *Probleme der Textgrammatik.* Berlin: Akademieverlag.

Daneš, F., and Viehweger, D. (Eds.). (1981). *Satzsemantische Komponenten und Relationen im Text.* Prague: Czechoslovakian Academy of Sciences.

Dorofeev, G. V., Martem'janov, J. S. (1969). Logičeskij vyvod i vyjavlenie svjazej meždu predloženijami v tekste [Logical inference and identification of intersentence relations]. *Mašinnyj perevod i prikladnaja lingvistika, 12,* 36–59.

Dressler, W. (1969). Eine textsyntaktische Regel der indogermanischen Wortstellung [A text-syntactic rule of Indo-European word order] *Zeitschrift für vergleichende Sprachforschung, 83,* 1–25.

Dressler, W. (1970). Textsyntax. *Lingua e Stile, 5,* 191–213.

Dressler, W. (1972). *Einführung in die Textlinguistik* [Introduction to text linguistics]. Tübingen: Niemeyer.

Dressler, W. (Ed.) (1978a). *Current trends in text linguistics*. Berlin: de Gruyter.

Dressler, W. (Ed.). (1978b). *Textlinguistik*. Braunschweig: Wissenschaftliche Buchgesellschaft.

Dressler, W., & Schmidt, S. J. (Eds.). (1973). *Textlinguistik: Kommentierte Bibliographie* [Text linguistics: Annotated bibliography]. Munich: Fink.

Drewnowski, A. & Healy, A. F. (1977). Detection errors on 'the' and 'and': Evidence for reading units larger than the word. *Memory and Cognition, 5*, 636–647.

Dubois, J. (1969). Énoncé et énonciation [Utterance and uttering]. *Langages, 13*, 100–110.

Enkvist, N. E. (1975). *Tekstilingvistiikan peruskäsitteitä* [Basic principles of text linguistics]. Helsinki: Gaudeamus.

Ertel, S. (1977). Where do the subjects of sentences come from? M. S. Rosenberg (Ed.), *Sentence production* (pp. 141–167). Hillsdale, NJ: Erlbaum.

Filipec, J. (1955). Byl to můj přítel, který . . . [It was my friend who . . .]. *Naše řeč, 38*, 193–198.

Firbas, J. (1957a). K otázce nezákladových podmětův současné angličtiné [On the problem of non-thematic subjects in contemporary English]. *Časopis pro moderní filologii, 39*, 22–42, 165–173.

Firbas, J. (1957b). Some thoughts on the function of word order in Old English and Modern English. *Sborník prací filozofické fakulty brněnské univerzity, A5*, 72–100.

Firbas, J. (1962). Notes on the function of the sentence in the act of communication. *Sborník prací filozofické fakulty brněnské univerzity, A10*, 133–148.

Firbas, J. (1964). On defining the theme in functional sentence perspective. *Travaux linguistiques de Prague, 1*, 267–280.

Firbas, J. (1966). Non-thematic subjects in contemporary English. *Travaux linguistiques de Prague, 2*, 239–256. Also in W. Koch (Ed.). (1972). *Strukturelle Textanalyse* (pp. 23–40). Hildesheim: Olms.

Firbas, J., & Golková, E. (1976). *An analytical bibliography of Czechoslovak studies in functional sentence perspective*. Brno: University of Brno.

Firth, J. R. (1957). *The technique of semantics* (Lecture, 1935.) In Firth, J. R. (1957). *Papers in linguistics. 1934–1951*, (pp. 7–33). London: Oxford.

Freedle, R. (Ed.). (1977). *Discourse production and comprehension*. Norwood, NJ: Ablex.

Freedle, R. (Ed.). (1979). *New directions in discourse processing*. Norwood, NJ: Ablex.

Fries, U. (1972). Textlinguistik. *Linguistik und Didaktik, 7*, 219–234.

Frith, U. (Ed.). (1980). *Cognitive processes in spelling*. London: Academic Press.

Fromkin, V. (1971). The non-anomalous nature of anomalous utterances. *Language, 47*, 27–52.

Fromkin, V. (Ed.). (1981). *Errors in linguistic performance*. London: Academic.

Garfinkel, H. (1960). The rational properties of scientific and common sense activities. *Behavioral Science, 5*, 72–83.

Garfinkel, H. (1967). *Studies in ethnomethodology*. Englewood Cliffs: Prentice-Hall.

Gentner, D. (1975). Evidence for the psychological reality of semantic components: The verbs of possession. In D. Norman & D. Rumelhart (Eds.), *Explorations in Cognition* (pp. 211–246). San Francisco: Freeman.

Gleitman, L. (1965). Coordinating conjunctions in English. *Language, 41*, 260–293.

Glinz, H. (1952). *Die innere Form des Deutschen* [The inner form of German]. Bern: Francke.

Glinz, H. (1965). *Grundbegriffe und Methoden inhaltsbezogener Text- und Sprachanalyse* [Basic concepts and methods in content-related analysis of text and language]. Düsseldorf: Schwann.

Grimes, J. (1975). *The thread of discourse*. The Hague: Mouton.

Grimes, J. (Ed.). (1978). *Papers on discourse*. Arlington, TX: Summer Institute of Linguistics.

Gülich, E. (1970). *Makrosyntax der Gliederungssignale im gesprochenen Französisch* [Macrosyntax of organizational signals in spoken French]. Munich: Fink.

Gülich, E., & Raible, W. (Eds.). (1972). *Textsorten* [Text types]. Frankfurt: Athenäum.

Gülich, E., & Raible, W. (1977). *Linguistische Textmodelle* [Linguistic models of the text]. Munich: Fink.

Halliday, M. A. K. (1964). The linguistic study of literary texts. In H. Lunt (Ed.), *Proceedings of the Ninth International Congress of Linguists* (pp. 302–307). The Hague: Mouton. Also in W. Koch (Ed.) (1972). *Strukturelle Textanalyse* (pp. 191–196). Hildesheim: Olms.

Halliday, M. A. K. (1967a). *Intonation and grammar in British English*. The Hague: Mouton.

Halliday, M. A. K. (1967b). Notes on transitivity and theme in English. *Journal of Linguistics, 3,* 37–81, 199–244.

Halliday, M. A. K. (1968). Notes on transitivity and theme in English. *Journal of Linguistics, 4,* 179–215.

Halliday, M. A. K., & Hasan, R. (1976). *Cohesion in English*. London: Longman.

Harris, Z. S. (1951). *Structural linguistics*. Chicago: Univ. of Chicago Press.

Harris, Z. S. (1952). Discourse analysis. *Language, 28,* 1–30, 474–494.

Hartmann, P. (1963a). *Theorie der Grammatik* [Theory of grammar]. The Hague: Mouton.

Hartmann, P. (1963b). *Theorie der Sprachwissenschaft* [Theory of language science]. Assen: van Gorcum.

Hartmann, P. (1964). Text, Texte, Klassen von Texten [Text, texts, text classes]. *Bogawus, 2,* 11–25. Also in W. Koch (Ed.). (1972). *Strukturelle Textanalyse* (pp. 1–22). Hildesheim: Olms.

Hartmann, P. (1975). Textlinguistische Tendenzen in der Sprachwissenschaft [Text linguistic trends in the science of language]. *Folia Linguistica, 8,* 1–49.

Harweg, R. (1968a). *Pronomina und Textkonstitution* [Pronouns and text constitution]. Munich: Fink.

Harweg, R. (1968b). Die Rundfunknachrichten [Radio news reports]. *Poetica, 2,* 1–14.

Harweg, R. (1968c). Textologische Analyse einer Zeitungsnachricht [Textological analysis of a newspaper report]. *Replik, 1,* 8–12.

Harweg, R. (1974). Textlinguistik. In W. Koch (Ed.), *Perspektiven der Linguistik* (Vol. II pp. 88–116). Stuttgart: Kroner.

Hasan, R. (1968). *Grammatical cohesion in spoken and written English*. London: Longman.

Hausenblas, K. (1964). On the characterization and classification of discourse. *Travaux linguistiques de Prague, 1,* 67–83.

Heger, K. (1976). *Monem, Wort, Satz und Text* [Moneme, word, sentence, and text]. Tübingen: Niemeyer.

Heidolph, K. E. (1966). Kontextbeziehungen zwischen Sätzen in einer generativen Grammatik [Context relationships between sentences in a generative grammar]. *Kybernetika, 2,* 274–281.

Hendricks, W. O. (1967). On the notion 'beyond the sentence'. *Linguistics, 37,* 12–51.

Hill, A. A. (1958). Beyond the sentence. In A. A. Hill, *Introduction to linguistic structures* (pp. 406–417). New York: Harcourt Brace.

Hjelmslev, L. (1943). *Omkring sprogteoriens grundlæggelse* [About the foundations of language theory. Copenhagen: Lunos.

Horálek, K. (1953). Několik poznámek o pořádku slov v ruštině ve srovnáni s češtinou [Some comparative notes on Russian and Czech word order]. *Sovětská Věda-Jazkověda, 3,* 540–544.

Ihwe, J. (Ed.). (1971). *Literaturwissenschaft und Linguistik* [Literary studies and linguistics]. Frankfurt: Athenäum.

Isačenko, A. (1965). Kontextbedingte Ellipse und Pronominalisierung im Deutschen [Context-dependent ellipsis and pronominalization in German]. In *Beiträge zur Sprachwissenschaft, Volkskunde und Literaturforschung* (Steinitz Festschrift) (pp. 163–173). Berlin: Akademie.

Isenberg, H. (1971). Uberlegungen zur Texttheorie [Deliberations on text theory]. In J. Ihwe (Ed.), *Literaturwissenschaft und Linguistik* (pp. 150–173). Frankfurt: Athenäum.

Jackson, L. A. (1971). *A transformation theory of context*. Unpublished doctoral dissertation, University of London.

Jelitte, H. (1973). Kommentierte Bibliographie zur Sowjetrussischen Textlinguistik [Annotated bibliography on Soviet text linguistics]. *Linguistische Berichte, 28,* 83–100.

Jelitte, H. (1974). Kommentierte Bibliographie zur Sowjetrussischen Textlinguistik [Annotated bibliography on Soviet text linguistics]. *Linguistische Berichte, 29,* 74–92.

Jelitte, H. (Ed.). (1976). *Sowjetrussische Textlinguistik* [Soviet text linguistics]. Frankfurt: Lang.

Jones, L. K. (1977). *Theme in English expository discourse*. Lake Bluff, IL: Jupiter.

Kallmeyer, W., Klein, W., Meyer-Hermann, R., Netzer, K., & Seibert, H. J. (1974). *Lektürenkolleg zur Textlinguistik* [Reading tutorial on text linguistics]. Frankfort: Athenäum-Fischer.

Kalverkämper, H. (1981). *Orientierung zur Textlinguistik* [Guide to text linguistics]. Tubingen: Niemeyer.

Karlsen, R. (1959). *Studies in the connection of clauses in current English*. Bergen: Eide.

Karttunen, L. (1968). *What makes noun phrases definite?* (Rand Memorandum P-3871). Santa Monica: Rand Corporation.

Kay, H. (1955). Learning and retaining meaningful verbal material. *British Journal of Psychology, 46,* 81–100.

Kintsch, W. (1977). *Memory and cognition*. New York: Wiley.

Kintsch, W. (1979). Concerning the marriage of research and practice in beginning reading instruction. In L. Resnick & P. Weaver (Eds.), *Theory and practice of early reading*. (pp. 319–330). Hillsdale, NJ: Erlbaum.

Kintsch, W., & van Dijk, T. A. (1978). Toward a model of text production and comprehension. *Psychological Review, 85,* 363–394.

Koch, W. (1965). Preliminary sketch of a semantic type of discourse analysis. *Linguistics, 12,* 5–30.

Koch, W. (1967). A linguistic analysis of a satire. *Linguistics, 33,* 61–81.

Koch, W. (1971). *Taxologie des Englischen* [Taxonomic model design for English]. Munich: Fink.

Koch, W. (Ed.). (1972). *Strukturelle Textanalyse*. Hildesheim: Olms.

Koch, W. (1973). *Das Textem* [The texteme]. Hildesheim: Olms.

Kuhn, T. S. (1970). *The structure of scientific revolutions*. Chicago: University of Chicago Press.

Kummer, W. (1975). *Grundlagen der Texttheorie* [Foundations of text theory]. Hamburg: Rowohlt.

Kuno, S. (1978). Generative discourse analysis in America. In W. Dressler (Ed.), *Current trends in text linguistics*. Berlin: de Gruyter.

Lang, E. (1977). *Semantik der koordinativen Verknüpfung* [Semantics of coordinative junction]. Berlin: East German Academy of Sciences.

Lenneberg, E. (1975). The concept of language differentiation. In E. Lenneberg & E. Lenneberg (Eds.), *Foundations of language development* (pp. 17–33). New York: Academic Press.

Leont'ev, A. A. (1969). *Jazyk, reč', rečevaja dejatel'nost'* [Language, speaking, speech activity]. Moscow: Proveščenie.

Lévi-Strauss, C. (1960). La structure et la forme. *Cahiers de l'Institut de Science Économique Appliquée, 99*, 3–36.

Longacre, R. (1976). *An anatomy of speech notions.* Lisse: de Ridder.

Luria, A. R. (1961). *The role of speech in regulation of abnormal behavior.* Oxford: Pergamon.

Luria, A. R. (1979). Neuropsychology of complex forms of human memory. In L. G. Nilsson (Ed.), *Perspectives on Human Memory* (pp. 279–289). Hillsdale, NJ: Erlbaum.

MacNeilage, P. (1970). Motor control and serial ordering of speech. *Psychological Review, 77*, 182–196.

Malinowski, B. (1923). The problem of meaning in primative languages. In C. K. Ogden & I. A. Richards (Eds.), *The meaning of meaning* (pp. 296–336). London: Oxford.

Marcel, A. (1980). Phonological awareness and phonological representation. In V. Frith (Ed.), *Cognitive processes in spelling* (pp. 373–403). London: Academic Press.

Marks, L., & Miller, G. A. (1964). The role of semantic and syntactic constraints in the memorization of English sentences. *Journal of Verbal Learning and Verbal Behavior, 3*, 1–5.

Mathesius, V. (1928). On linguistic characterology with illustrations from modern English. In *Actes du ler Congrés International des Linguistes,* 56–63.

Mathesius, V. (1947). *Čeština a obecný jazykozpyt. Soubor Statí* [The Czech language and general linguistics]. Prague: Melantrich.

Mathesius, V. (1961). *Obashový rozbor současné angličtiny na základě obecně lingvistickěm* [A functional analysis of contemporary English on a general linguistic basis]. Prague: Czechoslovakian Academy of Sciences.

Melčuk, I., & Žolkovskij, A. (1970). Towards a functioning meaning-text model of language. *Linguistics, 57*, 10–47.

Meyer, B. J. F. (1975). *The organization of prose and its effects on memory.* Amsterdam: North Holland.

Mitchell, T. F. (1957). The language of buying and selling in Cyrenaica. *Hesperus, 44*, 31–71.

Morgan, J. (1975). Some remarks on the nature of sentences. In *Papers from the Parasession on Functionalism* (pp. 433–449). Chicago Linguistic Society.

Morin, V. (1966). L'histoire drôle [Amusing stories]. *Communications, 8*, 102–119.

Mortara, B. G. (1974). *Aspetti e problemi della linguistica testuale.* Turin: Giappichelli.

Morton, J. (1980). The logogen model and orthographic structure. In U. Frith (Ed.), *Cognitive processes in spelling* (pp. 117–133). London: Academic Press.

Norman, D., & Rumelhart, D. (1975). *Explorations in cognition.* San Francisco: Freeman.

Osgood, Ch. & Bock, K. (1977). Salience and sentencing: some production principles. In S. Rosenberg (Ed.), *Sentence production* (pp. 89–140). Hillsdale, NJ: Erlbaum.

Palek, B. (1968). *Cross-reference: A study from hyper-syntax.* Prague: Charles University Press.

Pauliny, E. (1950). Slovosled a aktuálne vetné členenie [Word order and functional sentence perspective]. *Slovenská reč, 16*, 171–179.

Pecheux, M. (1969). *Analyse automatique du discours.* Paris: Seuil.

Petöfi, J. (1971). *Transformationsgrammatiken und eine ko-textuelle Texttheorie.* Frankfurt: Athenäum.

Petöfi, J. (1972). Eine Textgrammatik mit einer nicht-linear festgelegten Basis [A text grammar with a base not determined in a linear mode]. In van Dijk, T. A., Ihwe, J., Petöfi, J. & Rieser, H. *Zur Bestimmung narrativer Strukturen auf der Grundlage von Textgrammatiken* (pp. 77–129). Hamburg: Buske.

Petöfi, J. (1975). *Vers une théorie partielle du texte* [Toward a partial text theory]. Hamburg: Buske.

Petöfi, J. (Ed.). (1979). *Text vs. sentence: Basic questions in text linguistics*. Hamburg: Buske.

Petöfi, J. (1980). Einige Grundfragen der pragmatisch-semantischen Interpretation von Texten [Some basic questions of the pragmatic and semantic interpretation of texts]. In T. Ballmer & W. Kindt (Eds.), *Sprache und Logik* (pp. 146–190). Hamburg: Buske.

Petöfi, J. & Rieser, H. (1974a). *Probleme der modelltheoretischen Interpretation von Texten*. Hamburg: Buske.

Petöfi, J. & Rieser, H. (Eds.). (1974b). *Studies in text grammar*. Dordrecht: Reidel.

Pike, K. L. (1965). Beyond the sentence. *College Composition and Communication, 15*, 129–135.

Pike, K. L. (1967). *Language in relation to a unified theory of the structure of human behavior*. The Hague: Mouton.

Pilipenko, O. F. (1965). Intonacija nemestoimennogo voprosa v sopostavlenii s ukranskim jazykom [The intonation of questions without interrogative pronouns in regard to the Ukranian language]. *Phonetica, 12*, 182–185.

Plett, H. (1975). *Text und Textwissenschaft* [Text and text science]. Heidelberg: Quelle & Meyer.

Pospelov, N. S. (1948). Složoe sintakisčeskoe celoe i osnovnye osobennosti ego struktury [The complex syntactic unit and the fundamental characteristics of its structure]. *Doklady i soobščenija instituta russkogo jazyka, 2*, 43–68.

Propp, V. (1928). *Morfologija skazki* [The morphology of the folktale]. Leningrad: Academica.

Quirk, R., Greenbaum, S., Leech, G., & Svartvik, J. (1972). *A Grammar of Contemporary English*. London: Longmans.

Rieser, H. (1977). *Textgrammatik, Schulbuchanalyse, Lexikon*. Hamburg: Buske.

Rieser, H. (1978). On the development of text grammar. In W. Dressler (Ed.), *Current trends in text linguistics* (pp. 6–20). Berlin: de Gruyter.

Roggero, J. (1968). La substitution en anglais. *Linguistique, 2*, 67–92.

Rona, J. P. (1968). Für eine dialektische Analyse der Syntax. *Poetica 2*, 141–149.

Rubin, D. C. (1975). Within word structure in the tip-of-the-tongue phenomenon. *Journal of Verbal Learning and Verbal Behavior, 14*, 392–397.

Rüttenauer, M. (Ed.). (1974). *Textlinguistik und Pragmatik*. Hamburg: Buske.

Sacks, H., Schegloff, E., & Jefferson, G. (1974). A simplest systematics for the organization of turn-taking for conversation. *Language, 50*, 696–735.

Sanders, G. A. (1970). On the natural domain of grammar. *Linguistics, 63*, 51–123.

Saussure, F. de. (1916). *Cours de linguistique générale* [Course in general linguistics]. Lausanne: Payot.

Schank, R. & Abelson, R. (1977). *Scripts, plans, goals, and understanding*. Hillsdale, NJ: Erlbaum.

Schecker, M., & Wunderli, P. (Eds.). (1975). *Textgrammatik*. Tübingen: Niemeyer.

Schmidt, S. J. (1968). Zur Grammatik sprachlichen und nichtsprachlichen Handelns [On the grammar of linguistic and nonlinguistic actions]. *Soziale Welt, 3*, 360–372.

Schmidt, S. J. (1969). *Bedeutung und Begriff* [Meaning and concept]. Braunschweig: Vieweg.

Schmidt, S. J. (Ed.). (1970). *Text, Bedeutung, Aesthetik* [Text, meaning, aesthetics]. Munich: Bayrischer Schulbuchverlag.

Schmidt, S. J. (1973). *Texttheorie*. Munich: Fink.

Schmidt, S. J. (1982). *Foundations for the empirical study of literature*. Hamburg: Buske.

Sevbo, I. P. (1966). Ob izučenii struktury svjaznogo teksta [On studying the structure of connected texts]. *Lingvističeskie issledovani po obščej i slavjanskoj tipologii*, 16–31.

Sevbo, I. P. (1969). *Struktura svjaznono teksta i avtomatizacija referirovanija* [The structure of coherent text and automatic referencing]. Moscow: Nauka.

Sgall, P., Hajičová, E., & Benešová, E. (1973). *Topic, focus, and generative semantics.* Kronberg/Taunus, Germany: Scriptor.

Šimko, J. (1957). *Word order in the Winchester Manuscript and in William Caxton's edition of Thomas Malory's Morte d'Arthur (1485): A comparison.* Halle: Niemeyer.

Sinclair, J. McH., & Coulthard, M. (1975). *Towards an analysis of discourse.* London: Oxford.

Sitta, H., & Brinker, K. (Eds.). (1973). *Studien zur Texttheorie und zur deutschen Grammatik* [Studies in text theory and German grammar]. Düsseldorf: Schwann.

Skalička, V. (1961). Text, context, subtext. *Slavica Pragensia, 3,* 73–78.

Slama-Cazacu, T. (1961). *Langage et contexte.* The Hague: Mouton.

Šmilauer, V. (1940). Pořadek slov [Word order]. *Hovory o českem jazce, 8,* 39–51.

Smirnov, A. A. (1948). Psixologija zapominanija [The psychology of memory]. In A. A. Smirnov (Ed.), *Problemy psixologii pamjati* (pp. 7–35). Moscow: Prosveščenie.

Steinitz, R. (1968). *Nominale Pro-Formen* [Nominal pro-forms]. Report to the East German Academy of Sciences. Also in W. Kallmeyer, W. Klein, R. Meyer-Herman, K. Netzer, & H. J. Seibert (Eds.), (1974). Lektürenkolleg zur Textlinguistik (pp. 375–397). Frankfurt: Athenäum-Fischer.

Stempel, W. D. (1964). *Untersuchungen zur Satzverknüpfung im Altfranzösischen* [Investigations of sentence linking in Old French]. *Archiv für das Studium der neueren Sprachen und Literaturen,* supplement.

Stempel, W. D. (Ed.). (1971). *Beiträge zur Textlinguistik* [Contributions to text linguistics]. Munich: Fink.

Sumpf, J. (1969). Les problèmes des typologies. *Langages, 13,* 46–50.

Švedova, N. J. (1960). Strojaščiesja na osnove leksičeskogo povtorenija vtroye repliki dialoga [Second replies of a dialogue built on lexical repetitions]. In N. J. Švedova, *Očerki po sintaksisu russkoj razgovornoi reči* (pp. 280–362). Moscow: Academy of Sciences Press.

Svoboda, A. (1968). The hierarchy of communicative units and fields as illustrated by English attributive constructions. *Brno Studies in English, 7,* 48–102.

Todorov, T. (1966). Les catégories du récit littéraire [Categories of the literary discourse]. *Communications, 8,* 125–151.

van Dijk, T. A. (1969). Sémantique structurale et analyse thématique [Structural semantics and thematic analysis]. *Lingua, 23,* 28–53.

van Dijk, T. A. (1971). *Taal, tekst, teken: Bijdragen tot de literatuurtheorie* [Language, text, sign: Contributions to literary theory]. Amsterdam: Athenaeum, Polak, and van Gennep.

van Dijk, T. A. (1972). *Some aspects of text grammars.* The Hague: Mouton.

van Dijk, T. A. (1978). *Tekstwetenschap* (Science of Texts). Utrecht: Spectrum.

van Dijk, T. A. (1979a). *Macrostructures.* Hillsdale, NJ: Erlbaum.

van Dijk, T. A. (1979b). *Structures and functions of discourse.* Lectures at the University of Puerto Rico at Rio Piedras. (Spanish translation, *Estructuras y funciones del discurso,* Mexico City: Siglo XXI, 1980).

van Dijk, T. A., Ihwe, J., Petöfi, J., & Rieser, H. (1972). *Zur Bestimmung narrativer Strukturen auf der Grundlage von Textgrammatiken* [On determining narrative structures on the basis of text grammars]. Hamburg: Buske.

van Dijk, T. A., & Petöfi, J. (Eds.). (1977). *Grammars and descriptions.* New York: de Gruyter.

Vardul', I. F. (1955). O sceplenii samostojatel'nyx predloženij v japonskom jazyke [On the connection of independent sentences in the Japanese language]. *Trudy voenogo instituta po japonskom jakyke, 7*, 3–16.

Vater, H. (1968). Zu den Pro-formen im Deutschen [On German pro-forms]. *Sprachwissenschaftliche Mitteilungen, 1*, 21–29.

Weinrich, H. (1966). Tempusproblem eines Leitartikels [The problem of tense in a lead article]. *Euphorion, 60*, 263–272.

Weinrich, H. (1967). Syntax als Dialektik. *Poetica, 1*, 109–126.

Weinrich, H. (1971). *Tempus: Besprochene und erzählte Welt* [Tense: discussed and narrated world] (rev. ed.). Stuttgart: Kohlhammer.

Weinrich, H. (1976). *Sprache in Texten* [Language in texts]. Stuttgart: Klett.

Widdowson, H. (1978). *Teaching language as communication*. Oxford: Oxford University Press.

Wienold, G. (1969). Probleme der linguistischen Analyse des Romans [Problems of the linguistic analysis of the novel]. *Jahrbuch für Internationale Germanistik, 1*, 108–128.

Wienold, G. (1971). *Formulierungstheorie* [Theory of formulation]. Frankfurt: Athenäum.

Wirrer, J. (Ed.). (1977). *Textgrammatische Konzepte und Empirie* [Text-grammatical concepts und empiricism]. Hamburg: Buske.

Wunderlich, D. (1974). Textlinguistik. In H. Arnold & V. Sinemus (Eds.), *Grundzüge der Literatur- und Sprachwissenschaft* (pp. 386–397). Munich: DTV.

Zawadowski, L. (1956). Les fonctions du texte et des catégories de propositions [The functions of the text and of categories of propositions]. *Biuletyn polskiego towarzystwa językoznawczego, 15*, 31–63.

Žinkin, N. I. (1956). Razvitie pis'mennoj reči učaščixsja III-VII klassov [The development of the written word in pupils of the third to seventh grades]. *Izvestija Akademi Pedagogičeskix RSFSR, 78*, 141–250.

CHAPTER 4

Cognitive Psychology and Text Processing

Gordon H. Bower and Randolph K. Cirilo

INTRODUCTION

The goal of cognitive psychology is to understand how the mind works, how it manages to perform the small miracles of skill we see around us in everyday behavior. Cognitive psychologists take as mysteries what the layman accepts as common abilities—the ability to perceive the world as it is, to remember things, to comprehend social and linguistic events, and to act effectively to satisfy one's needs. Cognitive psychology is concerned with how people acquire and represent knowledge about their world, how they organize and use that knowledge. The ability to use language in speaking, listening, reading, and writing is one aspect of that knowledge. It is a complex cognitive skill that typically requires several years to acquire and several more to gain facility in.

This chapter focuses primarily on people's ability to listen to or read coherent texts, to comprehend them, to remember them, and to answer questions about them. In regard to people's ability to comprehend text, the goal of cognitive psychology is to describe the component processes involved, how they are organized and integrated to support the common feats of text understanding that people perform routinely. Of course, listening to or reading text admits of several different levels of analysis: neurological, phonetic, lexical, sentential, pragmatic. Cognitive psychologists are likely to skip over the neurological or phonetic levels in favor of the lexical or sentential levels of analysis.

Research on language within cognitive psychology falls mainly into three categories or styles. First are empirical studies designed to show that some variable influences language comprehension. An example would

HANDBOOK OF DISCOURSE ANALYSIS, Vol. 1
Disciplines of Discourse

be a demonstration that having a picture of a scene available improves the speed with which people can read a description of it with a given level of comprehension and memory. Another would be a demonstration that sentences with pronouns that have ambiguous referents take longer to comprehend.

The second style of research in cognitive psychology is concerned with specifying a small-scale theoretical model of the moment-by-moment operation of a subsystem of a person's language faculty. The subsystem is isolated and studied experimentally to gain understanding of its operation. An example of this would be the studies of Clark and Chase (1972) on how people verify a sentence (like *the star isn't above the plus*) in comparison to a simple picture (say, of a plus above a star). Experimental psychologists are most comfortable with just this type of situation—a circumscribed theory closely linked to a circumscribed experimental situation—and it provides a display case for their unique contributions. The presumption underlying such activities is that scientific understanding of a complex topic will proceed most rapidly by carving out manageable, small sections of the overall topic for intense investigation. The hope is that the type of theory developed for the subpart will be sufficiently general and consistent in principle with other miniature theories being developed to deal with other linguistic subsystems. The danger is that such miniature theories will become miniature islands isolated from a full scientific account of language competence.

The third style of research in cognitive psychology aims to construct a comprehensive theory of language understanding and text processing. The theory attempts to specify important processes and their organization in sufficient detail that a computer program could be written to simulate all or part of the theory. This characterizes the computer simulation approach followed by Winograd (1972), Schank and Abelson (1977; also Schank & Riesbeck, 1981), Anderson (1976), and Norman and Rumelhart (1975), to mention but a few practitioners. Computer models of natural language understanding attempt to specify sufficient mechanisms to perform designated linguistic tasks, relying upon common knowledge and linguistic intuitions to decide when the human task is being accurately simulated by the program. While attracted to such global models of language processing, experimental psychologists are somewhat put off by their apparent complexity, wondering whether the unfathomable human "blackbox" is being replaced by another blackbox (the program) that is just as complex and unfathomable. So, psychologists cull through the programs for basic principles, and then search for ways to collect discriminating experimental evidence for these principles.

In this chapter, we outline the basic cognitive system, its parts and organization, and then sketch briefly a view of how language is understood. We begin with a description of the cognitive system and its operation. We then consider how a single sentence is parsed and understood. Then we take up processing of interrelated sentences in a text.

THE COGNITIVE SYSTEM AND ITS ARCHITECTURE

The information processing approach assumes that perception and learning (from linguistic inputs or otherwise) can be analyzed conceptually into a series of stages during which particular mechanisms perform some elementary operation. Given a stimulus input to the system, the operation might be to isolate the figural stimulus from its background, to extract its significant features, to describe it in terms of perceptual primitives, to classify it as an instance of a certain kind, and to associate a meaning with the pattern. What gets passed along from stage to stage is an internal representation of the external stimulus and the context of its occurrence. Theories try to represent the causal flow of events in terms of a flow diagram in which blocks represent component processes, each labeled according to its typical function.

While several flow diagrams have been proposed, a prototypical one is shown in Figure 4.1. The interconnections between components are stipulated by the arrows representing both the flow of control and of information. The components can be divided roughly into a sensory system, a response system, a long-term memory (LTM), and a central processor (short-term memory [STM] and working memory) wherein occurs the active processes we identify with perceiving, memorizing, thinking, and deciding. The diagram is most quickly understood by describing how its parts operate in a simple stimulus-driven task such as reading a series of single unrelated words.

Pattern Recognition

The task instructions establish the goal to "read the words presented on a display screen." A plan to achieve that goal is entered into working memory. That plan consists of instructions to look at a certain place (controlling head and eye movements), to name any word presented there, and to continue doing so until told to stop. A word like *pencil* presented on the display is detected as a change in stimulus energies (a 'stimulus event'); contour-enhancing operations in the retina segregate the visual word as figure from its background. The pattern is laid down

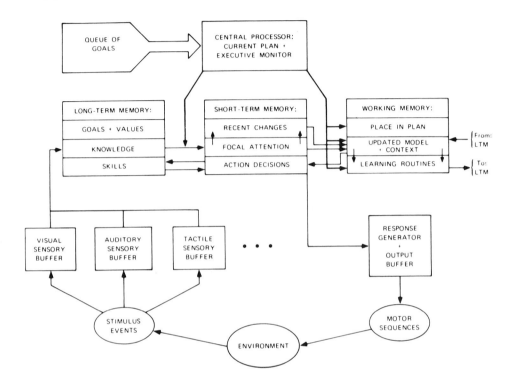

Figure 4.1   Information-flow diagram of the cognitive system. (From Bower, 1975 by permission.)

as an icon, or fleeting memory, in a visual sensory buffer, and a set of feature detectors located along the visual pathways begin extracting significant features from the stimulus. These features (vertical lines, angles, intersections) constitute a primitive description of the object.

Next, an identification stage ensues during which the system tries to classify the stimulus. Roughly speaking, pattern recognition is assumed to involve a weighted matching of the current feature list against a likely set of prototypes (idealized patterns) in LTM, with the input being classified according to the name of the best-matching prototype. Accuracy of identification depends on the quality of sensory information extracted and how many alternative prototypes are under consideration. A word will be identified more readily if it is probable and expected in the context. Thus, if the words in the list being read constitute a sensible sentence, then implicit predictions are made and those word prototypes are primed into readiness for matching against the input stimulus. This is why a familiar text, or a text about a familiar topic, is read more quickly. These expectations regarding the next word are being generated on-line from knowledge in LTM.

Short-Term Memory

To continue with our naming task, after *pencil* is identified, its internal code becomes active in STM. The plan sitting in working memory is basically a set of rules (technically, sets of condition–action productions) which, when fired, result in the person saying aloud the name of any word code entered into STM. Thus, the articulatory parameters for saying *pencil* are sent to the vocal apparatus, and the word is said. The system then prepares to read the next word and the task continues.

The STM in Figure 4.1 is the active part of the central processor that holds the internal symbols currently in the focus of attention and conscious processing. The STM need not be viewed as a "place" or "register" physically distinct from LTM; STM and LTM may only be two different states (or levels of current activation) of the same memory schemata.

The basic characteristics of STM are as follows: (1) it is the active partition of the memory system, (2) the processor has faster access to the items in STM than to items in LTM, (3) STM tends to preserve the surface perceptual properties of the stimuli as well as their temporal order, and (4) STM has a severely limited capacity, about four to seven symbols or coded items.

The capacity of STM is best characterized in terms of four to seven 'chunks' of information. A 'chunk' is defined as a stimulus pattern or sequence that the memory system recognizes as a familiar single unit for which a internal code already exists in memory. Thus, *cup* is a single unit to English readers whereas *ucp* is just three letters. The perceptual system appears normally to select the simplest, highest-level, discriminating description of the input sequence. Thus, *doghouse* is chunked as one unit rather than as two words or eight letters. Such units are identified by matching inputs to pattern schemata sitting in LTM.

Verbal items can be maintained in STM, if desired, by focusing attention on them and by rehearsing, covertly going over the items repeatedly. This rehearsal serves to maintain items in STM and to transfer some information about those items to LTM. The information transferred is typically the meaning and the context of occurrence of the items in question. Thus, in a memory span experiment (say, to remember *PZK*), the information transferred to LTM would be equivalent to the proposition 'List N consists of a token of letter *P* followed by a token of *Z* followed by a token of *K*'.

A critical aspect of rehearsal is that it is under 'strategic' control. The person's goals partly determine what he will select to attend to and rehearse (and consequently remember). Applying these ideas to a reader of text, the reader's goals would determine which textual information is relevant, important, and should receive special attention, rehearsal, and elaboration. This strategic component of STM may thus explain in part why the relevant, important parts of a text are better remembered.

Working Memory

Figure 4.1 also shows a working memory (or intermediate-term memory), which refers to memory structures that maintain information about the local context, but information that is neither in the focus of active memory nor in the distant edges of LTM. Working memory constructs and maintains an internal model of the immediate environment and events of the past few minutes. This local model serves as a framework or context within which dynamic (small) changes are recorded. The new information updates rather than casts aside the current model.

In regard to text processing, working memory would hold a list of foregrounded topics as well as a list of referents mentioned earlier in the text. Both are needed to look up connections for new expressions and statements. Thus, if a text states *John is a teacher,* later he can be referred to as *the teacher,* or as *he;* but to do so requires the reader to keep track of who is under consideration. The topics list in working memory helps resolve ambiguous expressions (*the bank*) and definite referents not mentioned previously, as in *I'm looking for a restaurant where the waiters wear tuxedos.* Many psychological studies have examined the process of reference establishment in comprehension; integral to their interpretation is the concept of working memory.

Also, as indicated earlier in our word-reading task, working memory holds the plan that the person is following in performing some task. The plan is typically a hierarchically structured set of goals, subgoals, and anticipated actions. In reading text, one can have various goals—to comprehend every sentence, or to skim for global gist, or to extract only a specific fact, or to look for typographic or grammatical errors, and so on. For each such goal, people have learned particular plans and routines that are activated in working memory and executed to achieve that goal.

Long-Term Memory

The LTM is conceived to be the repository of our more permanent knowledge and skills. It essentially includes all things that are in memory that are not currently being used. The LTM includes our knowledge of the language, of spatial models of our world, of properties of objects and people, of events of our lives, of perceptual–motor skills, and so on. A major enterprise in cognitive psychology is to indicate the types of knowledge people have, how that knowledge is to be represented, organized, accessed, and used. The two dominant representational formalisms are associative networks and production systems. Let us consider these briefly.

Productions

A production is an IF–THEN rule which states that in case a particular condition arises, then a particular action or series of actions is to be taken. An example would be *IF you drive up to a stop sign at a road intersection, THEN brake your car to a stop.* The conditions can be any patterns of activity represented in STM such as complex propositions; the actions can be either external or internal moves such as searching a memory location, fetching referents from memory, or activating other concepts into STM. This provides the power to model the flow of thought, problem solving, and plan following.

Each production is similar to an instruction in a computer program. In fact, computer programs can be viewed as a hierarchic sequence of productions. Productions thus provide the operational component in our models of cognitive systems: they form the "motor" that moves the "knowledge engine" through its skilled paces. Most cognitive models of motor and intellectual skills (typing, three-place subtraction) are written as production systems (see, e.g., Anderson, 1981).

Productions are typically learned (similar to stimulus–response habits), are strengthened by successful use, and weakened by nonreinforcement. Productions are stored in LTM; a production is selected and fired when its conditions are matched to the active contents of STM. When several productions are selected at the same time, some resolution or concordant action is required (e.g., choose the stronger one). We will not elaborate further details here; a volume edited by Waterman and Hayes-Roth (1978) illustrates many text-processing models realized as production systems.

Associative Networks

The most popular representation for information in theories of LTM is the associative (or semantic) network. The basic elements of the memory are concepts (nodes, symbols) and relations between concepts (propositions, symbol structures). A concept may be a perceptual primitive, an actional primitive, a primitive logical or semantic relation, or a higher-order concept built up by relations among these parts. The concepts can stand for generic terms as well as individual constants. The meaning of a concept is given partly by the configuration of its relations to other concepts and partly by the referential conditions necessary for the proper use and application of the term. In typical representations, concepts are represented as nodes (or cells in a computer memory) and relations between concepts as labeled arcs, arrows, or associations between the nodes.

In such a conceptual network, the learning of a new fact or new concept is solely a matter of recording a part of its representation in memory, which is accomplished through a specified configuration of relations among already-known concepts. An event is represented in memory in terms of a cluster of propositions describing features of the event. These are recorded in memory by establishing new associative connections among new instances (token nodes) of the concepts used in describing the event.

If the concept has many structured parts and several variables, with constraints on their fillers, then it is usually referred to as a 'schema' or 'frame'. A schema is a structured cluster of generic knowledge about some object or event. For example, our knowledge about a human face would be a schema composed of related slots (variable features) to represent the eyes, ear, nose, and so on. The eye color would be a variable (with values brown or blue, etc.) as would nose style and mouth size. The schema would specify prototypical information and correlations among features. Thus, people with black skin usually have brown eyes, those with red freckles usually have blue eyes, and so on. In encoding the face of a new acquaintance, the process is to call forth the generic face schema and to fill in its slots with the specific characteristics of the person. This process is called 'instantiation', and is the way generic schemata are employed in recording facts about particular individuals or events. Some theorists (e.g., Rumelhart, 1977b; Thorndyke, 1978) believe that text understanding is an example of the reader instantiating generic schemata regarding the type of text (folktale, nursery rhyme, detective mystery, etc.). We will later touch on this schema application view of text understanding.

Activation

It has already been stated that STM and LTM may only be two different states of the same memory nodes or schemata. This change in state occurs through the process of 'activation'. When the activation level of sensory elements, concepts, or propositions exceeds some threshold, they become the contents of consciousness (i.e., move from LTM to STM). Activation presumably spreads from one concept to another, or from one proposition to another, by associative linkages between them. A relevant analogy is an electrical network in which terminals correspond to concepts or event nodes, connecting wires correspond to associative relations with more or less strength, and electrical energy corresponds to activation that is injected into one or more nodes in the network. Activation of a unit can be accomplished either by presentation of the corresponding stimulus pattern or by prior activation of an associated thought.

To illustrate, a simple sentence like *An old man smoked a smelly cigar* would be represented graphically (and in LTM) as in Figure 4.2. The language parser (pattern recognizer) analyzes the sentence into atomic propositions and records these by subject–predicate links between the respective concepts. Thus, two entities (individual concepts) are created in memory, the nodes labeled *X* and *Y* in Figure 4.2. Then the atomic assertions are recorded by linking these new nodes to preexisting concept nodes by subject–predicate (S–P) (or relation–object) links: *X* is a man, *X* is old, *X* smoked *Y*, *Y* is a cigar, and *Y* is smelly. Each line in Figure 4.2 is to be conceived of as a new associative link to be learned (perhaps only briefly established while comprehending). The S–P labels are to be interpreted semantically as 'set membership': the referent of the S node is a member of the set of referents of the P node. Thus, in Figure 4.2, *X* is asserted to be a member of the set of things that smoked *Y* (smelly cigars).

Given such a linked structure in memory, it can be used to retrieve answers to questions by a spreading activation process. Thus, if asked *What did the old man smoke?*, activation of the queried concepts in

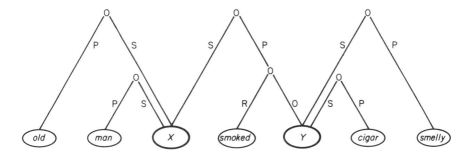

Figure 4.2 Node structure encoding the atomic propositions of *An old man smoked a smelly cigar*. S stands for subject and P for predicate.

STM is equivalent to direct access to the preexisting concepts of 'old' and 'man'; activation spreads out simultaneously from these two nodes and from the relation 'smoke'. Two of the activation processes intersect at node X (the concept of the specific old man), so it transmits activation along its link to intersect *smoke,* placing activation on node Y and thence to the *smelly* and *cigar* nodes. When these nodes receive activation above their threshold, the question-answering plan in working memory causes the person to report the names of these concepts as the answer to the question, that is, to say *smelly cigar*.

Spreading activation is a technique for retrieving associative concepts from memory. It has proven useful in explaining a number of experimental facts about simple question answering (see Collins & Loftus, 1975) and memory retrieval (see Anderson, 1976). Clearly, however, an intelligent processor and editor must be postulated that will discard the unwanted or irrelevant material churned out by an unguided spread of activation through a large, intertwined network.

As indicated, the representation of knowledge, its use in remembering, and the operation of the cognitive system are major topics of theoretical activity in cognitive psychology. Space limitations have prevented us from describing more than a fraction of the ideas in this area. For further reviews of this field, see Anderson (1976, 1980, 1981) and Rumelhart (1977a). We henceforth assume that the reader has enough familiarity with basic concepts to follow discussions in this chapter and other chapters in this *Handbook* written from the perspective of cognitive psychology. To illustrate this perspective, we take up the issue of linguistic parsing of single, isolated sentences. (Later we deal with sequences of sentences characteristic of text.) We focus on what is occurring in STM as an isolated sentence is parsed.

SINGLE-SENTENCE PROCESSING

We consider now the linguistic parsing and comprehension of a single sentence, either written or spoken. The parser and the lexicon in LTM take as input a linear string of words with surface features (order and intonation) and construct an interpretation and semantic representation of it. We may think of reading as the carrying out of a plan that causes the eyes to rapidly fixate successive words of a sentence. Measures of eye fixations indicate that careful readers fixate nearly all content words of a sentence at least once. A likely hypothesis is that the reader's eyes remain fixated on a word for as long as it is being processed (see Just & Carpenter, 1980). Thus, gaze durations provide information about on-line processing of single sentences or strings of sentences.

A likely hypothesis about comprehension is that the sensory input (words) is first organized in STM into surface constituents, then underlying propositions are extracted, then referents are looked up, then semantic interpretation of the sentence occurs and is deposited in working memory. Surface constituents are grammatical units like a word, a noun phrase, a verb phrase, a clause, and a sentence, often identified through surface syntactic clues (or intonation in speech). For example, the sentence *The old man smoked a smelly cigar* has such constituents as *man, old man, the old man, smelly cigar, smoked a smelly cigar,* and so on. Once surface constituents are segregated and their functions identified, the parser tries to coordinate underlying propositions to them. Thus, *man* is coordinated to the proposition 'There's an entity X that is a man'; *old man* is coordinated to 'X is a man and X is old', and so forth. The semantic network representation of such atomc propositions is illustrated in Figure 4.2. Eleven successive constituents are identified and corresponding propositions are extracted, and the parser builds continually in STM a hierarchic representation of the atomic propositions embedded in the larger matrix sentence, as Figure 4.2 illustrates. Once this translation into a semantic medium occurs, the surface string of words is allowed to decay from STM so that only the semantic interpretation is retained for very long.

The steps mentioned above—organizing words into surface constituents, extracting underlying propositions, setting up semantic structures in memory—go on cyclically and in parallel as the reader goes through a text sentence by sentence. The several levels of analysis cooperate and share partial results to help in one another's task.

Readers and listeners identify constituents by using a combination of syntactic and semantic knowledge. Psycholinguists have adopted different explanatory approaches to parsing. One approach supposes that readers or listeners have a loose-knit set of heuristic rules or parsing strategies that they use as the opportunity arises. An alternative approach tries to implement a complete computational model of parsing such as an augmented transition network. We briefly describe these two approaches.

The strategies approach (see Bever, 1970; Kimball, 1973) says that readers use linguistic clues to control syntactic expectations. Here are several heuristics and types of clues for English syntax (from Clark & Clark, 1977):

1. A function word indicates the beginning of a new constituent.
2. Use affixes to help decide whether a content word is a noun, verb, adjective, or adverb.
3. Use the first word (or major constituent) of a clause to identify the function of that clause in the sentence.

Here are a few semantic strategies:

1. Using content words alone, build propositions that make sense and parse the sentence into constituents accordingly.
2. Identify the verb and look for noun phrases that fit its semantic requirements.
3. Replace known definite noun phrases by their referents as soon as possible.
4. Expect 'given' information to precede 'new' information, unless the sentence is marked otherwise.

There is psychological evidence for the existence of each of these rules. For example, the last rule cited is supported by results showing slower and less accurate comprehension of statements when the order of mention of new versus given information is reversed in a sentence.

Despite the psycholinguistic evidence in its favor, a collection of strategies and rules such as these is incomplete and hardly performs adequately in parsing more than a subset of English or other languages. An alternative theoretical approach searches for a computational model that is both descriptively adequate and sufficient in so far as it can actually parse a significant portion of English sentences. Several computational formalisms have been proposed, including production systems (Anderson, 1976), word- or phrase-based programs (see Riesbeck, 1978; Wilensky & Arens, 1980), and augmented transition networks (ATNs) (see Kaplan, 1973; Woods, 1970). We discuss only the ATN formalism here as it is easiest to describe and has had the widest range of applications.

Augmented Transition Networks

An ATN is a computational algorithm that goes through a sentence left to right, classifying the part of speech of each word, trying to apply syntactic and lexical rules to arrive at the logical relations ('deep structure') being expressed in the surface sentence. The ATN consists of states that are connected by labeled arcs; the analysis of a sentence consists of passing from one state to another as successive words occur. The condition for a given transition is the occurrence of either a certain word (like *by* in English), or a word of a specified syntactic category (like verb), or a constituent of a specified kind (like noun phrase). To recognize a constituent like a noun phrase or verb phrase may require a call to an appropriate subnetwork, as shown in Figure 4.3. As parsing advances through a sentence, a chart accumulates hypotheses about the probable syntactic function of the words and constituents identified so far. Whenever a given transition occurs in the ATN, certain actions or changes in the

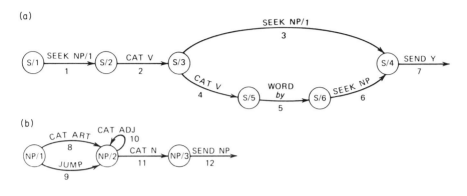

Figure 4.3 Augmented transition network for parsing active or passive declarative sentences in English. (a) sentence network; (b) noun phrase network. (Adapted from Rumelhart, 1977a by permission.)

developing chart are to be carried out by productions (see the table at the bottom of Figure 4.3). Figure 4.3, from Rumelhart (1977a), illustrates a simple ATN for parsing some active and passive declarative sentences. A more complete parser for English would have many more alternative paths through the network.

To illustrate the operation of this ATN, suppose the sentence to be parsed is *The old man was struck by a car.* The ATN begins in state S/1 looking for a noun phrase (NP). The NP label on this arc calls the NP subroutine; this finds that the first word *the* is an article, so arc 8 is taken; then *old* is found to be an adjective, so arc 10 is taken; then *man* is a noun, so arc 11 is taken. So far, the productions corresponding to the arcs taken (in the condition–action table below) will cause a structure to be built in working memory, assigning *man* as the HEAD of a noun phrase, with *the* and *old* as a determiner and modifier of that HEAD.

The next word is *was,* an auxilliary verb, which causes the ATN to take arc 12, to complete the NP subnetwork (thus completing arc 1 and arriving at state S/2), and to assemble the just-completed noun phrase. The *was* moves the system to state S/3. The next word, the verb *struck* moves the ATN along arc 4, causing its production in the table to fire, and to modify the chart by setting the ACTION to the current word (*struck*) and setting the OBJECT of the sentence to what formerly it believed was the SUBJECT (namely, the first noun phrase, *the old man*). The next word *by* causes arc 5 to be followed to S/6. Then a SEEK NP for arc 6 causes the NP subnetwork to be called to handle *the car*. When this arc 6 is finished, the arc action sets this noun phrase to be the logical subject (ACTOR) of the sentence. Arriving at S/4, the ATN notices there are no more words to be processed in the sentence, so arc 7 is taken, which assembles the logical deep structure, namely, ACTOR (*the car*), ACTION (*struck*), and OBJECT (*the old man*). Since the sentence is at an end and the ATN has moved from the initial state to its terminal state, we can say that the ATN has accepted or recognized this word string as a grammatical sentence according to its rules. If the sentence had been ungrammatical, then the ATN would have met some obstacles in the analysis and been unable to continue to the end.

ATN grammars are modular and can be built up piecemeal by adding more subroutines to analyze other grammatical constructions (relative clauses, complements, questions, etc.). Although no ATN grammar has ever been built capable of analyzing all of the English language, systems like that illustrated in Figure 4.3 have been expanded and elaborated to deal with a significant domain of English (see Woods, Kaplan, & Nash-Webber, 1972).

From a psycholinguist's perspective, an appealing feature of an ATN is the natural way the grammar of the language fits together with the rules for processing sentences. A second attractive feature of an ATN is that it gives a natural way to characterize readers' syntactic expectations about what is coming up next in a sentence. The arcs leaving a given state may be rank-ordered in terms of their expected uses; this forms the basis for syntactic heuristics. These differing expectations are revealed in many psycholinguistic experiments. Thus, in *the soldiers man the barricades,* the word *man* could be interpreted as a noun or verb, but after *soldiers* the ATN expects a verb, and so *man* is so interpreted. Such heuristics are misled by "garden path" sentences like *The old man the barricades* because *old* is interpreted first as an adjective and *man* as a noun (see the arcs of Figure 4.3), and the ATN halts when it comes to *the barricades* because it is looking for a verb. It then backs up, reinterprets *old* and *man* as a noun and verb, respectively, and continues with the new parse. Psychological experiments demonstrate that people do halt their reading at the points predicted by an ATN, and return to that point in the sentence where they went astray. Eye regression records reveal this process clearly.

Much psycholinguistic data about the difficulty of parsing is explained by an ATN. For example, an ATN explains why a right-branching construction like (1a) is much easier to understand than a center-embedded sentence like (1b).

(1)   a.   *The cat chased the mouse that lived in the house that Jack built.*

       b.   *The house the mouse the cat chased lived in was built by Jack.*

The center-embedded sentence requires the ATN to repeatedly call and interrupt the noun-phrase subroutine (see Figure 4.3) and then to pair off appropriately the stack of noun phrases with a stack of verb phrases. Further evidence for the ATN expectations is that when asked to continue a sentence fragment, people will fill in a word of the grammatical category predicted by the ordering of arcs in the ATN (see Stevens & Rumelhart, 1975). Similarly, when reading aloud, the errors people commit are invariably substitution of a word falling within the syntactic category that the ATN predicts at that point in the sentence.

Sentence parsing is an active research field, and current theories have led to many refinements of ATNs and beyond. There is also an active debate over how accurate ATNs are in accounting for psycholinguistic data (see Fodor & Frazier, 1980; Frazier & Fodor, 1978; Wanner, 1980). For our purposes here, the details of the parsing mechanism are not so important as is the form of its output. As noted before, the output of the parser is a cluster of propositions in working memory; these are represented in terms of labeled associations among the concepts (see Figure 4.2). This associative structure may be transferred to LTM; that is, the temporary links established during comprehension may become permanent. After a sentence is processed and its graph structure has been set up in working memory, its surface form in STM is permitted to fade. This fading occurs rapidly if attention is turned to a following sentence. In text, with streams of related sentences, the parser has the job of connecting successive sentences. We now turn to discussion of the processes that connect successive sentences in coherent text.

INTERPROPOSITIONAL CONNECTIONS

The view of comprehension presented thus far is in no sense unique to discourse. That is, most accounts of single-sentence parsing are just that: theories of the comprehension of single sentences isolated from any larger context. However, it should be clear that the meaning of a discourse cannot be adequately represented by a sequence of independent propositions (see de Beaugrande, this *Handbook,* Vol. 1). At the very least, a comprehender must recognize that the propositions are interconnected. In this section, an overview of the cognitive processes assumed to make interpropositional connections is given. Evidence for this picture is also provided.

Many sorts of interpropositional connections exist: referential, temporal, causal, and so on. Within psychology, however, most research has focused on the establishment of referential connections, perhaps because the to-be-connected elements are relatively obvious in discourse and, hence, amenable to a rather straightforward theoretical treatment.

Reference Establishment

As new propositions are processed, they must be integrated with earlier information in the text or with other knowledge present in LTM. At the referential level, this means that the comprehender must first determine whether a referent is given (information encountered earlier in the text) and, hence, already represented in working memory or new and, hence, not present in working memory (Clark & Haviland, 1977; Haviland & Clark, 1974). Cues in the text will often signal what is given and what is new (e.g., definite versus indefinite articles).

If the referent is taken to be new, then it cannot be linked to anything previously encoded from the text. Instead, a defining proposition (see Kieras, 1981) must be constructed for it, in essence, a new node in memory similar to 'X is a man' or 'Y is a cigar'. If the referent is given, however, such propositions are already present and the comprehender must search for the appropriate place to attach the new information. Just and Carpenter (1980) suggest that such searches are guided by several strategies. Comprehenders may first look for connections with antecedents that have been repeatedly referred to, are recent, or are topical. In fact, Kieras (1981) suggests that a topics list is maintained in STM for just such purposes. Consequently, the search for coreferents need not be a simple, linear one.

Moreover, the search will be constrained by the limits of the cognitive system (see Lesgold, Roth, & Curtis, 1979). That is, STM is limited in capacity. Hence, only a subset of the already-processed propositions will be active at any one time. If a referential connection can be made to an active proposition, the search will be relatively brief, leading to an immediate match. However, it may be that referential connections must be made to propositions that are no longer active. In such a case, the earlier memory structure must be reinstated in STM before an identification can be made. This is a reinstatement match. It relies upon the retrieval processes discussed earlier. Still, memory searches may fail. It may be that the cue to "given-ness" is inappropriate or the search cannot locate the needed memory structure. In such cases, inferential processes must be invoked to make the connection. This corresponds to Haviland and Clark's (1974) notion of a 'bridging inference'.

The evidence suggests that referential connections are made as soon as new referents are encountered. However, comprehenders occasionally make assignments that prove wrong on the basis of later information. Consequently, Just and Carpenter (1980) have held that a running representation of each clause is maintained with updates as each new word is processed. They also postulate that special processing occurs at the ends of sentences. Any gaps or inconsistencies that could not be resolved within the sentence are handled at this point.

This is only a rough outline of referential processing. In the following paragraphs, however, we consider some of the research that has been generated by this simple picture.

New Referents

First, consider the case of propositions whose referents are all new. As stated earlier, such propositions cannot be simply integrated with already processed material. Instead, new nodes must be created for the new referents. If this is so, then propositions containing new concepts should take more time to process than those containing previously mentioned concepts. A study by Kintsch, Kozminsky, Streby, McKoon, and Keenan (1975) supports this notion. They compared the reading times for passages with referential repetitions and pronominalizations to those for passages of the same length without such repetitions. As predicted, the passages with repetitions took less time to read. Kieras (1978) also found longer reading times for sentences containing only new referents. In short, when referents do not corefer with earlier concepts, extra processing is required. This is consistent with the creation of new nodes in memory.

Prior Coreferents

Next, consider the case of propositions that are coreferential with earlier propositions. As noted, referential ties can be drawn through immediate matches, if the propositions containing the critical referents are both in STM, or through reinstatement matches, if the earlier referent must be retrieved from working memory. Initially, it can be asked whether there is evidence that referential connections are being drawn during comprehension. Carpenter and Just (1977) have demonstrated this by examining eye fixations during reading. They assume that eye fixations can be external indicants of the internal integrative processes. If so, referential ties should be indicated by regressive eye fixations between the current referent and its earlier occurrence. Of course, this assumes the current referent unambiguously points to a single, earlier referent. If not, regressions should occur to any referent that could be appropriate. Just and Carpenter compared regressions from referents with singular and ambiguous coreferents. They found that regressions were more determinate in the former case than in the latter. Thus, regressions are obtained between coreferents, regressions that increase in specificity as the linguistic context dictates.

Immediate versus Reinstated Referents

Now consider the distinction between immediate and reinstatement matches. These two processes are differentiated by the activation state of relevant segments of text with respect to STM. Theoretically, one can influence this state by varying the distance between the current sentence and the earlier sentence containing the coreference of interest. The farther apart they are, the more likely it is that the earlier sentence has become inactive and, hence, will require a reinstatement match.

Clark and Sengul (1979) had subjects read a three-sentence context paragraph, press a button, read a target sentence, and then press a button when they had understood the target. They varied whether a referent in the target sentence was mentioned earlier in the first, second, or third sentence of the context paragraph and measured the time to understand the target (the time between button presses). They found comprehension time to be fastest when the referent was mentioned in the third sentence and slowest when in the first, comprehension time for a referent in the second sentence falling in between the two. Similarly, Carpenter and Just (1977) found that the time to decide if a sentence was consistent or contradictory with preceding information in a text increased with the number of intervening sentences between the target and an earlier sentence to which it had to be linked referentially. Thus, the more likely it is that referents must be linked on the basis of a reinstatement match, the longer it will take to understand the current sentence.

But is reinstatement actually taking place? Work by McKoon and Ratcliff (1980b) demonstrates this rather elegantly. They used an activation (or priming) procedure in which the subject read a paragraph sentence by sentence and was then presented with a single test word from the first sentence of the paragraph for recognition. They varied whether the last sentence of the paragraph referred anaphorically to the first sentence. If it corefers and there is reinstatement, then the earlier referent should be activated in memory and, hence, should be easier to recognize. This is what they found. Recognition time for a referent in the first sentence was faster when the last sentence had referred back to it than when it had not. Furthermore, the entire proposition was reinstated and not just the referent, for recognition time was also shortened for words in the same proposition as the referent of the anaphor in the last sentence. Thus, there is evidence for the occurrence of reinstatements.

As stated earlier, though, memory searches may fail. For example, when cues to "given-ness" are inappropriate, memory searches should occur even though there is no antecedent to be found. Haviland and Clark (1974) created sentence sequences in which definite references (which should be taken as given information) either did or did not have explicit antecedents. They found that the lack of antecedents resulted in longer comprehension times for the sentences containing the definite references. For example, *The beer was warm* (the definite article indicating "given-ness") takes longer to comprehend following *John got the picnic supplies out of the trunk* than following *John got the beer out of the trunk*. In the latter case, the connection between the two sentences is clearly defined by the recurrence of *the beer*. In the former case, however, there is no direct antecedent for *the beer,* rather a connection can only be made by inferring a relation between *picnic supplies* and *beer*. Hence, inappropriate signals to "given-ness" result in additional processing, the invocation of inferential processes to make the indicated connection.

There is also empirical support for special integrative processing at the ends of sentences. For example, when subjects read texts word by word or phrase by phrase, they tend to pause longer at the word or phrase ending the sentence (Aaronson & Scarborough, 1976; Mitchell & Green, 1978). In sum, there is ample evidence for the processing account given above (see also Cirilo, 1981; Vipond, 1980).

Referential Coherence and Integration

Referential coherence should be reflected in memory representations for texts. To use Kintsch and van Dijk's (1978) terminology, the product of the indicated processing is a coherence graph, a network of propositions interconnected referentially. Typically, coherence graphs are represented hierarchically. Propositions to which many others are connected occupy the higher levels of the graph.

If referential coherence is important in textual representations, information should be better integrated where coreference exists than where it does not. In an early test of this, de Villiers (1974) had subjects read a list of sentences that could form a referentially coherent passage but did not tell them this. For some subjects, the sentences contained definite articles, while for others they contained indefinite articles. Since definite articles should evoke attempts at referential integration, a coherence graph is more likely to be constructed in the former case than in the latter. The results supported this hypothesis. With definite articles, recall for the sentences was better and subjects tended to make more intersentence lexical substitutions (interchanging coreferents expressed by different words). In short, when readers have reason to believe that referential ties can be made, they will tend to do so, thus producing a greater degree of integration of the information.

This notion is further supported by Lesgold (1972), who studied pronominalization as a connective device. He compared the integration in memory for sentences whose propositions were or were not related by pronominal reference. Thus, *The postman whistled a tune and he (or George) was tired* links *tired* with *postman* in the *he* sentence but not the *George* sentence. Lesgold found that pronominal reference resulted in integrated representations (an equal likelihood of recall of lexical items in the same versus other underlying sentence propositions), while the lack of it resulted in incomplete integration.

Distance in a Coherence Graph

Although such research emphasizes the importance of coreference to memory for texts, it does not demonstrate that coherence graphs are an apt depiction of textual representations. For example, coherence graphs define different relative distances among propositions. Two propositions that corefer will be closer than two that do not. This should be true even when coreferring propositions are separated by several sentences in the surface text. Indeed, two propositions that are relatively close in the surface text may end up relatively distant in the coherence graph. Nonetheless, their closeness in the underlying coherence graph should indicate their psychological distance.

McKoon & Ratcliff (1980b) tested this distance implication using an activation (or priming) technique similar to that mentioned earlier. Specifically, the closer two propositions are in the coherence graph, the more the appearance of an item in one should prime or facilitate the subsequent recognition of an item from the other. Subjects read two unrelated paragraphs and then were tested on single words presented one at a time. Subjects had to decide whether or not each word had appeared in either of the paragraphs. However, the structure of the paragraphs was varied. Some had a linear structure (see Table 4.1). Thus, the amount of priming between two words appearing contiguously in the test list should depend only on the linear distance between them (e.g., *Tom* should be a better prime for *boy* than *flower*). Other paragraphs had a structure in which certain nouns were equally far apart in the surface text as other nouns but closer in the coherence graph (see Table 4.1). A noun close in the coherence graph to another noun should be a better prime for that noun than a noun that is equally distant at the surface level but more distant in the coherence graph (e.g., *nurse* should prime *cabinet* better than *patient* primes *ground*). The data were consistent with these hypotheses. In a subsequent study using the same procedure, McKoon and Ratcliff (1980a) also demonstrated that words from referentially connected propositions in LTM primed one another better than words from non-coreferential propositions in the same paragraph. In short, coherence graphs bear some relation to textual representations in memory.

Table 4.1

Examples of Two Different Text Coherence Graphs[a]

Linear structure
  P1   *Tom saw a boy.*
  P2   *The boy threw a ball.*
  P3   *The ball hit a dog.*
  P4   *The dog bit a girl.*
  P5   *The girl dropped a doll.*
  P6   *The doll smashed a flower.*

  P1——P2——P3——P4——P5——P6

Branching referential structure
  P1   *The doctor called a nurse.*
  P2   *The nurse pushed a wheelchair.*
  P3   *The wheelchair held a patient.*
  P4   *The patient had a cut.*
  P5   *The doctor opened a cabinet.*
  P6   *The cabinet contained a bottle.*
  P7   *The bottle struck the ground.*

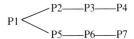

---

[a]Adapted From McKoon and Ratcliff, 1980b.

To summarize, referential links tend to be drawn when cues in the text indicate it. When such links exist, the result is a better integrated representation of the text. Furthermore, when referential processing should be more time consuming, evidence for such difficulties can be found.

As stated earlier, however, coreference is only one form of textual coherence relevant to comprehension. Unfortunately, relatively little psychological research has been done with connective devices in text other than coreference. For example, Haberlandt and Bingham (1978) have established the importance of verbs to coherence, while Black and Bern (1981) have studied the role of causal connections between sentences. Clearly, much more needs to be accounted for. Still, the ideas described above may provide a foundation on which to build more comprehensive accounts of text processing.

Macroprocessing

Another aspect of processing to be considered is macroprocessing (Kintsch & van Dijk, 1978), since it is often assumed to operate on coherence graphs. It has been hypothesized that, during comprehension, special processes reduce all the propositions contained in a coherence graph to a smaller set of high-level propositions or macropropositions. This set of propositions (which can be defined at several levels of abstraction) would describe the global organization of the text, its gist, thus making summarization and long-term memory of the ideas in the text manageable tasks.

To derive macropropositions, processes must be postulated that can abstract and generalize from the detailed text information to its more embracing concepts. These macroprocesses must occur simultaneously with the low-level processing. Indeed, to a certain extent, the two types of processing must be highly similar. That is, sequences of macropropositions must be coherent with one another. Hence, comprehenders must make referential connections among them. In particular, memory searches, reinstatements, and required inferences will influence processing at this level as well. Vipond (1980) has evidence supporting these ideas.

As to the actual creation of macropropositions, it is assumed that propositions are first differentiated according to their relevance to the topic of the text. To do this, comprehenders must use expectations about what sorts of things are relevant to the topic. Occasionally this is a matter of filling in the slots (values) of a schema or frame to deal with a particular type of text. Thus, newspaper stories about automobile accidents may call up a schema with variables to be filled with time and location of the accident, participants, its cause, extent of damage, and disposition of the victims. Once relevance assignments have been made, irrelevant propositions are deleted (or deactivated) while relevant propositions are incorporated into the macrostructure, perhaps after being modified by other macroprocesses, thus forming a macroproposition. The resultant macrostructures are hierarchical since macroprocesses can be reapplied. One of the macroprocesses is generalization over irrelevant details that are not preconditions for later understanding. This may involve deletion of qualifiers and of specific names, dates, places, or replacing constants by their superordinate categories (e.g., replace *apples* by *fruits*).

This aspect of comprehension is dealt with more thoroughly elsewhere (Kintsch, this *Handbook,* Vol. 2). Still, it should be noted that macroprocessing has not been studied as extensively as referential processing, for example. It is far more difficult to give a detailed process model that will yield macrostructures than one that will yield referential structures. As has been implied above, though, high-level knowledge structures, schemata, are crucial to the differentiation of relevant from irrelevant propositions. The nature and use of such schemata in text comprehension and memory are the subject of the next section.

GLOBAL TEXT STRUCTURES

A schema is a data structure for representing the generic concepts stored in memory (Rumelhart, 1980). Although schemata represent knowledge at many levels of abstraction, research in text comprehension has focused on schemata dealing with relatively high-level aspects of text structure. In this section, these schemata and their use is briefly described. Subsequently, some of the work bearing on these ideas is outlined.

Story Schemata

The schema familiar to most researchers in discourse is that assumed to describe stories (see Gülich & Quasthoff, this *Handbook,* Vol. 2, for a fuller treatment). This schema depicts the prototypical story and variations on it. It identifies the units that constitute stories, the sequencing of these units, and the types of connections that will typically occur between units. It is assumed to develop through experience with stories and the types of real-world event sequences found in stories.

Story grammars have been widely used to represent story schemata (Mandler & Johnson, 1977; Rumelhart, 1975; Stein & Glenn, 1979; Thorndyke, 1977). In story grammars, information about story structure is represented as a set of rewrite rules, essentially a set of rules for segmenting, identifying, and manipulating story constituents. Although this format is important, its use should not be taken as a claim that the story schema in the comprehender's head is a story grammar. Typically, one treats the formalism as though it specified the parts of the schema and their interrelationships in order to see if anything can be learned as a result (Bower, 1976). It provides a method of study rather than a complete theory. Consequently, those who argue against the formalism (e.g., Black & Wilensky, 1979) should try to indicate a more fruitful alternative for study.

The most common alternative to story grammars is the event schema (e.g., Lichtenstein & Brewer, 1980). Earlier we stated that the story schema must develop in part through experience with real-world event sequences. Consequently, it can be argued that story understanding is only a special case of event understanding. The claim would be that people understand story structures using their general knowledge about planning and problem solving found in event sequences (i.e., knowledge about how actions are related to one another to organize behavior) rather than by use of text-specific knowledge. Lichtenstein and Brewer support this view by demonstrating that memories for simple event sequences presented on film show properties very similar to memories for stories. Some would argue, then, that stories are no different from descriptions of other event sequences except for their evocation of particular emotional responses like interest, suspense, and surprise (Morgan & Sellner, 1980). Whatever the case, stories are assumed to be understood by way of the typical information patterns represented by schemata.

Expository Schemata

If this is true for stories, it would not be surprising that the same holds for expository prose. That is, there should be schemata which are used in comprehending different types of expository texts. In general, such schemata are hypothesized to be organized around prototypical patterns of argumentation (see Kopperschmidt, the *Handbook,* Vol. 2). However, the only theory of expository structures that has yet had any impact in psychology is that of Grimes (1975) and Meyer (1975). In this theory, the higher levels of text structure are characterized in terms of rhetorical predicates. These predicates relate textual information by specifying superordinate principles to which the rest of the text is made subordinate. Examples of top-level forms are problem–solution, question–answer, attribute–listing, and contrasting alternatives.

For example, the problem–solution rhetorical form defines two high-level ideas in a text: the statement of a problem and then the problem's solution. Hence, any crucial element of such a text should be either part of the problem statement or part of the solution.

In our account, these top-level structures are schemata which authors use to organize their texts. At comprehension, readers will use similar schemata to determine the text's global message and how this message organizes the rest of the content. In short, the understanding of exposition is no different from the understanding of stories except for use of schemata specific to such texts. Research finds that good readers who score high on comprehension also organize their recall using the rhetorical structure of the passage.

Schema in Comprehension

But how are schemata used in comprehension? According to Rumelhart (1977b), schematic comprehension consists of selecting schemata to account for the text to be understood and verifying the appropriateness of those schemata. Consider the case of a story. As its first sentences are read, they should activate certain schemata which in turn suggest that other, high-level schemata are appropriate for the text at hand. For example, the occurrence of *Once upon a time* . . . might activate a schema for the setting of a fairy tale. Consequently, the fairy tale schema should also be activated since the setting schema is one of its components. The activation of a high-level structure on the basis of something in the text itself (i.e., data-driven processing discussed by Bobrow & Norman, 1975) corresponds to schema selection. In essence, an initial hypothesis is made about which schema can account for the text.

Once the high-level schema has been activated, it will activate its subschema. The assumption is that these subschemata will be able to account for some of the input text. This activation from the top can be viewed as the creation of expectations about what will be found in the text (so-called conceptually-driven processing). In the case of stories, one would expect a series of episodes describing a protagonist's attempts to achieve some goal by overcoming obstacles. Of course, the activation of the episode schema results in the activation of its components, and so on.

The remainder of comprehension can be viewed as an interaction between these expectations and the input text. This is the substantiation procedure. That is, the expectations must be confirmed in the text (e.g., there must be some segment of the text that can be understood as an episode). With sufficient confirmatory evidence, the interpretation offered by the schema is substantiated. If enough disconfirmatory evidence is collected, however, the current schema is deactivated and a more promising alternative is found.

The product of comprehension will consist of an instantiation (possibly fragmentary) of the schema or schemata used during processing; this is essentially a copy of the schema with its variable slots filled by segments of the input text, with nonfitting elements noted. Retrieving such a representation would consist of finding these stored traces in memory and using the available schemata to reconstruct the original interpretation and/or the original text. That is, the traces must be found; then it must be determined what schema was used to encode them; finally, an attempt is made to fit the traces into the schema's component slots.

Whatever the plausibility of this specific theoretical account, it is apparent that schema processing will not always be successful. Texts will fail to be understood for many reasons; major reasons for failure are that they provide insufficient cues to the appropriate schemata or the comprehender does not possess the crucial schemata. Many studies with younger children (e.g., Kernan, 1977; McClure, Mason, & Barnitz, 1979; Poulsen, Kintsch, Kintsch, & Premack, 1979) show that their textual schemata are more poorly developed and used than those of older children. Clearly, we must be concerned not only with how schemata are used but also how they are formed. Rumelhart (1980) has offered several hypotheses as to how schemata develop.

To summarize, it has been argued that comprehension consists of building a schematic representation for a text. Later, if the text must be remembered, the representation and schematic knowledge will be activated and used to guide retrieval. This is a very rough picture, but a large body of research supports it. In the following, three lines of evidence are considered: studies dealing with schematically well-formed texts, studies dealing with schematically malformed texts, and studies dealing with schematic elaborations on texts.

Research Supporting Schema Theory

Well-Formed Texts

First, consider texts that conform to schematic expectations. By definition, such texts are well formed. Consequently, the schema should be maximally effective during comprehension. Moreover, the structural analysis provided by the schema should roughly describe the representation of a comprehended text in memory. If so, the properties of remembered texts will correspond to those of the schema. Much research has been motivated by the search for such correspondences.

Typically, the structural descriptions inherent in textual schemata are hierarchic. That is, some propositions are superordinate to or more important than others. If texts are processed in terms of such hierarchic structures, then this fact should be reflected in the reader's memory for them. Specifically, it has been argued (Bower, 1976; Thorndyke & Yekovich, 1980) that recall will start at the top of the hierarchy and work its way down by associative cuing. Retrieval paths will be longer to the low-level propositions. Hence, their retrieval probability will be lower. This has proven to be the most consistent finding in the literature. Whether a narrative schema (Rumelhart, 1977b; Thorndyke, 1977) or an expository schema (Meyer, 1975) is applicable, high-level ideas are recalled better than low-level ideas. Thus, the result of comprehension reflects the hierarchic nature of the structural descriptions.

Schemata also postulate constituent structures for texts. That is, well-formed texts are divisible into smaller constituents. Therefore, comprehenders should be sensitive to these units and encode texts in terms of them. The episodes found in narratives have been the most studied of these units.

For example, Glenn (1978) independently varied a story's length, as defined by its number of simple sentences, and the story's episodic structure, as defined by the types of information in the sentences and the intersentential relationships. She found that variations in length influenced the number of statements recalled but not the organization of those statements. On the other hand, variations in structure influenced the organization of information in recall but not the amount recalled. Similarly, Black and Bower (1979) have found that the recall of an episode's actions depends on the length of that episode but not on the length of other episodes in the story. Hence, story statements cluster into separate chunks (corresponding to episodes) in memory.

But even if hierarchic and episodic structures are evident at recall, it is not clear what the locus of the effects is. The schematic influence could be present at encoding, retrieval, or both. Recent studies, however, have indicated that analogous effects occur during encoding when retrieval is not an issue.

Structural Influences on Encoding

First, the hierarchic structure of a text is reflected in its immediate processing. Cirilo and Foss (1980) compared the reading time for a sentence when it occupied a high-level position in one story to the reading time for the same sentence when it occupied a low-level position in another story. They found that the sentence took longer to read when it occupied a high-level (important) position in the story structure. Just and Carpenter (1980) obtained a similar result with expository prose. Perhaps comprehenders spend less time on low-level propositions because they recognize them as irrelevant. Alternatively, high-level propositions may take longer to integrate into the accruing context than low-level propositions. Being globally relevant, perhaps they generate more connections to other parts of the text. Drawing more connections will take more time. Whatever the case, the hierarchic property of schematic representations is found both at encoding and retrieval.

The comprehension of episodic structures has also been investigated directly. Haberlandt (1980) measured the reading times for sentences constituting simple, two-episode stories. After subtracting extraneous contributions to reading time like the number of words in a sentence, he found that reading times were longer at the boundary nodes of an episode than would otherwise be expected. This was attributed to greater cognitive work in "wrapping up" or encoding the boundary nodes. Specifically, at the beginnings of episodes, there are often changes in perspective, characters, and the like, the establishment of which require extra cognitive resources. At the ends of episodes, the comprehender will attempt to organize the sentences into a single, high-level node, summarizing or wrapping up the gist of the episode. Again, the processing load will be greater at this point. In sum, the episodic structure of a story influences the course of comprehension and does not simply organize recall.

Processing Malformed Texts

So long as texts are schematically well formed, schema theory predicts they will be readily comprehended, with most readers agreeing on the relative importance of different sentences. However, suppose that a to-be-comprehended text violates the conventions of a textual schema. Such malformed texts should be difficult, if not impossible, to understand. In order to test this, the applicability of the appropriate schemata must be manipulated. The text's structure must be completely lacking or sufficiently distorted to prevent easy recognition. A number of techniques have been used to accomplish these aims.

One method of eliminating structure is to arrange the constituents of a well-formed story such that their order is nonschematic. This can be done at a number of levels. Thorndyke (1977) randomly permuted the sentences constituting stories. Stein and Nezworski (1978) created stories in which one story category occurred out of its ideal location. Mandler (1978) used pairs of two-episode stories in which during presentation the nodes constituting each episode were presented in interleaved fashion rather than separately. All of these studies found that comprehension and recall for the ideas in malformed stories was poorer than that for the same ideas in well-formed stories. Moreover, the greater the deviation from the ideal, the greater the decrease in recall accuracy. In short, when the relevance of a textual schema is not readily apparent, memory will be relatively poor.

Despite such problems, comprehenders still attempt to apply textual schemata to malformed texts. This is clear when the recall protocols are examined more closely. In particular, it is found that subjects tend to insert missing elements and reorder the story statements in recall to conform to their ideal order. In other words, schematic considerations influence how information is output such that the distortions at input are lost or corrected. However, this tendency decreases as schematic violations increase. Apparently, large deviations are not corrected, perhaps because the reader remembers that the text was substantially malformed.

A second method of eliminating schematicity relies on the cultural specificity of textual schemata. Other cultures may have very different conventions underlying their texts. When a text does not conform to the schema of one's own culture, comprehension should be poor. Accordingly, Kintsch and Greene (1978) found that for American college students the quality and intersubject agreement of summaries for stories corresponding to familiar schemata of European culture were better than those for Apache Indian folktales whose connections seem more arbitrary and less predictable. However, one must be careful in interpreting cross-cultural comparisons. Since Apache subjects were not tested, one could conclude simply that the European stories were more comprehensible than the Apache folktales to any readers regardless of their culture. Also, as Johnson and Mandler (1980) have noted, the Apache schema may be the same as ours but the interpretation of the content relies on other culture-specific knowledge which we do not have. Thus, there is as yet no convincing evidence that textual schemata differ fundamentally across cultures.

How do deviations from expected structures create difficulties? Violations upset expectations and cause comprehenders to spend more time explaining or resolving the unexpected elements than processing the rest of the story. However, the memory difficulty could also lie in retrieval. The parts of a well-formed text could act as cues for the retrieval of later parts. Such cues would not exist for texts which are structurally incoherent.

There is some evidence for the former account. Kintsch, Mandel, and Kozminsky (1977) scrambled the paragraphs constituting stories. They found that, when given free reading time, subjects summarized scrambled stories just as well as well-formed stories. However, scrambled stories took longer to read, suggesting that time was needed to resolve the confusions. Briefly, violations of schematic expectations create difficulties that are not seen when all the expectations are met.

Schema-Directed Elaboration

A final important aspect of schemata is that they contain information that not every text will explicitly realize. Consequently, comprehenders may elaborate on the presented material, generating plausible information consistent with the current schema but not necessarily true. Past experience is used to understand a text and as a result more information is added to its memory representation. For example, a comprehender may infer character motivations, embellish personality descriptions, and so on. The amount and type of elaboration will vary from person to person depending on his or her prior experience with related contexts. If the situation is highly regular (e.g., scriptal situations as described by Schank & Abelson, 1977), however, the nature of the elaboration will be highly similar across readers. According to Reder (1980), readers use such elaborations to find connections among sentences, generate expectations about later input, and aid in retention by creating a richer representation.

One common method of testing this view directs subjects to make certain elaborations (i.e., use certain schemata) rather than others. The expectations are that memory will be better for material consistent with the preferred elaboration and that inferences will be added to the representation on the basis of the preferred elaboration. Bower (1978), for example, reports an experiment in which subjects were given stories consisting of episodes. Half the subjects were given prior information that would suggest certain schemata were relevant, such as that the main character (a college coed) had recently discovered she was pregnant. The meaning of some of the episodes (e.g., going to the doctor) could be very different if the heroine is thought to be pregnant.

As predicted, subjects given the prior information produced more inferences at recall consistent with the pregnancy theme. Furthermore, they recalled more of the episodes related to the theme. This is to be expected if the prior information called up a schema used to make elaborations during comprehension. Similarly, manipulations of the reader's perspective or bias have also been shown to influence comprehension and memory (e.g., Anderson, Reynolds, Schallert, & Goetz, 1977; Pichert & Anderson, 1977; Schallert, 1976).

In sum, it is apparent that high-level knowledge structures are used in understanding and retrieving texts. Texts consistent with these structures are well remembered and easy to understand. Conversely, texts inconsistent with these structures are poorly understood and remembered, even creating a tendency for subjects to distort their memories toward more schematic forms. Finally, information in texts may be elaborated upon and remembered in terms of the schemata used at comprehension. Clearly, text understanding is as much a product of the knowledge structures of the reader as it is a product of the text itself.

CONCLUSION

In this chapter, we have given an overview of text processing as cognitive psychologists understand it. We have focused upon the architecture of the cognitive system, the cognitive processes that mediate comprehension, and the evidence gathered to test these views. In so doing, we have smoothed over the differences that exist among individual theorists. Some may choose to examine different aspects of the same problem. Others may examine the same aspects but in very different ways. We have attempted to capture the most commonly held picture of text processing.

However, it must be remembered that most of the psychological research in this area is of very recent origin. Consequently, the theoretical ideas must be regarded as preliminary and subject to refinement. In time, we may develop very different notions of the cognitive processes that operate on texts, the nature of textual representations, and so on. Despite this limitation, the empirical data generated thus far will always be relevent. Any new theory must be able to encompass results obtained within the frameworks of old theories.

Where, then, are the new theories coming from? Perhaps the most promising work is being motivated by the concern that scholars dealing with the same problem across disciplines should be interacting with one another. Although cognitive psychologists have drawn heavily from other disciplines in the past (e.g., ATNs from computer science and notions about textual structures from linguistics), only recently have more formal lines of communication been established. This is evidenced by the growth of the interdisciplinary field of cognitive science. It seems reasonable that this pooling of resources should significantly accelerate progress in the field. At this point, however, it is probably premature to point out any particular new approach.

Modern civilization demands that a person acquire and use language. It is imperative that we learn how it operates. This chapter represents only a single perspective on this issue. Consequently, we must continue the process of educating one another. That is the goal of this *Handbook*.

REFERENCES

Aaronson, D., & Scarborough, H. S. (1976). Performance theories for sentence coding: Some quantitative evidence. *Journal of Experimental Psychology: Human Perception and Performance, 2,* 56–70.

Anderson, J. R. (1976). *Language, memory, and thought.* Hillsdale, NJ: Erlbaum.

Anderson, J. R. (1980). *Cognitive psychology and its implications.* San Francisco: W. H. Freeman.

Anderson, J. R. (Ed.). (1981). *Cognitive skills and their acquisition.* Hillsdale, NJ: Erlbaum.

Anderson, R. C., Reynolds, R. E., Schallert, D. L., & Goetz, E. T. (1977). Frameworks for comprehending discourse. *American Educational Research Journal, 14,* 367–381.

Bever, T. G. (1970). The cognitive basis for linguistic structures. In J. R. Hayes (Ed.), *Cognition and the development of language.* (pp. 279–352). New York: Wiley.

Black, J. B., & Bern, H. (1981). Causal coherence and memory for events in narratives. *Journal of Verbal Learning and Verbal Behavior, 20,* 267–275.

Black, J. B., & Bower, G. H. (1979). Episodes as chunks in narrative memory. *Journal of Verbal Learning and Verbal Behavior, 18,* 309–318.

Black, J. B., & Wilensky, R. (1979). An evaluation of story grammars. *Cognitive Science, 3,* 213–230.

Bobrow, D. G., & Norman, D. A. (1975). Some principles of memory schemata. In D. G. Bobrow & A. M. Collins (Eds.), *Representation and understanding: Studies in cognitive science* (pp. 131–150). New York: Academic Press.

Bower, G. H. (1975). Cognitive psychology. An introduction. In W. K. Estes (Ed.), *Handbook of learning and cognitive processes.* (Vol. 1), (pp. 25–80). Hillsdale, NJ: Erlbaum.

Bower, G. H. (1976). Experiments on story understanding and recall. *Quarterly Journal of Experimental Psychology, 28,* 511–534.

Bower, G. H. (1978). Experiments on story comprehension and recall. *Discourse Processes, 1,* 211–231.

Carpenter, P. A., & Just, M. A. (1977). Reading comprehension as eyes see it. In M. A. Just, & P. A. Carpenter (Eds.), *Cognitive processes in comprehension.* Hillsdale, NJ: Erlbaum.

Cirilo, R. K. (1981). Referential coherence and text structure in story comprehension. *Journal of Verbal Learning and Verbal Behavior, 20,* 358–367.

Cirilo, R. K., & Foss, D. J. (1980). Text structure and reading times for sentences. *Journal of Verbal Learning and Verbal Behavior, 19,* 96–109.

Clark, H. H., & Chase, W. G. (1972). On the process of comparing sentences against pictures. *Cognitive Psychology, 3,* 472–517.

Clark, H. H., & Clark, E. V. (1977). *Psychology and language: An introduction to psycholinguistics.* New York: Harcourt, Brace, Jovanovich.

Clark, H. H., & Haviland, S. E. (1977). Comprehension and the given new contract. In R. O. Freedle (Ed.), *Discourse production and comprehension* (Vol. 1), (pp. 1–40). Norwood, NJ: Ablex.

Clark, H. H., & Sengul, C. J. (1979). In search of referents for nouns and pronouns. *Memory and Cognition, 7,* 35–41.

Collins, A. M., & Loftus, E. F. (1975). A spreading-activation theory of semantic processing. *Psychological Review, 82,* 407–428.

de Villiers, P. A. (1974). Imagery and theme in recall of connected discourse. *Journal of Experimental Psychology, 103,* 63–168.

Fodor, J. D., & Frazier, L. (1980). Is the human parsing mechanism an ATN? *Cognition, 8,* 417–459.

Frazier, L. & Fodor, J. D. (1978). The sausage machine: a new two-stage parsing model. *Cognition, 6,* 291–325.

Glenn, C. G. (1978). The role of episodic structure and story length in children's recall of simple stories. *Journal of Verbal Learning and Verbal Behavior, 17,* 229–247.

Grimes, J. (1975). *The thread of discourse.* The Hague: Mouton.

Haberlandt, K. (1980). Story grammar and reading time of story constituents. *Poetics, 9,* 99–116.

Haberlandt, K., & Bingham, C. (1978). Verbs contribute to the coherence of brief narratives: Reading related and unrelated sentence triples. *Journal of Verbal Learning and Verbal Behavior, 17,* 419–426.

Haviland, S. E., & Clark, H. H. (1974). What's new. Acquiring new information as a process in comprehension. *Journal of Verbal Learning and Verbal Behavior, 13,* 512–521.

Johnson, N. S., & Mandler, J. M. (1980). A tale of two structures: Underlying and surface forms in stories. *Poetics, 9,* 51–86.

Just, M. A., & Carpenter, P. A. Inference processes during reading: Reflections from eye fixations. (1978). In J. W. Senders, D. F. Fisher, & R. A. Monty (Eds.), *Eye movements and the higher psychological functions* (pp. 157–174). Hillsdale, NJ: Erlbaum.

Just, M. A., & Carpenter, P. A. (1980). A theory of reading: From eye fixations to comprehension. *Psychological Review, 87,* 329–354.

Kaplan, R. A general syntactic processor. (1973). In R. Rustin (Ed.), *Natural language processing* (pp. 91–102). Englewood Cliffs, NJ: Prentice-Hall.

Kernan, K. T. (1977). Semantic and expressive elaboration in children's narratives. In S. Ervin-Tripp & C. Mitchell-Kernan (Eds.), *Child Discourse.* New York: Academic Press.

Kieras, D. E. (1978). Good and bad structure in simple paragraphs: Effects on apparent theme, reading time, and recall. *Journal of Verbal Learning and Verbal Behavior, 17,* 13–28.

Kieras, D. E. (1981). Component processes in the comprehension of simple prose. *Journal of Verbal Learning and Verbal Behavior, 20,* 1–23.

Kimball, J. P. (1973). Seven principles of surface structure parsing in natural language. *Cognition, 2,* 15–47.

Kintsch, W., & Greene, E. (1978). The role of culture-specific schemata in the comprehension and recall of stories. *Discourse Processes, 1,* 1–13.

Kintsch, W., Kozminsky, E., Streby, W. J., McKoon, G., & Keenan, J. M. (1975). Comprehension and recall of text as a function of content variables. *Journal of Verbal Learning and Verbal Behavior, 14,* 196–214.

Kintsch, W., Mandel, T., & Kozminsky, E. (1977). Summarizing scrambled stories. *Memory and Cognition, 5,* 547–552.

Kintsch, W., & van Dijk, T. A. (1978). Toward a model of text comprehension and production. *Psychological Review, 85,* 363–394.

Lesgold, A. M. (1972). Pronominalization: A device for unifying sentences in memory. *Journal of Verbal Learning and Verbal Behavior, 11,* 316–323.

Lesgold, A. M., Roth, S. F., & Curtis, M. E. (1979). Foregrounding effects in discourse comprehension. *Journal of Verbal Learning and Verbal Behavior, 18,* 291–308.

Lichtenstein, E. H., & Brewer, W. F. (1980). Memory for goal-directed events. *Cognitive Psychology, 12,* 412–445.

Mandler, J. M. A code in the node: (1978). The use of a story schema in retrieval. *Discourse Processes, 1,* 14–35.

Mandler, J. M., & Johnson, N. S. (1977). Remembrance of things parsed: Story structure and recall. *Cognitive Psychology, 9,* 111–151.

McClure, E., Mason, J., & Barnitz, J. (1979). An exploratory study of story structure and age effects on children's ability to sequence stories. *Discourse Processes, 2,* 213–250.

McKoon, G., & Ratcliff, R. (1980a). The comprehension processes and memory structures involved in anaphoric reference. *Journal of Verbal Learning and Verbal Behavior, 19,* 668–682.

McKoon, G., & Ratcliff, R. (1980b). Priming in item recognition: The organization of propositions in memory for text. *Journal of Verbal Learning and Verbal Behavior, 19,* 369–386.

Meyer, B. (1975). *The organization of prose and its effect upon memory.* Amsterdam: North-Holland.

Mitchell, D. C., & Green, D. W. (1978). The effects of content and context on immediate processing in reading. *Quarterly Journal of Experimental Psychology, 30,* 609–636.

Morgan, J. L., & Sellner, M. B. (1980). Discourse and linguistic theory. In R. J. Spiro, B. C. Bruce, & W. F. Brewer (Eds.), *Theoretical issues in reading comprehension: Perspectives from cognitive psychology, linguistics, artificial intelligence, and education.* Hillsdale, NJ: Erlbaum.

Norman, D., & Rumelhart, D. E. (1975). *Explorations in cognition.* San Francisco: W. H. Freeman.

Pichert, J. W., & Anderson, R. C. (1977). Taking different perspectives on a story. *Journal of Educational Psychology, 69,* 309–315.

Poulsen, D., Kintsch, E., Kintsch, W., & Premack, D. (1979). Children's comprehension and memory for stories. *Journal of Experimental Child Psychology, 28,* 379–403.

Reder, L. M. (1980). The role of elaboration in the comprehension and retention of prose: A critical review. *Review of Educational Research, 50,* 5–53.

Riesbeck, C. K. (1978). An expectation-driven production system for natural language understanding. In D. A. Waterman & F. Hayes-Roth (Eds.), *Pattern-directed inference systems* (pp. 399–413). New York: Academic Press.

Rumelhart, D. E. (1975). Notes on a schema for stories. In D. G. Bobrow & A. M. Collins (Eds.), *Representation and understanding: Studies in cognitive science* (pp. 211–236). New York: Academic Press.

Rumelhart, D. E. (1977a). *Introduction to human information processing.* New York: Wiley.

Rumelhart, D. E. (1977b). Understanding and summarizing brief stories. In D. LaBerge & J. Samuels (Eds.), *Basic processes in reading: Perception and comprehension* (pp. 265–304). Hillsdale, NJ: Erlbaum.

Rumelhart, D. E. (1980). Schemata: The building blocks of cognition. In R. J. Spiro, B. C. Bruce, & W. F. Brewer (Eds.), *Theoretical issues in reading comprehension: Perspectives from cognitive psychology, linguistics, artificial intelligence, and education* (pp. 33–58). Hillsdale, NJ: Erlbaum.

Schallert, D. L. (1976). Improving memory for prose: The relationship between depth of processing and context. *Journal of Verbal Learning and Verbal Behavior, 15,* 621–632.

Schank, R. C., & Abelson, R. P. (1977). *Scripts, plans, goals, and understanding: an inquiry into human knowledge structures.* Hillsdale, NJ: Erlbaum.

Schank, R. C., & Riesbeck, C. K. (1981). *Inside computer understanding.* Hillsdale, NJ: Erlbaum.

Stein, N. L., & Glenn, C. (1979). An analysis of story comprehension in elementary school children. In R. Freedle (Ed.), *New directions in discourse processing* (pp. 53–120). Norwood, NJ: Ablex.

Stein, N. L., & Nezworski, T. (1978). The effects of organization and instructional set on story memory. *Discourse Processes, 1,* 177–194.

Stevens, A. L., & Rumelhart, D. E. (1975). Errors in reading. In D. A. Norman, D. E. Rumelhart, and the LNR Research Group. *Explorations in cognition.* San Francisco: Freeman.

Thorndyke, P. W. (1977). Cognitive structures in comprehension and memory of narrative discourse. *Cognitive Psychology, 9,* 77–110.

Thorndyke, P. W. (1978). Pattern-directed processing of knowledge from texts. In D. A. Waterman & F. Hayes-Roth (Eds.), *Pattern-directed inference systems* (pp. 347–360). New York: Academic Press.

Thorndyke, P. W., & Yekovich, F. R. (1980). A critique of schema-based theories of human story memory. *Poetics, 9,* 23–49.

Vipond, D. (1980). Micro- and macroprocesses in text comprehension. *Journal of Verbal Learning and Verbal Behavior, 19,* 276–296.

Wanner, E. (1980). The ATN and the sausage machine: Which one is baloney? *Cognition, 8,* 209–225.

Waterman, A., & Hayes-Roth, F. (Eds.). *Pattern-directed inference systems.* New York: Academic Press.

Wilensky, R., & Arens, Y. (1980). *PHRAN: A knowledge-based approach to natural language analysis* (Tech. Rep. No. UCB/ERL M80/34). Berkeley: University of California, Electronics Research Lab.

Winograd, T. (1972). *Understanding natural language.* New York: Academic Press.

Woods, W. A. (1970). Transition network grammars for natural language analysis. *Communications of the A. C. M., 13,* 591–606.

Woods, W. A., Kaplan, R. & Nash-Webber, G. (1972). *The lunar sciences natural language information system: Final Report* (Report No. 2378). Cambridge, MA: Bolt, Beranek, and Newman.

CHAPTER 5

Social Psychology and Discourse

W. P. Robinson

SOCIAL PSYCHOLOGY VIS-À-VIS LINGUISTICS: A BRIEF HISTORY

In discourse analysis, anthropologists and sociologists have been faster than social psychologists to stake claims to territory and to collaborate with linguists, and it may be instructive and constructive to note some reasons why the alliances and cooperative ventures are as they are. Historically, anthropologists and linguists have shared more than a common interest in language. Novitiate anthropologists were frequently trained by linguists, the better to come to grips with fieldwork in their target culture. Linguists interested in exploring languages other than their own would enlist the services of anthropologists and exploit their methods to gather and interpret data. Certainly in Great Britain the association was close and mutually beneficial—Malinowski (1935, 1949) and Firth (1958) both clearly exemplifying the intimacy of the two disciplines. Were the primary allegiances of Sapir (1921) and Whorf (1956) ultimately to linguistics or to anthropology? Extended living in the culture, with a notebook in hand, was a perceived desideratum for anthropologist and linguist alike. Forming and checking hypotheses about the characteristics, meanings, and significance of units and structures of cultural and verbal activity were treated as essentially similar tasks, each being necessary for the successful prosecution of the other.

Sociologists seem to have entered into collaborative arrangements with linguists from more than one source. Insofar as language intertwines with culture, and the boundaries of languages, dialects, and sociolects covary with cultural discontinuities and hierarchies, it would have been surprising if sociologists such as Bernstein (1971) had not associated themselves

HANDBOOK OF DISCOURSE ANALYSIS, Vol. 1
Disciplines of Discourse

with both linguists and anthropologists. Goffman's work (1959) seems to have initiated another strand of development. His demonstrations of the ways in which institutionally significant activities are realized in and through the face-to-face encounters of individuals did more than attempt to link the sociological to the social psychological. The approach emphasized the interpretive nature of perception, favoring a move towards the inclusion of more phenomenological and ethnomethodological approaches to interpersonal interaction. The subsequent microsociological concern with conversation per se coincided with and helped to stimulate or rekindle linguistic analyses of people talking and listening naturally. Whether such ventures are really sociological or attempts to colonize neglected areas of social psychology will be discussed later.

Somehow the social psychologists were left out. Why? In Europe especially, social psychologists have been products of psychology laboratories, which have trained them as experimentalists according to a tradition that has emphasized man's interaction with the physical rather than the social environment. In that tradition problems are presented as being most amenable to solutions if attacked with approaches and methods derived from either physiology or a distorted model of nineteenth century physics. Social psychologists have not usually been trained as ethologists or anthropologists. They have not been encouraged to describe and explain how and why people in their natural habitats think how they think, believe what they believe, feel what they feel, want what they want, do what they do, or say what they say. In a statistical sense, North America may have suffered somewhat less than Europe from the consequences of the traditions established by Helmholtz and Wundt (in his non-Volkspsychologie guise), but social psychology there has remained predominantly an experimentally oriented and laboratory-based discipline with the individual as its prime object of study.

As long ago as 1954, Gerth and Mills (1954) were suggesting that the relations between individuals and the societies in which they lived were the heartland of social psychology, but perhaps, partly as a result of the pronounced individualism of the cultures in which the study of social psychology arose, the study of man as an individual has been accorded more prominence than the relationships in which people are involved. What is more, individuals were frequently construed in terms of variations along relatively stable characteristics of values, motives, attitudes, or traits that in turn were used to describe or explain which of various alternatives would be realized in essentially single acts of behavior. These acts were not viewed as being strung together in more or less predictable sequences whose features were contingent upon the behavior of other people in the situation. The dynamics of the stream of behavior were generally neglected.

The study of the behavior of small groups (e.g., Cartwright & Zander, 1960) might have opened up both the relational and dynamic qualities of social interaction and simultaneously encouraged greater attention to sequences in verbal activities. Bales' (1950) interaction process analysis was strongly based upon observers recording what people in groups said. While some comments were made about typical sequences (Bales, 1950), the main interests became centered upon frequency counts of categories of utterances whose differential reception or use might be associated with role differentiation, for example, differences in reactions of leaders and followers. The frequency of occurrences of categories was also linked to the formation of norms and sentiments and used to predict the effectiveness and cohesiveness of the groups themselves. Some developments of this kind of analysis for descriptions of classroom interaction (Flanders, 1970) sought to specify adjacency pairs of utterances, but the primary focus remained on differential frequencies and their consequences for the attainments of pupils rather than upon the structure of the interaction or the meaning of the units.

Whereas the coding of Bales' categories and their developments in the area of classroom interaction (see Simon & Boyer [1974] for a range of such systems) might have been used to examine the sequential organization of appropriate forms of discourse, the techniques developed in the field of content analysis of texts necessarily summarized instances rather than sequences. The common activity was to count certain features in texts to give estimates of motivational and attitudinal variables, which ranged from assessments of the motivational states of individuals as indicated by stories they had written (Atkinson, 1964) to the attitudes of governments as indicated in their pronouncements through the mass media (Holsti, 1969). There is little doubt from the results that the technique does enable an analyst to capture bias and preferences in a publicly demonstrable and systematic manner, but while the attitudinal stance of the text as a whole can be portrayed, its sequential organization and relevance of this are left unrevealed and unevaluated. The same is true of estimates of motivation.

Another favored and relevant area of study in social psychology, particularly strong in the 1950s and 1960s, was attitudes and attitude change. Supported by vigorous contributions from Yale (Hovland, Janis, & Kelley, 1953; Hovland, Lumsdaine, & Sheffield, 1949; Janis & Hovland, 1959; Sherif & Hovland, 1951), questions were posed about conditions which facilitated attitude change in recipients of communications on topics ranging from international and national affairs to personal diets. Individual differences was a prominent basis for the development of more general theoretical propositions. Which kinds of recipients were most readily persuaded? Which kinds of persuaders were most influential? However, in this field the mode of transmission and characteristics of the message were not neglected, and a number of textual features were examined. (For reviews see Jaspars, 1978; Karlins & Abelson, 1970; Kiesler & Munson, 1975; McGuire, 1969.)

Locational effects of the primacy and recency of the critical propositions were demonstrated. Giving explicit conclusions of arguments was shown to increase influence. Appeals couched in emotional terms, including those arousing fear, were shown to have variable effects. The efficacy of including arguments for and against a position was contrasted with the power of one-sided presentations.

One unsurprising conclusion to emerge was that it was either difficult to isolate or misleading to claim main effects of message characteristics per se; the extent of their influence was a function of interactions with characteristics of recipients and perceived characteristics of their source. Insofar as claims were made about the relevance of qualities of the text, it has been concluded that these were small when compared with characteristics of recipients (McGuire, 1969). While it may be possible to show that qualities of the text can be a relatively weak source of influence when using small messages to first year undergraduates on issues about which their attitudes may have formed over many years, political, religious, and military leaders throughout history seem to have had more faith in the texts of their speeches, as have forensic experts. The reemergence of interest in communication in applied contexts as manifested in Volume 2 of this *Handbook* will hopefully be more vigorously supported by social psychologists in the future.

In the 1960s at least one other field of social psychology offered promise for cooperation with linguists and sociologists. Were there educationally important differences in the use of language between social groups, and were those differences important determinants of subsequent academic achievement? Bernstein's (1961) hypothesis linking the language use of members of the lower working class to a restricted code that was an unsuitable vehicle for the educational activities in contemporary schools offered a potentially powerful stimulus to collaborative research.

When sociologists and developmental social psychologists turned to linguistics for help with this research, what they needed were comprehensive linguistic descriptions at the levels of pragmatics, semantics, and lexicogrammar plus specifications of the linkages between units and structures across these levels. Bernstein's codes were defined at the semantic and pragmatic levels (Bernstein, 1971; see Robinson [1978] for a critical review), but unfortunately the linguistic descriptions extant were most powerfully developed at the phonological and lexicogrammatical levels.

Accordingly, most of the contrastive empirical counts made were of grammatical and lexical features which could be hypothesized to be symptoms of a symbolic representation of cognitive orientations and meanings, for example, depth of subordination as an indicator of holding an idea while qualifying it. Labov (1970) was particularly critical: "the cognitive style of a speaker has no fixed relation to the number of unusual adjectives or conjunctions that he uses . . . when we can say *what* is being done with a sentence, then we will be able to observe how often speakers do it" (p. 84). While the thrust of Labov's intention has force, it was both ill founded and misleading as a criticism. It was ill founded because the argument was stated in the opposite direction to Bernstein, who did not assert that what he was counting allowed direct and strong inferences back to codes. It was misleading because how often speakers use certain forms and constructions in certain contexts might well serve as a basis from which to hazard guesses about both what they are doing with their utterances and how effectively they are performing these functions. Further, the criticism was not constructive in that no alternative, more appropriate linguistic indices were offered. This rift remains—and children of various social groups continue to underachieve in the educational system.

If these issues are resurrected, discourse analysis may well have an important role to play, both because it is concerned with relations between form and function and because examination of the structure of texts may well yield important differences. Van Dijk (1972) suggests that "Children from lower classes do not receive enough training in the production and perception of different types of text . . . This lack in their training prevents them from manipulating the complex linguistic structures involved in textual performance" (p. 331). It is worth noting a parallel between this suggestion and the results of Bruck (Bruck & Tucker, 1974). In her comparisons of lower and middle class children at two different ages, Bruck found that some socioeconomic status differences manifested at the earlier age disappeared, particularly errors in phrase structure rules, but that others remained. Features that yield differences at one age may not differentiate at other ages, and as age increases so one might expect that the levels at which differences are manifested will move toward the textual. Joint work between linguists interested in text and social psychologists interested in similarities and differences among social groups might help to heal the rift between disciplines.

However, it was not only the social psychologists' passion for counting the incidence of linguistic units and a willingness to draw inferences about the skills and competencies of the speakers that disquieted linguists. Both our conceptual approach and our methods of data collection caused alarm. When we did lure linguists into providing us with classificatory systems for units and structures, we were disposed to ask them for a justification of the systems. Why these separations and not others? Were the linguistic categories psychologically real? When Labov published *The Social Stratification of Speech in New York City* (1966), social psychologists immediately wanted to know whether members of relevant speech communities normally attended to and used the markers described. Would they normally detect percentage differences of the orders listed? The whole field of 'markers' (see Scherer & Giles, 1979) suffers from frequent failures to distinguish between what machines or experts can detect and what ordinary people use to make inferences about motivational–affective states, personal identity, and social identity. We also asked questions about the selection of variables, the reliability of the scoring of the data, the representativeness of the samples of speech and persons, the role and influence of the observer or interviewer, and the propriety of the statistical analyses (where were the tests of significance?). This very influential work of Labov did not satisfy the standards of rigor required by a psychologically trained methodologist, any more than our inferences from the frequencies of use of certain speech features to psychological characteristics satisfied linguists.

We were operating from different methodological perspectives at the stages of collecting, processing, interpreting, and even reporting data. Psychologists preferred controlled conditions for data collection and were not necessarily responsive to the charge that such data are unnatural or artificial. Psychologists have to be able to demonstrate interjudge reliability of coding and rely on systematic statistical analyses of data; examples and apt illustrations are treated as illustrations only and not as evidence. Psychologists have to interpret and explain in terms of psychological concepts and principles rather than linguistic ones.

Of such kinds have been the conflicts. Rather than try to pass judgment on the rights and wrongs, it may be more helpful to point to some of the changes in social psychology since the early 1970s which may enhance the chances of future collaboration with linguists in general and discourse analysts in particular.

SOCIAL PSYCHOLOGY AND LINGUISTICS: THE CONTEMPORARY SCENE

The increasing acceptance by social psychologists of the sense and propriety of a wider range of methods of data collection and processing in social psychology through the 1970s stems in part from a shift in conceptions of what a person is. As has been mentioned, a person in society was usually treated as having some kind of unified identity, and the tasks of social psychology were seen as parallel to those of experimental psychology. The same processes of attention, perception, thinking, learning, remembering, and performance were the objects of study, except that social psychologists looked at these in relation to social rather than physical phenomena and occasionally at interactive relations between the social and physical. In both approaches a probabilistically determinist stance was common: forces outside the person impinged upon the sensory apparatus initiating essentially mechanistically mediated outcomes. Persons were victims of the physiological and anatomical properties of their biological characteristics. For the social psychologist, they were also victims of their social identity, determined by achieved or assigned roles arising out of their positions in the social structure. Such features as social class, age, and sex were seen as determinants of political or religious attitudes. These attitudes in combination with other mediating variables and situational factors determined behavior. What people said and did was treated as beyond their voluntary control and possibly outside their consciousness as well.

Disquiet about too strongly deterministic models of the person and arguments against investigations that relied solely on objective means of measurement in the controlled conditions of the laboratory had existed long before the 1970s, but at least for some social psychologists the publication of Harré and Secord's (1972) *The Explanation of Social Behaviour* was a signal for a change in orientation. The statements of these two authors were unequivocal: "Human beings must be treated as agents acting according to rule. . . . "Social behaviour must be conceived of as actions mediated by meanings. . . . "Reasons can be used to explain actions" (p. 29).

The approach that developed assigned a prime but not exclusive role to the collection of accounts of everyday living, with a view to the elucidation of the nature of the rules governing the sequences of actions that constitute the episodes of daily activity.

Such an approach had clear similarities to certain predilections of the discourse analyst. Both emphasized the need to segment the stream of human activity into the units and sequences that have meaning for the participants. Both sought to identify rules governing the organization of sequences and used people's accounts as a source of information about rules. They differed in that, as social psychologists, Harré and Secord included all behavior and not just speech. On the other hand the psychological perspective was narrower since its immediate focus was upon face-to-face activities only and not on the structure and content of extended texts in whatever situation they arose.

At the same time in Oxford, Argyle and his colleagues were conducting work on nonverbal communication and social skills and extending their interests into a study of the sequential structure of interpersonal social behavior. Initial interest was in the identification of the units of nonverbal communication and their functions, separately and as a system. Demonstrations of the significance of such variables as physical distance, orientation, and eye contact in defining role relations expanded into more specific investigations of the kinds of judgments of perceived friendliness (Argyle, Alkema, & Gilmour, 1971) or presumed power relations (Argyle, Salter, Nicholson, Williamson, & Burgess, 1970) made by respondents when presented with video recordings varying in facial expression, content of speech, and tone of speech.

Since Argyle and Kendon (1967), the idea had been extant that changes in eye contact were relevant to turntaking in conversation, and as the Oxford project became extended into an analysis of perceived differences and similarities in social situations (Argyle, Furnham, & Graham, 1981; Furnham & Argyle, 1981), it became necessary to ask about the temporal structure of activity as well as to study the variables operative at particular points in time. While retaining the basic features of his motor skill model of social performance, Argyle (1969), as illustrated in Figure 5.1, elaborated the representation to handle temporal sequences, repeated cycles, and multiperson situations. The importance credited to the goals and motivation of participants has also been increasingly emphasized, with elicited reasons for behavior considered potentially acceptable explanations of some of the phenomena.

This illustration of social psychology at Oxford may be geographically parochial, but its general import is not. The articulation of the approaches of Argyle and Harré introduced a number of changes to the narrower conceptions of social psychology. Methodologically, the demand for theories with tight predictive power has become tempered by a respect for

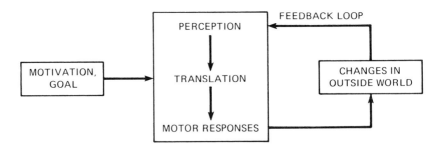

Figure 5.1   Motor skill model. (From Argyle, 1969.)

the value of explanations that might be less specific in their behavioral realizations and predictiveness but nevertheless remain valid at a higher level of generality. Social behavior is not to be treated as single acts predictable from measurements of attitudes, motivation, or traits but as sequences of actions contingently related to the actions of others, both being subject to the constraints of what is possible in, desired from, and proper to particular situations. What people say about what they are saying and doing or trying to achieve is to be treated as a source of evidence. Although experiments under controlled conditions are desirable ways of promoting the advance of understanding for some problems at certain stages, they need to be complemented by observations of natural behavior and may be neither necessary nor desirable for understanding some social activities whose descriptions and explanations can best be prosecuted by interrogation and observation. All of these developments would seem to be propitious for better collaboration between social psychologists and linguists concerned with discourse.

But what are the goals (in Figure 5.1) that individuals are seeking to achieve through their social behavior? What are the reasons they would give for doing what they do and saying what they say? There are of course many psychological classifications of motives, needs, and other similarly labelled concepts that are intended to explain both the intensity and direction of behavior (see, e.g., Hall & Lindzey, 1957; McGuire, 1980). Most such classifications structure motivation hierarchically, simultaneously allowing a regression and multiplicity of causation for particular actions and an elevation of the relatively specific to the more general. Such analyses are legitimate and necessary concerns of social psychologists seeking to explain why particular texts are created but by themselves will not serve to describe and explain the qualities of those texts. For a more complete story we have to start simultaneously from three different points of departure: from persons and their goals, from situations and their potential, and from language and its potential. And we need to know what functions language can and does serve in behavior. In their classifications of functions we find some authors preferring an emphasis on speakers' intentions and purposes and others emphasizing listeners' perceptions and interpretations. Both have their place, but we must also realize that both depend on a cultural consensus that enables identifiable communicative functions to be achieved through speech. In perfect communication the speaker's intention is realized through a message which is correctly interpreted by the listener—"Not to let a word get in the way of its sentence, not to let a sentence get in the way of its intention, but to send your mind out to meet the intention as a guest; THAT is understanding'' (Mencius).

But the relations between intention and message and between message and interpretation are both contingent and not necessary. Failures can occur. We need therefore to examine the cultural consensus about the language and its use. Later one can ask about the communicative competence of speakers and listeners.

FUNCTIONS OF LANGUAGE IN BEHAVIOR

It does seem that various attempts to diagnose functions have offered less than entirely satisfactory solutions. Sinclair and Coulthard (1975) faced the issue of plurality of functions of utterances (moves) but felt obliged to take refuge in requiring observers to recognize the primary function of an utterance. In describing functions of speech acts, Austin (1962) seems to emphasize the speaker's intention, while Searle (1975) includes the hearer's interpretation. Although it may be easier to describe speech acts from a single perspective, in reality all perspectives and possibilities must be incorporated into a comprehensive account, and any selectivity can be justified only in terms of particular questions being addressed. Ease of coding is no justification if it leads to a misrepresentation of the subjective realities of the participants.

The categorization of functions in Table 5.1 has no special sanctity, and it was not devised with problems of discourse analysis in mind. Its raison d'être has been defended elsewhere (Robinson, 1972). Suffice it to say here that the categories were intended to correspond to certain main divisions of interest assumed to have coherence in social psychology. However, some brief comments about which functions require supra-sentential linkages for their realization and which do not does highlight certain distinctions among them. Some which do require such cohesions appear to do so only in linguistically uninteresting ways. For example, the conglomeration of phonological and prosodic features that comprise accent may serve as a basis for marking social identity but does not involve significant linguistically interesting suprasentential organization for its maintenance. Occasional behavioral deviations from the norm may serve as signs that the presented identity is of recent or temporary assumption for example, but such deviations may result from mistakes rather than from any failure to follow discourse rules. Likewise, modifications of accent through time within an encounter, either in the direction of or away from that of the interlocutor, may mark attempts to define a role relationship as being more friendly or more distant, more unequal or more equal in power (Giles & Powesland, 1975), but these are not likely to be of special concern to discourse analysts per se. The same

Table 5.1
Functions of Language[a]

Functions	Everyday name of activity or products	Prime focus of verbal act	Essential linguistic forms		Basis of evaluation
			Description	Examples	
Avoidance worse activity	Escapism (verbal)	Participants	Any within constraints of context		Saved from other problems?
Conformity to norms	Speech and writing	Rule subscription	Any within constraints of context		Are the conventions observed? Did the corpus appear to be a speech, essay, etc.?
Aesthetics	Art, literature, drama, novel, rhetoric	Message form and content	Often well defined, but above rank of sentence. Beyond microlinguistics	Sonnets; tragedies; fables	Beautiful, insightful, moving?
Performatives	Promising, betting, etc.	Non-verbal accomplishments	A finite set of semantically associated verbs used in normatively and legally prescribed forms	*I name this ship the Bubbly Bosun*	Intended act performed?
Encounter regulation	Greeting, leavetaking	Participant interaction	A finite set of special words, noises, and phrases. Pausing, questions	*Hi! Jane! Caiou! What do you think?*	Attention attracted? Contact made? Flow maintained? Ending satisfactory?

(continued)

Table 5.1
Functions of Language[a] (Continued)

Functions	Everyday name of activity or products	Prime focus of verbal act	Essential linguistic forms			Basis of evaluation
			Description	Examples		
Expression of affect	Exclamations, swearing	Emitter	Vocatives, swear words, terms of endearment	*Oh my love! xxxx!*		Do you feel better?
Regulation of self (a) behavior (b) affect	Talking to oneself, etc.	Emitter	Abbreviated imperatives?	*Now, one teaspoon mustard. Pull yourself together*		Is performance in fact facilitated by talking? Is affective state changed or induced?
Regulation of others (a) behavior (b) affect	Commands, requests, threats, jibes, jokes	Receiver	Imperatives, closed questions, modal verbs, etc. A finite set of semantically associated verbs and phrases. Set forms of humor	*Jump! Will you…? You must…If… then…You creep.* Puns; sick jokes		Obedience obtained? Dissuaded? Humiliated? Made to laugh?
Marking of emitter (a) emotional state (b) personality (c) social identity	—	Emitter	Para- and extralinguistic features; overt statements. Phonology (accent) grammatical, lexical choices	*I, I, I think… I'm scared. 'otel, ain't no… lavatory*		Correct diagnosis made or impression conveyed?
Role relationship marking	—	Relationship emitter receiver	Rights and duties to use of socially prescribed forms of address, and forms of utterance	*Sir! Sweetie! Let us pray*		Choice and sequence right for accepted ways of defining roles?

118

Representation of nonlinguistic world involving: discrimination, organization, storage, and transmission, in sphere of knowledge: (a) logics (b) science (c) ethics (d) metaphysics (e) aesthetics	Many: stating, arguing, reporting, remembering, thinking(?), problemsolving, analyzing, processing, synthesizing	Correspondence of verbal act to nonverbal world	Declarative sentence forms	*The cat is on the mat. If A, then B! Doggie will bite! All gone, Daddy*	True or false within premises of universe of discourse? Is argument valid? Are rules of game followed?
Instruction	Teaching	Acquisition of new skills by receiver	Various	—	Did you learn?
Inquiry	Questioning	Acquisition knowledge for emitter	Interrogative form	*What is he on about?*	Does it serve to fill the appropriate gap in your knowledge?
Metalanguage functions	Linguistics, Psycholinguistics Sociolinguistics Philosophy English Language courses	Language and speech	—	—	Increase in knowledge of how language works?

*After Robinson, 1978.

argument will apply to socially linked choices of particular lexical items or grammatical constructions.

However, people are marked by the kinds of situations into which they enter, the kinds of texts they produce in these situations, and their reactions to the texts of others. When compared with other individuals, their competence to create texts evaluated against norms of some kind will serve to mark them as more or less competent, for example. It may therefore be instructive to comment briefly on those functions for which the production of whole texts of certain qualities is likely to be a necessary or contributory factor affecting the reactions of others.

Conformity to norms was introduced into the list of functions (see Table 5.1) as a category of dual significance. There is a time to speak and a time to keep silent. Space in newspapers has to be filled. One of the reasons why general conversation, for example, is a problematic activity for investigation is that its character may be rendered relatively amorphous and varied for the reason that many conversations take place only because the situation requires conversation; its actual structure and direction may be much less significant socially than that silence does not occur. If on the other hand the art of good conversation is the art of saying nothing well (Mahaffy, 1887), then to that extent such activity is an excellent object in which to study form unaffected greatly by content. (The charge of form without substance was of course the accusation leveled at the Sophists by Socrates in the *Gorgias,* and it was the development of the immense complexity of the rules of rhetoric that in part led historically to the reduction of its study and practice; Dixon, 1971.)

The aesthetic function is also at permanent risk of similar overspecialization into the roccoco, but, perhaps more obviously than any other function, the poetic has given rise to numerous conventions for the construction of definable literary forms. Questions of beauty are much more likely to be raised about texts than about single utterances, and the whole set of internal relations among units is a major consideration in assessments of aesthetic quality.

Encounter regulation necessarily involves problems of sequential organization. The appropriate ordering of units of speech and nonverbal activity defines the type and quality of interactions in both subinstitutional and institutional activities.

We remain ignorant of the possible efficacy of speech for the control of our own affective states and behavior. Certainly in the latter, those who subscribe to the belief that talking to oneself facilitates control are likely to engage in such talking when concerned not to omit items from sequentially ordered activities such as cooking or motor cycle maintenance.

In regulating the states and behavior of others one can immediately see a diversity of possibilities. Incitement to anger may be achieved by a single utterance, but politicians can talk for hours on end to accomplish the same effect. Making people laugh by telling jokes to them can turn critically on prosodic structure and timing. Some professionals and some competent amateurs can render prosaic material hilarious. Other people can kill the most promising story through a mismanagement of the same features. The study of rhetoric by the ancient Greeks focused in large measure upon problems of persuading others to accept beliefs, come to certain decisions, and/or act in certain ways. It was the structure and content of whole speeches that was discussed by Aristotle (Freese, 1926). Although abrupt commands issued by duly constituted authorities can suffice to regulate the actions of others, deliberative and forensic oratory depend for their efficacy upon a succession of speech acts organized into a coherent and cohesive text.

The expression of affect on the other hand is a function of language typically realized through short exclamations, for which structural rules at the suprasentential level are likely to have less significance.

Similarly, the marking of temporary emotional states, personal identity, and social identity may generally be served by features of speech and writing that are below as well as at the level of discourse structure, but the caveat has already been entered that judgments of competence, or trustworthiness, or other personality attributes may well depend in part on discourse features as well as lower-level features.

Role relationships are heavily defined in speech by rights and obligations to use specific forms, some of them simple lexical choices as in the case of nouns and pronouns, address, and reference. However, it is also true that some sentence forms are less likely to be used or deemed acceptable in certain role relationships. Asking questions, for example, is not expected of socially inferior partners in certain contexts. United Kingdom citizens are alleged to be advised that it is improper to pose questions to the reigning monarch. The discourse structure is likely therefore to be indicative of variations in power and solidarity (Brown, 1965).

A speech act serving the representational (referential) function of language is viewed by Searle (1975) as committing a speaker to believing the truth of any statement uttered—the purpose is to have any listener believe that the proposition is true. This definition has the advantage of providing immediate reasons for the utterance of true statements. Insofar as statements are linked together to provide descriptions, narratives, explanations, or arguments, they are subject to conventions regulating the order of their presentation and the qualities of the linkages between them. Since statements can be integrated to create books of great length as well as being short answers to isolated questions, the tasks for discourse analysts are prospectively Herculean.

Even from this brief exemplification of some of the functions of language in behavior for which suprasentential analyses will be necessary, it is clear that questions of hierarchical and sequential structure of texts have to be faced by social psychologists. The cursory differentiation can do no more than alert us to the need for systematic analysis, especially since the list of functions is misleading in several respects. The categories are not independent of each other, either as defined (Robinson, 1978) or in fact. The list ignores vertical stratification of functions as exemplified by the case study of Labov and Fanshel (1977). When we begin to examine both quality of function and generality, link them to the fact that remarks are necessarily multifunctional, and additionally remember that speakers and listeners may well be exploiting ambiguity and other linguistic devices as means of negotiating a future reality, we will perhaps abandon the notion that relations of function and form are either simple or infinitely variable. They are not, and we should not be seduced by statements to that effect which may be true at certain levels of generality only. Certainly Searle (1975) has begun to link form and function (at the level of speech act) in a persuasive manner, although he does omit some of the cruder yet valid social psychological points captured in Table 5.1.

If we introduce an additional distinction between doing something at all and doing it well or badly, the problems for both social psychologist and discourse analyst are multiplied. Initially it must be noted that some failures to follow the relevant discourse rules adequately could prevent a function from being performed at all. This does not seem to be simply an instance of the distinction between illocutionary and perlocutionary force. A joke told very badly might be deemed not to be a joke, just as a very bad essay might be said to fail to be an essay. In practice the boundaries of demarcation are likely to be fuzzy. For many kinds of text the constitutive rules are likely to have quantitative dimensions as well as qualitative categories, and the degrees of deviation from typical essays or from essays par excellence (Rosch, 1973) which lead to judgments that the text is not an essay at all will be reduced to matters of definition and preference. More interesting psychologically will be the investigations that seek to clarify the dimensions of judged excellence. Pirsig (1976) pointed to some of the difficulties that can surround the marking of student essays, but similar considerations will apply to all other socially related texts. Linguists may correctly insist that their discipline is descriptive, not prescriptive; social psychologists however have to analyze the evaluative judgments made by people and discover the bases and rationale for these. For any text in any genre social psychologists are obliged to examine human evaluations of its perceived functional efficacy, including individual and socially based differences in those judgments. All those who use speech or writing of persons as sources of information for assessment—and that is everyone—are chronically engaged in such judgments and have been from time immemorial. The bases of such judgments and the manner of their application have been matters of dispute for many years and will continue to be so, but as the analysis of discourse is advanced, it may become easier for social psychologists to use such findings to expose more of the criteria relevant to judgments of quality. While the educational system is an obvious context for such studies, similar problems arise for judgments of good conversationalists, good political speakers, and good players of any role involving the use of language.

Social psychologists have also to be equally concerned with children's development of communicative competencies in those roles and the examination of the internal and external factors which can be used to promote, retard, or prevent the achievement of such competencies. The possibilities for fruitful collaboration are infinite; the examples of such collaboration are all too rare.

Such contributions as have been made by social psychologists to the study of the intersection between language and social behavior have so far been mainly confined to language variables below the level of discourse (see, e.g., Giles, Robinson & Smith, 1980; Giles & St. Clair, 1979; St. Clair & Giles, 1980; Scherer & Giles, 1979).

Since conversation per se is the activity whose study has included a social psychological perspective, it is perhaps the best example available to represent some of the strengths (and weaknesses) that social psychologists can bring to discourse analysis. Undefined as it remains, and hypostatized to an extent that may eventually prove to be misleading, the study of conversation has attracted approaches from various perspectives. Three will be described and then compared and evaluated.

CONVERSATION

One Social Psychological Approach

Among many others, Clarke (1977) has argued that social psychologists need to describe and explain the temporal structure of the stream of interpersonal behavior. At least three main issues have to be tackled: the segmentation of that stream into appropriate units, the classification of those units, and the formulation of rules that will generate the orderly behavioral sequences which can and do occur. While these three problems may be separable for initial analytic purposes, the projected solutions for any one are contingent upon concurrent and complementary specifications of the characteristic features of the other two, and they must eventually be synthesized to form a consistent whole.

Clarke and Argyle (1982) enumerate similarities between these problems and those confronting linguists intent upon writing grammars. In each case what is needed is a "canonical generative representation of sets of sequences of discrete events arranged in time according to their type classes" (p. 161). It is necessary to maintain a distinction between the meanings of the units and structures and their lexicogrammar. Both the nonverbal and verbal behaviors are hierarchically organized systems in which higher-order plans generate the lower-order structures and units; the meanings of the latter can be inferred only from the higher-order plans. If this is so, then the methodological approach has to work from the top down rather than from the bottom up. To find out about plans requires the intelligent exploitation of the comments and judgments of competent members of the culture.

In certain respects lay native speakers may be able to be more helpful with suprasentential than subsentential analysis. For judgments about the grammaticalness or sense of subsentential strings, ordinary native speakers may be confined to assessments of what can and cannot be properly said. They may only be able to offer reactive replies: "Yes," "No," or "Perhaps." They may be able to segment strings into words but are likely to experience difficulty both below and above this level. Further, they are not likely to have a command over the linguistic terminology necessary for classifying units or structures into sets.

In contrast, native speakers may well be able to comment about speech acts in some detail. They may be able to specify necessary and sufficient conditions for the successful enactments of promises, bets, requests, complaints, and apologies, and these specifications may include structural and sequential features. At still higher order levels Everyperson may again be more likely to be incompetent. Determining what textual features make a sermon a sermon or a lecture a lecture may well require consultation with experienced practitioners rather than Everyperson, just as descriptions of literary texts will need the services of experts.

It is at the level of speech acts however that Clarke has experimented. Four main methods have been exploited:

Secondary Experimentation.   Natural conversations are collected and the recordings or transcripts are then mutilated in systematic ways. Native speakers can then be asked to perform a variety of tasks. They can be asked to construct utterances to replace deletions or to choose items from a given array. They can be asked to order utterances into acceptable sequences. They can be asked to classify extracts in terms of similarities or differences. In so far as the native speakers agree with each other, the experimenter is entitled to draw inferences about the propriety and likelihood of sequences, the appropriate segmentation of units and structures, and the classes into which they can be formed.

Inductive Procedures. Utilizing samples of natural discourse, the experimenter, as a specially trained native speaker and culture member, can try to extract and classify units and structures, count commonly occurring sequences, and then infer the meaning and significance of these through the principle of commutation—the rule that items that exchange for each other are of the same type. Clarke found the initial classification phase in this mode particularly difficult, since it presumes a knowledge of the relationships to be ascertained in the final phase of the sequence and, more important, because form–meaning linkages are so context dependent.

A Priori Modeling. It is possible to exploit current beliefs of experts about units and structures in various kinds of generative grammars in order to construct computer programs which, when fed with units and structures, may yield outputs that simulate discourse. Clarke has compared the differential efficacy of finite state, push-down stack, linear-bounded, and Turing automata models to this end.

Analyses and Modeling of Case Studies. This strategy relies upon generating a system that takes a set of case studies and derives a predictive model for these at the same time as it takes account of significant discriminating variables, for example, possible situational determinants. Programs can be tested against observed sequences.

Clark suggests that so far the first two approaches yield results more easily but that the results tend to be uninteresting and obvious, whereas the latter two are harder to make to work but yield more unexpected results when they are successful.

It is perhaps helpful to illustrate these considerations by describing some of the studies conducted by Clarke and reported by Clarke and Argyle (1982). Using dialogues recorded in waiting rooms, each utterance of 20-utterance extracts was typed on a single card and respondents were asked to sort these into a sequence that reconstructed the original conversation. The respondents were able to perform the task with massively greater than chance accuracy. Even when asked at the relatively abstract level of Bales' interaction process analysis categories to rank order which of the 12 categories was likely to precede or follow the emission of any particular category, the judgments of respondents correlated highly with the actually observed relative frequencies reported by Bales over 20 years earlier.

If utterances are in some measure predictable and themselves have predictive significance, over what span are these operative? Both Pease and Arnold (1973) and Clarke (1975) used the technique of providing respondents with one or more preceding utterances and require them to add to the text. The resultant texts were subsequently rated for plausibility. Both investigations found that plausibility ratings increased up to an order in which the subjects had a knowledge of up to four preceding utterances but not beyond.

A rather complicated design was used to try to define which features of earlier utterances were predictive of later ones. One group of subjects was shown the first 15 lines of a 20-line dialogue and asked to write a précis that would enable someone else to construct the last 5 lines. Members of a second group then used the précis to construct the last 5 lines, while members of a third group performed the same task with the original 15 lines as a guide. Members of the fourth group were provided with the versions of the last 5 lines generated from the second and third groups along with the original 5 last lines. They were also shown the original first 15 lines and rated each of the endings for the plausibility of their closeness to the original final 5 lines. Versions resulting from the précis were rated more highly than those from the other two sources.

In an attempt to specify the important features guiding choices, 22 scales were constructed that referred to such characteristics as topic, setting, and temporary and more stable cues about the participants. These were rated for perceived utility and correlated for each summary and the plausibility rating. The resultant matrix was factor analyzed. The pattern and size of loadings were interpreted to suggest that the content and the social roles of the participants were the best predictors of successful continuation of the dialogue.

Other similar experiments are used to infer that in conversation speakers first decide which of the previous remarks will be used as a springboard for their utterance and which of the possible reactions will be made. Narrative accounts by respondents of three conversational situations were used to extract a sequence of greeting–establish relationship–task–reestablish relationship–parting. When respondents were asked to name the units in the episodes, they tended to give labels for higher-order units, such as 'complaining', but offered extended descriptions of lower-order units. (Presumably the existence or absence of such brief lexical labels has social significance.)

Why these secondary experimentation and inductive procedures ought not to be disregarded by lovers of natural discourse will be discussed below. Suffice it to say at this stage that insofar as respondents can perform such tasks with a high degree of consensus, they must in fact be relying on their own versions of two theory-driven strategies: a priori modeling and the analysis and modeling of case studies. To be theory-driven, there must be theories of two kinds, one that segments and classifies discourse and one that generates the set of sequences which can occur but not other sequences. Various classifications of discourse units exist, but Clarke and Argyle have elected to work with speech acts deriving from Searle's (1969, 1975) developments of Austin's analysis (1962). Simple labels of speech acts do not in themselves offer sufficient information for judgments to be made readily about likely occurrence; for this they need to be tagged at least with speaker identification and some semantic cuing. Labels do enable us to see some of the relationships between speech acts themselves; for example, 'compliance' can be seen as a 'command' or 'request' followed by a performance. A priori (personal?) judgments were made as to which of 43 speech acts could or could not follow each other. Combined with distinctions between proactive and reactive speech acts and possibilities of speaker change, the model can generate dialogue. Judges in fact rated such dialogues as being more likely to be conversations than random sequences.

The case study work has concentrated on question-answer sequences with their possibilities of nesting and recursion. It has shown that none of the four models seems to be adequate in itself, a combination of the push-down stacks and linear bounding being necessary.

This kind of activity encounters two difficulties not experienced by analyses of subsentential grammars. First is the difficulty of deciding upon levels of analysis and classifications within those levels. Second is the difficulty that none of the four generative models combines both recursion and nesting with the interactive qualities, both of which are evident features of conversation.

A Microsociological Approach

It seems to be standard practice to acknowledge the contribution of microsociologists to our enhanced understanding of conversational activity (e.g., Schenkein, 1978; Sudnow, 1972), making particular reference to their analyses of turntaking (Sacks, Schegloff, & Jefferson, 1974), sequences of summons–answer (Schegloff, 1968), closing sequences (Schegloff & Sacks, 1973), side sequences (Jefferson, 1972), insertion sequences (Schegloff, 1972), and adjacency pairs (Schegloff & Sacks, 1973). Corsaro (this *Handbook,* Vol. 2) claims this work for sociology, and the reader might find it strange that we both devote space to turntaking. I have included it because I think it helps to define one parameter of the perspectives of social psychology by contrast: the approach helps to specify one set of limits within which people are free to choose their utterances.

In the introduction to his collection Schenkein (1978) mentions the novelties of using materials from actual interactions and of taking seriously the details of the interactions themselves. He notes that these materials are the tiniest sample of circumstances in which conversations are found and that they are for the most part conversations of the white middle class of North America and England. Investigators in the genre share an analytic mentality of a relatively unmotivated examination of materials, a concern with the details of interactions, and a preference for writing rules.

It is not too difficult to say why the approach is not social psychological. It is more difficult to say what kind of approach it actually is. The turntaking paper can be used to illustrate the issues. Sacks *et al.* (1974) list 14 facts about conversation to which any model of conversation must accommodate. They accomplish this accomodation with two rules. The first five facts cited are:

1. Speaker change recurs, or, at least, recurs;
2. Overwhelmingly, one party talks at a time;
3. Occurrences of more than one speaker at a time are common, but brief;
4. Transitions from one turn to the next with no gap and no overlap between them are common. Together with transitions characterized by slight gap or slight overlap, they make up the vast majority of transitions;
5. Turn order is not fixed, but varies.

To accomplish accommodation to these facts, two rules are proposed:

1. At initial turn-constructional unit's initial transition-relevance place:
   a. If the turn-so-far is so constructed as to involve the use of a 'current speaker selects next' technique, then the party so selected has rights and is obliged to take next turn to speak; no others have such rights or obligations, transfer occurring at that place.
   b. If the turn-so-far is so constructed as not to involve the use of a 'current speaker selects next' technique, selfselection for next speakership may, but need not, be instituted, with first starter acquiring rights to a turn, transfer occurring at that place.
   c. If the turn-so-far is so constructed as not to involve the use of a 'current speaker selects next' technique, then current speaker may, but need not, continue, unless another selfselects.
2. If, at initial turn-constructional unit's initial transition-relevance place,

neither 1a nor 1b has operated and, following the provision of 1c, current speaker has continued, then the rule-set a–c reapplies at next transition-relevance place and recursively at each next transition-relevance place until transfer is effected.

The authors suggest that the model is a local management system and an interactionally managed system and that conversation itself probably marks one pole of a complex gradation of speech exchange systems, the other end being marked by ceremonial activities where who says what to whom (and to some extent how) is institutionally prescribed.

Many questions can be asked about the specific and general quality of this account. The facts may be generally uncontentious, at least within the subcultural and contextual constraints examined. They could have been collected by the random or systematic sampling methods used by social psychologists rather than through the unsystematic agglomeration of data collected for other purposes. How representative they are of the white middle class of North America we cannot know since the universe of situations of which they purport to be a sample is not closely defined. Such a criticism is attenuated however by an establishment of general facts. If the generalizations represent reality, then the orderliness of that reality entails that the situations and people sampled are homogeneous in the relevant respects.

A Philosophical Stance

Although Grice (1975) is referred to frequently, his writing has not inspired social psychologists to develop his ideas into empirically examinable propositions, of which there could be two main kinds: those relating to the ground rules of conversation and those relating to the meanings to be assigned to various deliberate deviations from these ground rules. In respect of the former Grice asserts a very general cooperative principle: that participants necessarily in some measure recognize either a common purpose or at least a mutually accepted direction limiting the range of possible likely moves. This obliges speakers to make any contribution apposite to the accepted purpose or direction of the task exchange in which they are engaged. Grice extends this principle into maxims of quantity, quality, relation and manner which may be abbreviated

Quantity: Say as much as is required and no more;
Quality: Try to make contribution true (Do not tell lies. Do not make claims for which you lack adequate evidence.);
Relation: Be relevant;
Manner: Be perspicuous, avoid obscurity and ambiguity, and aim for precision and orderliness.

Doubtless more could be added (Be polite) (see Brown and Levinson, 1978), and those cited could be elaborated. The maxims are presented as obligations falling upon the speaker, but these obligations arise because they are expectations of the listener. What Grice appears to be offering are the culturally given ground rules—some basic assumptions underlying certain kinds of conversational activity. What status have these ground rules? Are they culture specific? How is it possible for Grice to make these assertions *ex cathedra* without offering adequate evidence? Scholars might become worried about the analysis, but ordinary people are perhaps more likely to say that the maxims are obvious once they are set down for consideration. One could argue that Grice is simply making explicit the most economical rational basis for communicative activity to proceed. If that is so, Grice does not need to cite particular evidence; his analysis commends itself because other conceivable ground rules would be seen as simple and efficient.

Once we turn to his suggestions about deliberate departures from the ground rules, the foundations of his argument may well rest on his competence as a member of a particular culture. He discusses the kinds of interpretations that are likely to be given when speakers are believed to be intentionally violating or flouting maxims, when they opt out, and when their intentions bring the maxims into conflict with each other. For example when the truth is not told, utterances may be examples of irony, metaphor, meiosis, or hyperbole. What Grice achieves in a few pages is a substantial extension of one of the early discourse analysis problems of formulating rules to explain when declaratives, interrogatives, and imperatives have which of the functions of stating, questioning, and commanding. He does not formulate rules for diagnosis, but he does alert us to the need for a thorough analysis of the circumstances in which transparent semantic content should not be interpreted literally and of conditions for deviations from the maxims of quantity, relation, and manner. His concept of 'conversational implicature' offers a point of departure for examining many important problems about the interface of semantics and pragmatics.

Conversation: A Comparison of Three Approaches

Orientation to Problems

Grice does not offer suggestions as to why people hold conversations and neither does he indicate how they do so. Rather he is, in the first instance, indicating the principles to be observed if conversations are to be held. Implicitly he is setting up what the sociologists call an 'ideal type'; if they are observed, his maxims specify conditions that a conversation must meet if it is to be a "good" conversation. His elaboration and exemplification of implicature indicate devices that can be used by masters of the art of conversation to achieve brevity or ambiguity and to mean without saying. In contrast, Sacks *et al.* examine the tactical problems of opening, maintaining, and closing conversations, in some sense summarizing how these are generally achieved. Clarke and Argyle are analyzing how conversation is constructed in terms of the ordering of speech acts, thereby emphasizing the semantic cohesiveness. All three are trying to cope with real problems, but more problems exist than their combined interests cover.

From the social psychological perspective the most obvious gap relates to more distal "why" of conversation. One strongly expressed general answer to this question is offered by Berger and Luckmann (1967): "In order to maintain subjective reality effectively, the conversational apparatus must be continual and consistent" (p. 174), and "one extreme possibility . . . sometimes approximated in primitive societies, is the definition of everything in social reality" (p. 120). Ignoring the fact that their position is exaggerated, we can at least accept that the idea has a possible kernel of truth to be investigated.

Less total is Malinowski's (1949) idea of phatic communion, "which serves to establish bonds of personal union between people brought together by the mere need of companionship and does not serve any purpose of communicating ideas" (p. 316). Conversation seen only as a vehicle of sociability would be insufficient in scope for explaining the activities of the persons under examination in the three approaches described above. Although conviviality of companionship may be a factor, more individualistic and varied motives are also likely to be operative. Meeting new people at gatherings and renewing old acquaintances provide opportunities for possible furthering of plans and hopes, ranging from gaining advice about medical or business problems and developing new interests through to establishing initial contacts with potential partners for life. Such gatherings are a mixing of potential developments for new relationships and activities and provide one mechanism for possible changes in people's networks of associates. They are aimless only insofar as the participants do not know in advance what they might be able to create.

All three approaches therefore stop short of formulating and testing hypotheses about the range of functions served by conversation; those functions will need to be defined in psychological terms and investigated through methods appropriate to social psychology, sociology, and anthropology.

Methodology

Are the three approaches intent upon description or explanation or both? Are they answering questions of 'what', 'how' or 'why'? Are the approaches predictive of future events or explanatory of previous ones? Both Clarke and Argyle, and Sacks *et al.* have to be concerned with 'what' questions in their efforts to classify units and structures. Likewise both are describing how conversation works: the two rules of Sacks *et al.* function to summarize observations rather than say why things are as they are, and to that extent they have the status of descriptive generalizations; Clarke and Argyle are also attempting to state what follows what, offering descriptive generalizations about sequences which could or do occur. In terms of the distinction between constitutive and regulative rules, both seem to be more concerned with the latter than the former. Grice, while also descriptive, is specifying principles and maxims, the explicit rejection of which would destroy the possibility of conversation taking place; the illustrations of more sophisticated manipulation of implicature are also constitutive. Since Grice's analysis is independent of time, questions of prediction do not arise. Neither do the rules of Sacks *et al.* have a temporal dimension, and they are certainly not predictive; they could not be used to generate components of conversational activity. Since the rules simply summarize probabilistic generalizatons, we have no idea what meanings participants would attribute to deviations from the rules (this contrasts strongly with Grice's analysis). Clarke and Argyle's analysis has the same indeterminacy but is predictive and generative; they are concerned to write programs and construct data tapes that can be used to produce conversations.

Demonstrations of the linguistic devices used to achieve cohesion in texts (e.g., Halliday & Hasan, 1976) seem to be simultaneously descriptions and explanations. The rules of anaphoric and cataphoric reference show how the devices work to organize the text and explain the cohesiveness. While there are fuzzy borders and possibly deep philosophical problems about the distinctions between descriptions and explanations, it does seem to be the case with language and social behavior that linguists can be satisfied by descriptions of what and how, whereas social psychologists have to proceed to ask why. If linguists do pose 'why' questions, the acceptable answers will relate to why the conventions are as they are, which in turn will lead them into historical–sociological analysis, into investigations of the actions of peoples in the past. Social psychologists have also to offer answers to 'why' questions about contemporary behavior, both specific and general. Why might X say what he is saying in the way he is speaking in this conversation? Why do X's generally use this form rather than that form in this situation, and what do selections of other forms mean? Both discourse analysts and social psychologists studying conversations are concerned to develop rules that will generate all that can happen in conversations, and that concern at least unites them in their efforts to achieve valid descriptions of segmentation, classification, and sequencing.

The discourse analyst will be additionally concerned with linguistic devices for achieving cohesion and a whole range of linguistic co-occurrences. The social psychologist will need to know what is being transacted between the participants and how and why the transaction is occurring. Neither can proceed without agreement about the units and structures of the texts.

Methods

Questions of the priority to be given to inductive and hypothetico-deductive modes of operation for generating and testing hypotheses might be more properly considered under methodology, but since an emphasis on one or the other is linked to methods of investigation, they can also be referred to in this context. Clarke and Argyle (1982) have utilized both approaches: their third and fourth approaches are heavily hypothetico-deductive, their first and second less so. Sacks *et al.* (1974) are heavily inductive, trying as much as possible to allow the natural data to speak for itself. They build up empirical generalizations and construct higher-order generalizations to summarize these. Their activities appear to cease at that point. No hypotheses are advanced to explain these generalizations, and no tests of their power are devised. The fits within the data, the first order generalizations, and the summarizing second order generalizations are the crucial considerations. While ostensibly (and properly) paring away their presuppositions, they are overestimating their open-mindedness. There is an implicit presupposition that conversation itself is an appropriate category for analysis. Also they necessarily bring to the data their knowledge as members both of the culture and of the speech. They bring their beliefs about linguistic categories to bear upon the data. These points are made not to criticize their procedures but to point out that the ideal of openminded ignorance is neither possible nor desirable as a stance for data collection and analysis. We necessarily have to bring our preconceptions to problems. What is important is that we do not allow these to distort our activities such that we claim correspondences between data and descriptions or explanations that are stronger than is merited by the evidence. What is important is that when data and concepts and their integration into principles do not match, we try to invent new concepts and new propositions that will match data.

We also have to be careful that the data have the status we believe them to have. The experiments of social psychologists have been criticized for the artificiality of the data they generate. In one sense this criticism is nonsense: behavior is behavior and speech is speech. People cannot display competence in the laboratory that they could not display outside it. (Of course they may well display competence outside a situational context that their behavior inside it fails to reveal.) The logical force of this argument is not always appreciated. The world is not divided into two kinds of situations, laboratories and the real world. Even the many situations of the outside world are but a sample of the possible. The world can change through time as well as across situations, just as individuals can change themselves and be changed through time.

Experimentally minded social psychologists do run risks in exchange for the gains of increased control over their respondents. They run the general risk of deluding themselves that they are controlling more variables than they are in fact. They run the risk that their procedures and materials are evoking activities and reactions that have no place in the real life of their respondents as these are currently experienced. Experiments tend towards the etic rather than the emic, except in so far as their results are used to deny rather than assert competencies and dispositions, in which case the reverse is true. (To deny possibilities on the basis of experimental evidence is always hazardous.) The answer however is not to abandon experiments, but to make sure that one is sufficiently acquainted with the lives of the respondents not to make wrong inferences.

Unfortunately, as was indicated early in this chapter, social psychologists are seldom trained in the ethological methods that would seem to be a matter of the highest priority for any student of human behavior, social or otherwise. If one is trying to describe and explain social behavior, proficiency in critical observation of that behavior would seem to be a necessary condition of success, for constructing explanations as well as for descriptions. Ritualizing the means and giving the appearance of an advanced science are no substitute for insightful, tentative comments based on the enlightened experience of social psychologists themselves or of others. Alas, such commentaries are unlikely to commend themselves to journal editors; Grice's (1975) article would have run into publication difficulties had it been submitted to certain social psychological journals, and yet it would seem to be an excellent insightful analysis of a social phenomenon.

For a thorough analysis of social psychological phenomena one would expect to find the whole range of methods deployed with data derived from natural as well as experimentally generated data. Within their linguistic tradition, discourse analysts are unfortunately likely to display the complementary bias and reject the kinds of data that experiments can yield.

The linguistic tradition also tends to place heavy responsibility upon the experts for the discovery or invention of the appropriate categories of analysis. While crediting participants with procedural competence, experts have relied more strongly on their own conceptions for the derivation of the propositional representations of the procedures. As was suggested earlier, this may be unnecessary in some areas of discourse analysis for, insofar as participants are relying on distinctions that the culture has made explicit in its lexis (e.g., promising, betting), then it may well be the case that culturally competent participants have this knowledge encoded propositionally as well as procedurally. Harré and Secord's injunction of "Why not ask them?" (1972, Chap. 6) could therefore be particularly appropriate for some discourse analysis. Participants in specialized subsystems of the culture (e.g., the legal, educational, political, and religious orders and likewise bridge players' clubs, coal miners, and ballet dancers) may have similar capacities for describing how and perhaps explaining why the texts they generate have the characteristics they do. Certainly constructive interviewing along such lines could be the simplest initial strategy for elucidating possibly significant categories and rules of sequence and for initiating further enquiries into the differences between high- and low-quality performances.

In our own work on the communicative competence of young children required to transmit or receive messages that identify particular items in an array, we find that most seven-year-olds and many younger children can explain communication failures arising from ambiguity in the messages (Robinson, 1981): they can say that the message needs to identify the referent uniquely for the listener to choose correctly. Although this awareness relates to semantic characteristics of single utterances only, the results show that propositional knowledge about the way language works in communication is not a prerogative of adults.

This is not intended to imply that people can necessarily retrieve such knowledge. The writings of Schank and Abelson (1977) as well as our own model of phases in the development of communicative competence (Robinson, 1982) offer reasons why much social behavior including speech may be reduced to routinized scripts. If behavior becomes automatized or heavily automatized, it is certainly possible that actions that were once the objects of deliberate and conscious consideration can become detached from such reflections, and the original products of the latter may cease to be available for retrieval.

Significant Omissions

By devoting space to general problems of methodology and methods, and then selecting some approaches to the study of some aspects of conversation to illustrate important issues, much has been omitted. Even within conversation, the social psychological contribution to nonverbal features associated with its structure and content has been neglected (Beattie, 1980; Clark, Ellgring, & Wagner, 1980; Dabbs, 1980; Monge & Cappella, 1980; Siegman & Feldstein, 1979). (See Scherer & Wallbott, this *Handbook,* Vol. 2.)

Research in institutionalized settings has not been referred to, although the legal order and its settings have certainly become popular for social scientists interested in discourse (see Danet, 1984, and this *Handbook,* Vol. 1. See Danet, 1981, for a bibliography.)

Comparable possibilities exist for the texts of any profession-based or specialized group. Doctor–patient communication has attracted attention (see Cicourel, this *Handbook,* Vol. 4), mainly from psychologists concerned with the effectiveness of communication and the social psychological factors related to this.

In terms of functions of language in behavior, each of these involves attention to the representational function, while recognizing its interaction with problems of regulating the affective state and behavior of others and the definition of role relationships (Pendleton & Hasler, 1983). As the study of textual organization expands to cover more and more types and settings of interaction, we shall be confronted with an escalation of data whose common features may become increasingly difficult to synthesize.

IMPLICATIONS FOR THE FUTURE

Unfortunately the implications for further work are infinite in more than one respect. Spatially and temporally there can be no end to studies that would be of practical use to individuals in their daily lives. What matters to individuals is the form and content of the discourse rules relevant to their personal spheres of activity. The greater their familiarity with the cultural specifics of Hymes' (1967) speaking factors in their own life spaces, the more likely individuals are to achieve their purposes. Their reactions to the texts they encounter and the texts they create will be more or less effective in promoting their ends. For such individuals it is as important to maintain familiarity with changes occurring through biographical time as it is to become familiar with changes across contexts at given times.

What is true for individuals and their particular procedural problems is comparably true for students concerned with the tasks of generating and testing descriptive and explanatory propositions in textual materials. Students have to be alert as to what is likely to change quickly and why, and what is likely to remain relatively stable and why. We have to remember that, unlike the phenomena of the physical sciences, those of the social sciences necessarily include the reactions and actions of human beings, who can themselves change and be changed as a function of the knowledge being constructed, discovered, and disseminated. Sociologists have been particularly disposed to point out that knowledge is power, and insofar as human beings are concerned to control the distribution of power at various levels in societies, they will act to promote or negate the consequences of any relevant knowledge that becomes available. Once one believes that the enemy has cracked a cipher, one changes to another cipher. Similarly once one knows that antagonists are noting the nonverbals to draw inferences, one tries to control and mask these. Once outgroup members can simulate the speech of ingroup members, the norms need to be changed for the ingroup to maintain the exclusiveness of its identity.

However, we always operate within limits. Our social behavior, including our discourse, is constrained by biological, psychological, social psychological, sociological-historical, and linguistic parameters. Although historically the nature of linguistic parameters has been noted mainly with respect to language features that are below the level of discourse, discourse studies will neglect such features only at their peril. Just as Laver and Trudgill (1979) have noted that certain components of voice quality can be changed only within limits, so we can see that the linguistic markings of the T/V distinction or the gender in pronouns in many Standard Average European languages function to prevent or retard the obliteration of such social features they might be used to mark. Some linguists write as though language changes do not occur, which is manifestly not the case. Some write to argue that change cannot be engineered. This latter view may indeed have empirical and historical force but logically it is not defensible. That language use is generally conservative is true, but changes could be made given the general will of a speech community, sufficient consensus about the desirability of particular changes, and a sustained effort to encourage the adoption of such changes.

However, given the numbers of people in a language community, the numbers who have a vested interest in maintaining their own competence against rising generations, the problems of reaching agreement as to which changes should be adopted and promoted, and the expense and effort involved in the dissemination and encouragement of the use of the new, it is perhaps hardly surprising that attempts to introduce changes have a high mortality rate. Many of the writing systems extant today are based on principles established by their original inventors, principles entirely sensible for the tools available and the materials on which the marks had to be made (Gelb, 1952). That they are less efficient for biros and paper, let alone typewriters and word processors, has not occasioned their demise and replacement. There is no doubt that would-be reformers have good reasons on their side for instituting change, but good reasons are not enough.

Whereas the stability of sound and writing systems, and that of grammar and basic lexis, is likely to be explained in terms of difficulties of achieving change, the stabilities of certain discourse rules are in some cases more likely to inhere in their rationality. Grice's (1975) exposition of the fundamental principles of conversation look to be empirically necessary conditions for efficient conversation to occur. The principles specified have a timeless rationality. It is the deviations from these that are linguistically and psychologically interesting. Similarly with face-to-face encounters. That there are cultural universals of opening and closing procedures would seem to inhere in the behavioral problem itself. The particular forms these take and their content are of social psychological and sociological interest. The conditions under which they are dispensed with are also of interest, but that they exist is not surprising in itself. Likewise, once telephones were invented one might have expected a standard procedure for initiating a call to be developed on rational grounds; calls cost money, and that fact in combination with the common reasons for making calls defines what will generally be a sensible way of proceeding to the business in hand. These procedures can be found posted in telephone booths and set out in telephone directories. It is not clear why Schegloff (1968) needed to collect data, unless he was interested in finding out when and why people deviated from the standard. Such rules are likely to be changed only if telephoning itself changes in some significant way. Discourse structure can be adaptive as well as stable, but the same principle of efficiency (or cost effectiveness) is likely to be operative. In situations where unambiguous information needs to be relayed quickly, the disourse structure devised will be designed against rational principles and then checked for its psychological soundness. If the discourse rules of air traffic control lead to planes crashing, they will be changed.

What is true of highly specialized settings may also be true of semi-institutionalized activities. If doctor–patient communication can be made more efficient and this is judged to be a worthwhile change, then doctors will be trained to be more efficient in their encounters with patients. Similar possibilities exist in the classroom. Enlightened contemporary practice will, other things being equal, be predicated upon current beliefs about instruction that are in turn contingent upon beliefs about conditions under which children learn efficiently. As the latter change so will the discourse structure.

Although there are signs of healthy assays into the study of the sequential structure of social behavior and its texts (the development of computers was certainly essential for tackling some of the problems in the field), one cannot but deplore the rarity of such interest. Neither is the progress in some areas that startling. Although in their review of persuasion Karlins and Abelson (1970) are able to cite many research studies on the topic in a way in which Aristotle could not have done, the theorizing about persuadability does not seem to have been substantially advanced since ancient times. Also, Artistotle has much to say about the structure, content, and functioning of texts that are germane to the study of the role of speech in the regulation of the affect and behavior of others. Aristotle, his immediate predecessors, and his successors through to Cicero and Quintillian offer comments about texts that social psychologists might find very helpful. But just as social psychologists need to broaden the range of resources they may draw on, so hopefully others working on texts will seek to find out whether social psychology can help with their particular problems.

EPILOGUE

I have deliberately concentrated upon perspectives, methodology, and methods rather than on theories in social psychology for what I hope are good reasons. It is not simply because the theories have largely ignored discourse in both their exegesis and investigatory activities. At the present time social psychology offers too many theories to permit summary reviews of their potential relevance to the study of discourse. McGuire (1980) has gone so far as to classify them against a grid that attempts to expose the weighting they give to different components of the individual: cognitive or affective end states of an internal or external nature, stability versus growth, and active versus reactive. All 16 cells have exemplars. Each provides a frame of reference that selectively delimits areas of behavior for special investigation, but none has been particularly successful in gaining and maintaining ascendancy over its rivals. As Gergen (1980) has ingeniously demonstrated, when students are provided with particular empirical results and are asked to devise arguments that permit these results to be derived from several theories, they are able to do so; the conclusion is that the theories generally lack discriminatory power. Theories that cannot be shown to yield better explanations than their rivals cannot be held up as better theories. By explaining too much they explain too little. Until this ceases to be the case, they are less useful than is desirable.

Theories in social psychology have also been strangely individualistic. As Tajfel (1978) has argued, social psychological theories should be concerned with the behavior of groups as well as behavior in groups. His own theory of intergroup behavior (Tajfel & Turner, 1979) attempts to achieve a description and explanation of the behavior of individuals qua group members and specify conditions under which group membership rather than individual characteristics will influence behavior. Complementary to such an approach is Harré's (1979) argument for the primacy of people as social beings. His view that people are constructed by their culture, which may or may not create conditions for agentive individuality to emerge, would likewise see the stress on individualism in Western social psychology as a culturally contingent fact that may itself be more a rhetorical myth than substantive reality. Harré asserts, but without offering evidence, that persons are made in the course of a wide variety of different language games. This adds a developmental strand to the views of Berger and Luckmann (1967) about the strong role of conversation as a source of definition of personal and social identity. If either argument is essentially sound in its orientation, then the texts of those communicative activities are a major component of social psychology. The work of Harré and of Berger and Luckmann will oblige social psychologists to bring behavior through real time back into their persective, to examine the interactions between texts and the maintenance and development of social relations, and to examine the interplay between these and problems of individual and social identity.

When that begins to happen, social psychology will be able to bring to bear on the study of discourse its methods, methodology, and perspectives. Its methods will include an insistence on systematic sampling of populations and variables as well as a predilection for systematic experimental testing of hypotheses. Where they are feasible, these experiments will be designed to probe descriptions and explanations for their validity and power, acting as an integral complement to the wide range of methods essential for the comprehensive study of social phenomena. The methodology of which its methods are one manifestation will emphasize efficiency of prediction as well as descriptions of contemporary states of affairs, while its ideals for theories will require these to be discriminating in their explanatory force.

The perspective should act as a counterweight to tendencies to reify language as an idealized system of rules existing independently of its users. Not only do social psychologists have to attend to paralinguistic and extralinguistic factors relevant to the structure and content of texts, they can never forget that language is used by people. While recognizing that the language itself, as well as cultural and biological heritage, imposes limits on human activities, social psychology draws attention to the exploitation and possible extensions of these limits.

ACKNOWLEDGMENTS

I would like to thank David Clarke and Howard Giles for their many criticisms of an earlier draft of this chapter—and Teun van Dijk and Malcolm Coulthard for having so few.

REFERENCES

Argyle, M. (1969). *Social interaction*. London: Methuen.
Argyle, M., Furnham, A., & Graham, J. A. (1981). *Social situations*. Cambridge: Cambridge University Press.
Argyle, M., Alkema, F., & Gilmour, R. (1971). The communication of friendly and hostile attitudes by verbal and non-verbal signals. *European Journal of Social Psychology, 2*, 385–402.
Argyle, M., & Kendon, A. (1967). The experimental analysis of social performance. *Advances in Experimental Social Psychology, 3*, 55–98.
Argyle, M., Salter, V., Nicholson, J., Williams, M., & Burgess, P. (1970). The communication of inferior and superior attitudes by verbal and non-verbal signals. *British Journal of Social and Clinical Psychology, 9*, 222–231.
Atkinson, J. W. (1964). *Introduction to motivation*. New York: Van Nostrand.
Austin, J. L. (1962). *How to do things with words*. Oxford: Oxford University Press.
Bales, R. F. (1950). *Interaction process analysis*. Cambridge, MA: Addison Wesley.
Beattie, G. W. (1980). The role of language production processes in the organisation of behaviour in face-to-face interaction. In B. Butterworth (Ed.), *Language production volume 1: Speech and talk* (pp. 69–107). London: Academic Press.
Berger, P. L., & Luckmann, T. (1967). *The social construction of reality*. London: Allen Lane.
Bernstein, B. (1961). Social structure, language and learning. *Educational Research, 3*, 164–176.
Bernstein, B. (1971). *Class, codes and control* (Vol. I). London: Routledge.
Bloomfield, L. (1935). *Language*. London: Allen and Unwin. (Original work published 1933).
Brown, P., & Levinson, S. (1978). Universals in language usage: politeness phenomena. In E. N. Goody (Ed.), *Questions and politeness*. Cambridge: Cambridge University Press.
Brown, R. (1965). *Social psychology*. Glencoe, IL: Free Press.
Bruck, M., & Tucker, W. (1974). Social class differences in the acquisition of school language. *Merrill Palmer Quarterly, 20*, 205–220.
Cartwright, D., & Zander, A. (Eds.). (1960). *Group Dynamics* (2nd ed.). London: Tavistock.
Clarke, A. H., Ellgring, H., & Wagner, H. (1980). Situational effects on the syntax of speech and gaze behaviour in dyads. In H. Giles, P. M. Smith, & W. P. Robinson (Eds.), *Language: Social psychological perspectives* (pp. 287–292). Oxford: Pergamon.
Clarke, D. D. (1975). The use and recognition of sequence in dialogue. *British Journal of Social and Clinical Psychology, 14*, 333–339.
Clarke, D. D. (1977). Rules and sequences in conversation. In P. Collett (Ed.), *Social rules and social behaviour* (pp. 42–69). Oxford: Blackwell.

Clarke, D. D., & Argyle, M. (1982). Conversation sequences. In C. Fraser & K. R. Scherer (Eds.), *Advances in the social psychology of language* (pp. 159–204). Cambridge: Cambridge University Press.

Dabbs, J. M. (1980). Temporal patterning of speech and gaze in social and intellectual conversation. In H. Giles, P. M. Smith, & W. P. Robinson (Eds.), *Language: Social psychological perspectives* (pp. 307–310). Oxford: Pergamon.

Danet, B. (1980). Language in the courtroom. In H. Giles, W. P. Robinson, & P. M. Smith (Eds.), *Language: Social psychological perspectives* (pp. 367–376). Oxford: Pergamon.

Danet, B. (Ed.). (1984). *Studies of legal discourse. Text 4* (special triple issue).

Dixon, P. (1971). *Rhetoric*. London: Methuen.

Firth, J. R. (1958). *Papers in Linguistics 1934–1951*. London: Longmans.

Flanders, N. A. (1970). *Analyzing teacher behavior*. Reading, MA: Addison-Wesley.

Freese, J. H. (1926). *Aristotle: The art of rhetoric*. London: Heinemann.

Furnham, A., & Argyle, M. (Eds.). (1981). *The psychology of social situations*. Oxford: Pergamon.

Gelb, I. J. (1952). *A study of writing*. London: Routledge.

Gergen, K. J. (1980). Towards intellectual audacity in social psychology. In S. Duck & R. Gilmour (Eds.), *The development of social psychology* (pp. 239–270). London: Academic Press.

Gerth, H., & Mills, C. W. (1954). *Character and social structure*. London: Routledge.

Giles, H., & Powesland, P. F. (1975). *Speech style and social evaluation*. London: Academic Press.

Giles, H., Robinson, W. P., & Smith, P. M. (Eds.). (1980). *Language: Social psychological perspectives*. Oxford: Pergamon Press.

Giles, H., & St. Clair, R. (Eds.). (1979). *Language and social psychology*. Oxford: Blackwell.

Goffman, E. (1959). *The presentation of self in everyday life*. New York: Doubleday.

Grice, H. P. (1975). Logic and conversation. In P. Cole & J. L. Morgan (Eds.), *Syntax and semantics* (Vol. 3) (pp. 41–58). New York: Academic Press.

Hall, C. S., & Lindzey, G. (1957). *Theories of personality*. New York: Wiley.

Halliday, M. A. K., & Hasan, R. (1976). *Cohesion in English*. London: Longman.

Harré, R. (1979). *Social being. A theory for social psychology*. Oxford: Blackwell.

Harré, R., & Secord, P. (1972). *The explanation of social behaviour*. Oxford: Blackwell.

Holsti, O. R. (1969). Content analysis for the social sciences and humanities. In G. Lindzey & E. Aronson (Eds.), *Handbook of social psychology* (2nd edition) (Vol. 2). Reading, MA: Addison-Wesley.

Hovland, C. I., Janis, I. L., & Kelley, H. H. (1953). *Communication and persuasion*. New York: Yale University Press.

Hovland, C. I., Lumsdaine, A., & Sheffield, F. (1949). *Experiments on mass communication*. Princeton: Princeton University Press.

Hymes, D. (1967). Models of the interaction of language and social setting. *Journal of Social Issues, 23*, 8–28.

Janis, I. L., & Hovland, C. I. (Eds.). (1959). *Personality and persuasability*. New Haven: Yale University Press.

Jaspars, J. M. F. (1978). Determinants of attitude and attitude change. In H. Tajfel & C. Fraser (Eds.), *Introducing social psychology* (pp. 277–301). Harmondsworth: Penguin.

Jefferson, G. (1972). Side sequences. In D. Sudnow (Ed.), *Studies in social interaction* (pp. 294–338). New York: Free Press.

Karlins, M., & Abelson, H. I. (1970). *Persuasion*. London: Crosby, Lockwood.

Kiesler, C. A., & Munson, P. A. (1975). Attitudes and opinions. *Annual Review of Psychology, 26*, 415–457.

Labov, W. (1966). *The social stratification of speech in New York City*. Washington, DC: Center for Applied Linguistics.

Labov, W. (1970). The study of language in its social context. *Studium Generale, 23*, 30–87.

Labov, W., & Fanshel, D. (1977). *Therapeutic discourse: Psychotherapy as conversation.* New York: Academic Press.

Laver, J., & Trudgill, P. (1979). Phonetic and linguistic markers in speech. In K. Scherer & H. Giles (Eds.), *Social markers in speech* (pp. 1–32). Cambridge: Cambridge University Press.

McGuire, W. J. (1969). The nature of attitudes and attitude change. In G. Lindzey & E. Aronson (Eds.), *The handbook of social psychology* (2nd ed.) (Vol. 3) (pp. 136–314). Reading, MA: Addison-Wesley.

McGuire, W. J. (1980). The development of theory in social psychology. In S. Duck & D. Gilmour (Eds.), *The development of social psychology* (pp. 53–80). London: Academic Press.

Mahaffy, J. P. (1887). *The principles of the art of conversation*. London: Macmillan.

Malinowski, B. K. (1935). *Coral gardens and their magic*. London: Allen and Unwin.

Malinowski, B. K. (1949). The problem of meaning in primitive societies. In C. K. Ogden & I. A. Richards (Eds.), *The meaning of meaning* (10th ed.) (pp. 296–336). London: Routledge. (Original work published 1923).

Monge, P. R., & Capella, J. N. (Eds.). (1980). *Multivariate techniques in communicaton research*. New York: Academic Press.

Pease, K., & Arnold, P. (1973). Approximations to dialogue. *American Journal of Psychology, 86*, 769–776.

Pendleton, D. A., & Hasler, J. C. (Eds.). (1983). *Essays on doctor-patient communication.* London: Academic Press.

Pirsig, R. M. (1976). *Zen and the art of motor cycle maintenance*. New York: Corgi.

Robinson, E. J. (1981). The child's understanding of inadequate messages and communication failure: a problem of ignorance or egocentrism. In W. P. Dickson (Ed.), *Children's oral communication skills* (pp. 167–188). New York: Academic Press.

Robinson, W. P. (1972). *Language and social behaviour*. Harmondsworth: Penguin.

Robinson, W. P. (1978). *Language management in education: The Australian context*. Sydney: Allen and Unwin.

Robinson, W. P. (1982). The child's development of understanding about ambiguity in referential speech. *International Journal of Psycholinguistics, 8*, 57–73.

Rosch, E. (1973). On the internal structure of perceptual and semantic categories. In T. E. Moore (Ed.), *Cognitive development and the acquisition of language* (pp. 111–144). New York: Academic Press.

Sacks, H., Schegloff, E. A., & Jefferson, G. (1974). A simplest systematics for the organization of turn-taking for conversation. *Language, 50*, 696–735.

St. Clair, R., & Giles, H. (Eds.). (1980). *The social and psychological contexts of language.* Hillsdale, NJ: Erlbaum.

Sapir, E. (1921). *Language: An introduction to the study of speech*. New York: Harcourt Brace.

Schank, R. C., & Abelson, R. P. (1977). *Scripts, plans, goals and understanding*. New York: Wiley.

Schegloff, E. (1968). Sequencing in conversational openings. *American Anthropologist, 70*, 1075–1095.

Schegloff, E. (1972). Notes on a conversational practice: formulating place. In D. Sudnow (Ed.), *Studies in social interaction* (pp. 75–119). New York: Free Press.

Schegloff, E., & Sacks, H. (1973). Opening up closings. *Semiotica 7*, 289–327.

Schenkein, J. (Ed.). (1978). *Studies in the organization of conversational interaction.* New York: Academic Press.

Scherer, K., & Giles, H. (Eds.). (1979). *Social markers in speech.* Cambridge: Cambridge University Press.

Searle, J. R. (1969). *Speech acts.* London: Cambridge University Press.

Searle, J. R. (1975). A classification of illocutionary acts. *Language in Society, 5,* 1–23.

Sherif, M., & Hovland, C. I. (1951). *Social judgment: Assimilation and contrast effects in communication and attitude change.* New Haven: Yale University Press.

Siegman, A. W., & Feldstein, S. (Eds.). (1979). *Of speech and time: temporal speech patterns in interpersonal contexts.* Hillsdale, NJ: Erlbaum Associates.

Simon, A., & Boyer, G. E. (1974). *Mirrors for behavior III.* Philadelphia: Research for Better Schools, Inc.

Sinclair, J. McH., & Coulthard, R. M. (1975). *Towards an analysis of discourse.* London: Oxford University Press.

Sudnow, D. (Ed.). (1972). *Studies in social interaction.* New York: Free Press.

Tajfel, H. (1978). Intergroup behaviour: individualistic perspectives. In H. Tajfel & C. Fraser (Eds.), *Introducing social psychology.* Harmondsworth: Penguin.

Tajfel, H., & Turner, J. C. (1979). An integrative theory of integrative conflict. In W. G. Austin and S. Worchel (Eds.), *The social psychology of intergroup relations* (pp. 33–48). Monterey, CA: Brooks/Cole.

van Dijk, T. A. (1972). *Some aspects of text grammars.* The Hague: Mouton.

Whorf, B. L. (1956). *Language, thought and reality.* New York: Wiley.

Zipf, G. K. (1935). *The psychobiology of language.* New York: Houghton, Mifflin.

CHAPTER 6

Artificial Intelligence: Modeling Memory for Language Understanding*

Roger Schank and Mark Burstein

INTRODUCTION

Consider the following story, which appeared recently in a newspaper:

> WASHINGTON—An Air Florida jetliner taking off from National Airport in a snowstorm crashed into a crowded bridge this afternoon and broke as it plunged into the Potomac River, leaving at least 10 people dead and more than 40 missing, according to unofficial police estimates.

If you saw another story about the same event in a different newspaper, it is quite likely that you would not read this second story as thoroughly as you read the first. Rather, you might skim the story, looking only for new information, having determined that it was indeed the same event being described.

Suppose, however, that it was not the same event. A few days after the above story appeared, the following event was reported in the newspapers:

> BOSTON—A World Airways DC-10 plane carrying 190 passengers skidded as it was landing during a winter storm at Logan International Airport last night, ending up partially in Boston Harbor, authorities said. Passengers were being taken by ambulances to area hospitals. Authorities were uncertain how many were injured.

People who read both stories were quite often reminded of the first story while reading the second. Clearly, we must be reminded of facts

* This work was supported in part by the Advanced Research Projects Agency of the Department of Defense, monitored by the Office of Naval Research under contract N00014-75-C-1111, and in part by the National Science Foundation under contract IST7918463.

HANDBOOK OF DISCOURSE ANALYSIS, Vol. 1
Disciplines of Discourse

we have learned from reading other stories when reading new accounts of the same event. Otherwise, the new account might be interpreted as describing a completely new situaion. But what is the value of being reminded of a story like the first one above when reading about a new situation? It seems we cannot help being reminded in these instances. Our claim is that such reminding is due to the nature of our memory-based understanding mechanism. Further, we claim that such reminding is at the root of how we learn.

Issues such as these have played an important part in shaping the direction of our research in natural-language processing over the last several years. Prior to that time, our work focused primarily on the development of representations for many of the aspects of meaning that would be needed in computer programs capable of the parsing and plausible-inference processes for building representations of the meaning of text. Our attempts to construct meaning representations for stories, as opposed to single sentences, made it clear that inferring the causal connections between events was an extremely important part of the understanding process. Since it was often impossible to determine from just the descriptions of two states or actions what the causal connections between them were, we were led to postulate the existence of a variety of complex memory structures, including scripts, plans, and goals, that could be used to represent the world knowledge needed to infer causal connections in those cases.

What the stories shown above demonstrate is the fact that language processing is dependent not only on general semantic and pragmatic knowledge of the world but also on the embodiment of that knowledge in a memory system that organizes memories of past experiences. This is crucial if learning and generalization are to take place. It is just as important for the language-understanding process.

Language understanding is essentially a memory-based process. We interpret new stories we read not just in terms of our general world knowledge but also in terms of our own related personal experiences. Our interest in a subject, and our knowledge of that subject, are both increased and refined by experience.

This relation between language and memory is important for verbal discourse as well as for reading. Arguments and everyday conversations appear coherent in part because the memory-based process of interpreting what the other conversant has just said can remind us of something related, from which a response can be formed. Most important, a usefully organized episodic memory can help us to understand more fully by filling in details using situations that we have abstracted from our own experience.

BACKGROUND

The first story-understanding programs developed at Yale were designed to illustrate some of the different levels of semantic and contextual knowledge that people regularly employ to understand stories and to show how that knowledge might be represented and used in the understanding process. Schank (1975) described a representational system for simple actions and states, and the causal relations that connect them (conceptual dependency). Schank and Abelson (1977) greatly expanded the inferential capability of the system by adding representations for packages of stereotypical action sequences called 'scripts,' various classes of intentional 'goals', sets of general 'plans' for achieving those goals, and 'themes' giving rise to basic human goals and classes of goals characteristic of different personality types. Computer programs implementing these constructs illustrated the role each plays in the process of understanding a text and at the same time pointed out problems and deficiencies in our system of representation for them.

When we read a story, we try to connect the events described into a coherent sequence. Sometimes this can be done using just our commonsense knowledge of simple causality. At other times we must resort to generalizations we have made from experience about what usually happens in a given situation. The SAM system (Cullingford, 1978, 1981) was based on the notion of a 'script', a knowledge structure representing a stereotypical sequence of events for some often-repeated situation. Scripts were used to represent knowledge about situations like taking a bus or going to a movie theatre. The prototypical example was going to a restaurant for dinner. SAM's representation of the restaurant script ($RESTAURANT) consisted of a set of simple actions described in conceptual dependency, together with the causal connections between those actions. The actions in a script were further organized into a sequence of scenes, which in the case of $RESTAURANT included entering the restaurant, ordering food, eating, paying, and leaving. Each script also had a set of roles and props characterizing the people and objects appearing in that script.

In processing a story about eating in a restaurant, SAM first had to recognize that the restaurant script was the relevant context for interpreting the story. Once the script was chosen, SAM would try to interpret each new sentence it read as part of that script. It did this by matching the conceptual representation of the new sentence against the actions represented in the script. When it found a match, it incorporated the sentence meaning into its representation of the story. It also filled in the script actions preceding the one matched. By this process, SAM inferred actions that were implicit in the story it was reading. Missing agents were inferred in sentences like *The food was served*, where the agent, a waiter or waitress, was characterized by his or her role in the script, and the action described was part of that role. Missing actions were automatically inferred from their description in the script. Thus, when SAM read the story

John went to the Fisherman's Grotto for dinner.
He ordered lobster. The bill was outrageous.

it included as part of its representation of the story that John actually ate his lobster, received a large bill, and paid it. From this representation, SAM could answer a number of questions about the story it had just read, including questions like *What did John eat?* and *Who paid the bill?*

PAM (Wilensky, 1978, 1981) dealt with situations that were not at all scriptlike. The levels of representation it addressed dealt with knowledge of human intentions. That is, PAM was concerned with analyzing stories in terms of the goals of the characters mentioned and discovering and tracking the plans they used to achieve those goals. Below is a simple story processed by PAM, a summary it produced, and several questions it answered showing how general knowledge of goals and plans helped it make sense of the story.

```
(UNDERSTAND STORY1)

John needed money. He got a gun and walked into
a liquor store. He told the owner he wanted some
money. The owner gave John the money and John
left.

WHO SHOULD TELL THE STORY? John

I needed to get some dough. So I got a gun, and
I walked down to the liquor store. I told the
shopkeeper that if he didn't let me have the
money then I would shoot him. So he handed it
over. Then I left.

Q: Why did John get a gun?
   JOHN HAD A WEAPON WHICH ENABLED HIM TO ROB
   THE LIQUOR STORE.

Q: Why did John threaten the shopkeeper?
   BECAUSE HE NEEDED TO GET SOME MONEY.

Q: What were the consequences of John threaten-
   ing the shopkeeper?
   THE SHOPKEEPER DIDN'T WANT TO GET HURT, SO HE
   GAVE JOHN THE MONEY.
```

In general, PAM had to do much more work that SAM did to understand a new story; it dealt with situations for which no script existed, requiring that many more separate inferences be made in the process of tying together the events of the story. However, by using knowledge of general plans for achieving goals in a wide variety of situations, PAM could construct a more complete explanation of what had occurred in a story, and why.

As it read the above story, PAM inferred that John was going to use a plan to threaten or overpower someone from its knowledge of his goal of getting money and his acquisition of a weapon, the gun. It could then explain that the shopkeeper decided to give John the money because his goal of preserving his own life took precedence over keeping the money. Recognizing internal goal conflicts such as this and competitions between story characters with similar goals is an extremely important part of the story-understanding process. Only by making inferences about the plans and goals driving characters' actions can such conflicts even be noticed.

INTEGRATING LEVELS OF THE UNDERSTANDING PROCESS

Both SAM and PAM dealt primarily with levels of the understanding process beyond what is generally considered a linguistic level of analysis (syntax and simple sentential semantics). In fact, both PAM and SAM relied on a conceptual analyzer, ELI (Riesbeck & Schank, 1976), to produce semantic representations of the actual text, one sentence at a time. On the other end, summaries and answers to questions were produced from the concepts that SAM or PAM incorporated into the final story representation.

While this was a necessary simplification at the time (and one that many language researchers make), it is in some ways unrealistic as part of a model of human language processing. For one thing, words in a text often have special meanings in specific contexts (e.g., compare *John ordered the hamburger.* with *The boy ordered the block by size.*). If a script or some other specific context is known before a sentence is read, then the meaning relevant in that context will be much preferred from the outset. In addition, words can refer directly to complex activities or to settings for complex events that must be retrieved from memory before the sentences in which they appear can be correctly interpreted. For example, *John caught the bus, Fred picked up the phone,* and *The plane landed* all describe specific actions that we can understand only if we know the normal uses of the objects mentioned (Lehnert, 1979; Lehnert & Burstein, 1979).

Another problem was that SAM and PAM each dealt only with a single level of interpretation. PAM did not deal with scriptlike situations, and SAM never made inferences about characters' goals and higher-level, more abstract plans. Clearly, there are goals associated with scripts. We usually go to restaurants when we are hungry. We go to doctors' offices when we are sick. In fact, knowing someone's goal is an important factor in determining whether a script is active or not. Consider the following stories:

> *Freddie the fish merchant only had two more deliveries to make before he was done for the day. When he arrived at Sal's restaurant, he was told the deliveries should be made at the rear entrance.*

> *Freddie the fish merchant hadn't had a good steak in months. When he arrived at Sal's restaurant, he was told the deliveries should be made at the rear entrance.*

Reading the second sentence of each story out of context, one would not be sure why the merchant was going to the restaurant. He could have several possible goals, one of which might be to get a good meal. Knowing his goal beforehand affects the degree to which we expect to see actions in the restaurant script and, therefore, the degree to which the second sentence in each story seems surprising. Clearly, then, these levels of interpretation are closely intertwined.

Other problems arose from psychological experiments on the nature of scripts in human memory. A number of experiments have confirmed the basic notion that stereotypical sequences are represented in memory (Abelson, 1980; Abbott & Black, 1980; Graesser, Gordon, & Sawyer, 1979; Nelson, 1979). However, one study in particular raised an interesting problem. A series of experiments reported by Bower, Black, and Turner (1979) showed that the presence of an underlying script in a story had significant effects on subjects' recall for that story. Specifically, they found that recognition confusions could occur between stories for which the underlying scripts were similar. For example, a story about a visit to a doctor's office was easily confused with a story about a visit to a dentist, particularly in recognizing details of the waiting rooms described in each case.

Intuitively, this result was not surprising, but it posed problems for our conception of scripts. The recognition confusions indicated that some single structure in memory was being used to store information from each story, at least in the scenes where the confusions occurred. Yet, postulating a HEALTH CARE VISIT script, or an even more general OFFICE VISIT script, meant that the script was being represented at a level of abstraction far enough removed from its experiential base to rob it of much of its value as an organizer of specific, detailed inferences about a given kind of situation.

What resulted from consideration of these issues was the development of the theory of MOPs (Memory Organization Packets) (Schank, 1980, 1982). In general terms, MOPs organize a group of scenes directed toward the achievement of a low-level goal. They are usually organized around a single scene that fulfills the purpose of the MOP.

The difference between this definition and the earlier definition of a script is mostly in the reformulation of the notion of a scene. Scenes, under the new definition, function as independent entities in memory. Many MOPs share some of the same generalized scenes, which serve a particular function in the plan implied by each MOP. However, they may also be colored by the MOP in which they appear with respect to props and other situation-specific information represented by that MOP. Scenes, then, are the principal organizers of specific memories of episodes. When there are many similar episodes organized around a scene, the result is a script describing the actions in that scene.

Another aspect of the MOP theory is what it implies about the process of understanding a story involving a script. As packagers of sets of scenes, MOPs provide the framework for dynamic creation of extended scripts, possibly involving several purposes. Several MOPs may be active at one time in order to understand a scene in a story. If the scene has several purposes for its characters, then the presence of several active MOP scenes provides several sources of expectations for the events described. Thus, scenes from different MOPs can simultaneously provide explanations for a single scene of a story. For example, a story about a business meeting in a restaurant may result in simultaneous expectations for the serving of food and the signing of a contract.

IN-DEPTH INTEGRATED UNDERSTANDING

Knowledge-source integration was the basis for a program called BORIS (Dyer, 1983; Lehnert, Dyer, Johnson, Yang, & Harley, 1983) developed at Yale during the early 1980s. BORIS was designed as a successor to SAM and PAM. It reads several 300-word narratives in great detail, making inferences at many different levels of representation as it parses the words and sentences of a story. In addition to script and goal inferences, represented in terms of a simplified form of MOPs, BORIS keeps track of story scenes in terms of structures called 'scenarios.' It makes use of a representation of affective states in combination with goal successes and failures to explain the emotional state of characters and to guide its summarization of what it reads. It also makes use of knowledge of interpersonal relationships (e.g., friendship) to explain things like the granting of favors, the desire for repeated communication between friends, and affective empathy for a friend's successes and failures.

Unlike PAM and SAM, BORIS is largely "bottom-up." That is, its inferential memory is no longer represented as a module or set of active modules looking at the output of a conceptual analyzer (although the first version of BORIS was structured in that way, rather unsuccessfully). Instead, the action of the parser results in almost continuous search of the system's memory for connections between possible meanings being constructed for the sentence it is currently reading and what it knows about the story so far.

Consider the following example:

```
PROCESSING PARAGRAPH 1
Richard hadn't heard from his college roommate
Paul for years. Richard had borrowed money from
Paul which was never paid back, but now he had
no idea where to find his old friend. When a
letter finally arrived from San Francisco,
Richard was anxious to find out how Paul was.

Who is Paul?
RICHARD'S FRIEND.

Did Richard want to see Paul?
YES, RICHARD WANTED TO KNOW HOW PAUL WAS.

Had Paul helped Richard?
YES, PAUL LENT MONEY TO RICHARD.

Why didn't Richard pay Paul back?
RICHARD DID NOT KNOW WHERE PAUL WAS.

How did Richard feel when the letter appeared?
RICHARD FELT GLAD BECAUSE PAUL AND HE WERE
FRIENDS.
```

Since the parser controls memory search in BORIS, it avoids one problem that ELI faced, that of generating erroneous intermediate representations for sentences because memory was not available to provide a context-based interpretation. For example, the phrase *pay back,* in the context of someone having borrowed money, refers specifically to the act of returning the money borrowed. In the context of a vicious prank, or, more generally, causing someone harm, *pay back* refers to the more abstract concept of revenge. By searching episodic memory for a recently mentioned act of borrowing before deciding on an interpretation, BORIS can construct a representation of the phrase that references a part of the active memory structure directly. As with SAM and PAM, this process automatically resolves many pronominal references in the English text as well.

In BORIS, the parser that reads the story is the same as the parser that answers questions about what it has read. While this seems like an obvious thing to have done, the parser used was originally designed only to answer questions about the story after it had been read by another, more modular program. The question parser was designed to actively search the representation of the story as parsing proceeded, with the result that the event referred to in the question was often found in memory before the parsing of the question was completed, or with very little effort afterward (Dyer & Lehnert, 1980). Once developed, this parser was modified to read the story as well as questions about it, simply by having it build a memory structure when the text referred to one that could not be found by searching the memory structures that had been built previously.

BORIS makes extensive use of the structure of MOPs in its design, interpreting each scene on many different levels. For example, later in the story shown above, Richard, who turns out to be a lawyer, meets Paul in a restaurant to discuss Paul's impending divorce. The scene is interpreted in terms of a scene in the restaurant script, a lawyer-client meeting, and as the reunion of two old friends. In a variation of this story in which a waitress spills coffee on Paul, it is interpreted both in terms of the action she was supposedly performing of delivering the coffee and as a violation of the more general DO-SERVICE structure, which explains why Paul refused to leave a tip.

Goal failures and plan violations are extremely important landmarks in a story, both because they represent situations occasioning strong affective responses and because they mark points of deviation from expectations. In *Dynamic Memory*, Schank (1982) describes a system of TOP's (Thematic Organization Points) for organizing memories of such failures. We claim these structures are needed to explain many kinds of cross-contextual remindings of similar failures and remindings of classic stories and fables depicting similar problem situations. Lehnert has described a system of affect-based plot units also based partially on points of goal failure and achievement, which proved to be a useful predictor of human narrative-summarization behavior (Lehnert, 1981; Lehnert, Black, & Reiser, 1981). Aspects of both of these systems have been combined by Dyer (1981) in his description of TAU's or Thematic Affect Units used in the BORIS system to infer characters' affective states and to generate summaries of the stories it has read. As with all other processing in BORIS, thematic and affective inferences are made during the parsing process. That is, words suggestive of affective states like anxious, relieved, grateful, cheerful, and so on that appear in a story will be related via TAUs to a character's goal failures and achievements.

PROGRAMS THAT SKIM TEXT

The interrelation between parsing and memory can be observed from many different angles. Another argument against the separation of parsing and memory retrieval is based on the observation that people often do not even read every word of every sentence they see. They can, often without significant loss of meaning, skip words or phrases, fail to finish sentences, or even skip whole paragraphs because of strong contextual predictions that make that extra work seem unnecessary or because they lack interest in what they expect to see. While this can lead to misinterpretations, the fact that people can read this way runs counter to any strict level-by-level model of language processing.

Skimming is an extreme case of reading from context. Several programs have been written at Yale to simulate forms of this process. The first was called FRUMP (Fast Reading, Understanding and Memory Program) (DeJong, 1979a, 1979b). FRUMP skimmed stories taken directly from news wire services. It used a simplified form of script called a 'sketchy script', which contained only representations of the concepts that FRUMP needed to extract from a story in order to produce a summary. In a sense, it only read the parts of a story that it was interested in.

FRUMP almost never read an entire sentence of a news story. Instead, it searched the story for words or phrases that could be interpreted as corresponding to an important concept in one of its scripts. Once it was reasonably certain which script best characterized the story, it searched only for phrases that would allow it to fill in the details of the concepts in that script, using syntactic cues only when necessary to help identify an item it was looking for. The remainder of the story was ignored completely. Once it had filled in the required information in the chosen script, it would generate a summary of the story from the concepts in that script. Because the summary was based on FRUMP's internal conceptual representation of the story, FRUMP could produce summaries in many different languages (Carbonell, Cullingford, & Gershman, 1978).

FRUMP had many of the same limitations that SAM had, since it could only "understand" stories that corresponded to one of its scripts. In addition, only about 50% of the stories that come over the news wire are "scripty" in the sense that they contain a fairly standard set of facts to be conveyed. Because it had neither all of the necessary scripts nor a complete dictionary, FRUMP could read correctly only about 20% of the stories it saw.

The combination of incomplete reading and lack of knowledge created a problem for FRUMP. Since FRUMP did not always have the script that best summarized a story, it would occasionally guess the wrong interpretation for a story by choosing another script that matched part of the story. For example, after reading the following news story,

> JERUSALEM (UPI)—A bomb exploded in the walled old city of Jerusalem Monday just about the same time the leaders of Egypt and Israel signed a peace treaty in Washington.
>
> A police spokeswoman said there were "some" casualties but no further details were immediately available.
>
> The bombing came despite increased security precautions by Israeli army troops and border guards against possible attacks by Arabs opposed to the treaty.

FRUMP, without a script for terrorist bombings, produced an English summary:

```
Egypt and Israel have agreed to a treaty.
```

Supplied with a summary that included a script for terrorist bombings, FRUMP produced

```
An explosion in Jerusalem has injured several
people.
```

Clearly, in principle FRUMP had the knowledge necessary to see several aspects of this story. However, it could only deal with one script at a time. It could not make connections between concepts or scripts if those connections were not already part of one of those scripts. It was also completely incapable of handling the third paragraph, which involved the Israelis' goal of preventing such attacks.

Another skimming program, IPP, tried to deal with some of these issues. IPP (Integrated Partial Parser) (Lebowitz 1980; Schank 1980b) was based on several important observations about the way people read. The first was that in reading with any speed, people do not have enough time to process every word completely and still finish interpreting each sentence within a short time after seeing the last word of that sentence. That is, they cannot consider every possible meaning of every word or make the inferences necessary to find every possible interpretation of each phrase before going on to the next word or phrase. Therefore, they must limit the amount of time devoted to processing each word and choose to pay more attention to some words than others. The second observation was what one gets out of a news story is largely governed by what one is interested in (Schank, 1979). A reasonable conclusion from these points it that more processing must be devoted to the interesting parts of a story. These hypotheses motivated a kind of 'wait an see' strategy for language processing that combines skimming with some careful reading.

The assumption that a relatively small number of words in the text convey most of the content suggests that a good strategy for reading quickly is to do very little processing of any words until a word or phrase referring to some large or interesting concept is seen. After such a concept is found, one can then justify further processing of modifiers of that word, using short-term lexical memory or even going back in the text if necessary. These concepts also establish a focus of interest for further processing, since they bring with them expectations for details. By continuing to be alert for other independently interesting concepts, in addition to concepts that are interesting because of some relation to an earlier part of the story, one can avoid the problem of being too "top down." This strategy causes temporary increases in the attention paid to phrases that relay significant information about a concept of interest, while allowing other phrases to be ignored altogether. The result is a system that is more flexible and sensitive to the actual text than FRUMP was, and one that suggests an important reason for variability in reading speed.

IPP was an implementation of this basic strategy for news stories in the domain of international terrorism. Below is a story from the *New York Times* processed by IPP:

> An Arabic-speaking gunman shot his way into the Iraqi Embassy here (Paris) yesterday morning, held hostages through most of the day before surrendering to French policemen and then was shot by Iraqi security officials as he was led away by the French officers.

A quick run through its processing of this story gives some idea of how IPP works. Using a default rule about adjectives, IPP quickly skipped along until it saw the word *gunman*, which it considered a priori to be interesting because of its relationship to the concept of death. This led IPP to collect more information about the actor by looking back at the modifiers it had skipped. Since the action a gunman is most likely to perform is shooting someone, IPP then assumed it might see a verb meaning "shot" and proceeded to set up expectations for who was shot. When this assumption was quickly confirmed by the verb, it began looking for reasons for that action by preparing to see indications that the gunman was engaged in a robbery, some terrorist activity, or a kidnapping.

When it saw that the shooting took place in an embassy, a politically significant location, it inferred that terrorism was the reason for the action. Once activated, this intentional level structure replaced the shooting as the principal point of the story and provided a higher level framework into which pieces of the story fit.

The inference that this story described a terrorist attack also caused IPP to prepare for a number of possible contingencies. It was thus prepared for such scenes as the taking of hostages, making demands, and certain kinds of countermeasures by police. The high interest word *hostages* activated the hostage scene and confirmed one of those expectations. The verb preceding it, *held*, was largely ignored, since it added nothing to the meaning.

The word *surrendering* confirmed another expectation. IPP was interested in the surrender scene, so it paid attention to the word *to* following *surrendering* since that indicated that a description of the captors, in this case some French policemen, would follow.

If the processing of this story had been done in a strictly top-down fashion, the remaining and most interesting part might well have been ignored, since there were no outstanding expectations. However, IPP continued to process the rest of the sentence: *and then was shot by Iraqi security officials*. It thus added to its final representation of the story an interesting, though unexpected, subsequent action. What follows is a pictorial version of the final story representation.

```
** MAIN EVENT **               ** UNEXPECTED EVENTS **
EV1 =                          EV4 =
  SCRIPT     T-TERRORISM          ACTION      PROPEL
  ACTOR      ARAB GUNMAN          ACTOR       IRAQI OFFICIALS
  PLACE      IRAQI EMBASSY        OBJECT      ARAB GUNMAN
  INTEREST   9                    ITEM        *BULLETS*
  CITY       PARIS                DIR-FROM    GUN
  TIME       MORNING              INTEREST    5
  SCENES                         AFTER        EV3
    EV2 =                        RESULT
      SCENE    $HOSTAGES           EV6 =
      PLACE    IRAQI EMBASSY       STATE     DEAD
      ACTOR    ARAB GUNMAN         ACTOR     ARAB GUNMAN
      INTEREST 7                   INTEREST  4
      TIME     DAY
    EV3 =
      SCENE    $CAPTURE
      PLACE    IRAQI EMBASSY
      OBJECT   ARAB GUNMAN
      ACTOR    FRENCH POLICEMEN
      INTEREST 6
      AFTER    EV2
```

IPP has successfully processed over 300 stories in the domain of in-ternational terrorism. Unlike previous programs, however, it did not simply summarize each story in isolation and then "forget" about it. IPP was also a model of how people classify and store such stories in memory, how generalizations are made from similar stories, and how those generalizations can affect the reading of new stories.

READING WITH A MEMORY

What do we remember of all of the news that we see and hear throughout our lives? We eventually forget the details of most stories, even those that we read carefully at the time. Yet we do get something useful out of what we have read. We develop a characterization of our world from the generalizations we make as we try to understand stories we read.

IPP also forms generalizations when it reads stories that have a lot in common (Lebowitz, 1981). Here are two stories that IPP read that led it to make a simple generalization.

> New Haven Register, 25 July 79, Israel—Nine people were wounded today by a bomb believed to be set by Palestinian terrorists near a snack bar, police said.

> UPI, 10 February 80, Israel–A bomb apparently set by Palestinian Guerrilas exploded in Petah Tikva today, and wounded at least 10 persons, the national radio said.

From these two stories, IPP was able to make the generalization that bombings in Israel are often carried out by Palestinians.

It is a fairly simple process to draw such conclusions when presented with two stories one right after the other. What makes IPP so interesting is the fact that it can make the same generalization no matter how many other stories it read in between its readings of these two. Once IPP has made a generalization, it will use it as a source of inferences when reading new stories. Both of these effects are a result of IPP's use of its memory as an integral part of the understanding process. They also depend on the nature of its memory organization system, which models an important aspect of human memory behavior. It gets reminded.

In understanding a story, as in our own experiences, we try to apply the knowledge structures in memory that best match, and hopefully best explain, what we see. These structures are an important part of what we know and will remember about the situation. It is reasonable, then, that we store episodic memories in terms of those structures. That is, we remember episodes as variants of previously formed generalizations, distinguishing them from the general structures on the basis of noticed differences from those structures and problems encountered in using them as sources of inferences and explanations for what we see. Thus, the structures used in understanding a new story are the principal organizers of our memories of that story.

What this means for the understanding process is extremely important. In the course of understanding a new story, we will naturally access structures we have used to store similar previous episodes. The very fact that we do this enables us to be reminded of similar previous episodes that either occurred not long before, shared important features beyond those captured in the general structure, or, most importantly, caused expectation failures similar to those that occurred when interpreting the earlier episode (Schank, 1981).

When we are reminded of an old situation, the two are naturally compared. Storing the new situation on top of the old one results in a new generalization in terms of which both experiences are remembered. Stories read after the formation of such a generalization, which have enough in common with the earlier ones, will automatically be interpreted in terms of that generalization, since it provides the most specific plausible inferences that can be made from what is known.

This is precisely why IPP's representation of a third story it read depended on its having seen the two stories above first.

> UPI, 2 May 80, Israel—A bomb ripped through a former hospital in the West Bank city of Hebron Friday, killing and injuring several people, the state-run television said.

Without the generalization made in the course of reading the earlier stories, IPP's summary of the third story was "A bombing of a former hospital in Hebron killed and wounded several people." After reading the two earlier stories, however, its summary also included the implicit assumption that the attack was made by Palestinian terrorists. IPP thus represents not only a model of an interested reader, but also in a limited sense a model of a reader whose depth of understanding changes as he reads.

STORAGE AND RETRIEVAL FROM EPISODIC MEMORY

Research on episodic memory organization also resulted in the development of the CYRUS system (Kolodner, 1980, 1981; Schank & Kolodner, 1979). CYRUS was a computer model of intelligent, heuristic-based reconstructive recall from long term memory. The CYRUS program answered questions posed in English about facts that could be derived from events stored in its memory. CYRUS' memory organized information about events in the lives of former Secretaries of State Cyrus Vance and Edmund Muskie. A large percentage of the events it had informtaion about were read directly from a news wire service by the FRUMP program. The rest of the data was added manually and consisted primarily of background biographical data. Here is a sample dialog with the CYRUS system.

```
ARE YOU INTERESTED IN VANCE OR MUSKIE? VANCE
BEGINNING DIALOG:
Q1: When was the last time you were in Egypt?
       inferring a diplomatic trip
       answering question using time context
    ON DECEMBER 10, 1978
Q2: Why did you go there?
       answering question using previous
       context
    TO NEGOTIATE THE CAMP DAVID ACCORDS.
Q3: Who did you talk to there?
       inferring undifferentiated political
       meeting
    WITH ANWAR SADAT.
Q4: Has your wife ever met Mrs. Begin?
       inferring a social political occasion.
    YES, MOST RECENTLY AT A STATE DINNER IN
    ISRAEL IN JANUARY 1980.
Q5: Who have you discussed SALT with?
       inferring a political meeting -- sM-MEETING
    searching memory for question concept
      additional information needed
        meeting could have occurred in USSR or USA
        searching for meeting in USSR
        searching for meeting in USA
    searching memory for episodes meeting could
    have occurred in
        searching I-NEGOTIATE for meeting
        searching for conferences about SALT
        searching for diplomatic trips to USSR
    searching memory for standard types of
    meetings
```

```
      searching for diplomatic meetings about
SALT
      searching for briefings about SALT
      searching for public relations meetings
CARTER, BREZNEV, GROMYKO, OTHER AMERICAN
AND RUSSIAN DIPLOMATS, AND MUSTAFA KHALIL,
```

CYRUS indexed events in memory, much as IPP did, in terms of their differences from general event categories called E-MOPs, based on Schank's MOPs. CYRUS dealt with a much wider range of events than IPP, which only read stories about terrorism, and was able to answer questions of varying degrees of specificity.

The model was based on the assumption that episodes are not generally accessible in memory as lists. This assumption is intuitively understandable if you have ever tried to perform any recall task like naming all of the museums you have ever visited. This constraint forced the CYRUS model to cross-index each episode at many levels of description, using structures representing several perspectives to ensure that they would be retrievable later.

As with IPP, storing two similar episodes using some set of indices led to the formation of a new generalization. In addition, if, after a reasonable number of episodes had been stored under an E-MOP, CYRUS noticed that most of them shared additional features, it would try to collapse both generalizations together, in effect reorganizing its memory to be useful in more siutations. When such a merger takes place, fewer features are required to retrieve the generalization and more information is made available when it is accessed later.

When CYRUS was asked a question, it first tried to find in memory those events that contained the necessary information for it to build an appropriate response. Memory search was initiated by building a description of a target event based on the question that was asked. CYRUS then applied a memory-search process called "traversal" to access episodes stored in terms of features found in the target event. In the traversal process, CYRUS used many different characterizations of the people and places mentioned in the question. This effectively varied the search pattern it was using to correspond to a number of the possible generalizations in terms of which episodes matching the target might have been stored originally.

Because CYRUS was designed to answer questions rather than read stories, it always tried to retrieve specific episodes from its memory. However, the questions it was asked often did not provide enough information for it to retrieve unique episodes, since it intentionally had no mechanism for linearly searching parts of its memory. If insufficient information was provided to CYRUS for it to access an episode directly by a series of discriminations, then its traversal process failed. Thus while question Q6 in the following example provided the traversal process with enough information for it to find an answer, that process could not be used to find answers to questions supplying less information like Q7.

```
QG: Have you ever attended a diplomatic meeting
    about the Camp David Accords with Dayan?
Q7: Have you ever attended a meeting in
    Jerusalem?
```

The target concept for question Q7 does not describe any situation explicitly enough for CYRUS to retrieve an episode from its memory, even though CYRUS had seen descriptions of many events that had occurred in Jerusalem. What CYRUS did in such cases was apply an inferential elaboration process to facilitate retrieval by generating plausible additional features for its description of the target event.

A number of heuristics were used to generate additional features and alternative contexts for search. Likely participants could often be inferred from the target event's location or the name of a participating organization, and vice versa. A topic of discussion at a meeting could provide an important clue as to where the meeting took place or who was involved, as in question Q5 above. Search could also be expanded by inferring larger and related contexts under which an episode might originally have been stored. A diplomatic meeting in Jerusalem, for example, might be found under "meetings in Israel" or as part of a longer sequence of negotiations in many locations on the topic of the Middle East.

The work on CYRUS was an important step in the examination of memory organization and retrieval heuristics for getting information from memory. It provides a framework in terms of which we can examine other, more goal-directed memory retrieval problems.

MEMORY IN ARGUMENTS

Episodic memory can also be shown to be an active part of the language understanding and generation processes we use in conversations and arguments. Forming a response in an argument, in particular, is highly dependent on one's ability to use memory effectively. Responding to a point requires understanding an opponent's statement and following its implications until recognizing an area of disagreement. If episodes are stored in memory in terms of the knowledge structures used for understanding and inference, then finding counterexamples should often be a natural consequence of memory-based understanding. This is clearly a useful result, since rebuttal by counterexample is an important form of argument.

Consider the following fragment of a mock argument between an Arab and an Israeli, both sides of which are modeled by a computer program called ABDUL (Birnbaum, Flowers, & McGuire, 1980; Mcguire, Birnbaum, & Flowers, 1980).

(1) Arab: Israel is trying to take over the Middle East.

(2) Israeli: If that were our goal, we wouldn't have given back the Sinai to the Egyptians.

(3) Arab: But then why haven't you given back the West Bank to the Palestinians?

In order to understand (1), the Arab's claim must be related to some knowledge structure representing imperialism or military aggression for territorial gain (hereafter called TAKE-OVER), and, if possible, to specific episodes supporting or refuting that claim.

Beginning with TAKE-OVER, the program searches its memory for evidence related to the Arab's assertion. Episodes involving aspects of the TAKE-OVER structure, including military build up, attacks on other countries, and military occupation, are examined in this process. This may lead to the discovery of many related facts. The Israeli may know that Israel was, in fact, trying to increase its military strength, though this action was justified by its right to pursue the goal of self-defense. He may be reminded that Israel had occupied territory, including the West Bank and Sinai, and that it had also agreed to return the Sinai to Egypt.

If (1) had been posed in the form of a question to an impartial observer or a program like CYRUS, all of these facts might have been used in answering the question. In the context of an argument, however, an appropriate response must satisfy the arguer's goal in the argument. In this case that involves effectively rebutting a claim that is bad for the arguer's own position. This conversational goal imposes constraints on the selection of the facts to be used in response. Here, the intention to occupy territory in general, represented by the TAKE-OVER structure activated in memory, is contradicted by the action of returning the Sinai, a description of which was found in searching memory for relevant facts about Israel occupying territory. Since it contradicts the Arab's claim, it is a valid rebuttal, and thus the program is led to respond with (2).

This process illustrates the point that just to understand statements like (1), most, if not all, of the work required to find an appropriate response in memory may already be done. We can be reminded of the facts needed to form an appropriate response as a side effect of our normal understanding process.

This process also explains the Arab's response (3) supporting his claim in (1) that was attacked in (2). The memory search that the Arab must do to form that response looks much like the search responsible for (2). However, since he was responding to an attack, his argument goal required that he find positive evidence of OCCUPY-TERRITORY rather than negative evidence.

Of course, not all rebuttals can be found so easily during the understanding process. Often, the focus of attack must be shifted to different points in the overall argument context. ABDUL represents that context in terms of an argument graph, describing evidential relations of support and attack that relate the statement made in the argument. Rules based on noticing patterns in the argument graph can be used to suggest new points to address when a particular point has been exhausted. This process is further described in Flowers, McGuire, and Birnbaum (1982).

CONCLUSION

This chapter provides an overview of the ongoing work at Yale on problems in natural language analysis. In describing the progression of this research, we have tried to motivate our growing concern with the nature and organization of human memory. This interest in the functioning of memory is due not only to its effects on the language understanding process but also to its implications for learning and the representation of meaning.

The programs described here all attest to the difficulty of maintaining modularity in describing the language-analysis process. They also lead to the conclusion that our understanding of language is far from static. Everything we read can affect our understanding because it affects the memory we will use to interpret what we read afterward. This in itself is not a surprising conclusion, but it is certainly an important point to remember as we study the reading process in detail.

The other aim of this chapter is to demonstrate how, through a succession of computer models, we can both discover and address interesting problems in the area of language analysis. The computer provides an excellent testbed for a number of ideas about language and its use, since it forces us to be specific both in our representation of meaning and in our descriptions of the processes that manipulate and abstract meanings from text. When examining issues relating to representation of knowledge in memory, the interactions between levels of language processing and inferential memory processing necessitate the construction of extremely complex models. The computer is an extremely useful tool in this endeavor.

REFERENCES

Abbott, V., Black, J. B. (1980, August). *The representation of scripts in memory* (Cognitive Science Tech. Rep. 5). New Haven: Yale University Cognitive Science Program.

Abelson, R. P. (1980, March). *The psychological status of the script concept* (Cognitive Science Tech. Rep. 2). New Haven: Yale University Cognitive Science Program.

Birnbaum, L., Flowers, M., & McGuire, R. (1980). Towards an AI model of argumentation. In *Proceedings of the First Annual National Conference on Artificial Intelligence* (pp. 313–315). Stanford, CA.

Bower, G. H., Black, J. B., & Turner, T. J. (1979). Scripts in memory for text. *Cognitive Psychology, 11,* 177–220

Carbonell, J. R., Cullingford, R. E., & Gershman, A. (1978). *Knowledge-based machine translation* (Tech. Rep. 146). New Haven: Yale University, Department of Computer Science.

Cullingford, R. E. (1978). *Script application: Computer understanding of newspaper stories.* Unpublished doctoral dissertation, Yale University.

Cullingford, R. E. (1981). SAM. In R. C. Schank & C. K. Reisbeck (Eds.), *Inside computer understanding: Five programs plus miniatures* (pp. 75–119). Hillsdale, NJ: Erlbaum.

DeJong, G. F. (1979a). Prediction and substantiation: a new approach to natural language processing. *Cognitive Science, 3,* 251–273.

DeJong, G. F. (1979b). *Skimming stories in real time: An experiment in integrated understanding.* Unpublished doctoral dissertation, Yale University.

Dyer, M. G. (1981). The role of TAUs in narratives. In *Proceedings of the Third Annual Conference of the Cognitive Science Society* (pp. 225–227). Berkeley, CA.

Dyer, M. G. (1983). *In-depth understanding: A computer model of integrated processing and memory for narrative comprehension.* Cambridge, MA: MIT Press.

Dyer, M. G., & W. G. Lehnert. (1980). *Organization and search processes for narratives* (Tech. Rep. 175). New Haven: Yale University. Department of Computer Science.

Flowers, M., McGuire, R., & Birnbaum, L. (1982). Adversary arguments and the logic of personal attacks. In W. Lehnert & M. Ringle (Eds.), *Strategies for natural language processing* (pp. 275–298). Hillsdale, NJ: Erlbaum.

Graesser, A. C., Gordon, S. E., & Sawyer, J. D. (1979). Memory for typical and atypical actions in scripted activities: Test of a script pointer + tag hypothesis. *Journal of Verbal Learning and Verbal Behavior, 18,* 319–332.

Kolodner, J. L. (1980). *Retrieval and organizational strategies in conceptual memory: A computer model* (Tech. Rep. 187). New Haven: Yale University, Department of Computer Science. (doctoral dissertation)

Kolodner, J. L. (1981). Organization and retrieval in a conceptual memory for events or CON54, where are you? In *Proceedings of the Seventh International Joint Conference on Artificial Intelligence* (pp. 227–233). Held at the University of British Columbia, Vancouver Canada.

Lebowitz, M. (1980). *Generalization and memory in an integrated understanding system.* Unpublished doctoral dissertation, Yale University.

Lebowitz, M. (1981). The nature of generalization in understanding. In *Proceedings of the*

Seventh International Joint Conference on Artificial Intelligence (pp. 348–353). Vancouver, British Columbia.

Lehnert, W. G. (1979). Representing physical objects in memory. In M. D. Ringle (Ed.), *Philosophical perspectives in artificial intelligence*. Atlantic Highlands, NJ: Humanities Press.

Lehnert, W. G. (1981). Plot units and narrative summarization. *Cognitive Science, 5*(4), 293–331.

Lehnert, W. G., Black, J. B., & Reiser, B. J. (1981). Summarizing narratives. In *Proceedings of the Seventh International Joint Conference on Artificial Intelligence* (pp. 184–189). Vancouver, B.C.

Lehnert, W. G. & Burstein, M. H. (1979). The role of object primitives in natural language processing. In *Proceedings of the Sixth International Joint Conference on Artificial Intelligence* (pp. 522–524).

Lehnert, W. G., Dyer, M. G., Johnson, P. N., Yang, C. J. & Harley, S. (1983). BORIS— An in-depth understander of narratives. *Artificial Intelligence, 20*(1), (15–62).

McGuire, R., Birnbaum, L., & Flowers, M. (1980). Opportunistic processing in arguments. In *Proceedings of the Seventh International Joint Conference on Artificial Intelligence* (pp. 58–60). Vancouver, British Columbia.

Nelson, K. (1979). How children represent their world in and out of language. In Seigler, R. S. (Ed.), *Children's thinking: What develops?* Hillsdale, NJ: Erlbaum.

Riesbeck, C. K. & Schank, R. C. (1976). *Comprehension by computer: Expectation-based analysis of sentences in context* (Tech. Rep. 78). New Haven: Yale University Department of Computer Science.

Schank, R. C. (1975). *Fundamental studies in computer science: Vol. 3. Conceptual information processing*. Amsterdam: North-Holland.

Schank, R. C. (1979). Interestingness: Controlling inferences. *Artificial Intelligence, 12*(3), (273–297).

Schank, R. C. (1980). Language and memory. *Cognitive Science, 4*(3), 243–284.

Schank, R. C. (1981). Failure-driven memory. *Cognition and Brain Theory, 4*(1), 41–60.

Schank, R. C. (1982). *Dynamic memory: A theory of reminding and learning in computers and people*. Cambridge: Cambridge University Press.

Schank, R. C. & Abelson, R. (1977). *Scripts, plans, goals and understanding*. Hillsdale, NJ: Erlbaum.

Schank, R. & Kolodner, J. (1979). *Retrieving information from and episodic memory, or why computers memories should be more like people's* (Tech. Rep. 159). New Haven: Yale University Department of Computer Science.

Schank, R. C., Lebowitz, M., & Birnbaum, L. (1980). An integrated understander. *American Journal of Computational Linguistics, 6*(3), 13–30.

Wilensky, R. (1978). *Understanding goal-based stories*. Unpublished doctoral dissertation, Yale University.

Wilensky, R. (1981). PAM. In R. C. Schank & C. K. Reisbeck (Eds.), *Inside computer understanding: Five programs plus miniatures* (pp. 136–179). Hillsdale, NJ: Erlbaum.

CHAPTER 7

Sociological Approaches to Discourse Analysis*

William A. Corsaro

INTRODUCTION

Since the beginning of the 1970s the study of human communication and discourse has progressed dramatically and become increasingly interdisciplinary with contributions from anthropology, linguistics, philosophy, psychology, and, to some extent, sociology. Although a growing number of sociologists have made contributions to this rapidly developing field, it is still fair to say that relatively few sociologists are aware of the sociological implications of discourse analysis. It is not that sociologists have ignored language; they have consistently made general references to the importance of language in the production and maintenance of social order. However, few sociologists have followed up these references with systematic attempts to integrate work on language and discourse with traditional sociological theory and research.

While relatively few sociologists have recognized the significance of work on discourse, a large number of researchers from other disciplines have become increasingly aware of the importance of social context for the analysis of discourse processes. Some of these researchers have come to recognize the limits of autonomous-rule systems for the study of discourse and the general tendency of analysts who propose autonomous rules to rely on imagined contextual information and their own tactic knowledge of social structure in the application of autonomous rules.

---

* This paper is a slightly revised and much shortened version of my article "Communicative Processes in Studies of Social Organization: Sociological Approaches to Discourse Analysis" (Corsaro, 1981a).

HANDBOOK OF DISCOURSE ANALYSIS, Vol. 1
Disciplines of Discourse

Several studies include references to information from several levels of abstraction as well as sociological concepts in the analysis of naturally occurring discourse events. Although the recognition of the limits of autonomous rules is a step in the right direction, these more comprehensive discourse models often rely on idealized concepts (e.g., status, role, norms) without grounding these notions in extensive ethnographic observations of the participants and social settings under study.

In this chapter I present a discussion and evaluation of three discourse models developed by sociologists (Sacks and Schegloff, Goffman, Cicourel) as well as two additional sociologically relevant models developed outside sociology (Labov and Fanshel, Gumperz). My purpose throughout this review is twofold. First, I hope the review calls attention to the theoretical and research potential of discourse analysis for sociology. If sociological theory is to advance beyond general references to the importance of language for the production of social order, there must be a commitment to the recognition and evaluation of theoretical developments in the study of human communication in other disciplines. A second goal of the review is to provide a sociological perspective regarding the strengths and limitations of integrative (and interdisciplinary) models of discourse and to evaluate the potential of these models and related research for analysis of discourse processes in substantive areas within sociology.

CONVERSATIONAL ANALYSIS: FROM PRACTICAL REASONING TO AUTONOMOUS RULES

Much research on conversational analysis has been contributed by sociologists (Jefferson, 1972, 1975; Sacks, 1972, 1973, 1974; Sacks, Schegloff, & Jefferson, 1974; Schegloff, 1972; Schegloff & Sacks, 1974; also see articles in Schenkein, 1978) and has primarily addressed the verbal structuring and organization of naturally occurring conversation. There are two distinct strands of research in conversational analysis. The first, which is most apparent in the work of Sacks (1972, 1973, 1978), is characterized by an emphasis on maxims of practical reasoning and social cognition, while the second, which appears most clearly in the work on turn taking, is characterized by an emphasis on autonomous-sequencing rules and psycholinguistic (rather than social) cognitive processing. The two strands of research also differ in terms of level of analysis. The first strand emphasizes maxims and reference rules that go beyond the recursive analysis of sentences to deal with the way members (speakers and hearers) recognize and maintain sociological descriptions over the course of interactive events or of topics and performances (i.e., stories, jokes) within events. The second strand of research uses the adjacency pair of utterances as the unit of analysis and emphasizes the identification of sequencing machinery that provides for orderly turn allocation in informal conversations.

Although it is generally agreed that Sacks and Schegloff's approach to conversational analysis developed out of ethnomethodology (especially the work of Garfinkel, 1967), the first, broader strand of research seems much more in line with Garfinkel's work than the second, more confined approach.[1] In much of his early work, Sacks, in line with Garfinkel, was interested in exploring properties of everyday practical reasoning. In particular, he was interested in how members (i.e., social interactants) produce and recognize descriptions of social events. In pursuing this aim, Sacks (1972) constructed a formal apparatus composed of several concepts, including the notion of membership-categorization devices. According to Sacks, such devices consist of collections of categories that may be applied to some population by the use of application rules. Application rules have important implications for discourse analysis because they specify how members connect different categories and thus arrive at adequate observations and descriptions of social events.

Although I do not have space to describe all of the rules, a brief review of Sacks' (1972) analysis of a young child's story (*The baby cried. The mommy picked it up.*) demonstrates three rules of application. Sacks argues that this story is an adequate description, and when we hear it, we hear that the *mommy* who picks up the *baby* is the mommy of that baby. This interpretation is based on our use of the economy and consistency rules plus a hearer's maxim. According to Sacks, the economy rule holds that if members use a single category from any membership-categorization device, then they can be recognized as making adequate reference to an element from that membership category (i.e., a single category can be referentially adequate). The consistency rule holds that if a category from some device's collection has been used to categorize a first element, then that category or other categories from the same device may be used to categorize further elements of the same population.

---

[1] It is difficult to argue that one strand of research appeared before the other, since much of Sacks' early work was unpublished. However, there seemed to be a move toward the second, formal turn-taking research in Sacks' collaborative research with Schegloff and Jefferson. But even here some of the work (see especially Schegloff & Sacks, 1974) contained features of both strands of research. Mehan and Wood (1975) also discuss these two research approaches in conversational analysis and argue that the work on turn taking involves a search for structures with no reference to structuring activities, which makes its classification within ethnomethodology difficult and controversial.

There is a corollary to the consistency rule, Sacks' 'hearer's maxim', which holds that if two or more categories are used to categorize two or more elements of some population, and these categories can be heard as categories from the same collection, then they should be heard as being from the same collection.

Applying these rules to the child's story (*The baby cried. The mommy picked it up.*), Sacks argues that a hearer can, in line with the economy rule, select the category 'baby' from the device 'family' or 'stage of life'. Having located these devices, the hearer uses the consistency rule and selects 'family' as the appropriate device because *baby* and *mommy* are both members of that device. Finally, using the hearer's maxim the listener is directed to hear *baby* and *mommy* as belonging to the same device and concludes that the mommy is the mommy of the baby.[2]

According to Cicourel (1974a), Sacks' model tacitly presupposes the social actor's use of interpretive procedures. Cicourel argues that speakers use interpretive procedures "to generate appropriate categories and assign them situational relevance," while the hearer "receives instructions for programming his own attributions of meaning and [for] generating responses" (p. 70). Sacks' work provides for the identification of categories and the connection between devices deemed appropriate by maxims and rules. In short, Sacks' model builds on earlier work on invariant interpretive procedures by providing mechanisms that facilitate the linkage of abstract social knowledge to specific features of unfolding interactive events.[3]

In the second strand of research in conversational analysis the focus is on the internal structure of conversation (see Sacks *et al.*, 1974). In their work on turn taking, Sacks *et al.* make two crucial assumptions, those being that turns of talk are valued in discourse and that informal conversation is the basic form of speech exchange systems. Although Sacks *et al.* recognize that turn-allocation procedures vary across speech exchange systems (e.g., informal conversation, interviews, public meetings, debates), they argue that other systems represent a variety of transformations on the conversation's turn-taking model (p. 730). Further, Sacks *et al.* claim that their model of turn taking is both context free and

---

[2] Detailed as this discussion has become, it still simplifies Sacks' (1972) analysis a great deal. He presented several additional concepts (e.g., duplicative organization and category-bound activity) and also described viewer maxims that show that interpretive rules go beyond speech.

[3] In later work Sacks (1978) presented an analysis of a dirty joke. The article, published after Sacks' death, was slightly edited by Gail Jefferson and was based on a series of four lectures Sacks originally presented in 1971. In this work Sacks further demonstrates how members use social knowledge to make sense of speech events and how different interpretations of events are related to values, norms, and concerns of various participants. See Corsaro (1981a) for a detailed discussion of this work.

context sensitive. This claim is necessary because conversation can accommodate a wide range of situations, participant indentities, and changes of situation, while it must be context sensitive to narrow "parameters of social reality in a local context" (pp. 699–700).

In generating a turn-taking device, Sacks *et al.* begin by isolating a set of facts that they argue were "grossly apparent" in their data (audio recordings of naturally occurring conversation). They then generated a device that accounts for those facts. I do not have space to cover all the facts which they discuss (see Sacks *et al.*, 1974, pp. 700–701); however, the following abbreviated list is useful for understanding the basis of the turn-taking device.

1. Speaker change occurs and usually recurs.
2. Although in almost all instances one party talks at a time, there are occurrences of brief overlaps of speech.
3. Transitions from one turn to a next with no gap and no overlap between them are common. Together with transitions characterized by slight gap or slight overlap, they make up the majority of transitions.
4. Turn-allocation techniques are obviously used. A current speaker may select a next speaker and parties may self-select in starting to talk.
5. Various turn construction units are employed. Turns can be one word long or, for example, they can be sentential in length.

Sacks *et al.* describe a turn-taking device which accounts for the above facts and is composed of turn-construction and turn-allocation components and a set of application rules. They maintain that turns are made up of units from the turn-construction component, the units are syntactically defined (sentences, clauses, phrases, words), and a speaker is initially entitled to one such unit. Given this psycholinguistic claim regarding syntactically based units, Sacks *et al.* go on to assert that recipients (supposedly because of linguistic competence and psycholinguistic processing) can project "transition-relevance places" where speaker transfer can occur during a current speaker's turn. Such projection is one example of "recipient design." According to this notion "there are a multitude of respects in which the talk by a party in a conversation is constructed or designed in ways that display an orientation and sensitivity to the particular other(s) who are coparticipants" (Sacks *et al.*, 1974, p. 727). The notion of recipient design has important discourse implications and, as Sacks *et al.* maintain, it is closely connected to the context sensitivity of their model (a point I return to below).

The turn-allocation component of the Sacks *et al.* model is made up of two groups of allocation techniques: (1) those in which a next turn is allocated by a current speaker selecting a next speaker, and (2) those in which a next turn is allocated by self-selection. Finally, there is a set of rules that govern turn construction, provide for allocation of a next turn to one party, and coordinate transfer to minimize gap (see Sacks *et al.*, 1974, pp. 703–704).

I would like to raise several issues regarding the implications of this turn-taking system for the study of discourse. First, the autonomous nature of the turn-taking system and the invariance of the rules are not made clear. Mehan and Wood (1975) have argued that the autonomous nature of the system is implied, given the similarity of the approach to abstract linguistics. It is true that both Sacks *et al.* and generative grammarians (see especially Chomsky, 1965) are primarily interested in describing generative devices that assign structural descriptions (to sentences for generative grammar and to conversation for Sacks *et al.*). However, the discovery methods of Sacks *et al.* seem much more inductive than those of generative grammar. In generative grammar the general form of the resulting system is given in advance and specific rules are deduced in line with these general assumptions. This is not the case for Sacks *et al.* They proceed by first isolating a set of facts in a corpus of data and then inductively generate a device (including a set of rules) to account for the facts. The Sacks *et al.* model seems closer to structural linguistics than to Chomsky's generative grammar. Structural linguistics is empiricist based and involves the gradual construction of a model by working inductively from data.[4]

Given the empiricist orientation of their approach, Sacks *et al.* face serious problems when confronted by facts that cannot be accounted for by their proposed model, since such facts cannot be handled by references to performance errors as in generative grammar. They show some sensitivity to this problem when they note that informal conversation is one of several types of speech exchange systems[5] and also when they argue that cross-cultural validity of their model is an empirical question.[6]

---

[4] See Chomsky (1977, pp. 115–119) for a further discussion of this distinction between structuralist and generative theories of grammar. It is also interesting that Chomsky does not see his approach as purely deductive, but as possibly in line with Peirce's notion of abduction (Chomsky, 1977, p. 71), which is an allegiance also made by Cicourel (1978, and see below).

[5] Sacks *et al.* argue, however, that turn-taking devices for other types of speech exchange systems are transformations of the more basic device in informal conversation (1974, p. 730). This claim is supported primarily by the belief that informal conversation is more natural than interviews, ceremonies, debates, and so on.

[6] Along these lines Sacks *et al.* (1974, p. 700) refer to several cross-cultural studies of conversations that they feel are in line with their turn-taking model. However, Phillips (1977) reports data on the structuring of disourse events among North American Indians that are qualitatively different from the data of Sacks *et al.* on white, middle-class Americans.

In addition to cross-cultural variability and variability across types of speech exchange systems, Sacks *et al.* also must face the problem of possible variation of the proposed rules across types of informal conversation. Although their data base is not described in detail, it is clear that much of the data is made up of telephone conversations and similar focused events (i.e., where participants come into contact primarily for the purpose of talk). Informal conversations also occur in settings where continuous talk is optional (e.g., when two or more parties are on a trip in a plane, jogging in the park, fixing a meal, watching the news on TV). The general problem is the premature claim of autonomy for their model. This was not the case in earlier work where Sacks (1972) often used the term "maxim" rather than rule. In any event, the Sacks *et al.* model is best seen as a set of strategies (rather than obligatory rules) that members use to generate structure in informal conversation.

A final point regarding the work of Sacks *et al.* on turn taking is its relation to Sacks' earlier work on member's use of social knowledge in discourse. Although the work on turn taking takes place at a microlevel, is more formalistic, and involves psycholinguistic rather than social (cognitive) processing, the notion of 'recipient design' is similar to concepts developed in Sacks' earlier work. Recipient design implies that conversation is produced as a result of the continuous (and often collaborative) structuring activities of participants. Sacks *et al.* (1974) argue that recipient design "is a major basis for the variability of actual conversations that is glossed by the notion of 'context sensitive' " (p. 727). Although the importance of recipient design and context sensitivity is evident in related work on closings in conversations (Schegloff & Sacks, 1974), it is less apparent in the later work on repair (Schegloff, Jefferson, & Sacks, 1977). Although the future of conversational analysis is clouded by the death of Sacks, contributions which focus on both structure and structuring activities in conversation will be most useful for the study of social-discourse processes.

GOFFMAN: SELF-PRESENTATION AND DISCOURSE PROCESSES

While the conversational analysts provide a discourse model nearly devoid of references to the social self, Goffman's *Frame Analysis* (1974) and later work on conversational structure (1976) can be seen as vehicles for further development of his early work on the presentation of self in everyday life (1959). In fact, Goffman's emphasis on self-presentation is the basis of both the strengths and limitations of his work on the analysis of discourse processes in sociology.

The major strengths of Goffman's approach are twofold. First, he has directed attention to the importance of units or boundaries of discourse. Second, Goffman has attemped to link the communicative abilities of individuals to frame and transform ongoing discourse to a range of impression-management strategies and rituals that he claims are a central part of American culture.

Goffman has addressed the question of units at the level of individual acts or 'moves' (1976) and speech events or 'face engagements' (1963). Regarding the latter, Goffman began by introducing the notion of 'territories of self.' Territories of self are important because social interaction depends on individuals "giving up some of the boundaries and barriers that ordinarily separate them" (Goffman, 1971, p. 52). What is of most interest for discourse analysis is how the protection and use of, as well as encroachment upon, territories of self affect movement toward the initiation or avoidance of discourse events.

Take, for example, Goffman's discussion of personal space in public settings like waiting rooms, buses, and elevators. In these settings the intruding into or giving up of personal space due to crowding is seldom questioned, but the return of space when crowding is alleviated is a more delicate matter. Thus, as a crowded elevator empties, passengers "acquire a measure of uneasiness, caught between two opposing inclinations—to obtain maximum distance from others and to inhibit avoidance behavior that might give offense" (1971, p. 38). I would argue in addition that it is at these points that a need for talk is heightened, even if for no longer than a single exchange. In short, realignments of territories of self can get conversation started by marking (or serving as boundaries for) stretches of discourse.

Once territories of self are relinquished, episodes or stretches of discourse can occur. Throughout his work, Goffman has referred to such episodes as 'encounters', 'focused activities', and 'face engagements'. Face engagements are defined as comprising "all those instances of two or more participants in a simple focus of cognitive and visual attention—what is sensed as *mutual activity* entailing preferential communication rights" (Goffman, 1963, p. 89).[7] What is important for discourse analysis is not simply Goffman's definition but also his recognition of the requirements and constraints for the production of face engagements. Goffman adds

---

[7] The reader should note that this definition is similar to Hymes' notion of the 'speech event' such as conversation at a party and is distinct from 'speech acts' such as a joke performed during a conversation (Hymes, 1972, p. 56). The main difference between Hymes and Goffman is Goffman's emphasis on self-presentation, which is apparent in terminology like 'face engagement'.

to what he calls the 'system constraints' developed by the conversational analysts and others (e.g., Sacks, *et al.*'s [1974] turn-taking procedures; Duncan's [1974] backchannelling devices; and Grice's [1975] conversational maxims) by introducing ritual constraints. These are constraints that govern "how each individual ought to handle himself with respect to each of the others, so that he does not discredit his own tacit claim to good character or the tacit claim of others, that they are persons of social worth whose various forms of territoriality are to be respected" (Goffman, 1976, p. 266).

According to Goffman, ritual constraints give rise to supportive and remedial interchanges. Supportive interchanges often serve bracketing functions within and around face engagements (Goffman, 1971, pp. 62–94). The most interesting of these are access rituals that are crucial for the initiation and termination of face engagements and that seem to be acquired early in life and may have universal features (see Corsaro, 1979; Ferguson, 1976; Schiffrin, 1977; Youssouf, Grimshaw, & Bird, 1976).

While supportive interchanges serve initiation, expressive, and termination functions, remedial interchanges are more directly tied to impression management. "The function of remedial work is to change the meaning that otherwise might be given to an act, transforming what could be seen as offense into what can be seen acceptable" (Goffman, 1971, p. 109). Remedial interchanges keep interaction running smoothly at points where an individual's behavior may potentially violate ritual constraints.

Supportive and remedial interchanges are important for discourse analysis because they are often intricately related and interwoven with other discourse functions. Thus, as Goffman (1976) suggests, individuals may be motivated to use these devices to preserve face, but they end up preserving orderly communication as well.

Regarding units of analysis within face engagements, Goffman (1976) discusses and rejects such units as the sentence, utterance, conversational turn, and Sacks' notion of the 'adjacency pair'. What is offered instead is a three-part series of moves making up an interactional unit. Moves are defined (loosely, according to Goffman) as "any full stretch of talk or of its substitutes which has a distinctive unitary bearing on some set or other of the circumstances in which participants find themselves" (1976, p. 272). The basic interactional unit is composed of three moves: mentionable event, mention, and comment on mention, with the first move quite likely not to involve speech at all (p. 290). Goffman argues that the first move is often overlooked in conversational analysis because of a reliance on audiotapes that cannot capture the precipitating phase of the interactional unit.

Although he focuses on units, Goffman does not mean to imply that discourse is simply a matter of chaining together a series of basic interactional moves. In fact, Goffman (1976) argues that responses (i.e., comments on mention and any additional comments) must have references. Therefore, it is the "cognitive activity of referencing (i.e., a sequence of response moves with each in the series carving out its own reference), rather than dialogic couplets and their chaining which ought to be the basic mode for talk" (p. 293). What we have in the end is a dynamic view of context in which "conversation becomes a sustained strip or tract of referencings, each referencing tending to bear, but often deviously, some retrospectively perceivable connection to the immediately prior one" (p. 309).

A second strength of Goffman's emphasis on self-presentation is his demonstration that the density, complexity, and fragility of social interaction is a reflection of the individual's ability to frame and transform ongoing social activity. Borrowing from Bateson (1972), Goffman defines frames as "the principles of organization which govern social events and the actor's subjective involvement in them" (1974, p. 10). According to Goffman, individuals not only frame ongoing strips of activity, but they can also transform frames by way of keyings and fabrications.

In *Frame Analysis,* Goffman (1974) presents a virtual legion of examples of framings including types of keyings, fabrications, frame breaks, misframings, and frame disputes. However, in the last two chapters of the book Goffman once again returns to a discussion of self and impression manangement. For Goffman, "self (then) is not an entity half concealed behind events, but a changeable formula for managing oneself during them" (p. 573). Goffman implies that at some point in human development individuals recognize the importance of self-staging, their abilities to stage appropriate selves, and the multiple threats to and vulnerabilities of self-presentations. The process of self-staging can take on a life of its own, and the individual's sense of a unique self, if it ever existed, soon dissipates into a myriad of performances.

What is most important for discourse analysis is not Goffman's conclusions about the nature of self (they can certainly be debated, see below), but rather his recognition of the communicative abilities that underlie self-presentation and the effects of self-staging on discourse processes. While other discourse theorists have systematically studied the importance of social context, background knowledge, and past interactional history in discourse, Goffman emphasizes the individual's tendency and ability to use discourse for the staging and maintenance of self.

Take, for example, Goffman's discussion of dramatization in everyday talk. The individual, says Goffman, spends most of his conversational time "providing evidence for the fairness or unfairness of his current situation and other grounds for sympathy, approval" (p. 503), and so on, while his listeners are primarily obliged to show audience appreciation. For Goffman, an individual engaging in ordinary talk can function as a principal, strategist, animator, and figure who seldom seeks a simple answer to a question or a compliance with a request but rather most often desires an "appreciation of a show put on" (p. 546). Furthermore, even while the individual's performances are underway, he can "frame himself from view" because self-displays in informal everyday talk "are properly to be attributed to a figure animated, not the animator" (p. 547). The complexity and looseness of everyday talk does not stop here, however, because "overlaid on the quickly changing frames of a speaker's talk may be another lattice of frame changes, this set introduced by the hearer—if sometimes only for himself. Adding perversity to polymorphousness" (p. 548).

While the emphasis on self-presentation is the source of the major strengths of Goffman's work for discourse analysis, it is also the root of several limitations of his approach. A frequently heard criticism of Goffman's work is that it is restricted to American culture and possibly even to the American middle class. Although Goffman often owns up to this criticism, the issue is seldom pursued in any detail. It would seem that the communicative abilities that underlie Goffman's (1974) notions of framings, keyings, and fabrications are part of human competence and are, therefore, universal. Could it be that these abilities appear across cultures but are manifested in different ways given variations in social-structural demands? In sum, the cultural limits of Goffman's work are real, but so are the opportunities for comparative research.

A second (and more serious) problem in Goffman's work involves the interrelationship between his analytic methods and his assumptions about the cognitive processing and communicative abilities of discourse participants. Goffman has always relied heavily on the generation of new concepts that are (or appear to be) supported by examples of data from unsystematic observation, the media, or literature. One problem with this method is that in Goffman's case it has become almost an art form in which all possible types or properties of each concept are pursued to their logical limits even when it appears they may have little to do with what transpires in social reality.

Goffman is personally aware of this problem. He acknowledges at the start of *Frame Analysis* that his analysis is "too bookish, too general, too removed from fieldwork to have a good chance of being anything more than another mentalistic adumbration" (1974, p. 13). But the problem runs deeper than this. Goffman makes major assumptions about what poeple do in discourse while seldom studying actual discourse. The logic of his analysis seems to be that if cognitive processing of linguistic, nonverbal, paralinguistic, ecological, and social cues can be carried out to arrive at social meaning of hypothetical events in periods of reflective, analytic thought (and perhaps that this process can be reconstructed by readers), then individuals can and do use the same processes in actual discourse. Such an assumption may be unwarranted. Surely, discourse is more demanding than isolated reflection in terms of the information processing, memory, and communicative skills required (Cicourel, 1978; and see below). The direct analysis of ongoing discourse processes is necessary to support many of Goffman's claims regarding the nature of self and the effects of self-presentation on discourse structure. It may be that we are much more self-conscious in reflection than in social interaction.

The above criticism is not meant to imply that impression management, role distancing, and other types of self-staging do not occur in discourse, but rather that they are matters for empirical investigation. Careful analyses of these processes in audio-video recordings of actual discourse that are preceded by extensive ethnography are crucial for both determining the validity of Goffman's claims about impression management and for isolating how self-presentations are accomplished in actual discourse events.

CICOUREL'S COGNITIVE SOCIOLOGY:
THE ROLE OF SOCIAL STRUCTURE IN
THE STUDY OF DISCOURSE

While Goffman has expanded on the formal rules of the conversational analysts in his attempt to bring self-presentation to the study of discourse, Cicourel has focused directly on the role of social structure in discourse processes. A major goal of Cicourel's (1980) work is to demonstrate that "the study of discourse and the larger context of social interaction requires explicit references to a broader organizational setting and aspects of cultural beliefs often ignored by students of discourse and conversational analysis" (p. 102).

In a recent series of papers, Cicourel (1975a, 1978, 1980, 1981) has outlined an interactive model for discourse analysis that stresses the interrelationships among linguistic, cognitive, and sociocultural elements in the study of language in society. Although there is some ambiguity in the description of specific features of the model,[8] the set of notions that Cicourel has presented is important in two respects. First, the interactive model integrates several theoretical approaches, and, second, it specifies research strategies for the initial testing, refinement, and further development of basic theory in discourse processes.

According to Cicourel, discourse involves several levels of information and more than one type of logical reasoning. Regarding logical reasoning, Cicourel (1978) argues that discourse models that rely primarily on references to autonomous syntactic, turn-taking, or entire-text or story grammar rules "must be understood as aspects of a general processing system that reflects on and interacts with information from a local communicative context" (p. 26). In short, Cicourel argues that the importance of formal structures of discourse is contingent on the local conditions of interaction in the assignment of semantic significance to what is said in specific discourse events.

Although discourse can be understood at many different levels of analysis, most approaches to discourse rely on top-down or bottom-up models. As Cicourel has argued, top-down models generally involve references to higher-order predicates that index constituent parts of the discourse such as general goals, beliefs, events, or procedures, or general relationships that exist between speakers (i.e., superordinate-subordinate alignments). Bottom-up models, however, are characterized by a focus on lower levels of abstraction like syntactic structure, propositional content of syntactic strings, and turn-taking procedures, with little reference given to status characteristics of participants or orgnizational features of interactive settings. In actual discourse, however, participants often make use of several levels of information at once. Additionally, Cicourel has argued that researchers also rely on their tacit knowledge of social structure as well as emergent features of interactive settings that go beyond the level of abstraction addressed in a given model. Therefore, Cicourel argues that an interactive model of discourse must address the abductive reasoning and cognitive processes that participants use in articulating various levels of information in actual discourse events.

In generating an interactive model to account for how participants use several types of logical reasoning and their ability to articulate multiple levels of information, Cicourel builds on classical notions developed by Peirce and more recent work on information processing by Rumelhart (1975, 1978, 1981). Cicourel (1978) argues that for Peirce the notion of 'abduction' "seems to be an inferential step that occurs in first stating

---

[8] This ambiguity that occurs in Cicourel's classification of various discourse models as top-down or bottom-up approaches is discussed in detail in Corsaro (1981a).

and then reflecting on a hypothesis that would choose among several possible explanations of some set of facts" (p. 28). Applying this notion to discourse, Cicourel maintains that the particular circumstances that exist during discourse provide for "the recognition or creation of facts that contextualize the inferential step of making guesses about what is happening" (p. 29) in the social exchange. From this perspective, the analysis of discourse must include references to autonomous rules, recognition of local features of the interaction setting, and properites of the logical reasoning and cognitive strategies that participants employ to link formal rules and higher-order predicates to specific features of ongoing interactive events.

Rumelhart's work (1975, 1978, 1981) on story grammars is also useful for attempting to discover properties of participant's abductive reasoning in discourse. According to Rumelhart (1978), as quoted in Cicourel (1978, p. 28), "a subject's understanding of a situation or the passage of a text or story becomes equivalent to having selected and verified the abstract representations or schemata that are said to characterize the central elements of the situation, story, or text." Summarization is seen as a key to understanding comprehension processes, and, according to Cicourel, an examination of participants' summarization processes of past interactive events can serve as important data for discovering properties of abductive reasoning.

In his model Cicourel addresses both macro- and microlevels of analysis and the autonomous and context-sensitive features of discourse rules or strategies, and he maintains that both researchers and social actors routinely rely on abductive reasoning in their analysis of and participation in discourse events. The interactive model is, however, underdeveloped and awaits substantive application and further specification regarding properties of abductive reasoning. However, given the specificity of Cicourel's illustrative application of the model in doctor-patient interviews and his discussion of research strategies, further development and detailed applications of the model may not be long in coming.[9]

A major strength of Cicourel's recent work is his extensive discussion of methodological issues in the study of discourse. In his discussion of the role of social structure in the analysis of discourse, Cicourel stresses the importance of embedding the collection and analysis of discourse materials in traditional field research or ethnography (see Corsaro, 1982;

---

[9] Recent applications of Cicourel's model to discourse between mid-level medical providers and patients (Drass, 1981) and among members of therapy groups (Vandewater, 1981) demonstrate that the model is highly useful for understanding discourse processes in social organizational settings.

Gumperz, 1976; Hymes, 1978; Mehan, 1979). Cicourel maintains that discourse events like classroom lessons, courtroom activities, doctor–patient interviews, and adult–child interaction are always part of more complex sociocultural conditions. These conditions "can provide organizational information of a conceptual nature that specify constraints for [the] analysis of discourse and textual materials" (Cicourel, 1980, p. 122).

When researchers extract discourse materials from organizational settings—without careful field entry, collection of background data on participants and setting, and intensive interviewing of participants regarding their perceptions and understanding of routine discourse events—two interrelated methodological problems arise. First, researchers relying only on extracted discourse materials must stay close to the interactive data. As a result, there can be "no explicit attempt to invoke higher level predicates which would identify the kinds of social interaction taking place, how this interaction reveals complex biographical conditions and interpersonal relations, and the way all of these elements reflect aspects of social structure or institutional constraints, beliefs, and practices" (Cicourel, 1980, p. 123). Data-driven analysis of extracted materials can distort the participants' intentions, understandings, and cognitive processing of discourse events. A second problem occurs when researchers (either explicitly or tacitly) go beyond the discourse materials and present interpretations that are based on idealized or stereotypical notions of social-structural features of the organizational setting or social and psychological characteristics of participants. When this type of expansion occurs, the problem is more one of reification than mere distortion because the analysis takes on a more extensive, theoretical character that is not based on valid ethnographic observation of the participants and settings under study.

Cicourel also argues that researchers should provide chronologies that account for how ethnographic data were collected and used in analysis of discourse materials. Regarding the latter point, researchers should account for all decisions and interpretations in analysis that involved linking different types and levels of data. For example, researchers should go beyond general references to field notes, conversations with discourse participants, and related research findings or theoretical concepts employed in their interpretations of discourse materials to identify specific features of the different levels of information that were the basis of their interpretations. In addition to accounting for how analyses are accomplished, researchers should provide accounts of how a research problem was formulated, a research site was selected, field entry was accomplished, obstacles to data collection were overcome, and problems of obtrusion and ethics were handled (see Corsaro, 1981b; Johnson, 1975, for examples of chronologies of this type). According to Cicourel, this second chronology provides readers with (and keeps researchers continually aware of) a framework for understanding the broader political and sociocultural conditions in the assembly of a data base. The chronology is important because these conditions generate restrictions that affect the interpretations, quality, and consistency of the more narrow data base (i.e., discourse materials).

In addition to these general methodological recommendations, Cicourel also proposes several specific strategies for data analysis. First, Cicourel (1980) suggests that researchers should attempt to collect contrastive ethnographic and discourse materials by focusing on societal, organizational, group, or bureaucratic occasions when routine transfers of information occur. To demonstrate the research potential of occasions of this type Cicourel (1974b, 1975a, 1978, 1981) has presented illustrative materials from doctor–patient interviews and medical summaries. In these examples, Cicourel offers a more sophisticated sociolinguistic version of a general analysis strategy first employed in earlier work in educational (Cicourel & Kitsuse, 1963) and criminal processing and courtroom settings (Cicourel, 1968). The general strategy is to attempt to trace the processes by which organizational members move from actual discourse events to written summaries of these events and eventually to organizational decision making. Once researchers obtain contrastive data, Cicourel stresses the importance of multilevel procedures. In particular, Cicourel (1978) recommends that researchers undertake and later compare analyses at a minimum of two levels of abstraction.

Finally, Cicourel also stresses the importance of assumptions about the reasoning processes of discourse participants in the analysis process. Here, Cicourel's recommendations are twofold. First, he suggests that discourse participants should take part in the analysis process. In his description of indefinite triangulation, Cicourel (1975b) suggests that researchers elicit multiple interpretations of discourse materials from participants and compare these data with their own (researchers') interpretations of the same and similar events. In this way researchers can check the validity of their interpretations and possibly discover properties of the reasoning abilities of social actors. Second, Cicourel (1980) has maintained that both discourse participants and researchers should be viewed as limited-capacity processors of information. He argues that researchers and informants "are constrained by their knowledge base and contingencies of using working and long-term memory under changing conditions of analysis and social interaction" (1980, p. 129). Cicourel suggests that researchers can avoid the inevitable reification that occurs when they insist on finding something inherently meaningful in everything said by discourse participants if they treat the processing limits of social actors as problematic aspects of discourse analysis.

In closing this section I want to emphasize the broad scope and vast potential of Cicourel's work as compared to the other sociological models discussed earlier. Given the scope of Cicourel's model, it is not surprising to hear complaints about the vagueness or obscurity of some of his theoretical statements. Although clarity and parsimony are commendable features of theoretical models, these features of theory should be evaluated in line with the complexity of the problem addressed. In the area of human communication and discourse, parsimonious, self-contained theoretical models can often reify the phenomena they seek to explicate.

COMPREHENSIVE DISCOURSE ANALYSIS

Labov and Fanshel's (1977) study of therapeutic conversation, which they refer to as comprehensive discourse analysis, is the most extensive substantive application of any discourse model yet to appear in the literature. I do not have space to consider Labov and Fanshel's study in detail here (see Grimshaw, 1979, for a detailed review). However, I do wish to (1) examine Labov and Fanshel's notion of expansion, (2) compare their research methods with those proposed by Cicourel (see above), and (3) evaluate the potential of the model for substantive studies of discourse in sociology.

Expansion is an analytic device by which Labov and Fanshel synthesize all information that will help in understanding the production, interpretation, and sequencing of particular utterances in discourse materials. The general goal is to expand the text beyond what is said to what is really meant. Expansion generally involves linking information of varying levels of abstraction. For example, there is often movement from more surface-level information (i.e., syntactic structure, propositional content, and paralinguistic and nonverbal cues) to information from past or future parts of the episode or episodes in which the utterance is embedded and, finally, to biographical and sociocultural information (e.g., discourse participants' role obligations in family relations).

Expansion is the crucial phase of analysis because it provides the basis for moving beyond actual speech to the identification of implicit or underlying propositions and eventually to a description of how interaction is accomplished in discourse. Expansion moves the analysis beyond isolated utterances and directly addresses the importance of context and hierarchical levels of abstraction. It will not be surprising to find that important work on discourse in the future contains some sort of expansion procedures.

There are several major strengths to Labov and Fanshel's methods of analysis. First, there is recognition of the need to work with naturally occurring discourse and to go beyond linguistic or turn-taking structure in the formulation of discourse rules. Labov and Fanshel argue that when researchers do not have specific knowledge of the context, they necessarily imagine it. As a result "the construction of such imagined context is an uncontrolled variable in the study, so that rules that appear to be quite general are, in fact, limited by those conditions that we necessarily construct unconsciously as we imagine how we would interpret the utterances in general" (Labov & Fanshel, 1977, p. 73). This recognition brings us to a second strength of Labov and Fanshel's model. Although the expansion process is open ended, Labov and Fanshel present their interpetations in such a way as to permit critical challenges from readers. Debates over interpretations of data are important because they can result in the expansion and refinement of discourse models and lead us toward more integrative approaches to discourse analysis.

The strengths of Labov and Fanshel's analysis far outweigh its weaknesses. There are, however, some problems in the application of the model. First, the wide scope of the model and the focus on multiple levels of abstraction does, at times, simplify the complexity of the linking of specific levels of information. For example, the articulation of text and paralinguistic cues is a complex process which often seems a bit too pat in Labov and Fanshel's analysis. The use of photographs of diplays produced by a spectrum analyzer is technically impressive and helps readers assimilate and interpret the paralinguistic information. However, the display has limitations that Labov and Fanshel acknowledge, and the authors also note that "assignment of semantic values to the paralinguistic cues is one of the more problematic and less objective parts of this analysis" (1977, p. 356).

A second problem in Labov and Fanshel's analysis is more serious. Although the analysis involves a recognition of the importance of hierarchical levels of information, the quality of the data beyond the discourse materials is suspect in two respects. First, when Labov and Fanshel go beyond the text and paralinguistic cues to consider information from past or future parts of episodes in which the text is embedded, they rely primarily on their own interpretations and (to an unspecified degree) the therapist's reactions to playbacks of the materials. In a general sense, the grounding of interpretations (or expansions) of specific utterances or exchanges in broader contextual data is a form of Cicourel's indefinite triangulation. However, in Labov and Fanshel's analysis neither the patient nor important members of her family is consulted.

This problem regarding the quality and depth of background data is also apparent when Labov and Fanshel reach out to more abstract information like notions of status and role. In drawing out this type of information, Labov and Fanshel rely on the patient's references to her family relations in the therapeutic interview and what Cicourel (1980) referred to as 'idealized' conceptions of role, a term borrowed from Goffman (1961, 1967). What is missing are additional ethnographic observations of the patient's family and their daily interactions. As Cicourel (1980) suggests, if analysis of discourse materials requires that the researcher reach out to higher levels of information like notions of status and role, then the researcher must worry about the empirical status of such concepts.

These limitations of Labov and Fanshel's analysis aside, their model has important implications for sociological theory and methodology. Regarding the latter, it has long been argued (see especially Cicourel, 1964) that traditional sociological research methods (survey, interview, and field observation) are based on implicit theories of language and communication. Labov and Fanshel's work (especially their use of expansion) could be an important aid for explicitly documenting and accommodating the role of language in the collection and analysis of sociological data. For example, the pretesting of survey items and interview schedules could benefit immensely from the application of some form of expansion analysis. Specifically, such a procedure could involve the expansion of audiotaped discussions with a subsample of respondents concerning their understanding of survey items.

Of even more interest are the theoretical implications of Labov and Fanshel's model for sociology. At the social psychological level many theoretical orientations (social exchange, attribution, and role theory among others) focus on why social actors behave the way they do with few references to how social interaction is accomplished. These theoretical approaches have obvious import, but we must also directly investigate how social order is produced. Labov and Fanshel's model could be useful in two ways. First, it can be employed to develop an understanding of how abstract concepts like self esteem and distributive justice are articulated with contextual features of real-life interactive settings. Second, once the expansion model uncovers propositions (recurrent communications), they could then be compared to the general assumptions and predictions of the various theoretical perspectives.

At the broader level, studies of discourse processes within organizations and institutions could lead to the identification of stable features of social structure. For example, the use of the expansion model could isolate underlying propositions in organizational decision making. These propositions could then be compared to official policy statements of organizational goals. In short, Labov and Fanshel's model has important implications for sociological research. One can only hope that sociologists' interest in and knowledge of the study of discourse will increase in the coming years to the point at which we can take advantage of these developments.

CONVERSATIONAL INFERENCE

According to Gumperz (1978b), conversational inference "is the 'situated' or context-bound process of interpretation, by means of which participants in a conversation assess others' intentions, and on which they base their responses" (p. 1). Like other models of discourse produced since the 1970s, Gumperz' notion of conversational inference is based on the assumption that individuals must articulate multiple levels of information in order to participate in discourse events. Gumperz has referred to the linking of various types and levels of information as a process of contextualization, which builds on the speaker's and hearer's ability to associate certain kinds of linguistic contextualization cues with propositional content on the one hand and with extralinguistic cues and background expectations on the other (Cook-Gumperz & Gumperz, 1976).

According to Gumperz (1978b), the term 'contextualization cue' refers to any aspect of the surface form of utterances which, when mapped onto message content, can be shown to be functional in the signaling of interpretive frames. Although most of the contextualization cues Gumperz (1978a, 1978b) refers to in his work are prosodic (e.g., intonation and stress) and paralinguistic (pitch, register, rhythm, loudness, etc.), many other signaling mechanisms of surface structure, such as lexical or phonological choice, use of formulaic expressions (e.g., greetings, interjections), and code switching, can function as contextualization cues.

Gumperz' analysis is similar to Labov and Fanshel's linking of text and paralinguistic cues and Cicourel's argument that autonomous rules must be articulated with local features of interactive settings. However, Gumperz takes the argument a step further. Gumperz notes that the linking of paralinguistic cues and propositional content is adequate for the interpretation of specific sentences or interactive scenes, but he argues that there is a need for a broader semantic concept that can account for thematic connections between elements of one of several scenes. Gumperz calls this semantic concept 'speech activities' (Cook-Gumperz, 1977).

Gumperz (1978b) characterizes speech activities with descriptive phrases like "discussing politics," "chatting about the weather," and "lecturing about linguistics." Speech activities are not bounded entities that can be labeled but rather function as guidelines for interpretation. Gumperz suggests that these guidelines can be seen as coocurrence expectations regarding certain constellations of contextualization cues that interactants develop through interactive experience in various speech activities. From this perspective, discourse involves multiple levels of signaling. Participants first listen to speech and interpret specific utterances by noting the co-ocurrence of various contextualization cues. They then form a general hypothesis about what routine or speech activity is being enacted on a more abstract level and then finally rely on social background knowledge and on coocurrence expectations to evaluate what is intended over the course of a speech event. There is a striking similarity between Gumperz' ideas regarding levels of interpretation and Cicourel's discussion of Peirce's notion of 'abductive' reasoning. I have discussed the convergence of the two approaches in some detail in a previous paper (see Corsaro, 1981a). In this context I wish to consider two additional features of conversational inference and briefly discuss the implications of Gumperz' work for sociological research.

Building on work on gestural and kinesic signals of conversational cooperation (Erickson, 1975, 1976; Kendon, 1977), Gumperz expands his model by arguing that the signaling of speech activities is not a matter of unilateral action but rather of coordination between speaker and listener. Participants, by the verbal style in which they respond and the listenership cues that they produce, implicitly signal their agreement or disagreement. Once a conversational rhythm has been established in this way, Gumperz (1978b) proposes that a "principle of strategic consistency takes over" (p. 25). In line with this principle, "speakers continue in the same mode, assigning negotiated meaning to contextualization cues, until there is a perceptible break in rhythm, a shift of content and cues, or until a mismatch between content and cues suggests that something has gone wrong" (p. 25).

As noted earlier, Gumperz argues that cooccurence expectations are a reflection of interactive experience. We should expect then that speech activities are signaled by culturally specific linguistic cues and that the ability to maintain, control, and evaluate conversation is a function of communicative and ethnic background. Given these features of conversational inference, we should expect to find communicative problems or breakdowns in speech events involving participants of differing cultural or ethnic backgrounds. Gumperz (1978a, 1978b) provides insightful analyses of breakdowns and miscommunication in such instances and specifies the differential interpretation of contextualization cues that were the source of the problems.

In his work on miscommunication, Gumperz (1978a, 1978b) not only identifed variation in the interpretation of contextualization cues across ethnic groups, but he also discussed the more general social-organizational effects of such problems. Here the sociological implications of Gumperz' work for the areas of intergroup relations, complex organizations, and sociology of work and occupations is quite apparent. For example, Gumperz found that minority group members (West Indian men and Pakistani women) in London have encountered communicative problems in service occupations. Certain elements of the minority group members' conversational styles are often interpreted as rude and threatening by speakers of British English (see Gumperz, 1978b). Gumperz notes that, since these minority group members are of a lower socioeconomic status, they have a hard time obtaining and keeping service jobs due to these communicative problems. Work such as Gumperz', when combined with more extensive ethnography in occupational settings, could result in useful changes in organizational policy and decision making regarding personnel issues of this type.

CONCLUSION

I have reviewed several theoretical models of discourse analysis. Although the models differ in a number of respects, the differences are primarily ones of emphasis. Indeed, there is general convergence in the models around three major points. First, all the models stress the importance of studying discourse in natural settings. As a result, the researchers (especially Sacks and Schegloff, Cicourel, Gumperz, and Labov and Fanshel) have all made important contributions regarding techniques for the collection, organization, and transcription of discourse materials. Their research has demonstrated that rich, detailed, and naturally occurring discourse events can be audio (and even video) taped with minimal disruption or obtrusion. Second, all the models stress the importance of social context and participants' abilities not only to adapt to but also to create and transform contextual features of discourse events. Third, the majority of the models reviewed emphasize the importance of multiple levels of information processing. The only possible exception is Sacks and Schegloff's turn-taking model; however, the emphasis on multiple levels of information is clearly evident in Sacks' work on social descriptions and practical reasoning. But even regarding turn taking, Sacks and Schegloff do not deny the importance of background information or the content of discourse events; rather they choose to identify context-free features of turn-taking systems before addressing other elements of discourse.

In addition to specifying theoretical aspects of the models, I have also discussed methodological issues and strategies in the study of discourse. Cicourel's work is the most important in this regard. In fact, Cicourel's recommendations regarding the importance of embedding discourse materials in extensive ethnography, producing chronologies of decision making in the research process, and collecting and analyzing information at several levels of abstraction can be seen as a major sociological contribution to discourse research. Although most sociologists have yet to appreciate the implications of discourse, they are well aware of the need to account for sources of variation in social-psychological and organizational processes as well as the value of comparative research. As more sociologists become involved in research studies of discourse processes, they will make important methodological contributions in terms of both data collection and analysis.

Finally, regarding directions for future research, there are a number of areas in sociology where the study of discourse could have almost immediate theoretical impact. The work of Gumperz (1978a, 1978b) and Erickson and Shultz (1981) demonstrates that subtle differences in communicative styles across ethnic and racial groups can have important effects on occupational mobility. Research of this type in other organizational settings, especially regarding different types of gatekeeping encounters, could provide important findings regarding the effects of social-class background on processing of individual cases and policy formation in social welfare, medical, and criminal justice organizations. To date (see Corsaro, 1981a) there has been much more research on discourse processes in childhood socialization and educational processes than in other substantive areas. Accordingly, there is a need for more basic descriptive studies of discourse processes in areas such as adult socialization and aging, and in legal, occupational, criminal justice, bureaucratic, and business organizations. There is now also a developing need for contrastive research on discourse and learning in multiple settings within and outside the school (e.g., the home, community, peer group; see Mehan, 1979). In addition, there is a need for comparative studies of discourse processes in childhood socialization across age groups, settings, and social class groups. As I mentioned earlier, sociologists may have much to offer in the design and accomplishment of comparative research of this type. It is my hope that a growing number of sociologists will become aware of the importance of work on discourse processes and eventually become major contributors to this highly significant area of research.

190 William A. Corsaro

REFERENCES

Bateson, G. (1972). *Steps to an ecology of the mind.* New York: Ballantine.
Chomsky, N. (1965). *Aspects of the theory of syntax.* Cambridge, MA: M.I.T. Press.
Chomsky, N. (1977). *Language and responsibility.* New York: Pantheon.
Cicourel, A. (1964). *Method and measurement in sociology.* New York: Free Press.
Cicourel, A. (1968). *The social organization of juvenile justice.* New York: Wiley.
Cicourel, A. (1974a). *Cognitive sociology.* New York: Free Press.
Cicourel, A. (1974b). Interviewing and memory. In C. Cherry (Ed.), *Pragmatic aspects of communication.* Dordrecht: Reidel.
Cicourel, A. (1975a, September–December). Discourse and text: Cognitive and linguistic processes in studies of social structure. *Versus: Quaderni di Studi Semiotici,* 33–84.
Cicourel, A. (1975b). *Theory and method in the study of Argentine fertility.* New York: Wiley.
Cicourel, A. (1978). Language and society: Cognitive, cultural and linguistic aspects of language use. In *Sozialwissenschaftliche Annalen,* Band 2, Seite B25–B28. Vienna: Physica.
Cicourel, A. (1980). Three models of discourse analysis: The role of social structure. *Discourse Processes, 3,* 101–132.
Cicourel, A. (1981). Discourse, autonomous grammars, and contextualized processing of information. In *Proceedings of a Conference on the Analysis of Discourse.* Institut fur Kammunikationsforschung und Phonetik, University of Bonn, Germany.
Cicourel, A., Jennings, S., Jennings, K., Leiter, K., Mackay, R., Mehan, H., & Roth, D. (1974). *Language use and school performance.* New York: Academic Press.
Cicourel, A., & Kitsuse, J. (1963). *The educational decision makers.* Indianapolis: Bobbs-Merrill.
Cook-Gumperz, J. (1977). Situated instruction: Language socialization of school age children. In S. Ervin-Tripp & C. Mitchell-Kernan (Eds.), *Child Discourse.* (pp. 103–121). New York: Academic Press.
Cook-Gumperz, J., & Gumperz, J. (1976). Context in children's speech. In J. Cook-Gumperz (Eds.), *Papers on language and context* (Working Paper No. 46). Berkeley: University of California, Language Behavior Research Laboratory.
Corsaro, W. (1979). 'We're friends, right?': Children's use of access rituals in a nursery school. *Language in Society, 8,* 315–336.
Corsaro, W. (1981a). Communicative processes in studies of social organization: Sociological approaches to discourse analysis. *Text, 1,* 5–63.
Corsaro, W. (1981b). Entering the child's world: Strategies for field entry and data collection in preschool settings. In J. Green & C. Wallat (Eds.), *Ethnography and language in educational settings* (pp. 117–146). Norwood, NJ: Ablex.
Corsaro, W. (1982). Something old and something new: The importance of prior ethnography in the collection and analysis of audiovisual data. *Sociological Methods and Research, 11,* 145–166.
Drass, K. (1981). The social organization of mid-level provider-patient encounters. Unpublished doctoral dissertation, Indiana University, Bloomington, IN.
Duncan, S. (1974). On the structure of speaker–auditor interaction during speaker turns. *Language in Society, 3,* 161–180.
Erickson, F. (1975). Gatekeeping and the melting pot: Interaction in counseling encounters. *Harvard Educational Review, 45,* 44–70.
Erickson, F. (1976). Gatekeeping interaction: A social selection process. In P. Sanday (Ed.), *Anthropology and the public interest: Fieldwork and theory* (pp. 111–145). New York: Academic Press.

Erickson, F. & Shultz, J. (1981). *Talking to the man: Social and cultural organization of communication in counseling interviews.* New York: Academic Press.

Ferguson, C. (1976). The structure and use of politeness formulas. *Language in Society, 5,* 137–151.

Garfinkel, H. (1967). *Studies in ethnomethodology.* New York: Prentice-Hall.

Goffman, E. (1959). *The presentation of self in everyday life.* New York: Doubleday.

Goffman, E. (1961). *Encounters: Two studies in the sociology of interaction.* Indianapolis: Bobbs-Merrill.

Goffman, E. (1963). *Behavior in public places: Notes on the social organization of gatherings.* Glencoe, IL: The Free Press of Glencoe.

Goffman, E. (1967). *Interaction ritual: Essays on face-to-face behavior.* Garden City, NY: Doubleday.

Goffman, E. (1971). *Relations in public: Microstudies of the public order.* New York: Basic Books.

Goffman, E. (1974). *Frame analysis.* New York: Harper & Row.

Goffman, E. (1976). Replies and responses. *Language in Society, 5,* 257–313.

Grice, H. (1975). Logic and conversation. In P. Cole & J. Morgan (Eds.), *Syntax and Semantics* (Vol. 1) (pp. 41–58). New York: Academic Press.

Grimshaw, A. (1979). What's been done—when all's been said? Review symposium on William Labov and David Fanshel, *Therapeutic discourse: Psychotherapy as conversation. Contemporary Sociology, 8,* 170–176.

Gumperz, J. (1976). Language, communication and public negotiation. In P. Sanday (Ed.), *Anthropology and the public interest: Fieldwork and theory* (pp. 273–292). New York: Academic Press.

Gumperz, J. (1978a). Dialect and conversational inference in urban communication. *Language in Society, 7,* 393–409.

Gumperz, J. (1978b). Sociocultural knowledge in conversational inference. To be published in the *28th Annual Round Table Monograph Series on Language and Linguistics.* Washington, DC: Georgetown University Press.

Hymes, D. (1972). Models of the interaction of language and social life. In J. Gumperz & D. Hymes (Eds.), *Directions in sociolinguistics* (pp. 35–71). New York: Holt, Rinehart & Winston.

Hymes, D. (1978). *What is ethnography?* (Sociolinguistic Working Paper No. 45). Austin, TX: Southwest Educational Development Laboratory.

Jefferson, G. (1972). Side sequences. In D. Sudnow (Ed.), *Studies in social interaction* (pp. 294–338). New York: Free Press.

Jefferson, G. (1975). Error correction as an interactional resource. *Language in Society, 3,* 181–199.

Johnson, J. (1975). *Doing field research.* New York: Free Press.

Kendon, A. (1977). *Studies in the behavior of face-to-face interaction.* Lisse, Netherlands: Peter De Ridder Press.

Labov, W., & Fanshel, D. (1977). *Therapeutic discourse: Psychotherapy as conversation.* New York: Academic Press.

Mehan, H. (1979). *Learning lessons: Social organization in the classroom.* Cambridge, MA: Harvard University Press.

Mehan, H., & Wood, H. (1975). *The reality of ethnomethodology.* New York: Wiley.

Phillips, S. (1977). Some sources of cultural variability in the regulation of talk. *Language in Society, 5,* 81–95.

Rumelhart, D. (1975). Notes on a schema for stories. In D. Bobrow & A. Collins (Eds.), *Representation and understanding: Studies in cognitive science* (pp. 211–236). New York: Academic Press.

Rumelhart, D. (1978). Understanding and summarizing brief stories. In D. La Berge & S. Sammuels (Eds.), *Basic processes in reading: Perception and comprehension* (pp. 265–304). Hillsdale, NJ: Erlbaum.

Rumelhart, D. (1981). Toward an interactive model of reading. Paper presented at Attention and Performance VI International Symposium, Stockholm, Sweden.

Sacks, H. (1972). On the analyzability of stories by children. In J. Gumperz & D. Hymes (Eds.), *Directions in sociolinguistics* (pp. 329–345). New York: Holt, Rinehart and Winston.

Sacks, H. (1973). On some puns with some intimations. In R. Shuy (Ed.), *23rd Annual Round Table, Sociolinguistics: Current Trends and Prospects* (pp. 135–144). Washington, DC: Georgetown University Press.

Sacks, H. (1974). An analysis of the course of a joke's telling in conversation. In R. Baumann & J. Sherzer (Eds.), *Explorations in the ethnography of speaking* (pp. 337–353). Cambridge: Cambridge University Press.

Sacks, H. (1978). Some technical considerations of a dirty joke. In J. Schenkein (Ed.), *Studies in the organization of conversational interaction* (pp. 249–269). New York: Academic Press.

Sacks, H., Schegloff, E., & Jefferson, G. (1974). A simplest systematics for the organization of turn-taking in conversation. *Language, 50,* 696–735.

Schegloff, E. (1972). Sequencing in conversational openings. In J. Gumperz & D. Hymes (Eds.), *Directions in sociolinguistics* (pp. 346–380). New York: Holt, Rinehart and Winston.

Schegloff, E., Jefferson, G., & Sacks, H. (1977). The preference for self-correction in the organization of repair in conversation. *Language, 53,* 361–382.

Schegloff, E., & Sacks, H. (1974). Opening up closings. In R. Turner (Ed.), *Ethnomethodology: Selected readings* (pp. 233–264). London: Penguin.

Shenkein, J. (Ed.), (1978). *Studies in the organization of conversational interaction.* New York: Academic Press.

Schriffrin, D. (1977). Opening encounters. *American Sociological Review, 42,* 679–691.

Vandewater, S. (1981). *The social organization of group therapy sessions.* Unpublished doctoral dissertation, Indiana University, Bloomington, IN.

Youssouf, I., Grimshaw, A., & Bird, C. (1976). Greetings in the desert. *American Ethnologist, 3,* 797–824.

CHAPTER 8

Sociocultural Dimensions of Discourse

Alessandro Duranti

INTRODUCTION

Throughout the 1970s, an increasing number of linguists have been arguing that certain sentence phenomena—word order, tense and aspect marking, verbal agreement, nominal case marking, to mention only a few—can be better explained through a study of their use in discourse. This line of research characterizes both synchronic and diachronic studies (e.g., Dixon, 1972; Givón, 1976, 1979a, 1979b; Hopper, 1982; Hopper & Thompson, 1980; Sankoff & Brown, 1976). Even within autonomous theories of grammar, there have been some attempts at utilizing discourse notions—see, for instance, Chomsky's (1977) introduction of the node 'topic' in the phrase structure rules of a generative grammar.

Most of these studies, however, have tended to conceive of discourse from a strictly structural or psychological perspective and not from a broader sociocultural perspective. Thus, for instance, the notion of 'topic', a key concept in many early contributions to discourse analysis, has usually been defined by referring to the position that a certain nominal may take with respect to a certain predicate, namely, the tendency for topics to appear in sentence-initial position (e.g., Creider, 1979; Givón, 1976, 1979a; Hawkinson & Hyman, 1974; MacWhinney, 1977), or by introducing psychological notions such as memory, consciousness, center of attention, and involvement (Chafe, 1976, 1979, 1980; Clark & Haviland, 1977; Li & Thompson, 1976). While most of these studies discuss the relation of speaker to hearer, the relation is either textual or cognitive but not sociological. Speaker and hearer are related in terms of dimensions of information processing but not in terms of the social function that they carry out or in terms of their cooperative construction of reality.

HANDBOOK OF DISCOURSE ANALYSIS, Vol. 1
Disciplines of Discourse

The questions asked are often the following: Is the conveyed information shared or nonshared, old or new, conventionally or conversationally implicable for the participants engaged in a particular discourse?

Several studies on word order patterns have, however, shown that it is possible and, in fact, profitable, to look at the sequence of elements in actual utterances as the product of structural, perceptual, and social factors.[1] Schieffelin (1981) and Feld and Schieffelin (1981) have shown that in Kaluli, a non-Austronesian language of Papua New Guinea, there are two allowable word orders (in transitive sentences with three full constituents): OBJECT–SUBJECT–VERB (OSV) and SUBJECT–OB-JECT–VERB (SOV). On the basis of naturalistic data from household interaction, it is demonstrated that the choice between the two word order patterns is not only conditioned by which element is in focus, but also by the particular genre and speech act in which the utterance is produced. The word order OSV is preferred in making requests, teasing, and tattling, while SOV is preferred in reporting or announcing action and in narratives and stories. Duranti and Ochs (1979) have shown that in Italian (as spoken in Rome among friends and colleagues), word order is sensitive to sequential organization of turns in conversation (see also Sacks, Schegloff, & Jefferson, 1974). So-called left dislocations—nominals that appear to the left of their unmarked position with a pronominal copy in the same sentence—are often found in turn-initial position and seem to be used as a warrant for gaining access to the floor. This is particularly true in multiparty conversation and in the course of decision making, where there is disagreement or need for foregrounding an assessment. Thus, the following transcript of an advanced linguistic seminar at the University of Rome, in which ten people participated, is laced wih left dislocations. In this example, members of the seminar are discussing whether or not the verb *fuggire,* 'to escape', can take a sentential com-plement. At this point, Speaker V introduces the term *rifuggire.* Once introduced, it is repeated by Speakers L, R, and F as they try to gain access to the floor. The last turn containing *rifuggire* is a left dislocation—*rifuggire già ce l'abbiamo* 'rifuggire we already have it (in our list of verbs)'—and closes the discussion.

(1)

    A: (. . .) *"fuggire da:l far qualcosa"*   *non mi sembra*
          escape from doing something   not to-me seems

---

[1] An integrated and interdisciplinary approach to the study of discourse has been proposed by researchers with fairly different interests and backgrounds, for example, Duranti and Ochs, 1979; Hymes, 1981; van Dijk, 1981.

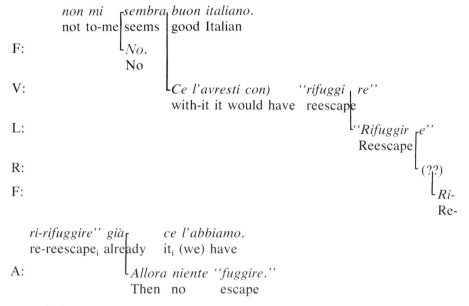

Translation

A: (. . .) "Fuggire dal far qualcosa" it doesn't seem good Italian.
F: No.
V: (You could do it with) "rifuggire".
L: "Rifuggire."
R: (??)
F: "Ri-ri-rifuggire" we already have it.
A: Then "fuggire" should be left out.

The relevance of social context of the type illustrated above is part of a vast array of sociocultural dimensions that enter in the very definition of discourse. In this chapter, I examine some of these dimensions by framing my discussion within the goals and orientations of the ethnographic approach advocated by Gumperz and Hymes (1964, 1972). I thus consider discourse as it relates to and is constructed by particular aspects of social organization and speakers' cultural constructions of the world.

To better understand the theoretical and methodological foundations of a sociocultural study of discourse, we must place this orientation within the more general context of the study of verbal behavior as defined by social and cultural anthropologists.

Social and cultural anthropologists studying discourse have manifested two main concerns. The first one is a continuous effort to relate a given text to its context. This concern is well represented in the following excerpt from Turner's review of Calame-Griaule's (1965) study of the Dogons' theory of language.

> Unless we present texts in terms of the circumstances under which they were obtained, from whom they were taken, and the social and psychological characteristics of their narrators, we are in danger of selecting concordant features from disparate accounts and producing a logically satisfactory synthesis which would perhaps be unintelligible to most members of the indigenous culture. (Turner, 1974, p. 159)

We could summarize this attitude by saying that for an anthropological study of discourse, one needs something more than texts. One needs an ethnography of discourse.

The second concern is the need for a characterization of speech not simply as a tool for describing the world but also as a tool for changing the world. In its most extreme formulation, this view goes back to Malinowski's concept of "language as an instrument of action," which he had first defined as characteristic of "primitive languages" as opposed to "civilized" ones (Malinowski, 1923) but later accepted as typical of language in general (Malinowski, 1935.)[2] The latter view is what we might call the pragmatic view of language. Such a view is currently reflected in sociolinguistics, which has distinguished itself from mainstream structural linguistics[3] by not favoring the so-called referential (or descriptive) uses of language over its social ones (see Halliday, 1973; Hymes, 1974; Myers & Brenneis, 1984; Romaine, 1981; Silverstein, 1976b, 1977). To make propositions about the world—what is usually called the referential or descriptive function of language—is seen by sociolinguists as only one of the many functions of speech and not necessarily the one through which other aspects of speech—the social ones—can be defined or explained.

The interaction between these two concerns, for a truly ethnographic study of discourse and for an explicit consideration of a wide range of functions realized by speech, has been often recognized by social and cultural anthropologists. We owe in fact to Malinowski, the father of modern ethnography, the notion of 'context of situation' (Malinowski, 1923) through which to understand the pragmatic uses of speech. This notion was later echoed by Hymes' (1964; 1972a) notion of speech event. Furthermore, symbolic forms have often been described as affecting

---

[2] The recognition of Malinowski's role in drawing attention to the pragmatic functions of language does not imply an acceptance of his (at times) extremely behavioristic concept of meaning. For a criticism of Malinowski's theory of meaning, see Henson, 1974; Pignato, 1981; and Sahlins, 1976. With the exception of the British linguist J. R. Firth, Malinowski had no followers among linguists (Hymes, 1964b; Lyons, 1966, 1977).

[3] For the purpose of this discussion, I am adopting Lepschy's (1970) view of generative grammar as a continuation of what is traditionally called "structural linguistics."

people's perception of the world, their behavior, and their very sense of social structure (Bernstein 1971; Cook-Gumperz, 1975; Dolgin, Kemnitzer, & Schneider, 1977; Lévi-Strauss, 1963, ch. 10; Whorf, 1956).

A Bridge

The absence of explicit and broader sociocultural concerns typical of most linguists' analyses of discourse becomes problematic if we are interested in a discourse grammar that would be something more than sentence grammar one step further (or higher) but would instead lead the way toward a communicative grammar that relates discourse as a linguistic structure and discourse as a social process. At the same time, many anthropologists do not seem interested in exploiting the potential richness of detailed linguistic analysis and thus fail to integrate their ethnographic knowledge with the linguists' knowledge and expertise in analyzing structural patterns of discourse. Anyone who starts from speech and tries to reach out to social context knows that it is a long and hazardous road; the more one gets involved in social interaction and cultural values the more difficult it becomes to look at the linguistic system as a separate code. One of Goffman's (1964) metaphors well illustrates these difficulties. He compared becoming interested in social context to crossing a bridge: When one gets to the other side, one often finds himself too busy to want to go back. It is essential, however, to have someone running back and forth across the bridge. It is important to try to maintain a link between discourse form and social conduct, between language and other symbolic systems, between Chomsky's ideal speaker–hearer and the actual members of a speech community. Those involved in the analysis of discourse seem ideal candidates for such an important role in interdisciplinary osmosis.

The question remains of how to provide a context for such interaction among different aspects and different approaches to the study of discourse. To accomplish such a task, the student of discourse must have access to units of analysis that would allow for different kinds of data (viz., linguistic expressions, social beliefs, social organization) to be integrated in a coherent and meaningful way. Whereas structural linguistics abounds in analytic categories (as well as in theoretical models), it has been difficult to establish useful and easily identifiable units for language use in social life. The task becomes even harder when we want to be able to move in and out of texts, not only to relate the parts (e.g., sentences, paragraphs) to each other but also to relate the text to its sociocultural context (e.g., its purposes, the invoked norms of interpretation, and social identities of the participants).

I suggest that, as a way of integrating linguistic, textual, and further sociocultural knowledge, we follow Hymes' (1964a) idea of starting from speech events. I will thus discuss some of the basic issues and concerns for a sociocultural study of discourse, relying on Hymes' (1972a) SPEAK-ING model. Though it is not supported by a theory of verbal interaction, such a model indicates some basic prerequisites of a theory of language use that aims at integrating and comparing, across societies, the different levels of linguistic and broader sociocultural knowledge employed by speakers in the construction, use, and interpretation of discourse units in daily social interaction.

The rest of this chapter is organized in the following way: In the next section I briefly outline Hymes' original program for an ethnographic study of language use and introduce the concept of speech event. I then discuss the basic components of a speech event and review some of the most salient contributions to an understanding of the sociocultural dimensions of discourse form and content. Finally, I draw some conclusions about possible directions for future research.

THE ETHNOGRAPHIC PERSPECTIVE

Before discussing the notion of 'speech event', it is necessary to outline the basic theoretical and methodological concerns of the ethnographic approach as originally defined by Hymes.

Trying to integrate the tools and goals of several disciplines, including cultural anthropology, linguistics, and literary criticism, Hymes (1962) called for an ethnography of speaking—later (Hymes, 1964a) to become an ethnography of communication:

> such an approach cannot simply take separate results from linguistics, psychology, sociology, ethnology, as given and seek to correlate them, however partially useful such work is. It must call attention to the need for fresh kinds of data, to the need to investigate directly the use of language in contexts of situations so as to discern patterns proper to speech activity, patterns which escape separate studies of grammar, of personality, of religion, of kinship and the like, each abstracting from the patterning of speech activity as such into some other frame of reference. . . . such an approach cannot take linguistic form, a given code, or speech itself, as frame of reference. It must take as context a community, investigating its communicative habits as a whole, so that any given use of channel and code takes its place as but part of the resources upon which the members of the community draw. (Hymes, 1964, pp. 2–3).

For Hymes, speech must be examined within the larger frame of reference of communication, which in turn, must be described through ethnography. As pointed out by Agar (1980), ethnography is an ambiguous term. It can refer to a process (viz., doing ethnography) or to a product (viz., an ethnography of certain people). As a process, ethnography traditionally involves a number of techniques for the description of a culture from the point of view of its members (Goodenough, 1964; Malinowski, 1922; Spradley, 1980). As a product, an ethnography is usually a monograph that covers many different aspects of the social life of a particular group. To say that the study of language must come under the more general goal of an ethnography of ways of speaking in a given speech community means at least two things: (1) One must use ethnographic techniques, for example, participant observation, interviews with the participants about norms and expectations about the use of speech, extensive recording of people's verbal activities across a number of different situations, transcription *in situ* of the recorded material with the assistance of members of the community able to understand the particular way of speaking used by the participants, (2) One has ethnographic concerns for the description of the form and content of verbal interaction. The latter involves, among other things, a concern for the way in which the participants themselves see their actions as well as for a culture-specific definition of the activities or some of their aspects (viz., ways of speaking) being studied (Agar, 1975; Basso, 1979; Fitzgerald, 1975; Mandelbaum, 1949; Myers, 1982).

Ethnographic concerns imply a different object of study from what is traditionally defined by mainstream linguistic theory. The field of ethnography of communication or ethnography of speaking (Bauman & Sherzer, 1974, 1975; Gumperz & Hymes, 1964, 1972; Hymes, 1974; Saville-Troike, 1982) has represented an attempt at defining a different object of inquiry along the lines suggested by Hymes (1962, 1964a). This enterprise has been succinctly characterized by Bauman and Sherzer:

> Grammars deal essentially with the structure of languages as abstract and self-contained codes, ethnographies with the patterns and structures of sociocultural life. There is much to be learned through correlation or conflation of these differentially focused products of linguistic and anthropological inquiry, but the ethnography of speaking centers its attention upon an entirely new order of information, bridging the gap between what is conventionally found in grammars on the one hand and ethnographies on the other: its subject matter is speaking, the use of language in the conduct of social life. (1975, pp. 95–96).

As Hymes wrote in reacting to Chomsky's (1965) definition of competence, a theory of language, as it is used by normal people in their daily lives, must go beyond the mere description of grammatical sentences:

> We have . . . to account for the fact that a normal child acquires knowledge of sentences, not only as grammatical, but also as appropriate. He or she acquires competence as to when to speak, when not, and as to what to talk about with whom, when, where, in what manner. In short, a child becomes able to accomplish

a repertoire of speech acts, to take part in speech events, and to evaluate their accomplishment by others. This competence, moreover, is integral with attitudes, values, and motivations concerning language, its features and uses, and integral with competence for, and attitudes toward, the interrelation of language with the other codes of communicative conduct (Hymes, 1972b, pp. 277–278)

It is this more sophisticated competence, that is, the ability to interpret and use language in socially and culturally appropriate ways, that Hymes has called 'communicative competence'[4] (see also Gumperz, 1981).

Within the ethnographic approach, the basic unit of analysis for the study of language use in a given speech community is the communicative event. The traditional trend of taking linguistic concepts to analyze social interaction or social structure is thus reversed[5] by adopting a social unit or, rather, a sociocultural construct, the event, as a unit for studying speech.

SPEECH SITUATIONS AND SPEECH EVENTS

An understanding of everyday language implies an understanding of the kinds of activities in which speech, in its various forms and contents,

---

[4] Hymes' definition of the scope of linguistics as the study of communicative competence is actually close to that of other linguists. Thus, for instance, Fillmore wrote "I take the subject matter of linguistics, in its grammatical, semantic and pragmatic subdivisions, to include the full catalogue of knowledge which the speakers of a language can be said to possess about the structure of the sentences of their language, and their knowledge about the appropriate use of these sentences. I take the special explanatory task of linguistics to be that of discovering the principles which underlie such knowledge" (1971: p. 1).

[5] For linguistics students it might be necessary to mention a few names and concepts to briefly illustrate the tremendous impact that linguistics has had on anthropology in the last 30 years or so. Pike's (1954) distinction between emic and etic, a dichotomy derived from the terms phonemic and phonetic, soon became a key word in American cultural anthropology, as attested by the rapid flourishing, in the 1960s and early 1970s, of the so-called ethnoscience or new ethnography, an approach to the study of cultural systems strongly influenced by linguistic terminology and techniques, above all componential analysis (Eastman, 1975; pp. 85–104; Langness, 1974, pp. 115–117; Tyler, 1969). Lévi-Strauss' debts to structural linguistics, mainly through Jakobson, are probably well known to almost everyone. A quotation from one of his early books, however, might well illustrate the supremacy of linguistics over anthropology, at least as perceived by one of the leading figures in contemporary social anthropology: "Although unquestionably one of the social sciences, linguistics has a very special place among them. It is not a social science just as the other, but that which has by far made the greatest progress; the only one, in fact, which can claim the name of science and which has succeeded, at one and the same time, in formulating a positive method and in knowing thoroughly the nature of the facts subject to its analysis" (Lévi-Strauss, 1964, p. 40).

is used by speakers in the context of daily interaction. A systematic ethnographic analysis of particular activities (Levinson, 1979) or communicative events (Hymes, 1964a) gives us an account of those features of communicative competence that are relevant for the study of discourse patterns in the conduct of social life.

Within the larger class of communicative events, Hymes (1972a) proposed to distinguish between speech situations and speech events.

Although there are many human activities in which speech occurs, only in a subclass of them does speech or, more specifically, the rules for verbal interaction define or constitute the interaction itself. In a class lecture, a trial, a Ph.D. defense, an interview, or a phone conversation, speech is crucial and the event would not be said to be taking place without it. Hymes calls this kind of event a 'speech event'. In many other cases, speech has a minor role, subordinate to other codes or forms of interaction. Hymes refers to the latter type of event as a 'speech situation'. Examples of speech situations are most sports events, a bikeride with a friend, going to the movies, and demonstrating in front of an embassy. Of course, there is a lot of variation, and speech can (and, in some cases, must) be used in all of these events, but speech does not define them. On the other hand, in such events as a class lecture, a trial, or an interview, talk must occur in order for the interaction to be considered an occurrence of such event types.

The distinction between speech situation and speech event can also be found within what might otherwise be viewed as the same event. Thus, one might want to distinguish between the speech situation 'train trip', which may or may not involve verbal interaction, and the specific speech events that might occur within such a situation, like, for instance, a conversation between passengers, the telling of a joke or story, the exchange of greetings at the beginning and end of the trip, or an exchange of compliments.

I propose eliminating the term 'speech situation' and using 'speech event' as a theoretical notion, referring to a perspective of analysis rather than to an inherent property of events. The perspective I am referring to is that of an analyst looking at a strip of social interaction from the point of view of the speech in it. This view may not be a new one. Gumperz' statement that "the speech event is to the analysis of verbal interaction what the sentence is to grammar" (Gumperz, 1972a, pp. 16–17) can be interpreted as meaning that speech events are abstract entities that exist only in the analyst's descriptive framework. They are, like sentences, types, not tokens (Lyons, 1972). This means that we should not expect to find speech events out there in the real world in the same way in which we should not expect to find sentences, or predicates, or adverbs in texts (we only find linguistic signs that can be classified in terms of such analytical notions). We do expect, however, to use the notion of speech event to make sense out of discourse patterns found in verbal interaction.

Given the ethnographic perspective adopted here, I assume that the event units identified by the analyst have a psychological reality for the actors (i.e., speakers) and are culturally recognized or recognizable units. How they can be recognized will be discussed below in the sections on ends and on spatiotemporal boundaries.

The notion of speech event presented here must be seen as an intended bridge between the macro- and the microlevels of sociocultural analysis. In the same vein, the order of things that I deal with represents in most part an intermediate level between the two poles of sociocultural order, namely, the modes of production, transaction, and exchange that characterize a particular society, and some particular processes of interpersonal communication, namely, daily verbal interaction. Social anthropologists would argue that it is important not to confuse "the surface forms manifest in a social universe at a particular historical moment with the structural principles that give rise to them" (Comaroff & Robert, 1981, p. 32). It is a basic goal of an ethnographic approach along the lines indicated in this chapter to try to make sense out of this complex, certainly problematic relationship. The speech event, discussed hereafter, seems a good candidate, although not necessarily the only one, for such an enterprise.

A SPEECH EVENT MODEL

On the basis of Jakobson's (1960) model of six constitutive factors in any speech event,[6] Hymes proposed, in successive versions (Hymes, 1962, 1964a, 1972a, 1974), a more extensive list of possible components of a speech event to be taken into consideration in analyzing language use. Such a list was originally conceived as an 'etic' grid, a tentative universal set of features that would provide a salient way of defining the interaction between language and sociocultural context. It was meant to allow for comparison within and across societies, leaving open to each ethnographer the task of making the original scheme into an 'emic' de-

---

[6] The original six factors or components are (1) addresser, (2) addressee, (3) message, (4) contact, (5) context, (6) code. To each of them corresponds a different function of language: (1) emotive, (2) conative, (3) poetic, (4) phatic, (5) referential, (6) metalingual. See Lyons (1977) for an historical account of the introduction of these notions in linguistics.

scription that would capture what was relevant to the participants in the event under discussion.[7]

A total of 16 components of speech events was grouped by Hymes into 8 main entries, to be remembered by using the word SPEAKING, as illustrated in the following scheme:

S	(situation)	1.	Setting
		2.	Scene
P	(participants)	3.	Speaker, or sender
		4.	Addressor
		5.	Hearer, or receiver, or audience
		6.	Addressee
E	(ends)	7.	Purposes—outcomes
		8.	Purposes—goals
A	(act sequence)	9.	Message form
		10.	Message content
K	(key)	11.	Key
I	(instrumentalities)	12.	Channel
		13.	Forms of speech
N	(norms)	14.	Norms of interaction
		15.	Norms of interpretation
G	(genres)	16.	Genres

As can be seen from the scheme, in making his descriptive framework more suitable for the complexity of daily verbal interaction, Hymes was forced to abandon the elegant one-to-one correspondence established by Jakobson between components of speech events and functions of language.

In my discussion of the speech event model, I rearrange and redefine some of the components listed above, using some recent contributions to a sociocultural understanding of discourse organization and discourse structure.

DEFINITION OF A SPEECH EVENT

The very characterization of one or more strips of social interaction as an event unit presupposes at least two things: (1) an understanding

---

[7] In fact, as pointed out by Philips (1977), researchers have usually assumed that their descriptions of speech events were done according to the native's point of view. Such an assumption, however, has not always been substantiated by the details of the descriptions.

of the type of activity of which the event is an instance, and (2) a spatiotemporal definition of the activity.

Ends

As pointed out by Levinson (1979), among others, to define a social activity we must have an understanding of its goals or ends (see also Castelfranchi & Parisi, 1980).

A distinction must be made, however, between the system's (or societal) goals (e.g., why does the system want me to use titles when I refer to or address certain people) and the actor's purposes (e.g., why do I address certain people using a title in some particular context?). Such a distinction is an old one in the social sciences. In sociology, the contrast between the study of the system's purposes as opposed to the actor's purposes can be epitomized by the contrast between a materialist perspective, that is, seeing the institutions working behind the backs of the actors (the so-called blind forces of society), and Weber's 'method of understanding' (*verstehen*), which was, at least in principle, to look at social actions and their functions in terms of the subjective intentions of the individuals who acted out those actions (see Gerth & Mills, 1946). In cultural anthropology, the most extreme trend in looking at the social and cultural patterns of a community from the perspective of an individual has been represented by the life history approach (Langness & Frank, 1981).

Whereas (British) functionalist anthropologists tended to pay more attention to the system's reasons for a given cultural phenomenon, failing thus to recognize a difference between functions and motives (Langness, 1974, p. 81), contemporary linguists, philosophers of language, and cognitive scientists have tended to couch their discussion of goal-oriented behavior in terms of the individual's goal(s), or, rather, his alleged intentions. Austin's performance analysis and Searle's speech acts theory are emblematic examples of this perspective.

Psycholinguists studying discourse (Castelfranchi & Parisi, 1980) and sociolinguists interested in how to define situation (Brown & Fraser, 1979) have followed a similar trend by adopting cybernetic models, like the 'hierachy of goals' proposed by Miller, Galanter and Pribram (1960). According to this model, a given task is seen as a set of different goals that are embedded in one another. The act of hitting a nail with a hammer is a subgoal of a higher goal, that of hammering the nail in the wall. The act of asking a question like *Do you have the time?* is seen as serving the higher goal of requesting information about the time.

When extended to naturally complex human interaction, however, the hierarchic model is likely to encounter several problems.

For one thing, the hierarchic model blurs the problematic but important distinction drawn by Searle (1965) between the actor's intentions in doing (in this case, with words) something and the conventional meaning of his actions and words. More generally, it is not clear how the hierarchy-of-goals model could recognize the same activity as having different goals according to whether we look at it from the perspective of the actors' interpretations and understanding of their own doings or we look at it from the standpoint of the social and cultural system in which the actors operate (unless we were to decide that, say, individual goals are always embedded in societal goals). In a hierarchy-of-goals model, multireadings are cooccurrent interpretations are possible only if hierarchically ordered. Thus 'talking to the receptionist' must be a subgoal with respect to the more global goal of 'seeing the doctor' (Brown & Fraser, 1979). But such a classification is not always as obvious as it looks. We can easily imagine someone falling in love with the receptionist and going to see the doctor in order to see the receptionist. In this case, we would want to differentiate between the particular goals of the actor and the conventional goal structure of the event 'going to the doctor', with respect to which 'seeing the receptionist' can still be seen as a subgoal of (or a condition for) 'seeing the doctor'. Other, more problematic cases can be found.

Finally, all the above mentioned approaches assume that someone's (either the actor's or the observer's) interpretations of certain actions and words will be not only unique but also constant over time. The latter assumption can be rejected on several grounds. Goodwin (1981), for instance, has shown that, in spontaneous conversational interaction, the illocutionary force of an utterance as projected by the speaker's words and intonation can change during the utterance itself. Thus, for instance, in one of the examples he discusses, when one of the participants realizes that the intended recipient of her utterance is not attending and, in fact, is already engaged in some other recognizable activity, she then modifies the illocutionary force of the on-going utterance to make it suitable to the new recipient. An original offer of information to someone who does not know the rules of a card game is changed into a request for verification from someone who already knows how to play (Goodwin, 1981, pp. 150–151). One could not simply say, however, that the speaker has completely changed her goal in the middle of her utterance—something that could still be handled by the hierarchy-of-goals approach. We must instead recognize that the speaker is reorienting her utterance to make it suitable for a new recipient while also maintaining its relevance for the original one.

A truly sociocultural perspective on goal-oriented behavior must handle the tension between verbal interaction as a cooperative achievement by all the participants and verbal interaction as social activity that can be understood only through the acceptance and interpretation of independent social norms and cultural expectations (Cicourel, 1974). Hymes' original distinction between societal goals and individual goals must then be preserved, although some refinements seem necessary.

Spatiotemporal Organization of an Event

The very definition of a speech event presupposes the possibility of determining when and where such an event takes place. Further, anyone who has ever looked at actual events from the point of view of the verbal interaction that goes on in them knows that the internal spatial and temporal organization of an event is always relevant to speaking patterns within the event (Philips, 1977; Yamamoto, 1979).

The two subcomponents 'setting' and 'scene' were introduced to deal with such temporal and spatial aspects of events. Both of them refer to the time and place of a verbal interaction, with setting capturing the actual physical circumstances of the interaction (e.g., at 10 o'clock in the morning, at the ticket counter of United Airlines at the L. A. airport), and scene referring to the psychological, culturally bound definition of the setting (e.g., buying a plane ticket for a business trip).

Although both the actors and the observers must assume the existence of some physical dimensions of an event, it should be clear that, by having to represent them through natural language and conventional ways of defining time and space, we are always very likely to end up with culturally bound descriptions. What is 'afternoon' for one culture, might be 'evening' for another; what could be described as 'the front door' by the member of one society might be described as 'the back door' by a member of another society. Finally, even within the same community, we might find differences according to whether, for instance, we take as a point of reference the common person's knowledge or the expert's knowledge.

Hymes' scene subcomponent can be integrated with what Goffman (1974) has called spatial and temporal boundaries, and the subcomponent setting with what I call "boundary markers." Such boundaries should be taken to be universal features of social events across societies, their existence (or psychological reality) being crucial for the participants to conduct themselves in the interaction and for the analysts to isolate the object of their inquiry (Philips, 1977).

Such boundaries should be defined from the perspective of the members of the society one is describing. Attention to boundaries and their conventional markers should help us provide accurate classifications of different types of events within and across societies.

Types of Boundaries and Boundary Markers

A few distinctions are necessary within the two general categories of temporal and spatial boundaries. First of all, we must distinguish between external and internal boundaries. External temporal boundaries refer to the beginning and ending of the event and correspond to Goffman's (1974, pp. 255–261) opening and closing temporal boundaries. Internal temporal boundaries I take to refer to potential division of the event into parts or episodes (Goffman instead reserves the same term for "time outs").

External spatial boundaries define the space within which the event takes place or, rather, the way in which participants perceive or represent to themselves spatial organization with respect to the outside. Spatial distinctions that participants make with respect to one another are defined by internal spatial boundaries. Thus, for instance, in the event 'class lecture', one would want to distinguish between the external spatial boundaries, corresponding to the boundaries of what is considered the classroom, outside of which there is no event 'class lecture' going on, and the internal spatial boundaries, such as the different areas allocated for the students to sit and the teachers to stand or sit or move around while they are talking.

Finally, one needs to distinguish between boundaries and boundary markers (with only the latter corresponding to what Goffman calls "brackets"). The distinction is meant to separate abstract, psychological, and cultural dimensions of experience (boundaries) from the overt, conventional ways of signaling the existence of such dimensions (boundary markers). In a class lecture, for example, one may say that the external spatial boundaries are conventionally marked by the walls of the room and the door or doorway (if the door is left open), and the internal spatial boundaries are usually marked by the teacher's desk area, the area in front of the blackboard, that is, the area not occupied by the students.

External temporal boundaries, that is, the beginning and closing of an interaction, are usually marked by conventional markers, which can be either verbal or nonverbal or a combination of the two. Thus, for instance, at many grocery stores in the United States, the cashier signals the beginning of the interaction with a particular customer through direct eye gaze and a conventional *Hi!* The interaction is concluded with a conventional *Have a nice day!* Any attempt by the customer to interact with the cashier outside of those boundaries runs the risk of being ignored.

The relation between spatial and temporal boundary markers is also important, given that, for instance, spatial positioning can be used to mark temporal boundaries and temporal boundaries can redefine spatial dimensions. Merritt (1980) discusses how, in service encounters, "the customer's entrance into the service area, and particularly his positioning himself at the service post, is the first step in the initiation of a service encounter." She further remarks that the use of spatial arrangement "is important to the overall structure of the service encounter and the continuities it preserves with respect to norms of social interaction generally" (p. 97).

An emblematic example of the culture-specific complexities of spatial and temporal arrangements in social interaction is provided by Frake's (1975) discussion of how to enter a Yakan house:

> Unlike our own culture, in which we have special settings for many kinds of events—classrooms for classes, churches for religious rites, law courts for litigation, concert halls for music—among the Yakan a single structure, the house, provides a setting for a great variety of social occasions. But a house, even a one-roomed Yakan house, is not just a space. It is a structured sequence of settings where social events are differentiated not only by the position in which they occur but also by the positions the actors have moved through to get there and the manner in which they have made those moves. (p. 37)

To move on from a descriptive grid toward an explanatory model, we must examine the possible correlates between boundaries and some specific discourse features.

First of all, the very idea of looking at speech events as discourse units defined by spatial and temporal boundaries allows for a new classification of events or, rather, event types. We should then look at the nature and content of boundary markers to see the extent to which participants use them to define or redefine their own interaction or, to ask with Goffman, "What's going on here?" Ritual events or formal events, for instance, might be characterized by highly elaborated and relatively long boundary markers (in some cases, the boundary markers might even be seen as events in themselves). More generally, events that are conceived of as different from other everyday activity, for example, sacred events, might need particularly elaborate external boundary markers. Thus, spatiotemporal demarcation or seclusion is typically used in ritual events for symbolizing differentiation from the ordinary or transition from one status to another (Durkheim, 1915; Leach, 1976; Turner, 1974; Van Gennep, 1909).

One might want to investigate the extent to which discourse patterns around as well as within boundary markers are different from the rest of the interaction. Thus, Schegloff and Sacks' (1973) study of telephone conversations suggest that speakers need more cooperative work to close than to open a conversation. In my own work on the Samoan *fono*—a political and judiciary assembly of title holders in a traditional village—I found that whereas the beginning of the event is sharply marked and highly predictable in its format and content, the end is less predictable and generally more open to negotiation. This asymmetry is reflected, at the discourse level, by the use of a well-defined oratorical speech genre at the beginning of the meeting and by a gradual return to more ordinary conversational style toward the end (Duranti, 1981). Irvine's (1974) discussion of Wolof greetings similarly suggests that the beginning salutation is more predictable and generally less open to individual variation than the rest of the interaction. The tendency for beginnings to be more predictable than endings appears to be characteristic across societies and certainly something worthwhile considering for further study.

Let us look now at some other dimensions of the speech event that seem relevant for the study of discourse within a sociocultural perspective.

Participants

As apparent in the scheme reproduced above, Hymes did not think that speaker and hearer would be sufficient for describing verbal interaction (as opposed to, say, speech). Consequently, the traditional speaker–hearer dyad was expanded into four categories of participants: speaker, addressor, hearer, addressee (see also Goffman, 1976).

In the social life of any speech community we can easily find instances of verbal interaction in which we need more than the two participants (speaker and hearer) to adequately describe what goes on. Let me illustrate this with a few examples.

In many societies, mothers often speak for young children. In middle-class American society, for instance, when an adult meets a friend with a child, it is considered appropriate to show interest in the child and engage in a brief conversation with him even if he is too little to talk. "What's your name?" people often ask while looking straight into a baby's eyes. At the point, the accompanying caregiver is expected to speak for the baby and answer the question. As described by Schieffelin (1979), among the Kaluli people of Mount Bosavi, in Papua New Guinea, speaking for a young child is a common type of activity in which mothers engage as a conscious way of teaching the child to speak and as a less-conscious strategy for directing older siblings to see infants as social beings with already developed identities, ideas, and intentions.

> Within a week or so after a child is born, the mother acts in ways that seem intended to involve the child . . . in dialogues and interactions not only with her but with others as well. Mothers hold the infant up, faced outward to other people, and while moving the child as if it were conversing with a third person, speak for the child in a special, high-pitched, nasalized register. (Schieffelin, 1979, p. 106)

In order to understand how such an interaction proceeds and how we can make sense of its linguistic features (e.g., the high pitch, the content of what is said), we must see the mother as only the speaker of the message and the baby as the addressor. Failing to recognize this interaction as one involving three participants—the speaker (the mother), the addressor (infant), and the addressee–hearer (usually an older sibling)—would impinge on our ability to describe what is going on and to relate this type of speech event to other aspects of Kaluli verbal behavior in particular and to their cultural system in general. Thus, for instance, the high pitch and the nasalized voice are used as keys (see below) to convey the metamessage that the mother is speaking for the baby; at the same time, the syntax and lexicon of the mother's utterances are not in baby talk (Ferguson, 1977), but are rather more like those of an older sibling (a three- or four-year-old). How can this be explained? First of all, we learn from Schieffelin that Kaluli speakers do not have baby talk as part of their repertoire; the absence of baby talk turns out to be not uncommon among the languages of the world (Ochs, 1982; Ochs & Schieffelin, 1982). Second, speaking somewhat like a three- or four-year old means to speak like the most common addressee of this kind of event, namely an older sibling. The imitation of some of the features of the addressee's speech is often used across languages to suggest and invoke solidarity as well as to improve understanding. It would also seem that in this case the mother uses this strategy as a way of establishing a bond between the two siblings.

Further examples of interactions in which one needs reference to a more complex network than the speaker–hearer dyad include talk to or from the dead (Feld, 1982; Keesing, 1979), spirit possessions (Schieffelin, 1981), and so-called mother-in-law (Dixon, 1972) or brother-in-law languages of Australia (Haviland, 1979a, 1979b), traditional oratory (see the papers in Block, 1975; Sherzer, 1974). In many societies, for instance, it is common to think of professional orators as speakers who often act on behalf of some higher-ranking individuals (e.g., chiefs). In such cases, like the Kaluli mother mentioned before, the orator is the speaker but not the addressor. A clear example of this kind of situation is offered by Firth's description of the selection of speakers at a Tikopia public assembly (*fono*):

> In general Tikopia chiefs do not orate or address public assemblies; they give instruction to their maru [the chief's main executive] to speak for them. They "hand over the speech" to their mouthpiece, and commonly are not even present at a fono where their orders are promulgated. (Firth, 1975, p. 35)

According to Firth, this procedure introduces a systematic ambiguity in the act of speaking and its possible consequences: the speachmaker cannot be held completely responsible for what he says and the chief avoids public face loss by not directly witnessing possible criticism or murmurs of dissent.

The identity of the hearer–receiver–audience also often needs to be parted. In political speeches in western societies, for instance, speakers often tell their supporters and sympathizers what is meant for their political opponents (e.g., answers to criticism from the opposition, clarification of earlier statements). Similarly, according to Brenneis (1980), in Indo-Fijian political speech performances, one must distinguish between primary and secondary audience:

> The primary audience is composed of the individuals or group at whom the performance is chiefly aimed, that is, those whom the performer hopes to influence directly. The secondary audience includes others who are present. It is not merely a residual category, however, as the secondary audience provides both evaluation and an element of control. The spectators limit and shape the performance. (p. 8)

All of the above examples show that there are speech events for which we need subtler distinctions than speaker–hearer. Despite the several cases cited above and the many more that could be found, it is still worthwhile considering whether the situation in which the speaker is the addressor and the hearer is the addressee should in fact be considered as the unmarked situation, and what kind of variation is found across events and societies. This is an aspect of verbal interaction that should be possible to relate to theories of personalities and of intentionality.

It is not uncommon, for instance, that even when there are some clear clues for the nonidentification of speaker with addressor (or that of hearer with addressee), some ambiguity still remains as to what extent the speaker is in fact also the addressor or as to what extent the hearer is in fact also an addressee. It is common to get angry at people who report bad news to us, and a fair amount of self-control and rationalization must be used not to see them as included in the party who sent the message. Although it seems fairly universal to see human beings as actors rather than as instruments (this is at least the case in the linguistic coding of agency across languages; see Silverstein, 1976a), cultures vary with respect to the extent to which an individual is, across situations, considered liable for his own actions.

Act Sequences

Under the heading 'act sequence', Hymes grouped two aspects of verbal interaction: 'message form' and 'message content'. Saville-Troike (1982, p. 137) suggested interpreting act sequences as separate from form and content and as referring to sequential aspects of communicative events, namely, turns in conversation. In my discussion, I follow her suggestion.

Conversational Interaction

Since the early 1970s a great deal of research has been carried out on several aspects of the sequential organization of turns in conversation. Such research has represented a real breakthrough in our understanding of the mechanisms used by speakers in sustaining a conversational interaction (Goodwin, 1981; Psathas, 1979; Sacks, Schegloff, & Jefferson, 1974; Schegloff, Jefferson, & Sacks, 1977; Schegloff & Sacks, 1973; Schenkein, 1978). At the same time, conversation analysts have claimed to assume no predetermined social structure and have focused instead exclusively on the emergent structure of patterns of interaction. This method gives us very good insights into the kind of work that language performs in interaction, but it avoids relating the details of conversational behavior to other aspects of the social organization in which conversationalists participate. As Hymes once put it,

> Admittedly, it is fascinating to discover the richness of speech, coming from a disciplinary background that has neglected it [sociology]; but it is a bit absurd to treat transcribed tapes of interaction as if they were the Dead Sea Scrolls. When a society is gone, we must glean all we can from texts that remain. . . . But . . . it is a bit absurd to invent an amateur philology to deal with the life outside one's door. (Hymes, 1974)

Conversation analysis describes speakers as people who display an ideology and a practice of interaction in which gaps, overlaps, and errors must be avoided, with a preference for self-monitoring and self-control over other-monitoring and other-control. One might ask to what extent this notion of 'self' is part of the analyst's ideology and to what extent it is part of the participants' ideology. From an ethnographic perspective, it is also crucial to ask whether the norms defined by conversation analysts can be considered universals of conversational interaction across societies or should be reframed as culture specific. Philips (1983), for instance, has argued that American Indians do not have exactly the same norms for turn-taking management that Anglos do:

> In everyday conversations the lesser extent of local management of topics is most apparent in Warm Springs Indians' responses to questions. While some questions are answered immediately, not all are. There does not seem to be the obligation that Anglos abide by to give some kind of response. Questions are often answered some time after they have been asked. There is accordingly less syntactic linking between a question and the utterance of the next speaker overall. (Philips, 1983, pp. 54–55)

Conversation analysis portrays overlapping in conversation as competitive (Sacks *et al.,* 1974). Brenneis (1982) has however suggested that overlaps in Fiji Indian gossip sessions should not necessarily be interpreted as jockeying for turns but rather as a strategy used to allow for a continuing flow of talk from speaker to speaker. We have here an example of something that, although similar from a structural or sequential point of view (both in English conversation and in Fiji Indian conversation overlaps are relatively rare and brief), turns out to be different in terms of its significance for the actors.

In Duranti and Ochs (1982), it is suggested that certain aspects of social structure may enter in the organization of other-correction or other-repair. In particular, we argued that in Samoan verbal interaction, across a number of different social contexts, there is a dispreference for higher-ranking parties to correct others. This aspect of verbal interaction seems consistent with the Samoan view of high-ranking individuals as the least mobile and generally emotionally distant participants. In fact, even in the village school, a student's mistake is usually not corrected by the teacher but by other students (prompted by the teacher).

Finally, another interesting case from a Polynesian society is represented by Besnier's (1982) study of the organization of repair in Tuvaluan informal conversation. Besnier points out that, in adult–adult interaction, despite the preference for self-initiation of repairs (Schegloff *et al.,* (1977), speakers often strategically invite the hearer's repair initiation as a way of adding drama and suspense, to stimulate the hearer's attention and involvement in the narrative, and, often, to emphasize the scandalous nature of what has been said (Besnier, 1982). Here are a couple of revealing examples:

(2)

    K: ((whisper)) *Ae (muimui) hoki naa   a   te- te:* ⌐ *((chuckle))*
              and follow   also there Foc the the |

    F: ((whisper, smiling))   L *A ai?*
                                             Foc who

(0.2)

K: ((high pitch)) *Afasene mo   Faaogaa.*
                  Afasene and Faaogaa

Translation:

K: And then comes along uh the- the- ((chuckle))
F: Who?
   (0.2)
K: Afasene and Faaogga!

(3)
→   A: *((fast)) A (ko) ou ta(a)gata ne olo ki te ulugaa fonu.*
              And Foc your men Pst go to the pair-of turtles

       (0.8)
→   L: *A   ai?*
          Foc who

       (0.2)

       A: *Haa   Teak(e). (0.1) Teake mo Filipo.*
          group Teake   Teake and Filipo

Translation

A: And they went to catch the two turtles.
   (0.8)
L: Who?
   (0.2)
A: Teake's group. (0.1) Teake and Filipo.

A sociocultural approach to the study of discourse invites precisely this kind of detailed and extensive recording and transcription of verbal interaction accompanied by a genuine understanding of the actors' goals and practices. To those who might object to the risks of rich interpretation, one should point out that often enough similar signs carry with them different meanings and what appears to be the same on a transcript need not be the same in people's intentions and evaluations. The analyst's involvement with interpretive procedures is dangerous but inevitable. The important point is to be aware of the risks, rather than hide under the cover of objective knowledge and observable (on a transcript) facts.

Message Form and Message Content

The stress that Hymes placed on form seemed more directed toward anthropologists than toward linguists, who have made their profession almost entirely coincide with the study of message forms. This is so true that even the early work of Labov, one of the most influential American sociolinguists, followed the structural linguists' trend by concentrating on the study of variable forms, that is, alternative ways of saying the "same thing" (Labov, 1969). We owe to Lavandera (1978) the first clear statement on the impossibility of extending such a study from phonological to syntactic variation. Lavandera's later work (1981, in press) demonstrated that perfect paraphrases exist only under very particular circumstances, if at all. In real life, change of form corresponds to change in the message being communicated. This means that a sociolinguistic study of discourse variants must rely on a study of the sociocultural contexts of speech in a given speech community. In normal social life, knowing what to say and knowing how to say it are intimately related (Hymes, 1972a, p. 59).

One could ideally interpret form as comprising everything one might want to read on a transcript of a given speech event. Such a definition, however, would not recognize that syntagmatic relationships (among the linguistic signs of a given text) are only a very small part of what one needs to know in order to move from form to content, the rest being embodied in the paradigmatic relationships between the existing (i.e., uttered) signs and their possible and impossible alternatives. For this reason, it is important to be aware of the need to always document a series of events, so that our reading of any transcript can be supplemented by the knowledge of a range of possible realizations and acceptable variants.

Content is even more problematic to define given that different disciplines, or even different orientations within the same discipline, can vary tremendously in their assessment of the content of a given sequence. Anyone who has ever participated in interdisciplinary seminars that involved reading a transcript should know this very well. Usually, in such settings, when the linguists think that they have said all there is to say about the content of some sequence, it is time for the cultural anthropologists to come in and start over. Some of the differences of opinion about what is being communicated might be intimately related to the problem of defining what the data are. An ethnographic approach does not define a priori what to study or where to terminate cultural analysis. Cultural interpretation is an inherently endless project (Geertz, 1973)— which, by the way, does not mean that generalizations cannot be made— and to stop in the middle of it is a conventional and often useful way of making our latest observations and speculations available to the scrutiny of others who are engaged in similar enterprises.

Key

In the course of social interaction, participants continuously offer each other cues as to how to interpret what follows or what is being communicated. The manner in which to perform or interpret speech is called "key." A change in volume, voice quality, intonation contour, dialect, and language being used are only some of the many key signals that are commonly employed to let others know that what we are saying should be interpreted literally, ironically, seriously, or playfully (see Gumperz' [1977, 1981] notion of 'contextualization cue'). Many nonverbal devices are also available to the participants in any speech event to confirm or change an existing key (Bateson, 1955; Goffman, 1974, Ch. 3; Hymes, 1972a, p. 62).

Key signals can be simple ones (e.g., sudden change of volume, overt clearing of the throat) or complex ones, (e.g., an opening speech may set the tone of an entire event, often by telling people whether they should enjoy themselves, express some serious concern, or be angry at some persons or institutions). Generally, complex key signals tend to occur at the external temporal and spatial boundaries of an event. More often they occur at the beginning, given that participants usually dislike ambiguity. A posteriori redefinitions of what just happened are possible (e.g., *I was joking*) but are relatively rare and potentially problematic.

There are several sentential phenomena ordinarily studied by linguistics that can be considered as keying devices. One of them is sentential stress, and, more generally, the devices used in languages to mark focus or new information. Another typical class of keys is constituted by so-called paralinguistic features, for example, whispery, breathy, husky voice, or laughing, giggling, crying while speaking (Crystal, 1969; Crystal & Davy, 1969). All these features tend to be classified by linguists as superimposed on other, more basic structures. And intuitively, this seems consistent with the idea of key signals as metamessages or framing devices (Bateson, 1955).

Instrumentalities

This component is divided into 'channels' and 'forms of speech'. Channel refers to the medium of transmission of speech (e.g., oral, written, telegraphic). It is important for a sociocultural study of discourse to consider the relationship between the channel being used and the form, uses, and content of verbal communication. It has become evident to researchers coming from different disciplines that channel and form of speech are closely related. Thus, for instance, the acquisition of literacy involves not simply a new medium for communicating (i.e., writing), but also a different form or style of communication as well as a different cultural concept of self and achievement (Cook-Gumperz & Gumperz, 1981; Duranti & Ochs, in press; Heath, 1981, 1982; Scollon & Scollon,

1981; Scribner & Cole, 1981). The appropriate patterns for the construction of a written text, once introduced, are not simply confined to the written language; they can influence and govern modes of oral communication as well. This discovery has consequences for the comparative study of discourse patterns across societies. Among other things, the researcher must be aware of the particular range of linguistic resources in any given community—what Gumperz (1964) calls repertoire—before assessing the social meaning as well as the appropriateness of a given discourse register to a given situation. This means, for instance, that one must be careful in using such concepts as 'formal' or 'informal' register without taking into consideration the entire repertoire of a speech community and the culture-specific meaning of particular choices within that repertoire. Thus, for instance, in traditional Samoan communities, the phonological register that characterizes writing is also used in certain formal settings such as classroom interaction and church services, but it is not used in the highly ritualized, oratorical speeches performed in the formal meetings of the village council (*fono*), where the same phonological register of casual household interaction is instead found (Duranti, 1981). Shore (1982) has suggested that the dichotomy between the two registers must be understood as an "opposition of Samoan culture as a whole with the introduced European sector of Samoan institutions, particularly those institutions related to technology and the Church" (p. 281). In Samoa, if one were to consider only, say, writing, family interaction, school instruction, and church services, one would miss this important aspect of the association of the writing register with western-related activities but not with traditional formal activities.

The potentially dynamic relationship between different registers must also be addressed. An ethnographic approach cannot a priori favor a particular register, channel, or genre (see below) over another. In this respect, Bloch's (1976) criticism of the ethnography of speaking as giving too great a place to ritual and artistic speech is appropriate. It is important, as he suggests, to pay attention to "the study of mundane ordinary speech intercourse in different cultures" (p. 233). One must also be aware, however, of the fact that ritual speech and conversation should not be seen as two discrete categories, necessarily independent from one another. Rather, it is increasingly apparent that ritual, formal, poetic, and other types of speech that characterize verbal performance across societies (Bauman, 1977) often share several features with casual, informal speech. As pointed out by Irvine (1979), one cannot predict exactly which linguistic features are going to be used to mark a certain style or genre as formal. There have been in fact some suggestions that the language of ritual may be in some respect quite mundane (Sherzer, 1977) and that within formal settings, such as the courtroom, participants may communicate in a much more direct and confrontative manner than in daily, supposedly casual interaction (Brown, 1981). Finally, Sherzer (1982) has suggested that the same unit, the line, could be used for describing both poetic and conversational speech.

Norms

Hymes' ethnographic approach is based on the assumptions that speech is rule-governed behavior and that the researcher's task is to infer such rules from the systematic observation and recording (in the form of handwritten notes, audio- or video-taping) of spontaneous verbal interaction. The researcher should also make use of techniques usually employed by social and cultural anthropologists (e.g., participation in the community life, discussion with members) and by linguists (e.g., elicitation of native speaker's judgments, creation of paradigms and crucial counterexamples, collection of texts).

Norms for interaction involve different levels of communicative competence, from the very basic rules for constructing processable sequences (e.g., possible word-order patterns in the particular language) to the use of the appropriate code or register (Andersen, 1977; Ferguson, 1975, 1977; Gumperz, 1964; Sankoff, 1972, 1980). Norms for interaction also include strategies for making apparent mistakes, such as, for instance, stopping in the middle of a word or sentence and starting a new sentence (Goodwin, 1981; Schegloff, 1979) or simply speaking as if one were "incompetent" (Albert, 1972).

Norms of interpretation, as pointed out by Hymes, assume cultural analysis. To know what was said as well as how and why means to know how the participants interpreted the form and content of the messages. This is where the explanatory power of our account is tested. An adequate account of a speech event must explain the choice among alternative forms, registers, or codes and the participants' cultural interpretation of it. This is one of the many places where discourse analysis coincides with ethnography, at least in its classic definitions of taking the perspective of the native (Malinowski, 1922, p. 25) and describing "whatever it is one has to know or believe in order to operate in a manner acceptable to (the) members" (Goodenough, 1964) of a given speech community.

The central issue for an ethnographically oriented study of discourse is the manner and the extent to which one can compare norms across societies. The most extensive study of verbal strategies for social interaction across societies is Brown and Levinson's account of politeness phenomena (Brown, 1979; Brown & Levinson, 1978; Levinson, 1977). Using Goffman's

(1967) notion of 'face'—the public self-image that everyone wants to claim for himself—and Grice's (1975) maxims for cooperative interaction, Brown and Levinson have proposed putative universals for strategic (verbal) interaction. Their work is based on the assumption that human beings are rational beings who ideally would want to exchange information in the most efficient way, namely, by being sincere, informative, relevant, and clear (Grice, 1975).[8] They argue that politeness is "a major source of deviation from such rational efficiency, and is communicated precisely by that deviation" (Brown & Levinson, 1978, p. 100). Their approach is somewhat reminiscent of interpretive science, as apparent from the similarity between the way they use the notion of 'norm' and Schutz' idea of normal form typifications (I am borrowing this quotation and the following one from Cicourel, 1974):

> as I confront my fellow-man, I bring into each concrete situation a stock of preconstituted knowledge which includes a network of typifications of human individuals in general, of typical human motivations, goals, and action patterns. It also includes knowledge of expressive and interpretive schemes, of objective sign-systems and, in particular, of the vernacular language. (Schutz, 1964, pp. 29–30)

Brown and Levinson's approach, however, lacks at times the awareness of the observer's role in the interpretive process that characterizes other interpretive approaches and does not distinguish between the participants' subjective intentions, the observer's reading of such intentions, and the culture-specific norms that precede the actors' interaction and their subjective motivations. To quote again from Schutz:

> The observer's scheme of interpretation cannot be identical, of course, with the interpretive scheme of either partner in the social relation observed. The modifications of attention which characterize the attitude of the observer cannot coincide with those of a participant in an ongoing social relation. For one thing, what he finds relevant is not identical with what they find relevant in the situation. (Schutz, 1964, p. 36)

The amount of data, from several speech communities, that Brown and Levinson are able to classify and explain within their framework is, however, unprecedented. For this reason and for the fine details of their analyses, their work deserves careful attention from ethnographers of speaking involved in different speech communities around the world.

---

[8] The alleged universality of Grice's (1975) maxims is challenged by Keenan's (1976) work on the Malagasy, who constantly violate Grice's 'be informative' norm. This leaves open the question of whether Grice's maxims define dimensions of universal relevance to ways of speaking or actual tendencies or principles (see also Hymes, 1980).

Genres

Speech genres are traditional units of discourse analysis in the study of verbal performance (Bauman, 1977; Cardona, 1976). Some researchers, particularly those engaged in the analysis of American Indian verbal art (Gossen, 1974) and of Black American speech performances (Abrahams, 1976; Kochman, 1972), have identified speech genres with speech events. In some cases, the terminological distinctions provided by the participants in a given community can be used for classifying ways of speaking even in other communities that do not use such terminology (Abrahams, 1976, p. 45). The underlying (or psychological) reality of these native classifications seems a better way of defining events than the researcher's own hypothesis about the goal of the activity (see the end of the preceding sections of this chapter). At the same time, we must be aware of the possibility of genre variation across events. As pointed out by Hymes,

> Genres often coincide with speech events, but must be treated as analytically independent of them. They may occur in (or as) different events. The sermon as a genre is typically identical with a certain place in a church service, but its properties may be invoked, for serious or humorous effect, in other situations. Often enough a genre recurs in several events. . . . A great deal of empirical work will be needed to clarify the interrelations of genres, events, acts, and other components. (Hymes, 1972a, p. 65)

Thus, for instance, in Samoa, the ceremonial speech genre *laauga* exhibits considerable variation in its form and content across social events. A careful speech-event analysis shows that such variation can, in fact, be explained by taking into consideration other components of the event in which the ceremonial speech is performed, such as the purposes of the event (viz., ends), the relative time at which the speech is delivered, the range of participants in the event, and, finally, the extent to which the speech is considered in the domain of performance (Duranti, 1983).[9]

CONCLUSIONS

In this chapter, I have discussed the notion of speech event as an analytical tool for the study of discourse from a sociocultural perspective. I have shown how discourse is part of the speakers' cultural construction of reality and must then be understood as relating to and defining such reality. Let me briefly summarize some of the main points.

---

[9] The relation between genre and social contexts is also a recurrent theme in Gossen's (1974) work on Chamula verbal performance.

I have suggested that a speech event can be identified as a unit (and therefore analyzed and compared to other similar or different events or activities) on the basis of two main features or sets of features: (1) the ends (or goals) of the event, and (2) its spatiotemporal organization. I have pointed out how, in both cases, we are concerned with the cultural definitions of those features. We assume that meaningful human interaction is always goal oriented. We must distinguish, however, between the system's or societal ends of an event and the participants' ends. The spatiotemporal organization of an event can be handled by adopting Goffman's (1974) notion of 'boundary.' After defining possible types of boundaries and after distinguishing between boundaries and boundary markers, I have indicated certain tendencies, across societies and events, in the relationship between boundaries and verbal interaction. Speech within boundaries is often used to define the type of activity embedded by the boundary markers. Speech at the opening boundaries is usually more predictable than speech at the closing boundaries. In any case, what constitutes the boundaries of an event as well as what are recognized as its ends or goals are cultural definitions, to be identified through ethnographic work. Generalizations and cross-cultural comparison are possible only after detailed emic descriptions.

In the section entitled Participants I have pointed out how the very definitions of speaker–addressor and hearer–addressee are also culturally bound and must be related to the particpants' understanding of a given event and their socioculturally defined ends. In the case of the Kaluli mothers talking for their young children, as well as in the other cases discussed, the correct identification of the different roles of speaker, sender, hearer, and addressee (audience) is dependent upon the cultural significance of the speech event. The meaning of the verbal interaction can be captured and properly decoded only after having assigned the culturally appropriate participant roles.

Within the section on Act Sequences I have discussed the organization of turns and the problematic message form and message content components of Hymes' model. I have stressed the need, from an ethnographic perspective, to relate the mechanisms of turn management to other dimensions of social (and, more specifically, verbal) interaction. The interest in the cooperative, emergent structure of conversational interaction should not prevent us from seeing (or looking for) the possible connection between the local organization of roles (viz., conversationalists) and its wider context (e.g., type of social organization). Finally, I have suggested that interpretive procedures are inevitable and the only way of avoiding imposing the analyst's ideology upon the actors' doings is to make such interpretive procedures explicit.

After a brief discussion of key and key signals, which are related to Bateson's notion of 'frame' or 'metamessage' and to Gumperz' notion of 'contextualization cue', I discuss the relevance of the channel or form of speech to discourse analysis. The notions of 'formal' and 'informal' speech are not only culture specific but are also influenced by the range of linguistic resources and channels available within a given speech community. Written language, for instance, can influence oral discourse, as in the Samoan case discussed by Shore (1982) and by Duranti and Ochs (in press).

In order to describe the norms through which participants perform and interpret speech in social interaction, discourse analysts must take the perspective of the participants. Brown and Levinson (1978), however, on the basis of Goffman's work on face and sacred self and Grice's maxims, have attempted a cross-linguistic, cross-cultural analysis of politeness phenomena that captures a vast array of clearly similar strategies in the use of certain classes of message forms and message contents across different speech events. Their work deserves careful consideration from ethnographers and students of discourse patterns concerned with the interaction of language structure and strategic interaction.

Speech genres are also another dimension for the study of systematic variation in speech performance and culturally defined discourse patterns. The rich literature on this subject, reviewed by Bauman (1977) and Cardona (1976), can offer important suggestions on the interpretation of discourse from the point of view of native taxonomies. Furthermore, the study of genre variation provides useful insights into the interaction of different components of speech events.

Throughout this chapter, I have pointed out several ways in which sociocultural knowledge and the interaction between speech and social context are relevant to the analysis of discourse. The approach advocated here should not be considered as an alternative to other differently oriented approaches, but rather as a body of knowledge and methods that needs to be integrated with current models and theories of discourse structure and discourse types within and across societies.

The ethnographic approach has been criticized for paucity of generalizations. It is apparent that the lack of universal claims characteristic of the ethnographic approach goes hand in hand with the cultural relativism that underlies the work of most contemporary cultural and social anthropologists (Leach, 1982). In my view, such a culture-specific approach to the study of discourse should not be fought or put aside. Rather, we should find a way of exploiting the explicit reference that such an approach makes to a vast range of sociocultural dimensions of verbal interaction and discourse structure. Models and theories tend to force data on a

Procrustean bed. The open-endedness of the ethnographic approach defines its limit but also its force. If we see the study of discourse as qualitatively different from the study of sentences in isolation—and this seems to me the meaning of discourse analysis—then we are committed to relating discourse to sociocultural context, speech to cultural beliefs, verbal strategies to social order, people as speakers to people as social actors. If so, we cannot but engage in the kind of interpretive enterprise that has characterized the history and methods of modern anthropology and bear the risks that go with it.

ACKNOWLEDGMENTS

I would like to thank the following people for providing helpful criticism and insightful comments on an earlier draft of this chapter: Edward Finegan, Elinor Ochs, Joel Sherzer, Donald Brenneis, and Richard Bauman. Many of the ideas and themes mentioned here were discusssed (sometimes vehemently) in 1980 and 1981 within the Working Group on Language and Cultural Context, at the Department of Anthropology of the Research School of Pacific Studies, at the Australian National University. I am particularly grateful to those in the group who shared their data and biases with generosity and enthusiasm: John Haviland, Steve Levinson, Penny Brown, Judy Irvine, Michael Silverstein, and Robert Van Valin.

REFERENCES

Abrahams, R. (1976). *Talking black*. Rowley, MA: Newbury House.

Agar, M. (1975). Cognition and events. In M. Sanches & B. G. Blount (Eds.), *Sociocultural dimensions of language use* (pp. 45–56). New York: Academic Press.

Agar, M. (1980). *The professional stranger: An informal introduction to ethnography*. New York: Academic Press.

Albert, E. M. (1972). Culture patterning of speech behavior in Burundi. In J. J. Gumperz & D. Hymes (Eds.), *Directions in sociolinguistics: The ethnography of communication* (pp. 72–105). New York: Holt.

Andersen, E. (1977). Learning to speak with style: A study of the sociolinguistic skills of children. Unpublished doctoral dissertation, Stanford University.

Basso, K. H. (1979). *Portraits of "The whiteman": Linguistic play and cultural symbols among the Western Apache*. Cambridge: Cambridge University Press.

Bateson, G. (1955). A theory of play and phantasy. In *APA Psychiatric research reports, II*. (Reprinted in *Steps to an ecology of mind*, 177–193. New York: Ballantine.)

Bauman, R. (1977). *Verbal art as performance*. Rowley, MA: Newbury.

Bauman, R., & Sherzer, J. (Eds.). (1974). *Explorations in the ethnography of speaking*. New York: Academic Press.

Bauman, R., & Sherzer, J. (1975). The ethnography of speaking. *Annual Review of Anthropology, 4*.

Bernstein, B. (1971). *Class, codes and control*. London: Routledge & Kegan Paul.

Besnier, N. (1982). Repairs and errors in Tuvaluan conversation. Unpublished manuscript, University of Southern California.

Bloch, M. (Ed.). (1975). *Political language and oratory in traditional society*. London: Academic Press.

Bloch, M. (1976). Review of R. Bauman & J. Sherzer (Eds.), *Explorations in the ethnography of speaking*. *Language in Society, 5,* 229–234.

Brenneis, D. (1980). Straight talk and sweet talk: political discourse in a community of equals. In R. Bauman & J. Sherzer (Eds.), *Working papers in sociolinguistics* (No. 71). Austin, TX. Southwest Educational Development Laboratory.

Brenneis, D. (1982). *Grogg and gossip in Bhatgaon: Style and substance in Fiji Indian conversation*. Paper presented at the Annual Meeting of the American Anthropological Association, Washington, DC.

Brown, P. (1979). Language, interaction and sex roles in a Mayan community: A study of politeness and the position of women. Unpublished doctoral dissertation, University of California at Berkeley.

Brown, P. (1981). *A courtroom case in Tenejapa*. Seminar given at the Australian National University, Department of Anthropology, Research School of Pacific Studies, Canberra.

Brown, P., & Fraser, C. (1979). Speech as a marker of situation. In K. R. Sherer & H. Giles (Eds.), *Social markers in speech* pp. 33–62. Cambridge: Cambridge University Press.

Brown, P., & Levinson, S. (1978). Universals in language usage: Politeness phenomena. In E. Goody (Ed.) *Questions and politeness: Strategies in Social Interaction* (pp. 56–289). Cambridge: Cambridge University Press.

Calame-Griaule, G. (1965). *Ethnologie et langage: La parole chez les Dogon*. Paris: Gallimard.

Cardona, G. R. (1976). *Introduzione all'etnolinguistica*. Bologna: Il Mulino.

Castelfranchi, C., & Parisi, D. (1980). *Linguaggio, conoscenze e Scopi*. Bologna: Il Mulino.

Chafe, W. L. (1976). Givenness, contrastiveness, definiteness, subjects, topics, and point of view. In C. N. Li (Ed.), *Subject and topic* (pp. 25–56). New York: Academic Press.

Chafe, W. L. (1979). The flow of thought and the flow of language. In T. Givón (Ed.), *Syntax and semantics, vol. 12: Discourse and syntax* (pp. 159–181). New York: Academic Press.

Chafe, W. L. (1980). The deployment of consciousness in the production of a narrative. In W. L. Chafe (Ed.), *The pear stories: Cognitive, cultural, and linguistic aspects of narrative production* (pp. 9–50). Norwood, Ablex.

Chomsky, N. (1965). *Aspects of the Theory of Syntax*. Cambridge, MA: MIT Press.

Chomsky, N. (1977). On Wh-movement. In A. Akmajian, P. Culicover, & T. Wasow (Eds.), *Formal syntax* (pp. 71–132). New York: Academic Press.

Cicourel, A. (1974). *Cognitive sociology*. New York: Free Press.

Clark, H., & Haviland, S. E. (1977). Comprehension and the given-new contract. In R. O. Freedle (Ed.), *Explaining linguistic phenomena* (pp. 91–124). Washington, DC: Hemisphere.

Comaroff, J. L., & Roberts, S. (1981). *Rules and processes: The cultural logic of dispute in an African context*. Chicago: University of Chicago Press.

Cook-Gumperz, J. (1975). The child as a practical reasoner. In M. Sanches & B. G. Blount (Eds.), *Sociocultural dimension of language use,* (pp. 137–162). New York: Academic Press.

Cook-Gumperz, J., & Gumperz, J. J. (1981). From oral to written: The transition to literacy. In M. F. Whiteman (Ed.), *Writing: The nature, development, and teaching of written* communication. *Volume 1. Variation in writing: functional and linguistic-cultural differences*, (pp. 89–109). Hillsdale, NJ: Erlbaum.

Coulthard, M. (1977). *An introduction to discourse analysis.* London: Longman.

Creider, C. (1979). On the explanation of transformations. In T. Givón (Ed.), *Syntax and semantics, vol. 12: Discourse and syntax*, (pp. 3–21). New York: Academic Press.

Crystal, D. (1969). *Prosodic systems and intonation in English.* Cambridge: Cambridge University Press.

Crystal, D., & Davy, D. (1969). *Investigating English style.* Bloomington: Indiana University Press.

Dixon, R. M. W. (1972). *The Dyirbal language of North Queensland.* Cambridge: Cambridge University Press.

Dolgin, J. L., Kemnitzer, D. S., & Schneider, D. M. (Eds.). (1977). *Symbolic anthropology: A reader in the study of symbols and meanings.* New York: Columbia University Press.

Duranti, A. (1981). *The Samoan FONO: A sociolinguistic study* (Pacific Linguistics, Series B, Vol. 80). Canberra: Department of Linguistics, Research School of Pacific Studies, Australian National University, Canberra.

Duranti, A. (1983). Samoan speechmaking across social events: One genre in and out of a *fono. Language in Society, 12,* 1–22.

Duranti, A., & Ochs, E. (1979). Left-dislocation in Italian conversation. In T. Givón (Ed.), *Syntax and semantics, vol. 12: Discourse and syntax,* (pp. 377–416). New York: Academic Press.

Duranti, A., & Ochs, E. (1982). *The social organization of other-correction in Samoan verbal interaction.* Paper presented at the annual meeting of the American Anthropological Association, Washington, DC.

Duranti, A., & Ochs, E. (in press). Literacy instruction in a Samoan village. In B. B. Schieffelin (Ed.), *Acquisition of literacy: Ethnographic perspectives.* Norwood, NJ: Ablex.

Durbin, M. A. (1972). Linguistic models in anthropology. *Annual Review of Anthropology, 1,* 383–410.

Durkheim, E. (1915). *The elementary forms of religious life: A study in religious sociology.* London: Allen & Unwin.

Eastman, C. M. (1975). *Aspects of language and culture.* San Francisco: Chandler & Sharp.

Feld, S. (1982). *Sound and sentiment: Birds, weeping, poetics, and song in Kaluli expression.* Philadelphia: University of Pennsylvania Press.

Feld, S., & Schieffelin, B. B. (1981). A functional basis for Kaluli discourse. In D. Tannen (Ed.), *Georgetown University Round Table on Languages and Linguistics 1981,* (pp. 350–370). Washington, DC: Georgetown University Press.

Ferguson, C. A. (1975). Toward a characterization of English foreign talk. *Anthropological Linguistics, 51,* 419–439.

Ferguson, C. A. (1977). Baby talk as a simplified register. In C. Snow & C. A. Ferguson (Eds.), *Talking to children* (pp. 209–235). Cambridge: Cambridge University Press.

Ferguson, C. A. (1982). Simplified registers and linguistic theory. In L. Obler & L. Menn (Eds.). *Exceptional language and linguistics.* New York: Academic Press.

Fillmore, C. J. (1971). *Santa Cruz lectures on deixis 1971.* Bloomington: Indiana University Linguistic Club.

Firth, R. (1975). Speech-making and authority in Tikopia. In M. Bloch (Ed.), *Political language and oratory in traditional society,* (pp. 29–43). London: Academic Press.

Fitzgerald, D. K. (1975). The language of ritual events among the GA of Southern Ghana. In M. Sanches & B. G. Blount (Eds.), *Sociocultural dimensions of language use* (pp. 205–234). New York: Academic Press.

Frake, C. O. (1975). How to enter a Yakan house. In M. Sanches & B. G. Blount (Eds.), *Sociocultural dimensions of language use* (pp. 25–40). New York: Academic Press.

Geertz, C. (1973). *The interpretation of cultures.* New York: Basic Books.

Gerth, H. H., & Mills, C. W. (Eds.). (1946). Introduction: The man and his work. In *From Max Weber: Essays in sociology.* New York: Oxford University Press.

Givón, T. (1976). Topic, pronoun, and grammatical agreement. In C. N. Li (Ed.), *Subject and topic* (pp. 149–188). New York: Academic Press.

Givón, T. (1979a). *On understanding grammar.* New York: Academic Press.

Givón, T. (1979b). *Syntax and semantics, vol. 12: Discourse and syntax.* New York: Academic Press.

Goffman, E. (1964). The neglected situation. In J. J. Gumperz & D. Hymes (Eds.), The ethnography of communication [Special issue] (pp. 133–137). *American Anthropologist, 66* (6) pt. 2.

Goffman, E. (1967). *Interactional ritual: Essays on face to face behavior.* Garden City, NY: Anchor/Doubleday.

Goffman, E. (1974). *Frame analysis: An essay on the organization of experience.* New York: Harper & Row.

Goffman, E. (1976). Replies and responses. *Language in Society, 5,* 257–313. Reprinted in E. Goffman (Ed.). (1981). *Forms of talk.* Philadelphia: University of Pennsylvania Press.

Goodenough, W. H. (1964). Cultural anthropology and linguistics. In D. Hymes (Ed.), *Language in culture and society* (pp. 36–39). New York: Harper & Row.

Goodwin, C. (1981). *Conversational organization: Interaction between speakers and hearers.* New York: Academic Press.

Goody, J. (1977). *The domestication of the savage mind.* Cambridge: Cambridge University Press.

Gossen, G. H. (1974). *Chamulas in the world of the sun: Time and space in a Maya oral tradition.* Cambridge, MA: Harvard University Press.

Grice, H. P. (1975). Logic and conversation. In P. Cole & J. L. Morgan (Eds.) *Syntax and Semantics,* Vol. 3, *Speech Acts,* (pp. 41–58.) New York: Academic Press.

Grimes, J. (1975). *The thread of discourse.* The Hague: Mouton.

Gumperz, J. J. (1964). Linguistic and social interaction in two communities. In J. J. Gumperz & D. Hymes (Eds.), The ethnography of communication [Special issue], (pp. 137–154). *American Anthropologist, 66* (6) pt. 2.

Gumperz, J. J. (1972). Introduction. In J. J. Gumperz & D. Hymes (Eds.), *Directions in sociolinguistics: The ethnography of communication,* (pp. 1–25). New York: Holt.

Gumperz, J. J. (1977). Sociocultural knowledge in conversational inference. In M. Saville-Troike (Ed.), *Georgetown University Round Table on Languages and Linguistics 1977,* Washington, DC: Georgetown University Press.

Gumperz, J. J. (1981). The linguistic basis of communicative competence. In D. Tannen (Ed.), *Georgetown University Round Table on Languages and Linguistics 1981,* (pp. 323–334). Washington, DC: Georgetown University Press.

Gumperz, J. J., & Hymes, D. (Eds.). (1964). The ethnography of communication [Special issue] *American Anthropologist, 66* (6).

Gumperz, J. J., & Hymes, D. (Eds.). (1972). *Directions in sociolinguistics: The ethnography of communication.* New York: Holt.

Halliday, M. A. K. (1973). *Explorations in the functions of language*. London: Arnold.

Haviland, J. B. (1979a). Guugu Yimidhirr brother-in-law language. *Language in Society*, *8*, 365–393.

Haviland, J. B. (1979b). How you talk to your brother-in-law in guugu Yimidhirr. In T. Shopen (Ed.), *Languages and their speakers* (pp. 161–239). Cambridge, MA: Winthrop.

Hawkinson, A., & Hyman, L. M. (1974). Hierarchies of natural topic in Shona. In *Studies in African Linguistics*, *5*, 147–170.

Heath, S. B. (1981). Toward an ethnohistory of writing in American education. In M. F. Whiteman (Ed.), *Writing: The nature, development, and teaching of written communication. Vol. 1. Variation in writing: Functional and linguistic-cultural differences* (pp. 25–45). Hillsdale, NJ: Erlbaum.

Heath, S. B. (1982). What no bedtime story means: Narrative skills at home and school. *Language in Society*, *11*, 49–76.

Henson, H. (1974). *British social anthropologists and language*. Oxford: Clarendon Press.

Hinds, J. (1979). Organization patterns in discourse. In T. Givón (Ed.), *Syntax and semantics, vol. 12: Discourse and syntax* (pp. 135–157). New York: Academic Press.

Hopper, P. J. (1982). *Tense-aspect: Between semantics and pragmatics*. Amsterdam: Benjamins.

Hopper, P. J., & Thompson, S. A. (1980). Transitivity in grammar and discourse. *Language*, *56*, 251–299.

Hymes, D. (1962). The ethnography of speaking. In T. Gladwin & W. C. Sturtevant (Eds.), *Anthropology and human behavior* (pp. 13–53). Washington, DC: Anthropological Society of Washington.

Hymes, D. (1964a). Introduction: Toward ethnographies of communication. In J. J. Gumperz & D. Hymes (Eds.), The ethnography of communication. [Special] (pp. 1–34). *American Anthropologist*, *66* (6) pt. 2.

Hymes, D. (Ed.). (1964b). *Language in culture and society*. New York: Harper & Row.

Hymes, D. (1972a). Models for the interaction of language and social life. In J. J. Gumperz & D. Hymes (Eds.), *Directions in sociolinguistics: The ethnography of communication* (pp. 35–71). New York: Holt.

Hymes, D. (1972b). On communicative competence. In J. B. Pride and J. Holmes (Eds.), *Sociolinguistics* (pp. 269–285). Harmondsworth: Penguin.

Hymes, D. (1974). *Foundations in sociolinguistics: An ethnographic approach*. Philadelphia: University of Pennsylvania Press.

Hymes, D. (1980). Forward to S. B. Shimanoff, *Communication rules: theory and research*. Beverly Hills, CA: Sage.

Hymes, D. (1981). *"In vain I tried to tell you"*. *Essays in Native American ethnopoetics*. Philadelphia: University of Pennsylvania Press.

Irvine, J. T. (1974). Strategies of status manipulation in the Wolof greeting. In J. Sherzer & R. Bauman (Eds.), *Explorations in the ethnography of speaking* (pp. 167–191). Cambridge: Cambridge University Press.

Irvine, J. T. (1979). Formality and informality in communicative events. *American Anthropologist*, *81*, 773–790.

Jakobson, R. (1960). Concluding statement: Linguistics and poetics. In T. Sebeok (Ed.), *Style in language* (pp. 350–373). Cambridge, MA: MIT Press.

Keenan, E. O. (1976). The universality of conversational implicature. *Language in Society*, *5*, 67–80.

Keesing, R. (1979). Linguistic knowledge and cultural knowledge: Some doubts and speculations. *American Anthropologist*, *81*, 14–36.

Kochman, T. (1972). Black American speech events and a language program for the classroom. In C. B. Cazden, V. P. John, & D. Hymes (Eds.), *Functions of language in the classroom* (pp. 211–261). New York: Teachers College Press.

Labov, W. (1969). Contraction, deletion, and inherent variability of the English copula. *Language, 45,* 715–762.

Labov, W. (1970). The study of language in its social context. *Studium Generale, 23,* 30–87.

Labov, W. (1971). Methodology. In W. O. Dingwall (Ed.), *A survey of linguistic science* (pp. 412–497). College Park, MD: Linguistic Program, University of Maryland.

Langness, L. L. (1974). *The study of culture.* Novato, CA: Chandler & Sharp.

Langness, L. L., & Frank, G. (1981). *Lives: An anthropological approach to biography.* Novato, CA: Chandler & Sharp.

Lavandera, B. (1978). Where does the sociolinguistic variable stop? *Language in Society, 7,* 171–182.

Lavandera, B. (1981). *The dialectic tension between equivalence and difference.* Paper presented at the winter meeting of the Linguistic Society of America, New York.

Lavandera, B. (in press). Creative variation. Shifting between impersonal and personal in Spanish discourse.

Leach, E. (1976). *Culture and communication: The logic by which symbols are connected. An introduction to the use of structuralist analysis in social anthropology.* Cambridge: Cambridge University Press.

Leach, E. (1982). *Social anthropology.* Oxford: Oxford University Press.

Lepschy, G. (1970). *A survey of structural linguistics.* London: Faber.

Levinson, S. C. (1977). *Social deixis in a Tamil village.* Unpublished doctoral dissertation, University of California, Berkeley.

Levinson, S. C. (1979). Activity types and language. *Linguistics, 17,* 365–399.

Lévi-Strauss, C. (1963). *Structural anthropology.* New York: Basic Books.

Lévi-Strauss, C. (1964). Structural analysis in linguistics and anthropology. In D. Hymes (Ed.), *Language in culture and society* (pp. 40–53). New York: Harper & Row. Translated by D. Hymes from C. Lévi-Strauss. (1958). *Anthropologie structurale.*

Li C. N., & Thompson, S. A. (1976). Subject and topic: A new typology of Language. In C. N. Li (Ed.), *Subject and topic* (pp. 457–489). New York: Academic Press.

Longacre, R. (1972). *Hierarchy and universality of discourse constituents in New Guinea languages: Discussion.* Washington, DC: Georgetown University Press.

Longacre, R. (1979). The paragraph as a grammatical unit. In T. Givón (Ed.), *Syntax and semantics, vol. 12: Discourse and syntax* (pp. 115–134). New York: Academic Press.

Lyons, J. (1966). *Introduction to theoretical linguistics.* Cambridge: Cambridge University Press.

Lyons, J. (1972). Human language. In R. A. Hinde (Ed.), *Non-verbal communication* (pp. 49–85). Cambridge: Cambridge University Press.

Lyons, J. (1977). *Semantics* (Vols. 1 & 2). Cambridge: Cambridge University Press.

MacWhinney, B. (1977). Starting point. *Language, 53,* 1352–1368.

Malinowski, B. (1922). *Argonauts of the Western Pacific.* London: Routledge. (Republished 1961 by Dutton, New York).

Malinowski, B. (1923). The problem of meaning in primitive languages. In C. K. Ogden & I. A. Richards (Eds.), *The meaning of meaning* (Supplement I) (pp. 296–336). New York: Harcourt, Brace & World.

Malinowski, B. (1935). *Coral gardens and their magic* (2 vols.). New York: American Book Company. (Republished 1961 by Dover Publications, New York).

Mandelbaum, D. G. (Ed.). (1949). *Selected writings of Edward Sapir in language, culture, and personality.* Cambridge: Cambridge University Press.

Merritt, M. W. (1980). *Service-like events during individual work time and their contribution to the nature of communication in primary classrooms.* (In collaboration with F. M. Humphrey) (Final grant report for the National Institute of Education). Arlington, VA, Center for Applied Linguistics.

Miller, G. A., Galanter, E., & Pribram, K. H. (1960). *Plans and the structure of behavior.* New York: Holt.

Myers, F. (1982). *Ethnography, language, and social value among the Pintupi.* Paper presented at the annual meeting of the American Anthropological Association, Washington, DC.

Myers, F. & Brenneis, D. (1984). Introduction. In F. Myers & D. Brenneis (Eds.), *Dangerous words: Language and politics in the Pacific* (pp. 1–29). New York: New York University Press.

Ochs, E. (1982). Talking to children in Western Samoa. *Language in Society,* 11, 77–104.

Ochs, E., & Schieffelin, B. (1982). Language acquisition and socialization: Three developmental stories and their implications. In R. Bauman & J. Sherzer (Eds.), *Working paper in sociolinguistics* no. 105. Austin, TX: Southwest Educational Development Laboratory. (Also to appear in *Culture and its acquisition,* R. Shweder & R. LeVine (eds.). Chicago: University of Chicago Press.

Philips, S. (1977). *The role of spatial positioning and alignment in defining interactional units: The American courtroom as a case in point.* Paper presented at the annual meeting of the American Anthropological Association, San Francisco.

Philips, S. (1983). *The invisible culture: Communication in classroom and community on the Warm Spring Indian Reservation.* New York: Longman.

Pignato, C. (1981). Suggestioni e spunti attuali nella riflessione di B. Malinowski sul linguaggio. *L'uomo. Società, tradizione, sviluppo,* 5, 135–172.

Pike, K. L. (1954). *Language in relation to a unified theory of the structure of human behavior* (preliminary edition). Glendale, CA: Summer Institute of Linguistics. (Published with the same title in 1967. The Hague: Mouton.)

Psathas, G. (Ed.). (1979). *Everyday language: Studies in ethnomethodology.* New York: Irvington.

Romaine, S. (1981). On the problem of syntactic variation: A reply to Beatriz Lavandera and William Labov. In R. Bauman & J. Sherzer (Eds.), *Working papers in sociolinguistics* (no. 82). Austin, TX: Southwest Educational Development Laboratory.

Sacks, H., Schegloff, E., & Jefferson, G. (1974). A simplest systematics for the organization of turn-taking for conversation. *Language,* 50, 696–735.

Sahlins, M. (1976). *Culture and practical reason.* Chicago: University of Chicago Press.

Sankoff, G. (1972). Language use in multilingual societies: Some alternative approaches. In J. Pride & J. Holmes (Eds.), *Sociolinguistics* (pp. 33–51). (Reprinted in G. Sankoff, 1980).

Sankoff, G. (1980). *The social life of language.* Philadelphia: University of Pennsylvania Press.

Sankoff, G., & Brown, P. (1976). The Origins of syntax in discourse. *Language,* 52, 631–666.

Saville-Troike, M. (1982). *The ethnography of communication: An introduction.* Oxford: Blackwell.

Schegloff, E. A. (1979). The relevance of repair to syntax-for-conversation. In T. Givón (Ed.), *Syntax and semantics, vol. 12: Discourse and syntax* (pp. 261–286). New York: Academic Press.

Schegloff, E., Jefferson, G., & Sacks, H. (1977). The preference for self-correction in the organization of repair in conversation. *Language,* 53, 361–382.

Schegloff, E. A., & Sacks, H. (1973). Opening up closings. *Semiotica,* 8, 289–327.

Schenkein, J. (Ed.). (1978). *Studies in the organization of conversational interaction*. New York: Academic Press.

Schieffelin, B. (1979). *How Kaluli children learn what to say, what to do, and how to feel: An ethnographic study of the development of communicative competence*. Unpublished doctoral dissertation, Columbia University.

Schieffelin, B. B. (1981). A developmental study of pragmatic appropriateness of word order and casemarking in Kaluli. In W. Deutsch (Ed.), *The child's construction of language* (pp. 105–120). London: Academic Press.

Schieffelin, E. (1981). *Spirit seances and the cultural construction of reality*. Unpublished manuscript.

Schutz, A. (1964). *Collected papers II: Studies in social theory*. The Hague: Nijhoff.

Scollon, R., & Scollon, S. B. K. (1981). *Narrative, literacy, and face in interethnic communication*. Norwood, NJ: Ablex.

Scribner, S., & Cole, M. (1981). *The psychology of literacy*. Cambridge: Harvard University Press.

Searle, J. (1965). What is a speech act?. In M. Black (Ed.), *Philosophy in America* (pp. 221–239). Allen & Unwin and Cornell University Press. Reprinted in P. P. Giglioli (Ed.), (1972). *Language and social context* (pp. 136–154). Harmondsworth: Penguin.

Sherzer, J. (1974). *Nomakke, Summakke, Kormakke: Three types of Cuna speech event*. In R. Bauman & J. Sherzer (Eds.), *Explorations in the ethnography of speaking* (pp. 262–282). Cambridge: Cambridge University Press.

Sherzer, J. (1977). The ethnography of speaking: A critical appraisal. In M. Saville-Troike (Ed.), *Georgetown University Round Table on Languages and Linguistics 1977* (pp. 43–58). Washington, DC: Georgetown University Press.

Sherzer, J. (1982). Poetic structuring of Kuna discourse: The line. *Language in Society, 11*, 371–390.

Shore, B. (1982). *Sala'ilua: A Samoan mistery*. New York: Columbia University Press.

Silverstein, M. (1976a). Hierarchy of features and ergativity. In R. M. W. Dixon (Ed.), *Grammatical categories in Australian languages* (pp. 112–171).

Silverstein, M. (1976b). Shifters, linguistic categories, and cultural description. In K. Basso & H. Selby (Eds.), *Meaning in anthropology* Albuquerque: University of New Mexico Press.

Silverstein, M. (1977). Cultural prerequisites to grammatical analysis. In M. Saville-Troike (Ed.), *Linguistics and anthropology*, Washington, DC: Georgetown University Press.

Silverstein, M. (1980). The limits of awareness. In R. Bauman & J. Sherzer (Eds.), *Sociolinguistic working papers* (No. 84). Austin, TX: Southwest Educational Development Laboratory.

Spradley, J. P. (1980). *Participant observation*. New York: Holt, Rinehart & Winston.

Turner, V. (1974). *Dramas, fields, and metaphors: Symbolic action in human society*. Ithaca: Cornell University Press.

Tyler, S. A. (Ed.). (1969). *Cognitive anthropology*. New York: Holt.

van Dijk, T. A. (1981). Episodes as units of discourse analysis. In D. Tannen (Ed.), *Georgetown University Round Table on Languages and Linguistics 1981* (pp. 177–195). Washington, DC: Georgetown University Press.

Van Gennep, A. (1909). *Les rites de passage*. Paris: Nourry.

Whorf, B. L. (1956). *Language, thought, and reality: Selected writings by Benjamin Lee Whorf*, J. B. Carroll (Ed.). New York: Wiley.

Yamamoto, A. (1979). *Culture space in everyday life*. Lawrence, KS: University of Kansas Publications in Anthropology.

CHAPTER **9**

Philosophy and Discourse Analysis

Asa Kasher

The purpose of the present chapter is to draw the attention of the reader who is interested mainly in discourse analysis to several related philosophical discussions.

Philosophy, that ancient "queen of arts, daughter of heaven," does not boast a special branch of discourse philosophical analysis or philosophy of discourse analysis. However, philosophy has taken a great interest in speech, acts, and speech acts and has also shown a perennial concern with knowledge and understanding in general and with sciences and their methodologies in particular. Such concern has brought forth a variety of observations, insights, and theories that bear on common human discourse and its systematic study. Several major examples are discussed in this chapter.

METHODOLOGY: LAUNCHING
A NEW DISCIPLINE

The creation of a new science must be a fascinating enterprise: The virgin soil swarms with new facts, distinctions that have passed unnoticed protrude unexpectedly, and regularities emerge from the seeming chaos.

The same holds for any attempt to make a given area of study significantly broader: Attention is paid to hitherto neglected phenomena, shattering frameworks, obsolescing laws, turning all apparently established theories into narrow and pale abstractions, much too remote from the interesting facts.

It is true that both cases carry a distinct revolutionary air, and revolutions are neither easily understood nor simply contained. Some reforms answer to the description suggested by Thomas Reed of what "is to be done,

HANDBOOK OF DISCOURSE ANALYSIS, Vol. 1
Disciplines of Discourse

in a way nobody knows how, at a time nobody knows when, that will accomplish nobody knows what," and too many revolutions carry the banner of "We have been naught, we shall be all." Are these two traits in the nature of revolution bound to appear when a scientific domain is created or made significantly broader?

Here is our first example of how discourse analysis, whether considered a new discipline or rather an extension of an old one, bears upon an underlying philosophical stratum.

Philosophers have realized that, in a very important sense, science is restricted. Not every endeavor to advance one's knowledge is scientific and not every pursuit of understanding is on a par with science. Entitled to be called scientific are just those inquiries that fulfill certain methodological conditions (Kuhn, 1962).

Before we discuss some of these conditions, two remarks have to be made. Notice, first, that "scientific" is not an honorific title, but rather one that marks a certain brand of human perusal of the world. Deep and rewarding as science is, it can by no means be considered the only worthwhile pursuit of knowledge and understanding. Daily common sense and military intelligence, on the one hand, and arts such as literature and painting, on the other hand, are all examples of human activities by which we might gain worthwhile knowledge and deep understanding. Philosophy of science is thus meant to be a philosophical analysis of the nature of science, rather than a systematic enterprise of praising science.

Hence, coming to think of discourse analysis as a branch of science is not tantamount to considering any other form of discourse inquiry as lacking in illuminative power.

Second, notice that philosophical discussions are seldom conclusive. In philosophy in general, views are lasting and unsettled disputes are abundant, and philosophy of science is no exception. Consequently, what is said in this chapter on the conditions imposed on any inquiry for it to be regarded as scientific does not reflect any common or official view held by philosophers of science, but rather a philosophy of science we happen to share with many other philosophers.

A Philosophical View of Science

Let us consider three major ingredients of scientific activity.

First, particular scientific activities involve certain problems of scientific understanding. Such a problem may take the form of a theory that explains some families of facts but is incongruous with other data. Under such conditions, a scientific effort is required in order to remove that incongruity without tampering with the theory in a way that would render it weaker in explaining those families of facts with which it is congruous.

A clash between a theory and some facts is an example of extreme incongruity: It might follow from one's theory that a certain utterance is appropriate for a certain context, whereas in fact it is not. However, incongruity may be more moderate. Sometimes a theory fails to provide explanation of a fact that clearly belongs to its sphere: If a theory about utterance–context relationships tells us nothing about a certain pairing of some utterance with some context, then the theory clearly fails in description and explanation. There is an incongruity between theory and the related realm of facts.

There are two major ways of resolving such an incongruity of a theory with a given family of facts. Usually, the theory is changed in order to accommodate it to the family of facts; sometimes, however, doubts are cast on what is given as fact, and the problem of incongruity is removed while the theory is left intact. The history of science is full of well-known examples of the former type. As for the latter, notice, for example, what happens when an alleged paranormal power of some person is presented as evidence against any entrenched theory of matter or radiation. According to the common, reasonable procedure, the alleged paranormality will be very carefully checked before any attempt is made at accommodating it to an appropriate theory that will, indeed, be radically different from the previous theory that is incongruous with paranormality of any kind.

When a theory collapses under the pressure of facts, how does one go about replacing it by a better one? Is there a general method of resolving incongruities?

Here is the second philosophical insight into scientific activity: The process of solving incongruity problems in science is not governed by any explicit canon of discovery, nor is there an implicit routine of scientific discovery of solutions. Scientific development is carried out by human creative powers of innovative problem solving. When the problem of incongruity of theory and facts arises, no restrictions should be imposed on the means the scientist may employ to find a solution to the problem. Quesions such as "Is the suggested solution of the given problem the best available one?" or "Is the purported solution a real one?" are important and interesting, whereas the question "Where has this or that solution come from?" is in a sense illegitimate.

The former questions are, indeed, fundamental to scientific activities. Given a scientific problem, one is commonly faced with a host of suggestions. The basic demarcation criterion would separate the solutions of the given problem from inadequate suggestions and seeming solutions. If several suggestions pass for real solutions of that problem, the basic ordering criterion would tell us which solution is preferable. Philosophers have gone deeply into the description of approximate demarcation and ordering criteria, and that gives rise to the third philosophical insight into scientific activity we would like to mention.

Roughly speaking, if a solution to a certain scientific incongruity problem of a certain theory with a certain family of facts replaces that theory by another one, then at least the following conditions should be fulfilled:

1. The previous incongruity does not arise in the new setting. If the incongruity took the form of incompatibility between the previous theory and a certain fact, then the new theory does not involve such an incompatibility with the fact.
2. Scientific problems that the previous theory has been shown to solve successfully should not be opened up by the new theory. Thus, an incongruity removed by the previous theory should not reappear in the new setting.
3. The new theory has to be testable. That is to say, the congruity of the new theory with new families of facts can be clearly checked. Total immunity from new scientific problems, no matter what new facts are brought in, is detrimental to scientific advance, because it reflects a suspicious insensitivity to new facts that a theory, which is about such facts, cannot afford to show.

When confronted with several solutions of the same scientific problem, pursuit of knowledge and understanding cannot proceed without an attempt being made to draw a conclusion as to which of the suggested solutions is superior to the others. Philosophical analysis of scientific activities shows us that there is no simple method of drawing such superiority conclusions, on the one hand, and that decisions about preferability of some solutions to others are not reached arbitrarily, on the other hand. The intermediate way is that of elaborately justifying each case of granting superiority of a certain solution over the alternative ones. Such justification commonly involves considerations of simplicity, fruitfulness, testability, and other methodological properties of the new theories put forward by the proposed solutions of the given scientific problem.

Undesirable Methods of Inquiry

These philosophical insights into scientific activity in general also apply to the particular case of discourse analysis. Instead of showing how each of the three points we have just presented can methodologically enlighten the discourse analyst, we would like to mention two methods of inquiry, present in discourse analysis as well as in other branches of similar scientific studies, that have to be excluded by anyone adhering to the above-mentioned philosophical view of science.

The first method may be dubbed "crude induction." In a sense, it views science as a very sophisticated kind of matchbox collection. Data are collected within a vaguely determined factual sphere and then sorted, arranged, and presented. Such compilation of facts is often followed by generalizations based upon that array of facts. When new facts are encountered, new arrangements and revised generalizations might be required.

Voluminous libraries of numerous types of recorded conversations exist. Orderly classifications of such data collections abound. Seemingly general, intricate descriptions of the data are also available, but many of these are barren of scientific depth because they fail to rest on a clear conception of the surrounding scientific framework: What is the scientific program within which the investigations are made? What is the incongruity problem to which a solution is sought? What is the theory and which are the facts that are incongruous with each other? What are the theoretical alternatives? Without proper answers to these questions it is not sufficiently clear which, if any, scientific purpose is actually being served by one's laboriously piling up data and classifications (Chomsky, 1980).

The second method may be dubbed "crude extension." Sometimes a successful new theory obviates some scientific incongruity problems by applying a brand-new conceptual framework or theoretical tool. A conspicuous example is Chomsky's transformational grammars. Such impressive novelties impel people, much too often, to use the new ideas somewhat opportunistically, regardless of the theoretical setting that has given rise to those novelties. Thus, efforts to write elaborate transformational grammars of some standard fragments of particular languages have been quite futile, serving no clear theoretical aim. If Chomsky's linguistic program is meant to shed light on the notions of 'rule of grammar of a psychologically possible human language', then an explicit representation of a certain fragment of, say, Hebrew might be theoretically worthless because it is bound to provide no insight into the concept 'rule of grammar'. Knowledge and understanding are never developed by formalizations of the obvious (Perry, 1980).

To conclude the present discussion with a few words of advice, we recommend that the reader not indulge in any project, paper, or discussion devoted to aspects of discourse analysis unless an outline of the theoretical setting is extractable. "What is the problem?" is a query that should always play a leading role when understanding is sought.

COMMUNICATION VERSUS ACTION:
FOUNDATIONS OF DISCOURSE ANALYSIS

In order to follow the advice we have just given, let us explain the problem to which we address ourselves in this part of the chapter.

Every scientific discussion—in fact, every significant discussion—rests on some working assumptions, that is to say, it rests on some factual statements that are taken for granted and centers on other claims that do not enjoy the critical immunity of the working assumptions. Many of these assumptions seem, indeed, self-evident, not worthy of serious discussion. For example, a moral discussion rests on the assumption that each person entertains some values, develops his opinions and tastes, and has a variety of moving emotions. Similarly, discussions of language share the conviction that, in a sense, language is completely rule-governed.

Philosophy is characteristicly interested in turning its critical eyes to what is taken for granted outside its confines. Hence, much of what is called "Philosophy of this-and-that" is actually a critical discussion of what is taken for granted in the respective field, for example, science, art, or religion.

Traditional Views

In the domain of language study, discourse analysis included, the notion of 'communication' has played a major role. It is the firm belief of many that language is a vehicle of communication, that is to say, a vehicle for transferring information from one person to another.

This seemingly innocuous belief carries ample consequences. For instance, if the study of language is actually an investigation of a vehicle for transferring information, then linguistic inquiry must include a method of representing the transferable information independently of language itself. To see that, consider other instruments. Design of water pipes rests on a rough characterization of the liquid to be conveyed through the pipes. Similarly, an explanation of the nature of a tobacco pipe hinges on some independent understanding of what tobacco is. Even the musical pipe cannot be fully described without resort to some possible representation of tunes, independently of the instrument. Many philosophers have asked themselves what form such a representation of information should take, since it must describe everything natural language can possibly do, in a form independent of natural language. Some philosophers are inclined to admit that such a representation is nonexistent; we shall see later what follows from this view.

Assuming there is a method of representing the information conveyed by whatever can possibly be said, rules are devisable that show how the information expressed in a given sentence depends on the structure of the sentence and on information conveyed when certain parts of the sentence are said. For example, the information conveyed by the a conjunction *He was born in Jaffa and she was born in Tel-Aviv* can be represented by the information conveyed by each of the conjuncts, *He was born in Jaffa* and *She was born in Tel-Aviv*, and by the function of *and*.

Similarly, on the assumption that a method exists for representing information conveyed by sentences, rules have been contrived to capture basic relations between sentences according to relations that hold between what is respectively conveyed. Such a basic relation holds between *There are red swans* and *There are no red swans*, or between *I was born in Jerusalem* and *I was not born in Jerusalem*. Another basic relation between the information conveyed by one sentence and that conveyed by another one is illustrated by the pair *If there is smoke, there is fire* and *If there is no fire, there is no smoke* or the pair *David is Solomon's brother* and *Solomon is David's brother*. Indeed, the former relation is that of negation (of a certain type) and the latter is an equivalence of some strict type. Descriptions of much more complicated and interesting relations abound in the literature.

Thus, the employment of notions such as 'communication' and 'information' leads us to a conceptual juncture at which one cannot choose but to follow either the philosophical track or the linguistic one. Opting for philosophical analysis would be making an attempt at adequate clarification of what we commit ourselves to by using communication-oriented theories: What are the hidden assumptions involved; what are the severe difficulties that arise when 'communication' and similar notions are explained. When we follow the philosophical track we are not as much interested in what one can accomplish when the legitimacy of the notions of 'communication', 'information', 'truth conditions' and the like are made use of as we are interested in the problem of the very legitimacy of such notions within an adequate theory.

However, serious obstacles might make it difficult to progress in understanding discourse, language and context alike, even if the linguistic track is followed and free use is made of communication-oriented theories.

An interesting way of depicting the informational content of a given sentence has been used by many theoreticians: The information contained in the sentence about the related state of affairs can be characterized in terms of the conditions that state of affairs has to fulfill for that information to be true. The suggestion that to know what is said by a sentence is the same as to know under what conditions it would be true has been found to be impressively fruitful in various parts of linguistics, discourse analysis included, as is explained in other chapters of this *Handbook*. However, a grave shortcoming of that approach is encountered once attempts are made at applying it to sentences used not for assertion but, say, for asking or commanding. Proposals for truth conditions for sentences such as *Who was the first president of the United States?*, *Don't shoot!* or *Pass the salt, please* are bound to fail, because such sentences are not used for describing some facets of appropriate states of affairs. It is quite clear that by describing such sentences as being on a par with sentences such as *Snow is white* or *A friend in need is a friend indeed* one misses an important distinction that is reflected in each and every natural language, that is, the distinction between asserting and other things done in words, such as requesting, congratulating, and promising. Even if the latter are taken to involve certain information transfers, much more has to be added about each of them for its description to be of even approximate linguistic adequacy (Austin, 1975).

When we have a suspicion that a given theory is actually built on flimsy conceptual foundations, we hasten to look for better foundations, that is to say, for a theory that would share the explanatory success of the previous one without raising the same or similar malign difficulties.

An Alternative Framework

We turn now to an outline of such alternative foundations. Again, we would like to draw the reader's attention to three ingredients of the present view, assuming that some understanding of the former will suffice for an informed impression about the latter.

First, the unit of language is taken to be a speech act, in a broad sense of the term (Searle, 1967) to be explained below. Neither single words nor complete sentences are considered to be more than just parts of what sustains a single appearance of language. A single instance of natural language use involves, first and foremost, a human action, done on purpose, with words and sentences, within an appropriate context. Thus, among the essential elements of the linguistic unit, one finds not only sentences but also several components of the context of utterance and various thoughts of the speaker about himself and about other components of the context.

What is the rationale for including such odd ingredients in the linguistic unit? Generally speaking, we never encounter self-sustaining words or sentences. Whenever language is "in presence," as we prefer to say what we are facing is never just a string of words; it is rather a sentence being used by a certain human being on purpose. What is done intentionally is done for some reasons, on the basis of the agent's ends and his assumptions as to the available means he can employ for attaining his end. To take the simplest example, when I address you, for whatever purpose I might have had in mind, I have useful assumptions as to which language should be used under the circumstances. Thus, when you evaluate my performance you must take into account not only which sentence I uttered, but also, for example, whom I addressed and what my assumptions were with respect to the language in which my addressee should be approached (Dummett, 1975, 1976).

To be sure, by saying that the unit of language is a speech act one has not done much more than point out an interesting direction to theoretical elaboration. One major problem, which looms large in the philosophical facet of the analysis of language, is that of characterizing and representing speech acts. Notice that the philosophical problem of answering the question "What is a speech act?" is much more difficult than that of answering the seemingly similar question "What is an act?" Whereas some understanding of what is shared by acts can be gained by probing causes and natures of bodily movements, no important insight into the essence of speech act will be gained by examining the physical qualities of utterances and the physical causes thereof.

As a first approximation to a framework for describing speech acts (and other intentional acts) we suggest the quadruple of ends, means, roles, and products. A type of speech act is characterized by a fixed quadruple, of ends and means, roles and products, of an appropriate form. A particular speech act of a certain type would be representable by a particular quadruple, of certain ends and means, roles and products, all directly connected to the related utterance and context of utterance. What are the constitutents of such quadruples of ends and means, roles and products? Roughly speaking, the ends of a speech act are the minimal ones: When I ask you *What is the time of the day?*, I entertain an appropriate intention concerning my own wish to know what the time of the day is, at the time of utterance, as well as my assumption about the possibility of eliciting from you a reply. On each occasion of my asking you *What is the time of the day?* I might, and indeed most of the times do, have a further goal in mind, beyond that of gaining knowledge of the time. Since, however, such goals are not minimal, in the sense that they are not shared by all instances of that question being uttered, it does not constitute part of what is included in the first member of the characteristic quadruple, namely end.

The means used in speech activity to attain given, minimal ends are of two kinds. Indeed, each sentence of the language, when appropriately uttered, is a means to a correlative end. An analysis of sentences as means to minimal ends would involve, first, the syntactic and semantic analyses of the sentences, as is clear from the role played by syntactic structures and by phrases of the form *I hereby V* in forming sentences that are typically used in forming questions, commands, and speech acts of some other kinds. Second and less obviously, contexts of utterance are used by speakers when they entertain certain minimal ends. To take a simple example, consider the use of demonstratives. The fact that Joanne is present at a context of utterance, with no other woman seen around or talked about, may be used by a speaker to say, for instance, *She is right,* meaning that Joanne is right.

However, the complete story of a felicitous speech act includes more than a detailed description of ends and means. Thus, for example, it takes more than an utterance of *Fire!* in presence of a person armed with a gun to issue a command. Real commands involve knowledge on both sides of the act, so to speak, that they are presently active within an appropriate hierarchy in which each "side" is ascribed a definite role. Only a person who plays a certain role in such a background hierarchy is in a position to use imperative sentences, under suitable circumstances, in order to issue a command. It is our view that every type of speech act involves some role ascriptions to the speaker and perhaps to some other persons present at the contexts of utterance, but the defense of that view is not attempted here.

Finally, each time a speech act is felicitously performed a typical product is created. To mention just one interesting example, consider the product of a sincere speech act of promising. Not much is gained by describing the product of such a speech act as being a promise, but deep understanding of that type of speech act might be gained if we notice that certain obligations are produced when promises are made.

According to the present view, then, to master any type of speech act is to acquire knowledge of the related ends and means, roles and products. More accurately, to master a type of speech act is to internalize a set of rules that determine the ends, means, roles, and products involved in speech acts of that type. The nature of these sets of rules is at the core of the second ingredient of the present philosophical view.

There have been many philosophical discussions of various types of rules and systems of rules. We would like to mention just one distinction between different types of systems of rules, one that has ample philosophical consequences with respect to speech and discourse analyses.

When we are presented with a description of a rule that belongs to a given system of rules, we may ponder over the very fact of that single rule belonging to the given system of rules. We may inquire into the reasons for including the rule in the system. There are two major ways of justifying the inclusion of a rule in a system. First, there is regulative justification, showing the contribution made by that rule to an attempt to achieve some purpose by employing the whole system of rules. Thus, each traffic regulation is meant to enhance the success of the whole system of traffic control in achieving optimal movement of vehicles and people. Second, there is definitional justification, which shows that a rule belongs to a system of rules by the very definition of the latter. The rule that specifies what checkmate is in the game of chess belongs to the system of the rules of chess, because it is part of the definition of the game. There is no independent standard by which one could have justified the rule of checkmate as part of the game of chess.

Philosophers have found the analogy between formal ways of activity, such as playing games, dueling, or creating coats of arms, on the one hand, and natural languages, on the other hand, to be very useful. The main insight so far is that a system of rules that characterizes a type of speech act, such as asserting or advising, is a definition of that type of speech act. Hence, when some rules specify certain conditions to be fulfilled by the ends or the means, the roles or the products of the related speech act for it to be a felicitous instance of, say, asserting, these rules are part of or follow from the definition of assertion. A felicitous performance of a speech act of promising creates an obligation, because by definition speech acts of promising create obligations if felicitously performed.

This view has an obvious consequence with respect to the nature of language and its study. A natural language is a family of systems of rules, each defining its own ends and means, roles and products. Different members of such a family share, first of all, an underlying system of syntactic and semantic rules that determine general properties and particular features of means used for performing speech acts. Moreover, all types of speech acts of a language share biologically determined, universal properties, namely those that any type of human act has to fulfill for it to be a psychologically possible type of speech act. The latter, universal properties are of particular interest to philosophers who have always been intrigued or infuriated by the possibility of there being human innate ideas that shape much of the form of our language and thought independently of the particular content of our experience.

Another consequence of the present view is related to discourse analysis in particular. Speech acts of almost any kind occur within broad spheres of human activity such as tuition, argumentation, and ritual. Relations between rule-governed speech activity and rule-governed activity of another type hold on two levels. First, formal ends and products of speech acts can serve further ends or more complicated products, respectively. For example, by performing an appropriately worded act of promising, an obligation is undertaken that, in turn, is instrumental in creating a legal bond of marriage. Second, by-products of a felicitous speech act sometimes serve the broader purposes at hand. For instance, a by-product of a comment on the weather is that the conversation is going on. To be sure, a by-product of a speech act can be an intended one, but since that speech act could have been performed without an accompanying intention to create that by-product, the latter intention cannot be regarded as part of the characteristic ends of the speech act. This relation between the rules defining a type of speech act and by-products of performing speech acts of that type is on a par with the relation holding between, say, the rules of chess and the pleasure one might feel playing the game. Although quite often that pleasure is the intended by-product of playing, it would be ludicrous to look for any note about it in the rules of the game.

We turn now to another consequence of the view that language is a family of related systems of definitional rules. This is the third ingredient of the present philosophical sketch. We mentioned earlier that each system of rules that serves as a definition of a type of speech act includes rules that define the form of the ends of performing a speech act of that type. Consequently, the all-embracing notions of 'communication' and 'information transfer' in the common parlance of the study of language are here replaced by individual ends determined by each member of the family of definitional systems of rules separately. If one does not have to explain every type of speech act in terms of information transferred by performing speech acts of that type, then one might realize that speech acts of major importance, such as assertion, can be interestingly described and explained without recourse to any form of intended communication.

Such a decentralized view of natural language carries some consequences concerning the study of language and discourse. First, the study of different types of speech acts, as well as that of different types of discourse, is a study of a family of highly independent phenomena. Therefore, it is much more difficult to put forward interesting generalizations about speech acts or about discourse than about, say, syntax, which is supposedly amenable to explanation in terms of a single, though highly complicated, system of rules. The prevalent fragmentary nature of most of the study of speech acts and discourse should, then, take none of us by surprise. However difficult it is to generalize, it is still not impossible, if one looks for generalizations at the right parts of the field. The most promising area for generalizations of some importance seems to be the counterpart of what Chomsky has called 'universal grammar'. Answers to questions such as "What is a psychologically possible type of conversation?," "What is a psychologically possible type of speech act?," or "What are the restrictions imposed on the class of concepts in terms of which rules of our linguistic capacities can define, for instance, ends and means of discourses or roles and products of speech acts?" will belong to the sought level of generalization. The current literature includes only preliminary studies of this type.

Second, an interesting problem arises when a variety of types of speech acts or discourse are under consideration, namely, to what extent would a full-fledged explanation of the given variety belong to an adequate presentation of our knowledge of our natural language. Whereas we take it for granted that one cannot be considered a speaker of any natural language as long as one has not mastered the rules that govern assertion, it is not self evident, if at all true, that advising and promising are also integral parts of the natural language. Similarly, if one does not know what it means to answer questions in some natural language, then one does not have the ordinary knowledge of that language that is common to all speakers of the language who have the capacity of conducting a conversation in the language. On the other hand, knowledge of intricate politeness forms of speech, of the legal significance of certain phrases, or of which words of the language are under some taboo is commonly not taken to be part of the knowledge of the language, although it is related to uses of certain expressions that belong to it. Demarcation problems arise as to what constitutes knowledge of a language, in contradistinction to knowledge of rules that govern social institutions that employ language in their activities.

Such a demarcation problem used to engage the attention of many philosophers, namely where, if at all, the line could be drawn between synthetic truths and analytic ones, that is, between those of a factual nature, their truth stemming from the way things in world happen to be, and those that are conceptual, their truth being a matter of linguistic or conceptual analysis, independent of the contingent facts. The dispute between those who confessed grave doubts as to whether this demarcation problem was solvable and their more optimistic opponents has not been definitely decided, but much has been gained in understanding the nature of language from the arguments pro and con. Thus, it seems worthwhile to raise the demarcation problems of speech acts and discourses: Which types of speech act are part of the language and which are just useful appendages? What part of the capacity to be engaged in discourses of certain types is purely linguistic? Philosophical work has been done concerning the basic linguistic nature of assertions and questions, but it still remains to be seen what significant results there are to be found in the field of demarcation problems.

PHILOSOPHICAL ANALYSIS
OF CONVERSATION

The most important philosophical contribution to theoretical analysis of discourse has been the systematic disclosure of underlying levels. In this section we present, in some detail, two concepts that have been shown to be of theoretical help in explaining why and how there is more in a conversation than meets the eye.

There is a variety of notions of 'presupposition' (Kempson, 1975; Stalnaker, 1978). Some of these notions are semantic in nature, denoting certain relations between contents of sentences. Such semantic relations are not discussed in this chapter, which is confined to pragmatic notions.

The main idea behind several notions of pragmatic presupposition is that there is a characteristic class of propositions whose truth is taken for granted as part of the appropriate background for a felicitous utterance of a given sentence. The assumption concerning some of these propositions is even stronger: their truth is taken for granted as part of the background for an utterance of a given sentence not only by the speaker but also by the other participants in the conversation within which the utterance of that sentence is embedded. According to such a sense of the notion of pragmatic presupposition, a felicitous utterance of any given sentence depends on a characteristic class of propositions that constitutes the mutual knowledge at hand.

Logico-philosophical studies of pragmatic presuppositions have been devoted to three problems: analysis and representation of the concept; the projection problem, namely the problem of defining the class of pragmatic presuppositions related to a complex sentence in terms of the classes of pragmatic presuppositions related to the simpler parts of that sentence; and applications of the notion to several philosophical problems.

One interesting method of capturing the idea of pragmatic presupposition in this sense employes the concept of "possible world." In a nutshell, a possible world is a way the world might have been. My typewriter in the actual world is red, but it might have been gray. Put differently, there is a possible world that is similar to the actual one, the only difference residing in the color of my typewriter: the fact that my typewriter in the actual world is red, whereas my typewriter in the other world is gray, and the consequences thereof. The possible-world parlance has been found useful in many logical and philosophical fields, though the concept itself is still in want of philosophical analysis that is free of basic difficulties.

In a given context of utterance, a speaker is ascribed his or her context set, that is to say, a class of possible worlds taken by the speaker as the present options. When I ask you for the identity of the person at your side, my context set at the moment includes a possible world in which the person is a visiting relative of yours, another possible world in which he is a partner of yours in some enterprise, and still another one in which you have never met him and you don't know who he is.

Now, a pragmatic presupposition of a speaker in a context of utterance is a proposition that is true in each member of the context set, that is, in each possible world the speaker takes to be a present option. For example, when I ask you *Who succeeded in solving the mystery?* in a certain context of utterance, my context set includes a possible world for each answer that I would accept from you. Part of what is common to all these possible worlds is that in each of them there is someone who tried to solve the mystery. That there is someone like that is then a pragmatic presupposition of myself as speaker when I ask you *Who succeeded in solving the mystery?*

When we examine a conversation we encounter the context sets of the different participants. In what has been dubbed "nondefective contexts," all the participants share the pragmatic presuppositions of their context sets. Thus, for example, when I ask you *who succeeded in solving the mystery?* in a nondefective context of utterance, both you and I share the pragmatic presupposition that someone has tried to solve the mystery.

If we assume that the surface form of a conversation is that of a series of speech acts, then for the sake of simplicity we consider first nondefective conversations, that is to say, those whose surface form is that of a series of felicitous speech acts, each performed under the conditions of a nondefective context of utterance. Corresponding to and underlying the surface series of speech acts is a series of the pragmatic presuppositions of them. Let us call the latter series "the pragmatic presuppositional depth representation" of the former series of speech acts or of the conversation itself. One way of studying discourses is to investigate the process of change that takes place when we move along the pragmatic presuppositional depth representation of a discourse. It has been suggested that assertions are attempts to reduce the present class of pragmatic presuppositions. Indeed, if a participant in a conversation asserts something that is then accepted by all the other participants as true, the context set of each of them is reduced, because by accepting a certain proposition as true one crosses out all possible worlds in his context set in which that proposition is false. Consequently, the class of shared pragmatic presuppositions is also being thus reduced. Upon reflection one realizes that a similar observation is possible of many nonassertoric speech acts as well.

A philosophical analysis of a different family of phenomena, also related to what happens behind the curtains, so to speak, of ordinary speech acts, has been developed around several notions of 'implicature'. We conclude this chapter by pointing out some of the major ingredients of the prevalent theories of conversational implicature (Grice, 1975, 1978).

The starting point of the discussion of implicature is the seemingly simple observation that speech acts are intentional, that is to say, performed for a reason. Ordinarily, a speaker of a language is in a position to provide on request answers to questions such as why he said what he said or why he put it the way he did rather than in any other way. The speaker's answers will, indeed, disclose his or her reasons for saying what was said, in the way it was said.

On many occasions there is no difficulty in grasping a speaker's reasons for performing a certain speech act in a certain context of utterance, but sometimes a want of reasons might be sensed. The latter occasions are presently much more interesting than the former. Consider, for example, sincere and literal utterances of sentences such as *He will either resign from the Cabinet or not, Have I liked the book? Well, yes and no,* or *A child is not an adult.* Why should anyone deem any context of utterance appropriate for what seems a truism, what is obviously right or obviously wrong? Notice that we are all inclined to ascribe to such utterances some interpretation in a way that renders the utterance under consideration appropriate to its context, in no particular need of further explanation. Thus, for example, we always interpret a *Yes and no* answer to a question as affirmative in one sense and negative in another. Our inclination to thus interpret such utterances rests, of course, on our global assumption that normally people have good reasons for saying what they say in the way that they say it.

It has been suggested that some order can be shown to exist behind the seemingly chaotic appearance of clever interpretations of utterances that call for special defense. Each speaker is taken to follow certain maxims and supermaxims under any normal circumstances of conversation. A supermaxim of 'quantity' prescribes contribution of the right amount of information when it is one's turn to participate in a normal conversation. A supermaxim of 'quality' instructs the speaker to attempt making only true contributions to the conversation in which he or she participates. The supermaxim of 'relation' recommends relevance, and maxims of manner direct the speaker to perspicuous, unequivocal expressions. When any of these maxims is apparently violated in a normal conversation, an attempt is made to save the speaker's adherence to them, so to speak, by supplementing the assumptions participants in the conversation hold with respect to the speaker with additional propositions such that under the new, enlarged class of assumptions about the speaker his utterance is well explained and no violation of any of the supermaxims is involved. Such additional propositions are called "conversational implicatures." For example, an utterance of the seemingly tautologous *He will either resign from the Cabinet or not* is apparently problematic, but if we assume that the speaker does not know which of the alternatives is going to be the case, nor does he have any evidence that one alternative should be regarded more probable or plausible than the other, then we can explain that utterance as an indirect way of expressing the speaker's being utterly noncommittal with respect to that resignation. His being thus noncommittal is an implicature of his utterance. Many interesting phenomena in different types of discourse have been explained by resort to a theory of conversational implicatures.

A problem arises at the foundations of any theory of implicatures concerning the justification of the assumption that under normal conditions of conversation the above-mentioned maxims and supermaxims do hold. The standard defense of the latter rests on Grice's cooperative principle: "Make your conversational contribution such as is required, at the stage at which it occurs, by the accepted purpose or direction of the talk exchange in which you are engaged" (Grice, 1975, p. 45). However, it is difficult to take talk exchanges that have an accepted purpose or direction as typical. Consequently, if the whole implicature theory hinges on the assumption that the cooperative principle obtains in the contexts of utterance under discussion, then not much is gained in understanding the logic of conversation from an elaboration of a theory of implicatures. Fortunately, the cooperative principle can be successfully replaced by a more general rationality principle, namely: "Given a desired end—a minimal purpose—make that linguistic action which most effectively and at least cost attains that purpose" (Kasher, 1979, p. 47). By recourse to a general rationality principle and to particular consequences thereof, it is possible to substantiate many supermaxims and maxims of conversation. From such a point of view, speech acts and conversations are intentional, completely on a par with many other human intentional actions. To the latter as well as to the former one not only may, but actually has to, apply the general principles of practical reasoning (Raz, 1978).

REFERENCES

Austin, J. L. (1975). *How to do things with words* (2nd ed.). Oxford: Clarendon Press.

Chomsky, N. (1980). *Rules and representations*. Oxford: Basil Blackwell.

Dummett, M. (1975). What is a theory of meaning? (I). In S. Guttenplan (Ed.), *Mind and language* (pp. 97–138). Oxford: Clarendon Press.

Dummett, M. (1976). What is a theory of meaning? (II). In G. Evans & J. McDowell (Eds.), *Truth and meaning* (pp. 67–137). Oxford: Clarendon Press.

Grice, H. P. (1975). Logic and conversation. In P. Cole and J. L. Morgan (Eds.), *Syntax and semantics* (Vol. 3) (pp. 43–58). New York: Academic Press.

Grice, H. P. (1978). Further notes on logic and conversation. In P. Cole (Ed.), *Syntax and semantics* (Vol. 9) (pp. 113–127). New York: Academic Press.

Kasher, A. (1979). What is a theory of use? In A. Margalit (Ed.), *Meaning and use* (pp. 37–55). Dordrecht and Boston: D. Reidel.

Kempson, R. M. (1975). *Presuppositions and the delimitation of semantics.* Cambridge: Cambridge University Press.

Kuhn, T. S. (1962). *The structure of scientific revolutions.* Chicago: University of Chicago Press.

Perry, T. A. (Ed.) (1980). *Evidence and argumentation in linguistics.* Berlin and New York: Walter de Gruyter.

Raz, J. (Ed.) (1978). *Practical reasoning.* Oxford: Oxford University Press.

Searle, J. R. (1967). In F. E. X. Dance (Ed.), *Human communication today* (pp. 116–129). New York: Holt, Rinehart & Winston.

Stalnaker, R. C. (1978). Assertion. In P. Cole (Ed.), *Syntax and Semantics* (Vol. 9) (pp. 315–332). New York: Academic Press.

CHAPTER 10

Historical Discourse

Nancy S. Struever

INTRODUCTION

Words make history. The historian who has discarded the old and invidious insistence that history deals with real action and not mere words now may turn to pragmatics, the initiative of the philosophy of language that treats words as acts and regards communicative action as the strongest model of social interaction (Apostel, 1980, p. 240). Discourse analysis is the formalist program that describes what pragmatics wishes to explain—the systematicity of the activities and events of discursive practice (Parret, 1980, pp. 46-47).

First, then, the discourse analysis project is of obvious interest to the historian since both discourse analysis and pragmatics are prominent instances of the movement of rehistoricization in contemporary language study. Both attempt an account of the totality of language competence, the reconstruction of language as a communicative, intersubjective, social phenomenon (Parret, 1980, p. 3). Both focus on recognizably historical topics: the relation of the phrase as primary language unit to those who enunciate and interpret it, the specification of the situation of enunciation, and the presence of such investing factors as illocutionary force, implication, presupposition, insinuation. Further, discourse analysis is of interest as a compendious project in the field of formal study. That is to say, while there is a specifically discursive level of analysis—the domain of large discursive structures such as argumentative strategies, rhetorical tactics, mechanisms of intervention by the speaking subject—linguistics (the various modes of lexical and syntactic analysis within the phrase) is to be folded into the discourse analysis project, and semiotics (the general study of all systems of signification, nonverbal as well as verbal) is to be instructed

HANDBOOK OF DISCOURSE ANALYSIS, Vol. 1
Disciplines of Discourse

by the model of exchange, distribution, and consumption developed in discourse analysis.

Investment in discourse analysis technique, then, is an economical expenditure for the historian. But more importantly, it is an analytic mode that is heuristic on two levels; it can function as both critique and self-critique. First, it functions as a tool of inquiry in the traditional task of interpretation of source, the exploitation of the archive of pertinent discourses that the historian uses to reconstruct the past. It is a formalist project that promises direct access to significant social process; the formal description of the functioning of a discursive practice is at once the description of the structures and processes of social action. Second, analysis of the discourse of the historians themselves reveals the discursive strategies of presentation and thus the uses the historian makes of techniques, including discourse analysis itself. This promises a description of history as discipline, of the activities and events of history writing; here discursive self-definition should make a significant contribution to the definition of proper historical inquiry, to a theory of history.

DISCOURSE ANALYSIS AND THE ARCHIVE

Perhaps a symptom of the essential, not trivial, historicity of discourse analysis is its susceptibility to nationalist fashions, for it is relatively easy to discern three major initiatives in historical discourse research: a discourse analysis *manqué* (Anglo-American), a mainstream discourse analysis (French), and a revisionary moment (German).

Anglo-American Historians and the Study of Discourse

Anglo-American discursive research is marked by strong inconsistencies. The epithet *manqué* derives from the resistance to the premise of the systematicity of discourse and its lack of commitment to the usefulness of purely formal analysis. Yet the analytic philosophy of language, and particularly the later work of Wittgenstein, is profoundly suggestive for the historical study of discourse (Apel, 1967; Tiffoneau, 1977). The postulates of Wittgenstein have an economical elegance: he rejects a separation between concepts and language, mental activity and discursive activity, and thus eschews the depiction of a private mental realm for the study of public, accessible discursive activity. The unit of study is the language-game, a unit that is both historically specific and holistic, self-subsistent. Further, the language game is a manifestation of a 'form of life', a premise that functions as a powerful claim that linguistic forms express the most basic sociohistorical structures.

The most articulate theoretician is Quentin Skinner, who invokes the work of the philosophers Austin, Grice, and Searle, work that can be seen as a modification of Wittgensteinian theory (Skinner, 1972). The historian no longer deals in propositions but speech acts, not sentences but utterances, with, in sum, discourse, not texts. Austin claimed that in any utterance an agent does something in saying something; an utterance has an illocutionary or perlocutionary force. For Skinner, this means that historical explanation is illocutionary redescription, a process of recovering the agent's intended illocutionary act by decoding the social conventions that govern the linguistic exchange.

But the ambivalence of the theory is manifest in an oscillation between the temptation of Skinner and his followers to regard a private realm of meanings as primary and a devotion to the Wittgensteinian concern with public usage. The ambivalence generates, on the one hand, Dunn's (1972) statement that private intentions close the circle of context, and on the other hand, Dunn's claim, obviously Wittgensteinian in emphasis, that the product of a history of Cartesian philosophy is not a summary of a set of propositions embedded in the Cartesian text but an account of Cartesian philosophizing as activity. The confusion invests the collection of theoretical essays, *Action and Interpretation* (Hookway & Pettit, 1978), which is bemused with the problem of the indeterminacy of translation (Quine, 1960) as the central methodological issue. This is a bemusement with meaning and thus is a pseudoproblem, according to Parret, since it denies discourse as having its own empirical systematicity and thus reduces discourse analysis to an act of translating from one realm of mental entities to another, realms which are opaque and private (Parret, 1980, 53–54).

But it is in the practice of discursive research that the difficulties of this school are most apparent. A resistance to system and to formalist studies at times seems an antagonism to precision and rigor and seems to motivate the rejection of specific projects such as the classification of illocutionary acts in a discourse, projects the French easily accommodate (Slatka, 1971).

Further, there seems to be a disjunction between theory and practice, for instance, between the spirited theorizing of Skinner and his very traditional, nonanalytic approach in his survey, *Foundations of Modern Political Thought* (1978). Then, in practice, theoretical constructs lose their analytic promise. The key construct of what Pocock calls the "Cambridge School" of political history, which includes Skinner, Pocock, and Dunn, is that for any age there is a range of available languages that determine thought (Pocock, 1981). But in their usage, the word "language" is vacuous, almost metaphorical; there is no recognition of formal lexical and syntactic constraints as pertinent. The languages are akin to vocabularies that, in turn, are lists of thematic units very close to the unit-ideas of the traditional history-of-ideas approach of Lovejoy (1948). The project slips back into a neo-Kantian project of a history of conceptual structures; the description of a range of available languages produces a Platonic array of possible thematic choices rather than an analysis of the actual discursive practices of a historical period.

The practice, in sum, does not develop a program. Pocock (1957) proceeds, for example, in an intuitive manner, relying on his tact and his great erudition in his close readings of texts. The most outstanding historical monograph that uses analytic philosophical categories is Kahn's *The Verb "Be" in Ancient Greek* (1973), and this work is marked by eclecticism, since he uses the methods of Harrisian discourse analysis and classical philology as well. In striking contrast to the strong claims of Pocock's tact is the unconvincing dishevellment of Sewell's approach in his *Work and Revolution in France: The Language of Labor* (1980). Sewell either ignores or blurs the splendid French analytic work on the language of the laboring classes during and after the French Revolution (Dubois, 1962; Matoré, 1967; Ranciére, 1976; Tournier, 1973); his account seems afflicted by what Bourdieu calls "essaisme" and thus seems resistant not only to formal research and its premise of systematicity but also to theory, *tout court*.

Contemporary French Discourse Analysis

The contrast between Sewell and the French analysts exemplifies the contrast between the confused and tentative, if suggestive, nature of Anglo-American inquiry and the coherence and rigor of the French project.[1]

---

[1] Besides the collections cited in the text (Greimas & Landowski, 1979; Conein *et al.*, 1981; Guilhamou, 1974) readers should be aware of the many serial publications which have dealt with issues pertinent to historical discourse analysis at great length. I speak, of course, of *Langages,* especially *13* (1969) "Analyse du discours"; *23* (1971) "Le discours politique"; *37* (1975) "Analyse du discours, langue, et idéologies"; *41* (1976) "Typologie du discours politique"; *53* (1979) "Le discours juridique; analyses et méthodes"; *55* (1979) "Analyse du discours et linguistique générale." Also *Langue française,* especially *9* (1971) "Linguistique et société"; *15* (1972) "Langage et histoire"; *43* (1979) "Dictionnaire, sémantique, et culture." And, of course, the *Bulletin du Centre d'Analyse du Discours,* published by the University of Lille, especially No. 2 (1975) "Sur la Révolution française"; No. 3 (1976–1978) "Discours et Enseignements"; No. 5 (1981) "Accuser et Juger aux XVIIIe et XIXe siècles."

The French work is the richest development of discourse analysis as historical inquiry, and it draws its strength from two major initiatives: the post-structuralist movement of the transcendence of the text, with its insistence on the pertinence of extra-linguistic factors such as the speaking subject and the enunciative situation in all their historical specificity (Dubois, 1969; Kristeva, 1971), and Marxist historical materialism, which welcomes an emphasis on the materiality of discursive practices and on the facticity of its social occasions, interventions, and effects.

However, neither the transcendence of the rigid demarcations of linguistic structuralism nor Marxist materialism inhibits the robust formalism that invests both theory and practice in France. Robin's *Histoire et Linguistique* (1973) stated the assumptions guiding the work of the previous decade: first, the object of analysis is to reveal a hidden, not a patent structure; in Maldidier's words, "L'inasserté gouverne toujours l'asserté" (Maldidier, Normand, & Robin, 1972, p. 137). While the tissue of self-conscious thematic statements (content) is relegated to the surface, the hidden structure is a complex of formal constraints that constitute the internal economy of the system (Robin, 1973, p. 139). The assumption of the systematic nature of discursive functioning entails two further postulates: that only a formal, rigorous analysis, not an intuitive method, is useful, and that this analysis is integrated and holistic (Robin, 1973, pp. 139, 196). Discourse analysis is both species and genus; while there is a specifically discursive level of research, exemplified by Pecheux's (1969) analysis of discursive syntax, a mode Pecheux derives from Harrisian transformational analysis, discourse analysis is not one method but all methods integrated into a program of exhaustive, technically precise description of whole practices. Integration as program combines taxonomic initiatives—the classification of dominant types of predicate, the sorting of categories of verbs of action or of types of speech act—with ambitious attempts to map entire discursive domains: projects such as the description of the discursive strategies of major political confrontations such as that between Turgot and the Parlementarians (Maldidier & Robin, 1974) or the reconstruction of the complex rhetoric that guides the discursive reception of one culture by another (Marandin, 1979). Studies of discursive syntax disclose elementary social strategies: They depict the constitution of social solidarity and party opposition, the development of centrifugal and centripetal rhetorical processes, and increases in specificity or reductions in ambiguity that force the reader to make connections or assent to distinctions in crucial political definitions. Also, choices of narrative forms are shown as reversing attributions of activity or passivity to historical agents, while argumentative choices effect shifts in performative types of discourse—apologetic, polemic, eulogistic, and so on. Discursive strategies control semiotic nonverbal activity as well; Ozouf's (1976) analysis of French revolutionary fêtes reveals an overarching discursive tactic of imposition of a false utopian consciousness, a pedagogic coercion.

But the key question for any historian who wishes to employ discourse analysis is how one maps discursive practice onto other social practices. Two different French approaches to this question are those of Foucault and of the Althusserian Marxists. All of Foucault's work can be seen as an elaborate justification of the importance of the study of discourse in history (Foucault, 1971), although it is impossible to reduce his method to discourse analysis, since his techniques are personal and inimitable, and resist description even by his own *Archéologie du Savoir* (1969). Foucault's complicated methodology corresponds to a complex theory. He sees discursive forms as both cause and effect, active and passive, responsive to transhistorical factors, yet molding institutions and roles.

For this reason, Marxists feel that Foucault simply juxtaposes discourse practice and other practices; he explains nothing. Marxists stipulate a tight relation of effect and cause between discourse and politics. Discursive formations are the material production of the process of winning adhesion to an ideology (with ideology defined as a system of notions and beliefs that control the behavior of interlocutors toward reality); the discursive system has an extralinguistic as well as intralinguistic source (Conein, 1981, pp. 181, 200). The Marxist task for discourse analysis is the revelation of the internal economy of an ideology; it is a project of unmasking, and Marx's *Eighteenth Brumaire* is the archetypal exposition of the relation of discourse, ideology, and power (Robin, 1973, pp. 100ff.). But the Foucaultians attack Marxist analysis as an oversimplification. They claim that the Marxist approach is as question begging as the standard history of ideas approach, for both prophesy their results by sharply limiting their problematic. The historian of ideas can only find the presence or absence of his chosen themes, while the Marxist can only describe ideological manipulation and exploitation through discourse since he has no vocabulary to describe well-motivated discursive initiatives.

If we turn away from these theoretical problems to French practice, we notice at once the very high proportion of research of Marxist orientation. Many of the studies, for example, relate to issues of class interest and revolutionary politics. The privileged periods for analysis are the French Revolution, 1848, 1870, the Algerian crisis, and May 1968. There are also privileged types of discourse; much of the analysis deals with political rhetoric or with the description of the raw popular idioms of the struggling classes. And it is certainly the case that a great deal of French analysis takes place within a polemical frame. If a study holds the Marxist premise that discursive forms share the structure of ideology, that is, they are illusory or delusory manifestations of false consciousness, then discourse analysis is necessarily highly politicized itself, since it is engaged in disclosing falsity and arguing the truth of revolutionary goals (Robin, 1973, p. 15; Sumpf, 1979).

Yet the range of definition of French projects is very great; discourse analysis has stimulated both broad redefinition and ingenious specialization. Furet (1978), for example, wishes a total reorientation of the history of the French Revolution based on his assumption that "the semiotic circuit is the absolute master of politics" (p. 72); thus discourse confects revolt. One of the most fruitful of the specific projects is the redescription of the historical agent. Conein, for example, criticizes the historians' tendency to reify abstractions such as the 'revolutionary masses'. Analysis replaces such naive predictions with precise accounts of the creation of agency in successive discursive formulations; discourse anticipates and defines events in which the collectivities are deemed actants (Conein, 1981, pp. 55ff.; see Landowski, 1976). Foucault's *Naissance de la Clinique* (1963), an account of the institutions, roles, and rituals of medical discourse in the nineteenth century, is a very rich redescription of continuity and change in the competence and performance of the physician, especially in doctor–patient relations.

We also may note the mutual and fruitful reinforcement of historical problematic and discourse-analysis technique. On the one hand, the Annales school of French historiography, with its preoccupation with the *longue durée* rather than the heroic episode as the domain of significance, and description of the *mentalité collective* rather than the biography of an elite, has expanded the range of pertinent texts. The analyst must confront archival documents hitherto read only for statistical information as well as the accounts and monuments of ceremony and ritual, wills, testaments, and other popular legal discourse. At the same time, the analytic mode that focuses on discursive practices in their historical specificity has forced a return to the *histoire événementielle* that had been rejected by the Annales school and thus has fostered a double commitment to both heroic event and the *longue durée* of collective mentalities. The historical analyst needs to describe not only the invention of a new discourse but also the power of group memory in maintaining discursive convention over long periods of time.

Finally, we notice that the central concern of French discourse analysis with system can translate into a historical focus on disjunction. The premise of systematicity generates descriptions of integral, holistic practices, and, in turn, the descriptions of distinct formal economies help demarcate the individuality of a culture. Proper history, Kuentz (1981, pp. 35–36) claims, assumes the *illisibilité*, the radical difference of an earlier discourse, but insists that the accessibility of this unreadable discourse is stipulated by its systematic nature. The paired assumptions of difference and formal accessibility subvert anachronistic attempts to force present usages or perennial constructs on past practice and also permit counterintuitive, intriguing accounts, rather than mere affirmations of the expected; formal, relational results can constitute surprises.

German Revisionary Moments

Dällenbach (1979), in his preface to the *Poétique* issue devoted to current German literary research, notes the parallelism of German initiatives in *Rezeptionsgeschichte* and French initiatives of "transcendence of the text" (p. 258). But the particular emphasis in German research is on inclusiveness, on the inextricability of production, distribution, and reception modes, an emphasis that can function as a revisionary moment in discourse study. A historicist revision: To the historian, the German initiative seems most sensitive to the danger that formalist accounts may become accounts of ahistorical structures rather than of historical activities and practices. The focus on reception is a focus on phenomena of interaction. Thus while Apostel (1980, p. 306) claims that any discourse, no matter how monologic in form, is dialogic in operation, Stierle (1977) claims that any writing is a practice of reading. Indeed, his point is a stronger one: Discourse originates in reception, not production; "a reader is never content to simply confront a text, but organises it immediately into discourse" (p. 426). He states that text is an artifice, a confection of the investigator, while discourse denotes the living reality of linguistic exchange.

Further, the Marxist premises and goals that invest the movement constrain the discourse analyst to confront pragmatic issues on two levels: first, he must give a formal account of communicative interaction; second, he must give an account of the processes of articulation of normative values that motivate discourse (Apel, 1980; Habermas, 1974). Like the Anglo-American historians, Marxists employ speech act models of analytic philosophy to describe linguistic conventions as social constraints (Apel, 1967); their descriptions of significant segments of discourse—a genre, an ongoing parliamentary debate—reveal a shared "horizon of expectations", as well as modifications by the discursive exchange of that horizon. Form is not limited to aesthetic tactics; instead, precise, formal descriptions of agents, functions, and plots reveal the vital interchanges, the rituals and arguments that constitute the issues, and the nodes of affirmation and acquiescence, as well as the cleavages of revision and revolution of a society.

This conjunction of aesthetic and political interests assures a nourishing relation between literary historical technique and historical problematic.

The privileged topic for research becomes the genre, the domain in which formal choices are most explicitly political choices as well. Analysis of a specific text is deemed incomplete without consideration of the genre rules to which a practice attempts to conform, of the genre or genres it attempts to replace or subvert, and of the genres that surround it and thus modify its function. Genre research imposes the necessity of dealing with peripheral as well as central texts: the minor forms of audience response, the minor discourses to which the central text responds.

Stierle's (1972, 1977) studies of genre translate formal inclusiveness into historical ambition; his studies of Renaissance genre shifts are contributions to a political history of intellectual elites. The processes of the formation of the lyric or of new historiographical modes are described as a succession of reworkings of old genres that generate new goals and procedures, new roles and institutions in academic inquiry. The first chapter of Paul Feyerabend's *Against Method* (1978) can be seen as a genre analysis, a dissection of Galilean argumentative discourse as it constrains the development of a new scientific community and its patrons. Feyerabend claimed that an anarchist freedom of argument generates progress in theory; discursive procedures reveal institutional change.

The German initiative, then, is both inclusive in problematic, and exclusively formal in mode. Gumbrecht's (1979) analysis of the funeral orations for Marat in 1793 claims to demonstrate that the historian can move from "how" to "why" questions; analysis can bring to light implicit, not-conscious processes veiled by surface structures. His analysis leads to a revision of the naive attribution by historians of a desire for Terror to the Sans-culottes; instead, he claims, the orations reveal strategies that aim to refute doubts about the future of the Revolution by perpetuating a myth of consensus and to stabilize a relation between pretended equals. The tactic creates a shared interest in the Terror by invoking an external danger (aristocratic plot) as a reason for internal menace (the Terror). In comparison with French modes, Gumbrecht's generic definition of the speaking subject includes a typology of production and reception situations, comprising attitudes of reception (contemplation, judgment), situations of communication (fete, funeral), and speech acts accomplished (praise, blame). He is able to define epideictic as a strategy of closure, a refusal of problems, a mythic refutation of rational doubts.

An Agenda for Historical Research

Granted, then, that the goal of discourse analysis is the reconstruction of historically specific discursive economies insofar as they are linguistic actions (Parrett, 1980, p. 47), a specific agenda of tasks and issues would be useful. Just as the French has produced the largest portion of analysis, so they have produced the largest number of suggestions for revision and refinement.

Revisions seem to stem from two major reversals of emphasis. First, the corollary of the axiom that systematicity is necessary to the production of significance in discourse is the axiom that subversions and infractions of the system also produce significance. The strong Derridean (deconstructionist) and Marxist (demystificationist) impulses reinforce the program of mapping inconsistencies, contradictions, and falsifications in discursive activity. In this vein the summary colloquy in *Matérialités Discursives* (Conein, 1981, pp. 177ff), suggests a range of major and minor tasks: It raises the issue of the *porte-parole,* the spokesman and his relation to the social entities (e.g., working class, masses) for which he purports to speak. The metaphor of language as a kind of currency with an exchange value suggests the task of identifying counterfeit as well as veraciously valued discourse. If there can be exchange value, there can also be false exchange, such as Hitlerian rhetoric, which employed a revolutionary verbal coinage to establish a counterrevolutionary economic program. Robin (1973, p. 110) had already recognized that ideology does not always control discourse efficiently, like some kind of infernal machine; rather, all discourse is qualified by contradictory, self-subversive moments.

The second reversal of emphasis is the shift from a preoccupation with productivity, which in literary history has been an obsession with poeticity or the definition of a peculiar literary competence, to a focus that includes distribution and reception as analytic problems (Kuentz, 1981). In harmony with German *Rezeptionsgeschichte,* the French demarcate the domain of *interdiscours* as a "process of incessant reconfiguration of discursive function" (Courtine & Marandin, 1981, p. 24). Thus the new problematic questions not only the efficiency of the ideological manipulation by elites but also the simplistic characterization of non-elite reception as passive. De Certeau (1980) sets the task of describing the production of discourse by consumers, the tactics members of the underclass employ in molding and reorienting the elite discourse addressed to them; he points to Foucault's *Surveiller et punir* as concerned not with the production, but with the subversions of the consumption of power.

Interdiscours suggests a problematic analogous to that of intertextuality; the historian must map the interrelations of discourses that are radically different. Exemplary is Bakhtin's (1968) study of the employment of popular discursive conventions in a high culture text such as *Gargantua and Pantagruel.* The medievalist, for instance, who uses literary texts may not ignore the structure and motives of folklore; the historian of folklore must note the transformations of folklore themes into literary texts (Rosenberg, 1979). An obvious problem for the social historian is the confrontation of literate and nonliterate culture (Cressy, 1980). How, precisely, are literate conventions transposed by an oral culture? Raison-Jourde (1977) describes this confrontation of indigenous oral language and introduced script as a power confrontation. Obviously, this task demands a specific competence for the reconstruction of oral cultural practices and transcription of oral sources (Samuel, 1981; Vansina, 1968). Samuel warns of the highly confected nature of transcripts. Lastly, specialized histories, say, legal or medical history, must recognize the interaction between the discourse of jurisprudence or medicine and general conventions of a dominant rhetoric (Bourcier, 1979; Morel, 1977; Viehweg, 1974).

Conclusion

One may put the discourse-analysis initiative in perspective by considering the extraordinary success of three contemporary histories: Le Roy Ladurie's *Montaillou* (1975); Ginzburg's *Il Formaggio e i vermi* (1976); and Samuel's *East End Underworld* (1981). Their popularity relates, I think, to their central strategy of close-reading a single rich document or type of document (in the case of Ginzburg and Ladurie an inquisitorial archive) that purports to filter out little and seems to transmit in a translucent manner the articulations of the silent masses of history.

But we find a straight social historian, N. Z. Davis, pointing out in her review of *Montaillou* (1979) that Le Roy Ladurie has paid insufficient attention to formal analysis. She faults his reading as formally naive: there is no consideration of the narrative structures of the witnesses and their contribution to the confection of the past; there is no stylistic analysis; and there is in particular no account of the vernacular register in use, a deficiency related to a lack of awareness of the complexities of the relation between vernacular witness and Latin transcription.

Davis' sense of loss corresponds, I think, to Ginzburg's sense of a gain that derives from a significant convergence of research topics and research methods in contemporary history (Ginzburg, 1980). Ginzburg, in fact, suggests that discourse analysis itself instigates a new kind of investigative tact by correcting an overly mechanical notion of system as well as an immodest scholarly detachment. He asserts that the study of practices must begin with the assumption of the subtlety, complexity, and ingenuity of that very large share of discursive economies that exist outside the texts of high culture: it recognizes that this discursive domain is made up by small interventions, petty decisions, and ephemeral confrontations, rather than the salient events of voting or manning the barricades; it is a domain where stratagems, ruses, and tactics of complicity and compromise rule (Detienne & Vernant, 1974). Ginzburg proposes, in short, the replication of the discursive modes by the modes of historical reconstruction. The matching of strategies investigated with the investigating strategies avoids the dysfunction of reduction of these complex texts to rationally coherent schemas, which is the dominant strategy of standard intellectual history dealing with the canonic texts of high culture. He assumes synchrony between a low intuition (as opposed to high, mystical intuition) that characterizes a large mass of historical events and a modest methodology; this is a method of flexible formality, of elastic rigor, as opposed to reduction.

In addition to Ginzburgian tact, discourse analysis seems to make at least three other contributions to the historical enterprise. First, it refines historical categories such as 'period'. For example, wills of the seventeenth and eighteenth centuries may be treated together, but not wills of the fourteenth through the eighteenth centuries. The continuities disclosed by discourse analysis of the seventeenth and eighteenth centuries are such that one can talk about change within this period in a nontrivial way, while to speak of change between the fourteenth and the eighteenth centuries is vacuous.

Second, discourse analysis, by dealing with conventions and with public and publicly accessible rules and constraints, elides the problem of privacy, the chore of attempting to describe private intentions or states of mind. At the same time, discourse analysis is specific and "eventful," since it sees that individual practices may modify conventions such a genre rules and thus does not bog down in the confection of amorphous and anonymous collective mentalities. It also focuses on process, on the meshing of discursive economies with the economy of phenomena (Parret, 1980, p. 47).

Lastly, it makes demands on the historian; Lacapra (1980, pp. 273–275) has argued for a more 'performatory' notion of reading and interpretation; he defines interpretation as a form of political intervention but denies that this reduces history to a presentist monologue. Rather, he insists on the text as a network of resistances that acts as a dialogic partner. Just so, the kind of self-consciousness stimulated by the procedures of discourse analysis forces the historian to recognize a shared susceptibility to analysis, and to the eventful, time-specific nature of his own discourse.

DISCOURSE ANALYSIS AND THE PRACTICE OF WRITING HISTORY

It seems probable, then, that discourse analysis as a formalist project with the task of contributing to a strong theory of linguistic practice as social action can also function as a formalism with the duty of contributing to a strong theory of history as an account of past action. So far, we have considered the use of discourse analysis as a technique of historical research, an interpretative tool employed by historians. A second and more interesting project is the analysis of the discourse of history, the precise description of the discursive practice of the historians' community. This requires a shift from a focus on the modes of acquisition of knowledge to a focus on the use of acquired knowledge in the confection of the historical account. The historian needs not only a technique for describing the pragmatic dimension of the discursive documents he employs as sources but also a mode of describing the pragmatics of his own language, the constraints and conventions that produce either well-motivated or ill-motivated inquiry. The analyst should raise such questions as: Is there a specifically historical kind of discourse? What are the implications for a theory of history of asserting a claim to define proper historical discourse?

Contemporary Theories of Historical Discourse: Three Models

History as Narrative

In the lengthy and often illuminating contemporary discussion of history as discourse, three major hypotheses have dominated. Barthes' seminal article, "Le Discours de l'histoire" (1967), which claimed history as narrative, was brilliantly suggestive. Barthes proposed descriptive tactics that include the formulation of lists of substantives (existents) and actions (occurrents) dominant in each text as well as the analysis of modes of discursive self-definition of the historian, for example, the suppression of the authorial "I" in standard modern histories as a claim to objectivity by asserting impersonality. His distinction between *histoire narrans* and *histoire narré* enunciates the enabling distinction of the analytic project, since it postulates the functional autonomy of historical discourse when it insists that history as account inhabits an entirely different domain than history as event.

Anglo-American analytic philosophy has also made a case for discursive structure as an essential, nontrivial aspect of the historical project and has also focused on the logic of narration. Mink quotes Gallie as indicating that story is the form of history: "a historical narrative does not demonstrate the necessity of events but makes them intelligible by unfolding the story which connects their significance" (Mink, 1970, p. 545). For Mink, finding a historical truth is grasping in a single act or cumulative series of acts a relation that can only be experienced seriatim (1970, p. 548). For Gallie

(1964, pp. 12–13), to produce or "follow a story," or for Mink (1970, p. 546), "to have followed a story," describes the central historical act of investigation and of exchange of investigative results within the historical community. Ricoeur (1980), in his appreciation of Gallie and Mink, approves their focus on historical competence as narrative competence; the historian works with concrete patterns and must assign an action to a particular configuration of events, connected by a network of overlapping descriptions. The description of the tactics of configuration and of the succession of networks thus becomes the description of historical procedure.

What is most significant is that both Anglo-American analytic philosophers and French hermeneuticists are making strong claims about narrative as a complex construct of serious investigation. Mink asserts that the autonomy of historical understanding derives from narrative form. Ricoeur's article appears in *La Narrativité,* a collection of papers that discusses narrative as archetype. In the introduction to this collection the editors claim that it is the narrative dimension that in the last analysis distinguishes history from the other social and human sciences; therefore, Ricoeur seems to argue, the contemporary rejection of narrative is one tactic of the modern strategy of reducing history to a social science. All are claiming that the generation of narrative is a primary mental operation; narrativity demarcates not only a discursive but a cognitive style, and thus to disclose narrative structure is to reveal cognitive strategy.

History as Rhetorical Style

White (1973) also focuses on discursive styles as cognitive styles but claims that his analysis of history as rhetoric is more inclusive, narrative, or emplotment, being only one form of rhetoric. His tropological analysis reveals one of the four master rhetorical tropes—metaphor, metonymy, synecdoche, irony—as hegemonous in the historical text. These tropic structures constitute an exhaustive list of fundamental mental structures, very like the preperceptive sets of Gestalt psychology, that generate primitive strategies of connection and disjunction and thus create both discursive form and thematic content.

Yet White's project, instead of being more inclusive, is reductive in the extreme. Since his method assumes the total coherence of historical, literary, and cognitive styles, he reduces rhetoric to stylistics, thus diminishing the importance of the traditional rhetorical concerns with invention, disposition, and judgment, the practice of argumentation. His poetics of history does not confront the task of defining the discourse of well-motivated inquiry and betrays the more inclusive discourse analysis project in at least two ways. First, he concentrates on the problem of poeticity or the production of stylistic effect and depicts the historian as the demonic manipulator of tropes, the reader as the passive recipient of tropic effect. Second, as an analysis of the text in its "textuality," White's poetics cannot focus on the discursive practices of the historians in their historical specificity.

History as Argument

The third mode, which assumes that the primary discursive structure in history is argument, attempts to retrieve the total project of traditional rhetoric but also provides a more generous model for the modern project of discourse analysis. Both the narrative model and White's poetics of history generate endless debate on the relation of history to fiction, since they cannot formally distinguish between history and fiction. But to claim that the hegemonous structure of historical discourse is argument has the advantage of revealing the formal constraints on historical discursive practice that exclude fiction, thus focusing on history as discipline, on the historical communication community (Apel 1980). And where White's strategy deals only with poeticity, with issues of the production of texts, the concern with argument necessarily confronts the issues of the distribution, exchange, and reception of historical information and insight.

This model, of course, originates in a very broad discussion on the nature of inquiry. The thesis that history is argument may be simply an extrapolation from the Collingwood (1970) postulate that history is an informal logic of question and answer that attempts to reveal the logic of question and answer that motivates all historical action. The hypothesis is also consistent with initiatives in the historiography of science by Kuhn (1977), Feyerabend (1978), and Hesse (1978). All three are concerned with how a paradigm or theory achieves dominance in science, and all use characterizations of scientific discourse to explain success. Kuhn describes an essentially authoritarian model of disciplinary exchange, where it is "the abandonment of critical discourse which marks the transition to science" (1977, p. 273); Feyerabend insists that the truly generative theoretical stance is philosophical anarchism, which is enabled by freely structured argumentative practice; Hesse sees an overarching debate on usefulness, on the pragmatic values of science as controlling both theory and observation initiative.

On the one hand, then, the argumentative model seems to stipulate the unity of inquiry; there is no formal or logical difference between scientific or humanistic modes because all ultimately depend on the structure of informal argument for the discipline that assures success; to prevail requires the use of the kind of flexible argumentative procedures described by Toulmin in his *Uses of Argument* (1964). Toulmin's procedures, indeed, are of a piece with the very simple disciplinary model proposed by Fish (1980). Fish, confronting the theoretical disarray in the linked projects of literary history and literary criticism, has claimed that the ultimate sanction of historical or critical activity is the basic one of "making your case;" Fish argues that dynamic obsolescence must invest the discursive practices of inquiry.

On the other hand, Veyne (1971) insists on specificity and points to the very highly structured arguments that characterize the practice of the moral and political sciences, and thus of history. And certainly, we can see an intricate relation between argumentative and narrative modes; unlike the storyteller, the historian must not only narrate arguments, he must also argue narratives. This argued narrative makes demands. The discursive criterion that distinguishes narrative history from historical novel is that history evokes testing behavior in reception; historical discipline requires an author–reader contract that stipulates investigative equity. Historical novels are not histories, not because of a penchant for untruth, but because the author–reader contract denies the reader participation in the communal project.

Further, historical argument has a very complicated relation to contemporary moral–political argument. French analytic practice, for example, in attempting to describe the relation of specific historical texts to specific discursive contexts, not unexpectedly posits that the external constraints of ideology, rather than the internal constraints of "making your case," dominate. Giroud (1979), for instance, describes, by means of structural analysis, the central function of an article of Lucien Febvre as polemical; he reveals it as a tissue of apologetics. Floch (1979) describes formal choice as a tactic of ideological manipulation in a text of Pierre Francastel. The analytic description of the embeddedness of historical discourse in the larger domain of sociocultural practices does not require a capitulation to the rigid Marxist thesis that history writing is an ideological mechanism, a simple reflection of class interests. Yet the description does compel the historian to acknowledge that his own discourse in ineluctably related to and cannot be insulated from the lexical and syntactic constraints of contemporary civil debate; the historian, committed to producing statements about the civil significance of structures and events of the past, must produce public truths, conclusions about possibly remote social processes that are accessible to the public of his own discourse.

Historiographical Practice: An Agenda of Analytic Projects

It should be reassuring to the historian that the discourse analysis of historical texts is an essentially historicist project, since it describes specific acts of exchange of information, reinforcement or consolidation of hypotheses, and argumentative changes of goals and premises of research, as well as the place of historical discursive structures in the wider domain of moral–political discourse. Further, the analysis should serve the historian engaged in self-critique as both diagnostic tool and source of therapeutic suggestion. Its description of the conventions and rules that constrain the historical account may be used to discriminate between successful and unsuccessful inquiry. A priority of this project, of course, is the development of an agenda of analytic tasks.

Intratext Analysis: Function and Disfunction within the Historiographical Text

The Issue of Narrative Form.   Ricoeur (1980), as mentioned above, suggested that since narrative form is the essential mark of historical inquiry, the contemporary social scientific strategy that rejects narrative destroys history. Specifically, the Annales school, which stipulates the *longue durée* as topic and rejects *histoire événementielle,* deems the narrative that delineates character and plot in a succession of events as inadequate for the presentation of the large, synchronous, and anonymous forces that truly govern history. Furet (1978), for example, sees narrative as merely commemorative, disallowing serious investigative moments, and subjective, not permitting the establishment of a critical distance on the part of the investigator. Yet pertinent questions concerning Annaliste discourse can be raised: Can statistical description achieve "thick" description of a cultural practice? Are problems of scale introduced by oscillations within the account between collation of minutiae and the use of very broad generalizations? Does the attenuation of narrative form enhance or detract from argumentative structure?

The Problem of the Footnote: The Nature of Upper and Lower Text Relations.   Gossman (1976), in his discussion of the historiography of Thierry, has pointed out the problematic relation between the upper text on the page, the argument or narrative, and the lower text, or footnotes. This relation is a strategic one: A historian may relegate opponent's arguments to the notes; he may qualify his own argument with exceptions and limitations; he may supplement the upper text with parallel or even subversive arguments. Gossman sees the relation between upper narrative and lower sources as very often a difficult one. And recall that the edited history produces the interesting situation where the upper text must subsist in relation to a double lower text, one that represents both authorial and editorial presences.

Cliometrics: Quantification and Its Discontents. The quantification initiative in modern historical research would seem to offer a clear instance
of a strategy not so much of diminution of narrative as of augmentation
of argument. Yet Fogel, in an article entitled "The Limits of Quantitative
Methods in History" (1975), claims that quantification techniques may
serve to disguise the criteria and hypotheses that guide research. Fogel
points to a disjunctive effect: As one equation supports or opposes one
hypothesis, a series of equations produces either linking arguments or
disjoined generalizations. Further, since dependence on counting is often
expressed as a dependence on charts, graphs, tables, and maps, quantitative
history raises the issue of the integration of discursive and semiotic
descriptions, the relation of figure to narrative or argumentative matrix.
Certainly, the format that eschews narrative for a presentation of non-
discursive observation schemas is familiar; it may be the case that discursive
matrices no longer function as bearers of the primary message. One must
balance this phenomenon with Ricoeur's (1980, p. 13) insistence that any
critical discontinuities must be woven into the narrative web.

Intertext Analysis: The Relation of the
Historiographical Text to
Discursive Practices

The Historical Account as Use of Texts. Maldidier and Robin's "Du
Spectacle au Meurtre de l'Événement" (1976) is a comparative formal
account of a range of newspaper reports of a single event of political
crisis. The newspapers as documents are submitted to an analysis that
discloses the formal discursive markers of the ideological techniques and
results. They describe a range of very different characterization and
emplotment tactics; the neutral discourse of journalistic reporting is revealed
as a pastiche of persuasive and judgmental initiatives. The implied argument
of the article is that historians are not aware of this systemic ideology
of newspaper accounts. The analysis points to a peculiar intimacy that
can subsist between historical narrative and documentary source; the
analyst may detect the historian in a posture of protecting or privileging
his source, since he does not assume the source as discursive context
for his own text.

   The employment by the historian of metadiscursive texts, the sources
that purport to resolve historical language issues, poses a separate problem
of privilege. Lexicology, the theory of the inquiry into lexical usage,
requires the analysis of dictionary texts as discursive practices; the analyst
must describe the modes of interposition of the dictionary practice between
the historian and his source (Rey & Delesalle, 1970; Rey, 1977). The
embedding of metadiscursive information and hypotheses within the his-

torical text suggests the task of discourse analysis of discourse analysis itself. The discursive practices of the semiotic and linguistic analysts seem to have enjoyed a peculiar immunity to analysis, a privilege which is surely ill-motivated.

The Historical Text and Historical Discipline: Discursive Structures of Diffusion and Exchange. The analysis of the discursive practice of historians is a mode of investigating the roles and institutions of history as discipline. Foucault (1971) has selected as key practices in the development of modern discipline the confection of the role of author with its obligations and privileges, the creation of the pivotal genre of commentary, and the development of the scholarly journal as mode of exchange. But additional tasks suggest themselves. The rhetoric of quantitative history is a good example of an intratextual problem becoming an intertextual difficulty. Fogel's (1975) observation that schematic forms obscure argument becomes Erikson's (1975) conclusion that the quantitative historical monograph has often fostered belligerence, not rapprochement. At the same time, the irrefragable problems of historical observation militate discursive goodwill: Dunn (1978) states that "social complicity (the taking in of one another's washing) has much to do with the maintenance of optimism among social scientists" (p. 161).

The task of describing history as discipline requires, indeed, a commitment to a *Rezeptionsgeschichte* of historical accounts. A specific project would be an account of the discursive practice of peer review, for example, the publishing conventions and rules of bookreviewing, or the use of the symposium or colloquy to promote or revise theory and method. Revisionist strategies, indeed, control a great deal of historiographical activity. The analyst who discloses similarity and difference in the formal structure of accounts can disclose a false revisionism, where opposing historians are locked into a structure of shared premises and procedures; here revision may secure only a mild oscillation between two approved, traditional positions. Conversely, discourse analysis, in its description of historical debate, may find itself engaged in defining the complex structure of innovative debate and modes of discovery.

CONCLUSION

Obviously, the discourse analysis that attempts to describe the rules of innovative historical discourse has prescriptive as well as descriptive claims; the ability to describe argument is the ability to discriminate between good and bad argument. Indeed, the German hermeneuticists, with Apel as exemplary, are less interested in the description of ideological procedures than in the prescription of goals; they claim that the values of historical argument derive from the minimal ethics that make possible all communication. Therefore, they would seem to claim that the task of discourse analysis is to define, and thus mandate, equity in discipline.

But equity to the past seems a much more interesting problem. Dunn (1978) has characterized justice as the primary obligation of the social scientist and historian: "If we claim to know about other men, we must try as best we can to give them what is their due, their right. This is a simple moral duty, not a guarantee of epistemological prowess" (p. 174). Discourse analysis can be seen as one of a range of formal options that turns this simple injunction into a formal technique, a mode of achieving equity; it replaces piety with a protocol. The main thrust of discourse analysis is anti-anachronistic, the elimination of "our" habits of usage by means of precise accounts of "their" actual practice.

But the ultimate justice to the past is to assume its creativity, to see the relation of investigator and investigatee as in some way reciprocal, as in the hermeneuticists' model of a dialogue or conversation with the past. If we stipulate the governing assumption of historical discourse analysis to be Kuentz' paired premises of first, the *illisibilité* of the past, and second, the systematic nature, and thus accessibility to analysis, of the past, we can see that formalist access to the radically disjoined cultural practices of the past offers an account of radically different and potentially enriching cultural problematics. In contrast, the Whig model of cultural history encapsulates the issues of, say, investigative loss and gain, scientific success and failure, in a linear progress model. Whig definition of progress is hindsight, a simple development of a constructed anticipation. But Kuentz' formalism projects innovation as pluralist, as a potential of all historical domains, rather than as determined by a place in a temporal succession of domains. A gain in descriptive accuracy can become a gain in problematic. Kuentz replaces the Whig metaphor of condescension with an act of equity. Discourse analysis, then, promises not simply counterintuitive accounts of past cultural systems, but a confirmation of history as not merely commemorative, but as a serious mode of inquiry, capable of making useful contributions to a range of investigative practices.

BIBLIOGRAPHY

Apel, K.-O. (1967). *Analytic philosophy of language and the Geisteswissenschaften.* Dordrecht: Reidel.

Apel, K.-O. (1980). *Towards a transformation of philosophy.* London: Routlege & Kegan Paul.

Apostel, L. (1980). Communication et action. In H. Parret (Ed.), *Le langage en contexte* (pp. 193–315). Amsterdam: Benjamins.

Bakhtin, M. (1968). *Rabelais and his world*. Cambridge, MA: Massachusetts Institute of Technology Press.

Barthes, R. (1967). Le discours de l'histoire. *Information sur les sciences sociales*, 6(4), 65–75.

Bourcier, D., *et al.*, (Eds.). (1979). Le discours juridique; analyse et méthodes, *Langages*, 53.

Collingwood, R. G. (1970). *Autobiography*. Oxford: Oxford University Press.

Conein, B. (1981). Décrire un événement politique. In B. Conein *et al.*, *Matérialités discursives* (pp. 55–64). Lille: Presses universitaires de Lille.

Conein, B., *et al.* (1981). *Matérialités discursives*. Lille: Presses universitaires de Lille.

Courtine, J. J., & Marandin, J.-M. (1981). Quel objet pour l'analyse du discours? In B. Conein *et al.*, *Matérialités discursives (pp. 21–33). Lille: Presses universitaires de Lille*.

Cressy, D. (1980). *Literacy and the social order; Reading and writing in Tudor and Stuart England*. Cambridge: Cambridge University Press.

Dällenbach, L. (1979). Actualité de la recherche allemande, *Poétique*, 32, 258–260.

Davis, N. Z. (1979). Les conteurs de Montaillou, *Annales, E.S.C., 34*(1), 61–73.

Delesalle, S., & Rey, A., (Eds.). (1979). Dictionnaire, sémantique, et culture. *Langue française, 43*.

de Certeau, M. (1978). *L'écriture de l'histoire*. Paris: Gallimard.

de Certeau, M. (1980). *L'invention du quotidien: I, Arts de faire*. Paris: UGE,10/18.

Detienne, M., & Vernant, J.-P. (1974). *Les ruses de l'intelligence; La métis des Grecs*. Paris: Flammarion.

Dubois, J. (1962). *Le Vocabulaire politique et sociale en France de 1869 à 1872*. Paris: Larousse.

Dunn, J. (1972). The identity of the history of ideas. In P. Laslett et al., (Eds.), *Philosophy, politics, and society; Fourth series (pp. 158ff)*. Oxford: Blackwell.

Dunn, John (1978). Practising history and the social sciences on 'Realist' assumptions. In C. Hookway and P. Pettit, (Eds.), *Action and interpretation* (pp. 145–176). Cambridge: Cambridge University Press.

Erickson, C. (1975). Quantitative history: A review article. *American Historical Review, 80*, 351–365.

Feyerabend, P. (1978). *Against method*. London: Verso.

Fish, S. (1980). *Is there a text in this class?* Cambridge, MA: Harvard University Press.

Floch, J.-M. (1979). Communication ou manipulation? Analyse du discours socio-esthétique de Pierre Francastel. In A. J. Greimas & E. Landowski, (Eds.), *Introduction à l'analyse du discours en sciences sociales* pp. 177–192. Paris: Hachette.

Fogel, R. (1975). The limits of quantitative methods in history. *American Historical Review, 80*, 329–350.

Foucault, M. (1963). *Naissance de la clinique*. Paris: Presses universitaires de France.

Foucault, M. (1969). *L'archéologie du Savior*. Paris: Gallimard.

Foucault, M. (1971). *L'ordre du discours*. Paris: Gallimard.

Furet, F. (1978). *Penser la révolution française*. Paris: Gallimard.

Gallie, W. B. (1964). *Philosophy and the historical understanding*. New York: Schocken.

Ginzburg, Carlo (1976). *Il formaggio e i vermi*. Turin: Einaudi.

Ginzburg, Carlo (1980). Morelli, Freud and Sherlock Holmes: Clues in scientific method. *History Workshop, 9*, 5–36.

Giroud, J. C. (1979). Apologie pour l'historien: analyse d'un article de L. Febvre. In A. J. Greimas & E. Landowski, (Eds.), *Introduction à l'analyse du discours en sciences sociales* (pp. 129–39). Paris: Hachette.

Gossman, L. (1976). *Augustin Thierry and liberal historiography. History and Theory*, Beiheft 15.

Greimas, A. J., and Landowski, E., (Eds.). (1979). *Introduction à l'analyse du discours en sciences sociales.* Paris: Hachette.

Guilhamou, J., *et al.,* (1974). *Langage et idéologies: Le discours comme objet de l'histoire.* Paris: Les Éditions Ouvrières.

Gumbrecht, H. U. (1979). Persuader ceux qui pensent comme vous; Les fonctions du discours épidictique sur la mort de Marat. *Poétique, 39,* 362–384.

Habermas, J. (1974). *Theory and practice.* London: Heinemann.

Hesse, Mary (1978). Theory and value in the social sciences. In C. Hookway & P. Pettit (Eds.). *Action and interpretation* (pp. 1–16). Cambridge: Cambridge University Press.

Hookway, C., & Pettit, P. (Eds.). (1978). *Action and interpretation; Studies in the philosophy of the social sciences.* Cambridge: Cambridge University Press.

Kahn, C. (1973). *The verb 'be' in ancient Greek.* Dordrecht: Reidel.

Kristeva, J. (1971). Du sujet en linguistique. *Langages, 24,* 107–24.

Kuentz, P. (1981). Les 'Oublis' de la nouvelle rhétorique. In B. Conein *et al., Matérialités discursives* (pp. 35–43). Lille: Presses universitaires de Lille.

Kuhn, T. S. (1977). *The essential tension.* Chicago: University of Chicago Press.

Lacapra, D. (1980). Rethinking intellectual history. *History and Theory, 19,* 245–276.

Laclau, E. (1981). La Politique comme construction de l'impensable. In B. Conein *et al., Matérialités discursives* (pp. 65–74). Lille: Presses universitaires de Lille.

Landowski, E. (1976). La mise en scène des sujets de pouvoir. *Langages, 43,* 78–89.

Landowski, E., & Greimas, A. J., (Eds.). (1979). *Introduction à l'analyse du discours en sciences sociales.* Paris: Hachette.

Le Roy Ladurie, E. (1975). *Montaillou; Village occitan de 1294 à 1324.* Paris: Gallimard.

Lovejoy, A. O. (1948). *Essays in the history of ideas.* Baltimore: Johns Hopkins University Press.

Maldidier, D., Normand, C., & Robin, R. (1972). Discours et idéologie; Quelques bases pour une recherche. *Langue française, 15,* 116–142.

Maldidier, D., & Robin, R. (1974). Polemique idéologique et affrontement discursif en 1776; Des grand édits de Turgot et les remontrances du Parlement de Paris. In J. Guilhamou *et al., Langage et idéologie* (pp. 13–80). Paris: Les Éditions Ouvrières.

Maldidier, D., & Robin, R. (1976). Du spectacle au meurtre de l'événement; Reportages commentaires et éditoriaux de presse à propos de Charléty, (Mai 1968), *Annales, E.S.C., 33*(3), 552–588.

Marandin, J. M., & Courtine, J. J. (1981). Quel objet pour l'analyse du discours? In B. Conein *et al., Matérialités discursives* (pp. 21–33). Lille: Presses universitaires de Lille.

Marandin, J. M. (1979). Problèmes d'analyse du discours; Essai de description du discours francaise sur la Chine. *Langages, 55,* 17–88.

Matoré, G. (1967). *Le vocabulaire et la société sous Louis-Philippe.* Geneva: Slatkine.

Mink, L. (1970). History and fiction as modes of comprehension. *New Literary History, 1,* 542–558.

Morel, M. F. (1977). Ville et compagne dans le discours médical sur la petite enfance au XVIIIe siècle. *Annales, E. S. C., 32*(5), 1007–1024.

Ozouf, M. (1976). *La fête révolutionnaire, 1789–1799.* Paris: Gallimard.

Parret, H. (1980). Connaissance et contextualité. In H. Parret, (Ed.), *Le langage en contexte* (pp. 9–189). Amsterdam: Benjamins.

Parret, H., (Ed.). (1980). *Le langage en contexte, linguisticae investigationes:* Supplementa 3. Amsterdam: Benjamins.

Pecheux, M. (1969). *Analyse automatique du discours.* Paris: Dunod.

Pettit, P., & Hookway, C., (Eds.). (1978). *Action and interpretation; Studies in the philosophy of the social sciences.* Cambridge: Cambridge University Press.

Pocock, J. G. A. (1957). *The Ancient constitution and the feudal law*. Cambridge: Cambridge University Press.

Pocock, J. G. A. (1981). The Reconstruction of discourse; Towards the historiography of political thought. *Modern Language Notes, 96*, 959–980.

Quine, W. V. O. (1960). Translation and meaning. In W. V. Quine, *Word and object* (pp. 26–79). Cambridge, MA: Massachusetts Institute of Technology Press.

Raison-Jourde, F. (1977). L'échange inégal de langue, La pénétration des techniques linguistiques dans une civilisation de l'oral. *Annales, E.S.C. 32*,(4), 639–669.

Ranciére, J. (1976). *La parole ouvrière, 1830–1851*. Paris: UGE, 10/18.

Rey, A. (1977). *Le lexique: Images et modèles*. Paris: Colin.

Rey, A., & Delesalle, S., (Eds.). (1970). Dictionnaire, sémantique, et culture. *Langue francaise, 43*.

Ricoeur, P. (1980). L'histoire comme récit. In D. Tiffoneau, (Ed.), *La narrativité* (pp. 5–24). Paris: Centre National de Recherche Scientifique.

Robin, R. (1973). *Histoire et linguistique*. Paris: Colin.

Robin, R., & Maldidier, D. (1972). Discours et idéologie. *Langue française, 15*, 116–142.

Robin, R., & Maldidier, D. (1974). Polemique idéologique. In J. Guilhamou *et al.*, *Langage et idéologies* (pp. 13–80). Paris: Les Éditions Ouvrières.

Robin, R., & Maldidier, D. (1976). Du spectacle au meurtre. *Annales, E.S.C., 33*(3), 552–588.

Rosenberg, B. A. (1979). Folkoristes et médiévistes face au texte littéraire. *Annales, E.S.C., 34*(5), 943–955.

Samuel, R. (1981). *East End underworld, 2: Chapters in the life of Arthur Harding*. London: Routledge & Kegan Paul.

Sewell, W. H. (1980). *Work and revolution in France; The language of labor from the Old Regime to 1840*. Cambridge: Cambridge University Press.

Skinner, Q. (1972). Social meaning and the explanation of social action. In P. Laslett *et al.*, (Eds.), *Philosophy, politics, and society; Fourth series* (pp. 136–157). Oxford: Blackwell.

Skinner, Q. (1978). *Foundations of modern political thought*, 2 vols. Cambridge: Cambridge University Press.

Slatka, D. (1971). L'acte de 'Demander' dans les Cahiers de doléances. *Langue française, 9*, 58–73.

Stierle, K.-H. (1972). L'histoire comme exemple; L'exemple comme histoire, *Poétique, 10*, 176–198.

Stierle, K.-H. (1977). Identité du discours et transgression lyrique, *Poétique, 32*, 422–441.

Sumpf, J. (1979). À quoi servir l'analyse de discours?, *Langages, 55*, 5–16.

Tiffoneau, D., (Ed.). (1977). *La sémantique de l'action*. Paris: Centre National de Recherche Scientifique.

Tiffoneau, D., (Ed.). (1980). *La narrativité*. Paris: Centre National de Recherche Scientifique.

Toulmin, S. (1964). *The uses of argument*. Cambridge: Cambridge University Press.

Tournier, M. (1973). La vocabulaire de pétitions ouvrières de 1848. Étude de parentage statistique. In R. Robin (Ed.), *Histoire et linguistique* (pp. 261–303). Paris: Colin.

Vansina, J. (1968). *Oral tradition; A study in methodology*. Chicago: Aldine.

Vernant, J.-P., & Detienne, M. (1974). *Les ruses de l'intelligence*. Paris: Flammarion.

Veyne, P. (1971). *Comment on écrit l'histoire*. Paris: Seuil.

Viehweg, T. (1974). *Topik und Jurisprudenz*. Munchen: Beck.

White, H. V. (1973). *Metahistory*. Baltimore: John Hopkins University Press.

CHAPTER 11

Legal Discourse

Brenda Danet

INTRODUCTION

In the 1970s legal discourse became a topic of interest to social scientists, linguists, and sociolinguists working in the United States, Britain, Sweden, West Germany, and Israel. While language is central to all human affairs, it is particularly critical in the law. Physicians work with physical substances and entities; in contrast, the work of lawyers and judges is symbolic and abstract. In a most basic sense, law would not exist without language.

The Domain of Legal Discourse

When most people hear the word "legal," they probably think of courts, lawyers and judges. Indeed, the other two chapters in this *Handbook* that deal with legal matters focus on police–judge–defendant discourse (Wodak, Volume 4), and on courtroom interaction (Drew, Volume 3).[1] I propose to define the domain of legal discourse broadly enough to include relevant phenomena in preliterate societies without legislature, courts, or legal personnel. The study of legal discourse is concerned with "the nature, functions and consequences of language use in the negotiation of social order" (Danet, 1980, p. 449). The two primary functions of law are (1) the ordering of human relations, and (2) the restoration of social order when it breaks down. With regard to the

---

[1] Apart from the chapters by Wodak and Drew, other chapters in this *Handbook* that are especially relevant include those by McDowell (Volume 3), Seidel (Volume 4), Schiffrin (Volume 3), and Atkinson (Volume 3). Apart from my own review essay (Danet, 1980), on which I draw in this chapter, other general sources are O'Barr (1981), O'Barr (1982, Chap. 2), and Levi (1982).

HANDBOOK OF DISCOURSE ANALYSIS, Vol. 1
Disciplines of Discourse

ordering function, there are two complementary tasks. Law defines relations and tells us which activities are permitted and which are not. It also provides recipes for creating relations where none existed before (e.g., marriage ceremonies). These are, respectively, the regulative and facilitative functions of law.

"Restoration of social order" is another term for dispute processing. Here we are concerned with the ways language usage affects both substantive and procedural justice in the disposition of cases of conflict or trouble, whether between one citizen and another (civil law), or between the individual and the state (criminal law). The same social processes are at work in the fleeting, informal "remedial interchanges" of everyday life (Goffman, 1971) and in the highly formalized setting of the modern trial, in both its adversary and its inquisitorial versions (see, e.g., Damaska, 1975; Thibaut & Walker, 1975).

Play, Ritual, and the Serious: Three Keys in Legal Discourse

It is useful to think of three basic keys of discourse—play, ritual, and the serious—and the ways they relate to law. We tend to think of dispute processing as belonging to the realm of the serious, because of its supposed concern with facts. However, there are genres of disputing with little or no concern for "facts" or truth, such as Eskimo song duels (Danet, 1980, pp. 499–508; Hoebel, 1954; see also McDowell, this *Handbook*, Volume 3).

Since the other two chapters on legal discourse in this *Handbook* both focus on spoken discourse and on dispute processing, I devote the remainder of this chapter to a discussion of written forms of legal discourse and their role in the ordering of human relations.

The Social Critique of Legal Discourse

The emerging study of legal discourse is a product both of intellectual developments within the academic world and of more general social trends. Since the 1970s there has been much criticism of the uses and misuses of language in public life and of the power and status of the professions. The language of bureaucracy, advertising, politics, and the professions has come under attack. Critics have argued that the professions use language in ways that mystify citizens and keep them dependent.

Legal language, at least legal English, has been attacked at least since the sixteenth century (see Mellinkoff, 1963). Jonathan Swift savagely satirized lawyers and legal language in *Gulliver's Travels*. In our own century, the critics have included political scientists, sociologists, and anthropologists, and, more recently, a handful of linguists (see, e.g., Carlen, 1976; Charrow, Crandall, & Charrow, 1983; Edelman, 1972; O'Barr, 1981; Shuy & Larkin, 1978; Wright, 1981).

In the privacy of their in-house professional journals, lawyers and judges have occasionally debated whether legal language should be reformed. More recently, this debate has spilled over into publications meant for a more general audience. Lawyers of a more radical persuasion, like Caplan (1977) or Lefcourt (1971), see legal language as a major barrier to responsive legal services and call for linguistic reform. Other legal analysts debate whether mystification may actually be necessary (e.g., Arnold, 1935; Frank, 1930) in order to create a sense of security and certainty or to mask the irrationalities in human decision making.

The critique of legal language, and of public language generally, has given rise to the plain language movement. Just as the consumer movement is posited on the idea that consumers have a right to obtain their money's worth and to complain when justice is not done, so the plain language movement is posited on the premise that citizens have a right to understand and to be understood. Beginning in the early 1970s, the Scandinavian countries, notably Sweden, pioneered in promoting the reform of legal and bureaucratic language. The United States and Britain have followed suit, and other countries are joining the bandwagon.[2]

THE LEGAL REGISTER

Dialect, Register, or Sublanguage?

Modern legal language has become so highly differentiated a variety that one can debate whether it should be called a separate dialect, sublanguage, or register. Since there is very little comparative work on legal discourse, I restrict this discussion to legal English. Both O'Barr (1981) and Charrow, et al. (1982) believe that the linguistic differentiation of legal English may be great enough to warrant calling it a separate dialect or sublanguage. My own preference is to call it a register, in the light of Bolinger's (1975) suggestion that register is mainly a matter of formality.

Genres of Legal Discourse

Table 11.1 cross-classifies genres or types of language use in legal settings according to two criteria: (1) the modes of language use—written,

---

[2] A good source for information on the plain language movement both in the United States and elsewhere is *Simply Stated,* a newsletter published by the Document Design Center, American Institutes of Research, 1055 Thomas Jefferson St., Washington, DC 20007.

Table 11.1
A Typology of Situations in Which Legal English Is Used, by Style and Mode[a]

Mode	Style			
	Frozen	Formal	Consultative	Casual
Written	Documents: insurance policies contracts landlord-tenant leases wills	Statutes Briefs Appellate opinions		
Spoken–composed	Marriage ceremonies Indictments Witnesses's oaths Pattern instructions Verdicts	Lawyers' examinations of witnesses in trials and depositions Lawyers' arguments, motions in trials Expert witnesses' testimony	Lay witnesses' testimony	
Spoken–spontaneous			Lawyer–client interaction Bench conferences	Lobby conferences Lawyer–lawyer conversations

[a] Danet (1980, p. 471); based on Joos (1961).

spoken though composed in advance, or spoken and spontaneous; and (2) the degree of formality of the style used. Following Joos (1961), I have distinguished between frozen, formal, consultative, and casual styles (intimate style has been omitted, as by definition it is not applicable to a public setting).

Thus various kinds of documents, like contracts or wills, are formulaic, frozen written uses of legal English. Formal written genres include such types as statutes, lawyers' briefs or appellate opinions. Spoken–composed genres include marriage ceremonies or witnesses' oaths to tell "the truth, the whole truth, and nothing but the truth." These are fixed formulas that are spoken aloud. Unlike the frozen spoken genres, where content is fixed, the formal spoken–composed genres allow for variation in content but require planning. This category includes the interrogation of witnesses, by lawyers in the adversary system, and by judges in the inquisitorial system. The testimony of witnesses is included under the consultative heading, while that of expert witnesses is listed under formal spoken, since it may be planned ahead to a greater extent.[3] Finally, casual legal discourse that is characterized by a high degree of informality, including perhaps some slang, might characterize lobby conferences between judges and attorneys, or lawyer–lawyer conversations out of the earshot of their clients.

Table 11.1 groups these various genres into two larger categories, the first of which incorporates all written and spoken-composed genres; all the others are spoken varieties with at least some degree of spontaneity and variation in content allowed. The features of the legal register are most prominent, then, in the frozen, formulaic genres, where matters are virtually all form and no content and the words are performative: A will written in the wrong formula is not a will at all, and a marriage ceremony performed faultily is not "happy," to use Austin's (1970) phrase. Though we lack empirical information on the style of lawyer-client communication (see Bogoch & Danet, 1984), this cross classification suggests that those with an authoritarian approach will communicate in a more formal style, while those committed to a democratic, participatory ideology may incorporate elements of casual style (see Rosenthal, 1974).

Legal English as a Form of Diglossia

The concept of 'diglossia', first introduced by Ferguson (1964), provides a useful way of analyzing the linguistic status of the legal register. He

---

[3] Direct examination of one's clients or witnesses in the adversary model may be highly planned and even rehearsed; however, cross-examination of the opposing side's witnesses is almost totally unplanned, by definition.

originally used the concept to describe the relation between high and low varieties of the same language, say, Arabic or Greek; in such situations, one variety is superposed on the other. Ferguson identified 10 features of diglossia, nearly all of which are strikingly applicable to the situation of modern legal discourse. For example, the high variety enjoys high prestige (at least in certain circles) and is acquired only through formal education; it is never the speaker's native language. The high variety is also grammatically far more complex, though the two varieties share the same sound system (O'Barr, 1981). The two varieties live in a situation of stable functional differentiation until there is a call for reform and more effective communication between those commanding high and the rest of society.

TOWARD A LINGUISTIC DESCRIPTION OF THE LEGAL REGISTER

To date, no adequate linguistic description of legal English or of the legal register of any other language has been carried out. The first to attempt a partial description were Crystal and Davy (1969, Chap. 8), who analyzed two documents, an endowment–assurance policy and a hire–purchase agreement. Gustafsson (1975) analyzed the syntactic properties of British and American legislative language. Her doctoral dissertation perhaps comes closest to a formal description and includes comparison of the incidence of various features of legal English with several other genres of English prose. Charrow and Charrow (1979) identified the linguistic features of American jury instructions, focusing particularly on those that cause comprehension difficulties. Two other teams have also studied jury instructions (see Elwork, Sales, & Alfini, 1977; Sales, Elwork, & Alfini, 1977; Severance & Loftus, 1982). Shuy and Larkin (1978) discussed the linguistic problems that arise in the reform of insurance policy language. Finegan (1982) investigated the relation between form and function in testament language. The same volume includes a paper by Arena (1982), reporting on the development of a clause-analysis technique to measure the stylistic complexity of the legal writing of patent attorneys.[4]

More recently, seven papers in a special issue of the journal *Text,* which I have edited, pursue the nature of the legal register in written

---

[4] The conclusions of Crystal and Davy; Gustafsson; Charrow and Charrow; Sales *et al.;* and Shuy and Larkin are summarized in somewhat greater detail in Danet (1980, pp. 474–482). Finegan and Arena may be short-changed because the volume in which their papers appear (Di Pietro, 1982) was not available to me at the time of writing.

genres of Swedish, English, and Hebrew (see Danet, 1984a). Westman (1984) and Gunnarsson (1984) both write about Swedish legislative and administrative language. Kurzon's (1984) materials included five genres of British legal English: a court order, a statute, a deed, a will, and a house-purchase agreement. Vargas (1984) widened the range of genres to include appellate opinions and law textbooks, as well as legislation. Papers by Hiltunen (1984) and Gustafsson (1984) continue the concern with legislative English. My own paper examined the language of a Hebrew insurance policy (Danet, 1984b).

Despite the paucity of systematic studies on the legal register, we can already point to distinctive lexical, syntactic, prosodic, and discourse-level features. How generalizable the conclusions of the various studies are remains, of course, a matter for debate and future research. To illustrate some of these features, I draw on the first 60 or so lines of one example of British legal English, a document known as an Assignment (see Figure 11.1), in which a debtor unable to pay bills transfers property to a trustee so that the trustee can manage or sell the property in order to pay the creditors. I have chosen this document because it is an extreme example—almost a caricature—of the legal register and probably displays its features with more intensity than most written documents in British legal English.[5]

Lexical Features

Technical Terms.   Every occupational specialization has its own technical terms, or "terms of art," as lawyers call them. Examples in the Assignment, shown in Figure 11.1, are *real property* (line 36), *forfeiture* (line 32) and *fee simple* (line 39).

Common Terms with Uncommon Meanings.   Legal language has a penchant for using familiar words but with uncommon meanings. Thus, *assignment* means not simply 'something assigned, a task or duty', but 'the transferance of a right, interest or title'. And the debtor is called the *beneficial* owner, not because he benefits others, but because as owner, he is the one who benefits.

Archaic Expressions.   The Assignment is remarkably full of multiple appearances of ten different archaic expressions, which have come down from Old English: *hereinafter, hereto, herein, hereby, hereof, thereof, therefor, aforesaid, whatsoever,* and *wheresoever.*

---

[5] About half of the text of the Assignment is displayed in Figure 11.1. I have included two of the fourteen sections in order to show what appear to be two giant legal register sentences, the first of which ends just before *Whereas* in line 13.

This Assignment is made the _____ day of

197 ___ **Between**

(hereinafter called "the Debtor " which expression shall where the context admits if more persons than one are parties hereto of the first part include each or either or any of them alternatively so that every assurance covenant declaration appointment and agreement by the Debtors herein contained or implied shall be several as well as joint but shall where joint relate only to property hereby assured which belongs to or can be appointed by the Debtors jointly and where several relate only to property hereby assured which belongs to or can be appointed by the party making such assurance covenant declaration appointment or agreement separately) of the first part

(hereinafter called " the Trustee " which expression shall where the context admits include his representatives or other the trustees for the time being hereof) of the second part and the several PERSONS COMPANIES AND PARTNERSHIP FIRMS being Creditors of the Debtor whose names and addresses are set forth in the Schedule hereto and all other persons (if any) who are now Creditors of the Debtor and shall assent hereto in writing or otherwise (all of which parties are hereinafter called " the Creditors " which expression shall where the context admits include the persons respectively deriving title under them) of the third part **Whereas**:—

(1) The Debtor indebted to the Creditors respectively in the divers sums of money set opposite to their respective names in the Schedule hereto (such debts where more persons than one are parties hereto of the first part being unless otherwise described in that Schedule the Debtors' joint debts) and to other persons in divers sums of money and being unable to pay the same in full ha proposed to make such provision for the payment thereof as is hereinafter contained:

(2) The Creditors have agreed to accept such proposal and to enter into the covenants on their part hereinafter contained

Now in pursuance of the said agreement and for the consideration aforesaid **This Deed Witnesses** and it is hereby declared as follows:—

1. **The** Debtor as Beneficial Owner do hereby convey assign and appoint unto the Trustee (and as to real estate) in fee simple **All** the real and personal estate whatsoever and wheresoever which belongs to the Debtor beneficially (except as follows):—

   (a) property held by the Debtor for any term of years (not being a mortgage term) or shorter term
   (b) interest in and charges on land the title to which is registered under the Land Registration Acts
   (c) all shares standing in the name of the Debtor which are not fully paid up or to the holding of which some liability is attached
   (d) any interests in property which cannot be transferred by this Deed or which cannot be transferred without creating a forfeiture and
   (e) the tools of trade (if any) of the Debtor and the necessary wearing apparel and bedding and other personal necessaries of the Debtor and h famil not exceeding (in the case of each Debtor) the value of pounds

And also (by way of conveyance and not of exception) **All** property whether real or personal which the Debtor now ha power by deed or writing (otherwise than by Will only) to appoint as the Debtor may think fit Together with all books of account vouchers papers and writings relating to the affairs of the Debtor

To hold as to real estate Unto the Trustee in fee simple and as to personal estate Unto the Trustee absolutely **Upon trust**:—

   (a) To carry on the business (if any) of the Debtor and to call in collect and receive or sell and dispose of all or any part of the property either by public auction or private contract with liberty to give time for the payment of any purchase money or to take any security for the same or any part thereof and with full power to bring defend compromise or abandon any legal proceedings relating to the trust estate or any part thereof and to give time for the payment of any debts owing to the Debtor and to accept payment thereof by instalments composition or otherwise and to abandon any debts which shall be considered bad and generally to adjust and settle all accounts questions and disputes relating to the trust estate or any part thereof between the Trustee and the Debtor or any other person in such manner and upon such terms as the Trustee shall think fit.

   (b) Out of the money to be so realised—
      (i) First to pay the expenses of the collection realisation and conversion into money of the said estate:
      (ii) Secondly to pay all costs charges and expenses of or incidental to convening and holding any meeting of the Creditors held before the execution hereof and the negotiations therefor and the investigation of the affairs of the Debtor and preparing executing stamping and registering this deed and the execution of the trusts hereof and carrying the same into effect including the professional charges of the Trustee (to which the Trustee shall be entitled in the same manner as if he were not a trustee and had been employed as agent to perform the services rendered by him):
      (iii) Thirdly to pay and discharge all claims which would be required by law to be paid in full in priority to other debts if the Debtor had become and been adjudged bankrupt on the date hereof:
      (iv) Subject as aforesaid to divide the residue of the said money rateably amongst the Creditors in proportion to the amounts of their respective debts in like manner in all respects as the said money would be divisible under the law of bankruptcy if the Debtor had been on and at the date hereof duly adjudged bankrupt (and where more persons than one are parties hereto of the first part according to the law of administration in bankruptcy of the joint and separate estates of joint debtors):
      (v) To pay the residue (if any) of the said money to the Debtor according to the respective rights and interests affecting the same.

Figure 11.1 A sample of British legal English: an Assignment. This document was obtained from "Oyez" Law Stationery Shop, Chancery Lane, London. Approximately one-half of the full text is displayed here.

Doublets.   The historian of legal English, Mellinkoff (1963), made much of the frequent incidence of what he and others call *'doublets'*, or word pairs. Common ones are *cease and desist, will and bequeath, aid and abet*. The Assignment is full of such pairs; however, unless the pairs are fixed in the mind as frozen expressions, typically irreversible, they should be treated as aspects of form, that is, of syntax, rather than of content or lexis. See the discussion of binomial expressions below.

Formality.   Many characteristic expressions in legal English show a proclivity for high formality, where a choice is possible. Note the preference for *shall* over *will* in the Assignment (lines 3 and 4: *'the Debtor'* which expression **shall** . . .*include; shall assent*, in line 12). Another instance is the present emphatic, in *The Debtor as Beneficial Owner do(es) hereby* **convey assign and appoint** (line 24), along with the use of *hereby*, the common mark of the performative in English (Austin, 1970). *Unto* in the continuation of line 24, *unto the Trustee*, continues the effect of high formality.

Unusual Prepositional Phrases.   Charrow and Charrow (1979) noticed the frequency of the phrase *as to* in the variety of American legal English they studied. In the bit of legal English used to illustrate my discussion in Danet (1980), I noted the use of *in the event of default*, instead of the simpler *If the borrower should default*. In the Assignment, *as to* occurs twice in line 39.

Frequency of *Any*.   The word *any*, which frequently appears to be redundant, is common in legal English. In the 66 lines of the Assignment included here, it appears a remarkable 18 times.

Syntactic Features

Syntactic features are probably more distinctive of legal English than are lexical ones, and certainly account for more of the difficulties of lay persons in comprehending it (see below). At least 11 such features are easily identified.

Nominalizations.   Crystal and Davy (1969), Gustafsson (1975), Charrow and Charrow (1979), and Shuy and Larkin (1978) all found nominalizations to be prominent in the materials they studied. The sample of legal English used in Danet (1980), a sentence from a loan form of the Citibank of New York, contained 11 different nominalizations. Similarly, the text used here contains phrases like **make such provision** *for the payment* instead of **provide** *for the payment* (line 18), or *give time for the* **payment** *of any debts* instead of *give time for persons owing debts* **to pay** (lines 44–45).

Passives. The prominence of passive constructions was noted by Sales *et al.* (1977), Charrow and Charrow (1979), and Shuy and Larkin (1978). The Citibank sentence contained several instances where an active verb might have been more natural. The British Assignment employs *it is hereby declared* (line 23) and *not fully paid up* (line 29). Passives are not always translatable into the active, as the example in line 31 shows: *any interests in property which cannot be transferred by this Deed* could not be changed to the active, because no specifiable agent of the action is identifiable.

Whiz Deletion. The omission of a *wh*-form plus some form of the verb *to be,* as in *agreement . . . herein* [*which is*] *contained or implied* (line 5), is fairly common. There are four instances of whiz deletion in the 66 lines in Figure 11.1. The Citibank sentence also contained some examples (see Danet, 1980, p. 479).

Conditionals. Complex conditionals are common in the legal register. Among previous writers on legal English, only Crystal and Davy noted this feature. The Citibank sentence contained six conditions on the main clause. In the Assignment, complex conditionals are set out in the parenthetical parts of the first few lines—they attempt to specify, for instance, who is included in the term *Debtor* if more than one person is involved.

Prepositional Phrases. A prominent feature of legal English is the high incidence of prepositional phrases, strung out one after the other, as in lines 41 to 48: *to call in collect and receive or sell and dispose of all or any part of the property either by public auction or private contract with liberty to give time for the payment of any purchase money.* Another common feature is the fact that prepositional phrases are often misplaced, at least in contrast to what we experience as normal usage (see Charrow and Charrow, 1979).

Sentence Length and Complexity. Even the most unpracticed eye instantly spots the unusual length and complexity of legal register sentences. In Gustafsson's (1975) corpus, the average sentence contained about 55 words, almost twice as many as the average sentence of scientific English, and nearly eight times the number in dramatic texts. The Citibank sentence contained 242 words. In the Assignment, it is quite problematic to decide what constitutes a sentence. The first one ends, perhaps, in line 14, just before the word *Whereas.*

Length and complexity of structure tend to go together. In Gustafsson's (1975) corpus, there was an average of 2.86 clauses per sentence, and only a fifth of the sentences contained a single independent clause. The most complex sentence in the jury instructions studied by the Charrows contained nine subordinate clauses (1979, p. 1327). Hiltunen (1984) analyzed four main types of clausal embedding, left branching, right branching, left nested, and right nested, in 373 sentences of a British law. Right branching was found to be by far the most frequent. Some of the peculiar flavor of the legal register may derive from the rather unusual point in a clause where the embedding is inserted. Consider lines 1–4 (inserted // indicates the relevant clause): *This assignment is made . . . between* _____ *(hereinafter called 'the Debtor' which expression **shall** // where the context admits if more persons than one are parties hereto of the first part // **include** . . .*

Unique Determiners.   The legal register has a propensity to use the unfamiliar *such* and *said* as determiners (Charrow & Charrow, 1979; Crystal & Davy, 1969; Danet, 1980; Shuy & Larkin, 1978). There are five instances of *such* in the Assignment text (lines 16, 18, 20, 48) and five of *said* (lines 22, 50, 61, 65). A typical example is in line 20: *The Creditors have agreed to accept **such** proposal.* (See the discussion of anaphora below.)

Impersonality.   Even when texts are intended as a communication between two parties, they are typically cast in the third person. Loan forms used by banks speak of the borrower and the lender, for instance. A switch to first and second person is often preferred by language reformers, though it obviously would not be appropriate to other genres of legal English like that of legislation.

Negatives.   Negatives, especially multiple negatives, are prominent in legal English. They are expressed not only in *not, never,* or prefixes like *un*, but in terms like *unless* and *except*. There are several negatives in the Assignment; a rather difficult one to digest is in line 37: ***otherwise than by Will only***.

Binomial Expressions; Parallel Structures.   The legal register is striking for its use of elaborate parallel structures, a feature most often discussed by students of poetics, oral tradition, and literature (e.g., Jakobson, 1960). Binomial expressions (Danet, 1984b; Gustafsson, 1975, 1983; Malkiel, 1959) are a special case of parallelism; they are sequences of two words belonging to the same form class, which are syntactically coordinated and semantically related (Gustafsson, 1984). Gustafsson found binomials to be four to five times more frequent in legal English than in other types of prose; they are typically a pair of nouns functioning as an adverbial in the rhematic part of the sentence. There were eight different binomials in the Citibank sentence (Danet, 1980). The Assignment text contains a remarkably high 30 different ones, of which 14 are nouns and 9 are verbs, thus corroborating Gustafsson's findings about distribution by form class. Several expressions are in fact multinomials, for example, *assurance covenant declaration appointment or agreement*. Other types of analysis of binomials have focused on such matters as the type of semantic relationships (synonymy or near-synonymy, contiguity, antonymy, and enumeration; see Gustafsson, 1975; Koskenniemi, 1968). Binomials are also extremely common in legal Hebrew. Both English and Hebrew binomials may ultimately derive from Biblical Hebrew (Danet, 1984b).

Prosodic Features

Little attention has been paid to possibly distinctive prosodic features of the legal register. Mellinkoff (1963) casually referred to occasional alliteration or love of a good phrase among lawyers. Both the Citibank sentence and a sentence taken from a Hebrew insurance policy showed evidence of preoccupation with assonance, alliteration, rhyme, rhythm, meter, and even phonemic contrast (Danet, 1980, 1983). These features of poetization may occur mainly in binomial expressions and in the critically performative parts of documents.

Assonance, Alliteration, and Phonemic Contrast. In the Assignment, expressions like *each or either or any* (line 4), and *assurance covenant declaration appointment or agreement* (lines 4 and 5) contain assonance of /e/ and of /a/, respectively. In *call in collect and receive or sell and dispose* (line 41), we have, first, alliteration of /k/ and /l/, and then of /s/.

Rhyme, Rhythm, and Meter. Among the binomial expressions in the Assignment, *whatsoever* and *wheresoever* (line 25) rhyme. *Contained or implied* (line 5) has the same rhythm in each member, with the stress on the second syllable of each, as do *convey, assign* and *appoint* (line 24). While I fail to find any obvious instance of regular meter in the Assignment, the Citibank sentence opened with a pattern of three beats, the first two unstressed, the third stressed:

$$\overset{x}{\text{In}} \; \overset{x}{\text{the}} \; \overset{x\,\acute{}}{\text{event}} \; / \; \overset{x}{\text{of}} \; \overset{x}{\text{de}} \overset{\acute{}}{\text{fault}} \; / \; \overset{x}{\text{in}} \; \overset{x}{\text{the}} \; \overset{\acute{}}{\text{pay}} \; / \; \overset{x}{\text{ment}} \; \overset{x}{\text{of}} \; \overset{\acute{}}{\text{this}} \; / \; \overset{x}{\text{or}} \; \overset{x}{\text{any}} \; \overset{\acute{}}{\text{o}} \; / \; \overset{x}{\text{ther}}$$
$$\overset{x\,\acute{}}{\text{obliga}} \; / \; \text{tion.}$$

End Weight. Gustafsson (1975), Koskenniemi (1968), and Danet (1984b) have all discussed the extent to which their materials conform with the principle of end weight, whereby there are more beats, or more phonetic material, in the second half of a two-part expression. At least some of the binomials in the Assignment conform to the principle of end weight, for example, *belongs to* / *or can be appointed by* (line 6), *deed* / *or writing* (line 37), and *joint* / *and separate* (line 64). Reversals, where the shorter term appears second (e.g., *convening* / *and holding* in line 52), appear to occur less often than either those conforming to the principle of end weight or those having an identical number of syllables.[6]

Discourse-Level Features

Analysis of discourse-level features of legal discourse has hardly begun. There is growing consensus that the true distinctiveness of legal discourse may lie at the discourse level.

Cohesion. Shuy and Larkin (1978), Crystal and Davy (1969), Sales *et al*. (1977) and Kurzon (1983) have all speculated that legal discourse may be low in cohesive devices, notably anaphora. More likely, the types of devices featured are distinctive. Application of a typology of cohesive devices like that of Halliday and Hasan (1976) presupposes clear sentential boundaries, a matter that is clearly problematic in the Assignment. Nevertheless, all five of their types are present in this sample.

1. Anaphora. The dominant pattern in the Assignment is certainly to avoid pronouns and to repeat *debtor, creditors* and *trustee,* presumably to avoid ambiguity. However, in lines 56 and 57 we do find instances of *he* and *him,* respectively (referring to the trustee). The various instances of *said* and *such* as in *such proposal* (line 20), and *the said estate* (lines 50–51) are peculiar to legal discourse, as noted above.

2. Conjunction. We find, for instance, *first...secondly...thirdly* (lines 50, 52, 58). And terms like *hereinafter* (lines 3, 9, 19, etc.), *aforesaid* (line 22), and *said* (as in *the said estate,* (lines 50–51) all provide cohesion.

3. Substitution. Substitutions may be generally rare in legal English, though in the Assignment we do find a transition from *has proposed* (line 18) to *such proposal* (line 20), a switch from an active verb to a nominalization.

4. Ellipsis. Intersentential ellipsis may be lacking because of the concern for precision and explicitness, though we saw an example of *intra*-sentential ellipsis in the use of whiz-deletion (see the discussion of syntactic features above).

5. Lexical cohesion. There is apparently much lexical reiteration, partly because of the avoidance of pronouns; in addition, there is little use of synonyms, near synonyms, and superordinate or general terms to replace items mentioned in previous sentences. The As-

---

[6] And of course the well-known *signed, sealed and delivered,* which concludes the Assignment (not included in Figure 11.1), conforms to the principle of end weight.

signment clearly illustrates this feature. This stands in sharp contrast to the use of synonyms and near-synonyms within binomial and, especially, multinomial expressions.

Thematic Organization.   Several approaches to the study of thematic organization have been applied to legal discourse.

1. Thematic progression. Kurzon (1983) has employed the concepts and methods of the Prague linguists (Daneš, 1974; Firbas, 1974) for the study of thematic progression. His analysis of five genres of British legal English led him to conclude that such texts do have identifiable thematic structure, provided a hypertheme is identified, often known only to experts.

2. Foregrounding and backgrounding. Vargas (1984) finds that there are two distinctive types of American legal discourse, one containing both backgrounding and foregrounding, thus resembling everyday discourse, and one with little foregrounding. Transitivity is considered to signal foregrounding.[7] Both supposedly go with a concern for specific episodes between individuals, while low transitivity and backgrounding are signs of a more abstract approach—a concern with the social structure in which categories of participants are related.

3. Extreme propositional density; lack of redundancy. The unusual length and complexity of legal English sentences carry with them the feature of extreme propositional density. The maze of embedded clauses and prepositional phrases in the Assignment makes this evident. Propositional density, in turn, entails a striking lack of redundancy in information communicated—every word counts.

Comprehensibility of the Legal Register

Much of the interest in description of the features of legal discourse is obviously motivated by a search for what makes comprehension difficult. Work on comprehensibility of legal discourse has become increasingly sophisticated, focusing in turn on superficial readability, vocabulary, syntax, textuality, and, most recently, the interdependence of text, situation, and function.

---

[7] This chapter cites two rather different uses of the terms 'foregrounding' and 'backgrounding'. In the usage of Vargas (1984) and of Hopper and Thompson (1980) on whose work she draws, the terms refer to what is important and subsidiary, respectively, in a narrative. In the structuralist usage, foregrounding has to do with the calling to attention of language qua language. See the discussion of thickening in the legal register below.

Lexical and Syntactic Features
Affecting Comprehensibility

In Charrow and Charrow's (1979) study of the comprehensibility of jury instructions, replacement of 36 difficult technical terms by easier ones improved the mean score on correct paraphrases from 34 to 50%.[8] Material in their corpus containing nominalizations was less well understood than material without them. Moreover, removing them significantly improved comprehension. Passives, on the other hand, did not affect comprehension adversely; removing them improved comprehension only in subordinate clauses. The 12 instances of whiz deletion in their materials received only 25% correct responses, while portions containing misplaced phrases received the lowest single average of correct responses (24%) of any of the syntactic or lexical variables studied. Moving them to more natural places, as well as removing the difficult *as to* also improved comprehension. Sentence length was not important, though comprehension did decrease with the number of embeddings. Among negatives, only multiple negatives appeared to affect comprehension.

Interdependence of the Reader, Reading
Purpose, and Reading Situation

In a persuasive critique of previous research, Gunnarsson (1984) rejects the concern with lexis or syntax, which stopped at memorization or ability to paraphrase (the Charrows' study), and develops a theory of functional comprehensibility focusing on perspective and function orientation (implications for action). Guided by her theory, she prepared revised versions of portions of a Swedish employment law and then tested the ability of ordinary citizens, trade union members, and law students to apply them to specific cases.

How Much Can Linguistic Reform
Improve Comprehension?

It is by no means clear how much comprehension can be improved, particularly if a broad view is held of the notion 'comprehension'. Overall, the Charrows improved comprehension from 45 to 60%, as measured by ability to paraphrase. This is still not very good, if one happens to be

---

[8] The vast body of relevant psycholinguistic research is not cited in this chapter; see the chapters in this *Handbook* by Bower and Cirilo (Volume 1), and by Kintsch (Volume 2).

the defendant in a trial. In the Severance and Loftus study (1982), which tested ability to use jury instructions, reform resulted in a high 80% correct responses. Gunnarsson's experiment also required subjects to apply materials; the average number of correct responses improved from 5.7 out of 15 to only 6.8 for all groups together. Law students did best, whether materials were reformed or not, and even they scored only about 11 out of 15 on the reformed materials. In sum, progress in the improvement of comprehension by law persons is still limited.

Societal Limitations on Reform

Prospects for long-term social change through reform of the legal register are probably not particularly good, and may be primarily symbolic in value. Plain language reformers identify with citizens as underdogs but may fail to recognize that linguistic simplification is no substitute for substantive justice. Moreover, most contracts (like airplane tickets or insurance policies) are not negotiated. Thus, language simplification will probably not alter the fundamental weakness of citizens vis-à-vis modern institutions.

"THICKENING" IN THE LEGAL REGISTER: WHERE DOES IT COME FROM?

Each of the many features of the legal register should be viewed as a separate variable along a continuum from high to low. Many features no doubt covary, or entail one another, in differing patterns in different subgenres. Although work on linguistic description of the legal register is still so fragmentary, we know enough to be puzzled as to the origins of such convoluted, opaque language. Lawyers would argue that the legal register has evolved as an efficient tool for the specification of precise, technical meanings. Cynics might claim that lawyers intentionally use opaque language to mystify the public and to preserve their own power.

In my own view, syntactic complexity and the play with prosodic features are evidence of a preoccupation with language qua language. In the structuralists' sense of the terms, we have a foregrounding of language, and a backgrounding of referential meanings. This type of foregrounding apparently characterizes many genres in the keys of play and ritual, but especially the latter. It is as if lawyers—or perhaps persons in earlier times, before the modern legal profession emerged—added "cornstarch" to language, to thicken it, to give it body, so as to create the illusion of certainty in an uncertain world. Convoluted legal language may in part derive from preliterate times, when elaborate verbal formulas were considered a kind of word magic (see Danet, 1980, pt. V; 1984b).

TOPICS FOR FUTURE RESEARCH

I conclude this chapter with a brief listing of topics for future research. An obvious project would be a systematic, comparative description and analysis of the legal register in different languages. A topic that begs to be studied is how law students learn to produce and to comprehend the legal register. A third topic is how the legal register integrates given and new information and how this affects comprehension (Clark & Haviland, 1977; Glatt, 1982). A topic not touched on at all in this chapter, yet obvious from a glance at the Assignment reproduced in Figure 11.1, is the role of visual layout, typography, and indentation, in organizing a legal text. Fifth, I believe it would be enlightening to compare legal language with the language of religion, with respect to the trend toward stylization discussed in this chapter. Finally, work needs to be done on the ways in which legal language resembles or differs from the language of bureaucracy, a subject on which work has only recently begun.[9]

REFERENCES

Arena, L. A. (1982). The language of corporate attorneys. In R. Di Pietro (Ed.), *Linguistics and the professions* (pp. 143–154), Norwood, NJ: Ablex.

Arnold, T. W. (1935). *The symbols of government*. New Haven: Yale University Press.

Austin, J. L. (1970). *Philosophical papers*. New York: Oxford University Press.

Bogoch, B., & Danet, B. (1984). Challenge and control in lawyer–client interaction: A case study in an Israeli legal aid office. *Text, 4*, 249–275.

Bolinger, D. (1975). *Aspects of language*. New York: Harcourt Brace Jovanovich.

Caplan, J. (1977). Lawyers and litigants: A cult reviewed. In I. Illich, I. K. Zola, J. McKnight, J. Caplan & H. Shaiken (Eds.), *Disabling professions* (pp. 93–110). London: Marion Boyars.

Carlen, P. (1976). *Magistrates' justice*. London: Martin Robertson.

Charrow, R. P., & Charrow, V. R. (1979). Making legal language understandable: A psycholinguistic study of jury instructions. *Columbia Law Review, 79*, 1306–1374.

Charrow, V. R. (1982). Language in the Bureaucracy. In R. Di Pietro (Ed.), *Linguistics and the professions* (pp. 173–188). Norwood, NJ: Ablex.

Charrow, V. R., Crandall, J. A., & Charrow, R. P. (1982). Characteristics and functions of legal language. In R. Kittredge & J. Lehrberger (Eds.), *Sublanguage*. Berlin: Walter de Gruyter.

Clark, H. H. & Haviland, S. E. (1977). Comprehension and the given-new contract. In R. O. Freedle (Ed.), *Discourse production and comprehension* (pp. 1–40). Norwood, NJ: Ablex.

---

[9] But see Charrow, 1982; Danet, 1984a; Holland and Redish, 1981; and Redish, 1981.

Crystal, D. & Davy, D. (1969). *Investigating English style*. London: Longman.

Damaska, M. (1975). Presentation of evidence and factfinding precision. *University of Pennsylvania Law Review, 123*, 1083–1106.

Daneš, F. (1974). FSP and the organization of the text. In F. Daneš (Ed.), *Papers on functional sentence perspective*. Prague: Academi.

Danet, B. (1980). Language in the legal process. *Law and Society Review, 14*, 445–564.

Danet, B. (1983). Language in legal and bureaucratic settings. In "Language as a social problem," special issue of *Transaction-Society* (A. Grimshaw, ed).

Danet, B. (Ed.). (1984a). Studies of legal discourse [Special issue]. *Text, 4*, nos. 1–3.

Danet, B. (1984b). The magic flute: A prosodic analysis of binomial expressions in legal Hebrew. *Text, 4*, 143–172.

Di Pietro, R. (Ed.). (1982). *Linguistics and the professions*. Norwood, NJ: Ablex.

Edelman, M. (1972). *Political language*. New York: Academic Press.

Elwork, A., Sales, B. D., & Alfini, J. J. (1977). Juridic decisions: In ignorance of the law or in light of it? *Journal of Law and Human Behavior, 1*, 163ff.

Ferguson, C. (1964). Diglossia. In D. Hymes (Ed.), *Language in culture and society* (pp. 429–439). New York: Harper & Row.

Firbas, J. (1974). The Czechoslovak approach to FSP. In F. Daneš (Ed.), *Papers on functional sentence perspective*. Academi: Prague.

Frank, J. (1930). *Law and the modern mind*. New York: Brentano's.

Glatt, B. S. (1982). Defining thematic progressions and their relationship to reader comprehension. In Martin Nystrand (Ed.), *What writers know* (pp. 87–104). Academic Press: London.

Goffman, E. (1971) *Relations in public*. New York: Harper & Row.

Gunnarsson, B. L. (1984). Functional comprehensibility of a Swedith law: An experiment. *Text, 3*, 71–106.

Gustafsson, M. (1975). *Some syntactic properties of English law language* (Publication No. 4). Turku, Finland: University of Turku, Dept. of English.

Gustafsson, M. (1983). The syntactic features of binomial expressions in legal English. *Text, 4*, 123–142.

Halliday, M. A. K., & Hasan, R. (1976). *Cohesion in English*. London: Longman.

Hiltunen, R. (1984). The type and structure of clausal embedding in legal English. *Text, 3*, 107–122.

Hoebel, E. A. (1954). The law of primitive man. New York: Atheneum.

Hopper, P. J., & Thompson, S. A. (1980). Transitivity in grammar and discourse. *Language 56*, 251–299.

Jakobson, R. (1960). Concluding statement: Linguistics and poetics. In T. A. Sebeok (Ed.), *Style in Language* (pp. 350–377). Cambridge, MA: MIT Press.

Joos, M. (1961). *The five clocks*. New York: Harcourt, Brace & World.

Koskenniemi, I. (1968). *Repetitive word pairs in Old and Early Middle English prose* (Annales Universitatis Turkuensis No. 107). Turku, Finland: Turun Yliopiston Julkaisuja.

Kurzon, D. (1984). Themes, hyperthemes, and the discourse structure of British legal texts. *Text, 4*, 31–56.

Lefcourt, R. (Ed.). (1971). *Law against the people*. New York: Random House.

Levi, J. M. (1982). *Linguistics, language and law: A topical bibliography*. Bloomington, IN: Indiana University Linguistics Club.

Malkiel, Y. (1959). Studies in irreversible binomials. *Lingua, 8*, 113–160.

Mellinkoff, D. (1963). *The language of the law*. Boston: Little, Brown.

O'Barr, W. M. (1981). The language of the law. In C. A. Ferguson & S. B. Heath (Eds.), *Language in the U.S.A.* New York: Cambridge University Press.

O'Barr, W. M. (1982). *Linguistic evidence*. New York: Academic Press.

Redish, J. C. (1981). *The language of the bureaucracy* (Tech. Rep. No. 15). Washington, DC: Document Design Center.

Rosenthal, D. (1974). *Lawyer and client*. New York: Russell Sage.

Sales, B. D., Elwork, A., & Alfini, J. (1977). Improving jury instruction. In B. D. Sales (Ed.), *Perspectives in law and psychology 1*. New York: Plenum.

Severance, L. J., & Loftus, E. F. (1982). Improving the ability of jurors to comprehend and apply criminal jury instructions. *Law and Society Review, 17,* 153–197.

Shuy, R. W., & Larkin, D. K. (1978). *Linguistic considerations in the simplification/clarification of insurance policy language. Washington, DC: Georgetown University and Center for Applied Linguistics.*

Thibaut, J., & Walker, L. (1975). Procedural justice. Hillsdale, NJ: Erlbaum.

Vargas, D. M. (1984). Two types of legal discourse: Transitivity in American appellate opinions and casebooks. *Text, 4,* 9–30.

Westman, M. (1984). On strategy in Swedish legal texts. *Text, 4,* 57–70.

Wright, P. (1981). Is legal jargon a restrictive practice? In S. M. Lloyd-Bostock (Ed.), *Psychology in legal contexts* (pp. 121–145). London: Macmillan.

Biographical Notes

ROBERT DE BEAUGRANDE is a professor of English and linguistics at the University of Florida, Gainesville. He is author or coauthor of some 70 scholarly books and papers on discourse and related issues, including *Text, Discourse, and Process, Text Production, Factors in a Theory of Poetic Translating, Introduction to Text Linguistics* with Wolfgang Dressler, (also published in German, Italian, Rumanian, and Japanese), and papers in such journals as *Poetics, PTL, Empirical Studies of the Arts, Discourse Processes, Text, Word, Journal of Pragmatics, Reading Research Quarterly, Psychoanalysis and Contemporary Thought, IRAL, College Composition and Communication,* and *Journal of Technical Writing and Communication.* He is now preparing a volume that surveys major linguistic theories within a unified conception, and another that treats literary theories in the same way.

GORDON H. BOWER holds the A. R. Lang Distinguished Professorship in the Department of Psychology at Stanford University, where he was chairman for four years. He has published over 150 experimental and theoretical articles on human memory, including studies of narrative comprehension and memory. He has coauthored *Theories of Learning* with E. R. Hilgard and *Human Associative Memory* with J. R. Anderson. His honors include election to the U. S. National Academy of Sciences and the American Association of Arts and Sciences; Distinguished Scientific Contributions Award and Division-3 presidency of the American Psychological Association; presidency and member of the Governing Boards of the Psychonomic Society and the Cognitive Science Society.

MARK BURSTEIN received his B.S. in mathematics from the Massachusetts Institute of Technology in 1976 and his Ph.D. in computer science from Yale University in 1983. He has written several articles concerned with issues in memory, learning, and natural language processing.

His thesis presented a cognitive model of the use of multiple analogies in the learning of new concepts.

RANDOLPH K. CIRILO received his Ph.D. in human experimental psychology from the University of Texas at Austin in 1980. He spent one year at Stanford University on a postdoctoral fellowship in cognitive science from the Sloan Foundation. Currently, he is faculty advisor in psychology and education for Century University, a nontraditional educational institution. His fields of interest are psycholinguistics and cognitive psychology, particularly the comprehension and memory of natural language texts.

WILLIAM A. CORSARO received his Ph.D. in sociology from the University of North Carolina, Chapel Hill. He was an NIMH post-doctoral research fellow at the University of California, Berkeley, and is presently an associate professor of sociology at Indiana University, Bloomington. Corsaro is the author of *Friendship and Peer Culture in the Early Years,* which will be published by Ablex in 1984. He is also the author of a number of articles on childhood socialization, discourse analysis, and qualitative methods. He will be a Fulbright senior research fellow in Italy in 1983–1984, where he will continue his work on childhood socialization and children's cultures.

BRENDA DANET is an associate professor of communications and sociology at the Hebrew University of Jerusalem and until recently served as the director of its Communications Institute. During the 1982–1983 academic year she was an academic visitor in the Department of Social Psychology of the London School of Economics and Political Science. Her interests in language and law developed during the Watergate scandals. She has carried out studies of courtroom questioning in Boston and in Jerusalem, as well as of lawyer–client communication in Jerusalem's legal aid office. Her review essay "Language in the Legal Process" was commissioned by the American Law and Society Association for a special issue of its journal, the *Law and Society Review* ("Contemporary Issues in Law and Social Science") and appeared in 1980. More recently, she served as guest editor for a special issue of *Text* on legal discourse.

ALESSANDRO DURANTI teaches at the Istituto di Glottologia, University of Rome. He received his laurea in Modern Letters from the University of Rome in 1974 and his Ph.D. in linguistics from the University of Southern California in 1981. In 1978–1979 and again in 1981, he carried out fieldwork in a traditional village in Western Samoa, studying language structure, language use, and communicative competence. His dissertation, an ethnography of speaking of a political event, was published as a monograph of the Series B (Vol. 80) of *Pacific Linguistics (The Samoan Fono: A Sociolinguistic Study)*. He has published articles on several journals, including *Language in Society, Journal of the Polynesian Society,* and *Rivista di Grammatica Italiana*. His publications include works on Samoan discourse literacy, Spoken Italian, and Bantu syntax. He is currently editing a film on the acquisition of communicative competence and the effects of literacy instruction on Samoan children.

CHARLES J. FILLMORE earned his B.A. degree at the University of Minnesota, his M.A. and Ph.D. degrees at the University of Michigan. His first teaching position was in the Linguistics Department at the Ohio State University, where he served from 1961 to 1970; in 1971 he moved to the University of California, Berkeley, where he is currently a professor of linguistics. His best-known work is the 1968 article, "The Case for Case." He has published numerous papers on deixis, pragmatics, lexical semantics, idiomaticity, and text semantics. He is currently preparing a booklength manuscript on the principles of empirical semantics.

ASA KASHER received his M.Sc. in mathematics and philosophy of science and Ph.D. in philosophy from Hebrew University in Jerusalem. He is a professor of philosophy (Tel-Aviv) and editor of *Philosophia*. His main interests are philosophy of language, particularly pragmatics, philosophy of religion, and the methodology of linguistics. Books he has authored or edited include *Linguistics and Logic; Conspectus and Prospects, Philosophical Linguistics* (with S. Lappin), and *Language in Focus: Foundations, Methods and Systems*. He has also contributed to various journals and collections in philosophy of language, philosophy of religion, philosophy of art, and philosophy of law, as well as to many publications in Hebrew periodicals, both professional and popular, on ethics and current affairs.

W. P. ROBINSON has been a professor in the School of Education at the University of Bristol since 1977. His interest in language and its use was stimulated through conversations with Basil Bernstein at the London School of Economics after he had completed his doctoral studies in social psychology at Oxford. Work with Bernstein led to the publication of two books, *A Question of Answers* and *Language Management in Education*, while a more general concern with the social psychology of language was expressed through the publication of *Language and Social Behaviour*. A subsequent shift of interest to a developmental social perspective has focused on the child's coming to understand that representational speech acts can be ambiguous, which is viewed as a potentially fruitful transition in which to examine the relevance of children's understanding about language to their development of mastery over its resources.

ROGER SCHANK is a professor of computer science and psychology at Yale University, and chairman of the Computer Science Department. He received his Ph.D. in linguistics from the University of Texas in 1969, and was an assistant professor of linguistics and computer science at Stanford from 1969 to 1974. He then spent a year as a research fellow at the Institute for Semantics and Cognition in Castagnola, Switzerland, before coming to Yale in 1975. Professor Schank was a cofounder of both the Cognitive Science Society and its journal, *Cognitive Science*. He has written many articles and several books on the subjects of artificial intelligence and natural language processing, including *Scripts, Plans, Goals, and Understanding,* with Robert Abelson, and *Dynamic Memory: A Theory of Reminding and Learning in Computers and People.*

NANCY SCHERMERHORN STRUEVER holds a joint appointment at the Johns Hopkins University in the History Department and the Humanities Center. She is a specialist in Renaissance intellectual history, with a strong interest in the history of language theory and, in particular, the history of rhetoric. She has published *The Language of History in the Renaissance* and is currently writing a book on ethical discourse in the Renaissance.

TEUN A. VAN DIJK is professor of discourse studies at the University of Amsterdam, from which he received a doctorate in linguistics. After earlier work on linguistic poetics, text grammar, and discourse pragmatics, he did research (with Walter Kintsch) on the psychology of discourse processing. This work is currently extended toward the field of social cognition, with applications in the analysis of ethnic prejudice in discourse (media, textbooks, conversations) and of news in the press. His books in English include *Some Aspects of Text Grammars*; *Text and Context*; *Macrostructures*; *Studies in the Pragmatics of Discourse*; *Strategies of Discourse Comprehension,* with Walter Kintsch; *Prejudice in Discourse*; and *News as Discourse* (in preparation). He has edited several books and special journal issues and founded and edited *Poetics* and *Text.*

Index